HOTELS AND COUNTRY INNS
OF CHARACTER AND CHARM
IN ITALY

While every care has been taken to ensure the accuracy of the information in this guide, time brings change, and consequently the publisher cannot accept responsibility for errors that may occur. Prudent travelers will therefore want to call ahead to verify prices and other "perishable" information.

Published in the United States by Fodor's Travel Publications, Inc.
Published in France by Payot /Rivages

Fodor's is a registered trademark of Fodor's Travel Publications, Inc.

ISBN 0-679-03160-X
Second Edition

**Hotels and Country Inns
of Character and Charm in Italy**
Translator: Mark Ennis
Rewriting: Marie Gastaut
Cover design: Fabrizio La Rocca
Front cover photograph: Relais La Suvera, Pievescola di Casole (Tuscany);
back cover: Villa Cimbrone, Ravello (Campania)

Printed in Italy by Litho Service
10 9 8 7 6 5 4 3 2 1

Fodor's RIVAGES

HOTELS AND COUNTRY INNS
of Character and Charm
IN ITALY

Founding editors:
Simonetta Greggio
Michelle Gastaut

Fodor's Travel Publications, Inc.

New York • Toronto • London • Sydney • Auckland

BIENVENUE

Welcome to the world of hotels with character and charm in Italie. This edition contains 392 hotels, 34 properties appear in the guide for the first time. All have been selected for charm, quality of welcome, food and hotelkeeping. They range from the comparatively simple to the luxurious.

When choosing among them, remember that you cannot expect as much of a room costing 90,000L as you can of one costing 180,000L or more. Please also note that the prices given were quoted to us at the end of 1995 and may change.

When you make your reservation be sure to ask for the exact prices for half board *(mezza-pensione)* or full board *(pensione)* as they can vary depending on the number in your party and the length of your stay. Half board is often obligatory. Note that rooms are generally held only until 6 or 7PM; if you are going to be late, let the hotel know.

STAR RATING

The government's hotel roting organisation assigns stars, from one to four, based on the comfort of a hotel, with special weight given to the number of bathrooms and toilets in relation to the number of rooms. This star rating has nothing at all to do with subjective criteria such as charm or the quality of the hospitality which are among our most important criteria. Some of the hotels in this guide have no stars–and that is because the hoteliers have never asked the gouvernement to rate them.

HOW TO USE THE GUIDE

Hotels are listed by regions, and within each region order by district. The number of the page on which a hotel is described corresponds to the number on the flag that pinpoints the property's location on the road map and to the numbers in the table of contents and index. The phrase "major credit cards" means that Diner's, Amex, Visa, Eurocard and MasterCard are all accepted.

PLEASE LET US KNOW . . .

If you are impressed by a small hotel or inn not featured here, one that you think ought to be included in the guide, let us know so that we can visit it.

Please also tell us if you are disappointed by one of our choices. Write us at Fodor's Travel Publications, 201 E. 50th Str., New York, NY 10022.

CONTENTS

L A T I U M   A B R U Z Z I

L I G U R I A

L O M B A R D Y

PIEMONT   VALLE   D'AOSTA

P U G L I A / A P U L I A

S A R D I N I A

S I C I L Y

TRENTINO - DOLOMITES

V E N E T O

Blay - Foldex

for traveling in France and around the world

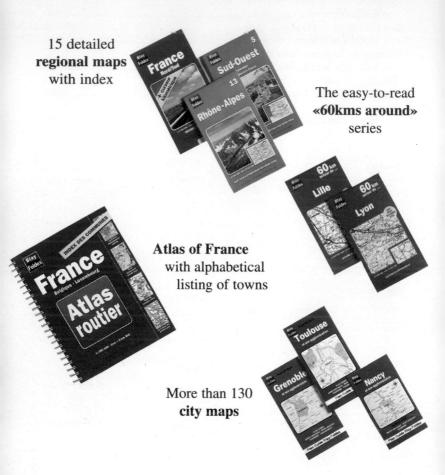

15 detailed
regional maps
with index

The easy-to-read
«60kms around»
series

Atlas of France
with alphabetical
listing of towns

More than 130
city maps

maps-plans-guides
40-48, rue des Meuniers
F - 93108 MONTREUIL cedex (FRANCE)
Tél. : (1) 49 88 92 10 - Fax : (1) 49 88 92 09

Blay
Foldex

KEY TO THE MAPS

Scale: 1:1,000,000
Maps 30 & 31: scale: 1:1,180,000

MOTORWAYS

❶ Interchange
❷ Half-interchange
❸ Toll-barrier

Kilometre-distance
❶ in total
❷ partial

Motorway
❶ under construction
❷ projected

ROAD WIDTH

4 carriageways

3 lane or
2 wide lane

2 lane

Narrow road

Kilometre-distance
❶ in total
❷ partial

ROAD CLASSIFICATION

Dual-carriageways

High traffic road

Trunk road

Other road

Road ❶ under construction
     ❷ projected

BOUNDARIES

National boundary

County boundary

TOURISM

Picturesque locality — Chenonceaux

Very picturesque locality — **Amboise**✱

Interesting site or natural curiosity — Roches de Ham

Historic castle

Ruins of outstanding beauty

Abbey

National park

TOWNS CLASSIFICATION

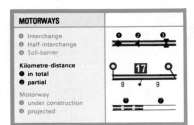

❶ by the population

— less than 10,000 inhabitants ○
→ from 10.000 to 30.000 ○
— from 30.000 to 50.000 ◉
— from 50.000 to 100.000 ●
— more than 100.000 ●
— towns with over 50.000 inh. ⬠

❷ Administrative
— Chief-town of department — **TARBES**
— Main subdivision of department — **CARPENTRAS**
— Districts — **Combeaufontaine**
— Commune, hamlet — Andrézieux-Bouthéon

DIVERS

Civil Airport

Dam

Canal

Car-ferries

Motorail

Pass — 1045

Summit — ▲ 2392

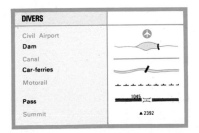

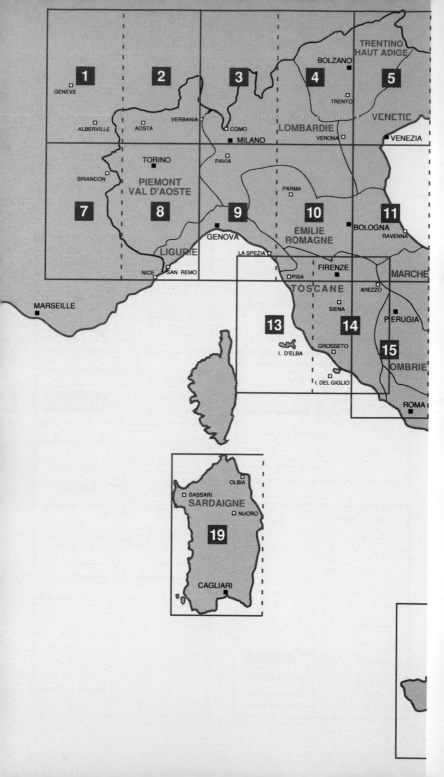

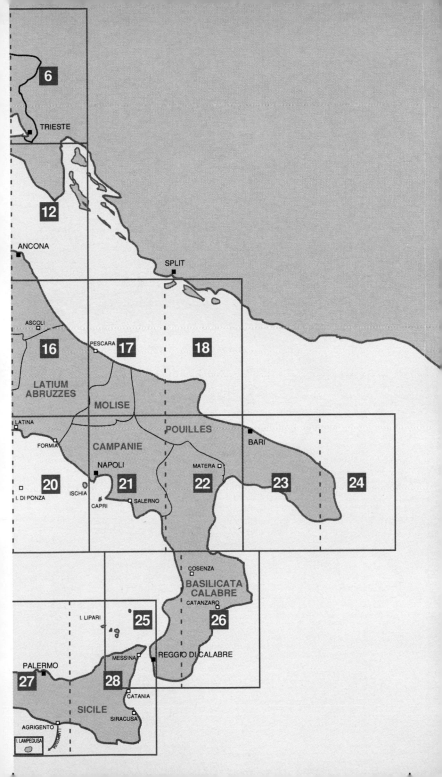

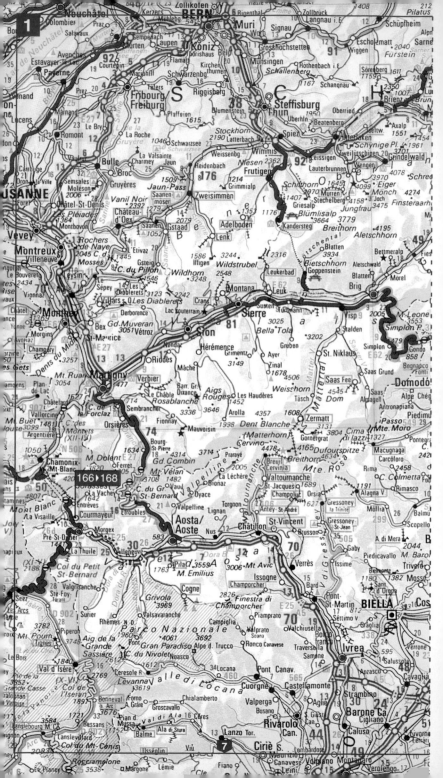

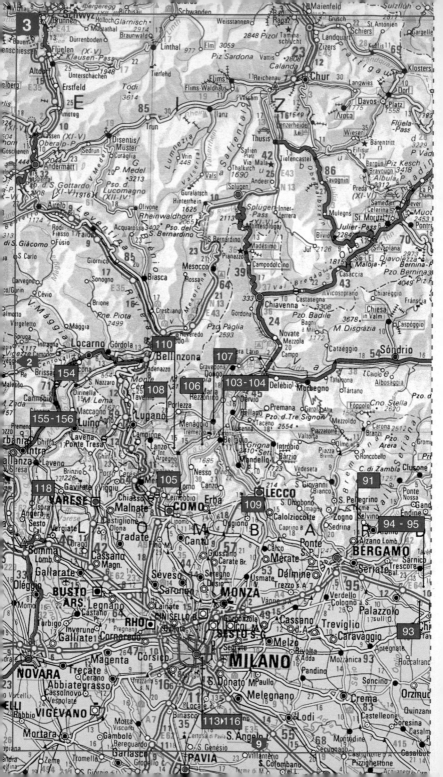

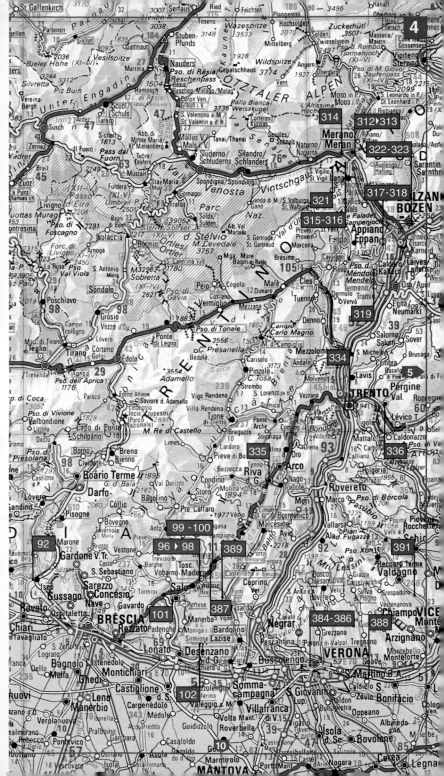

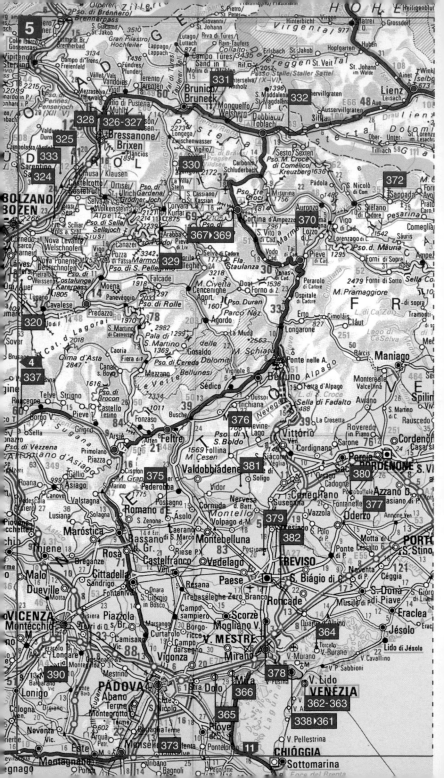

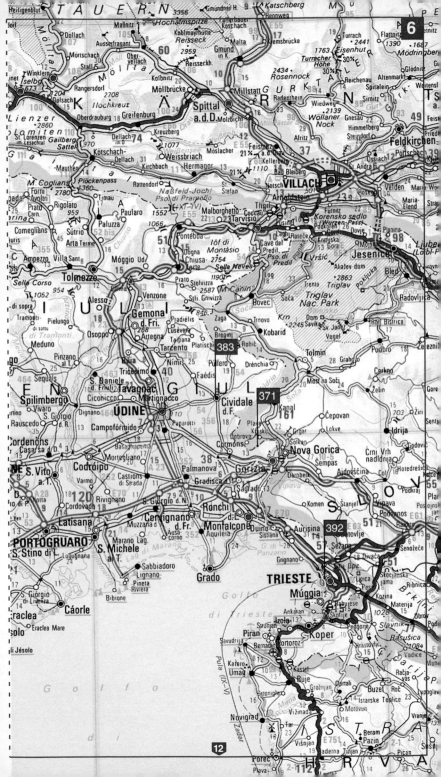

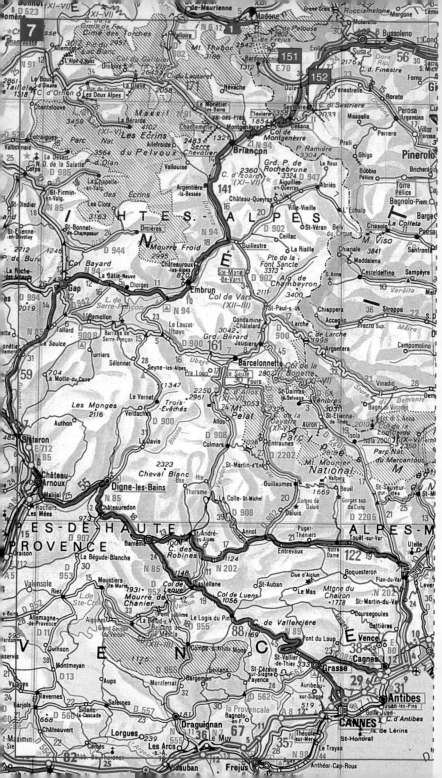

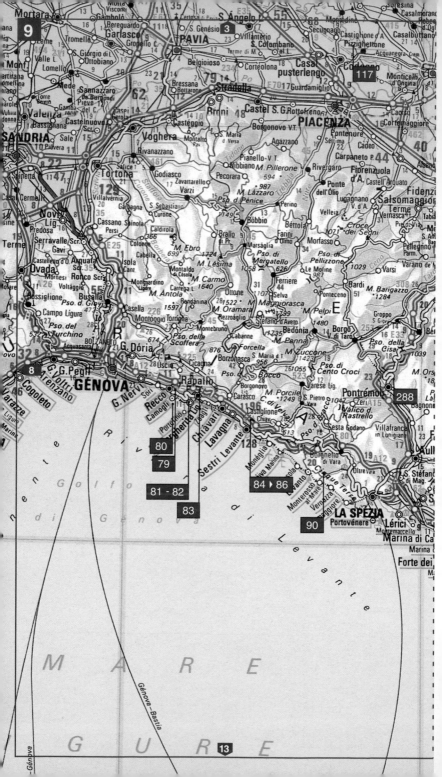

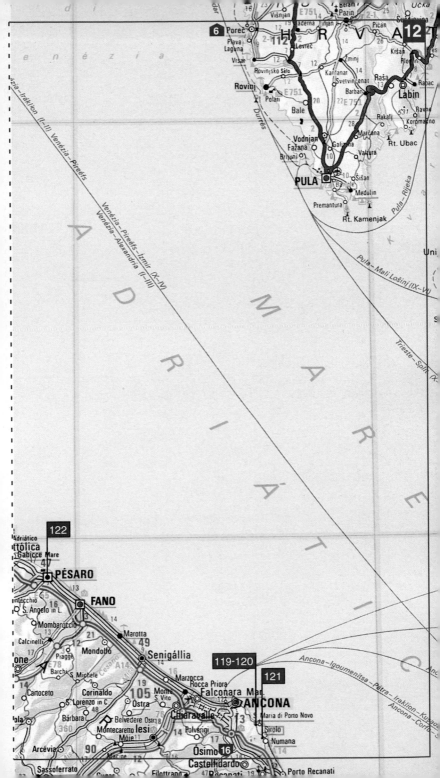

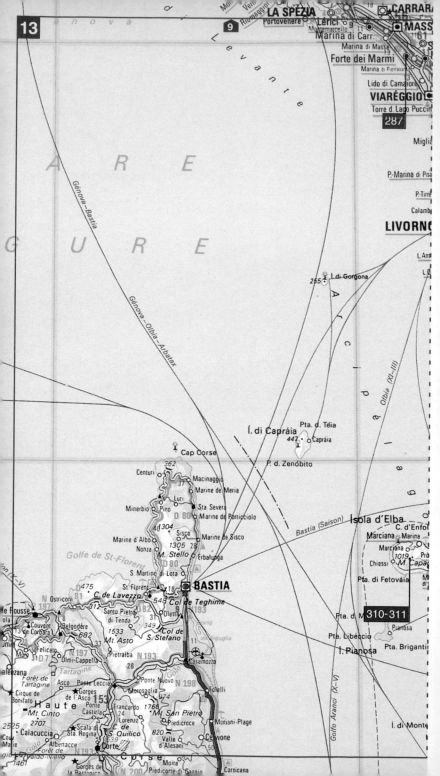

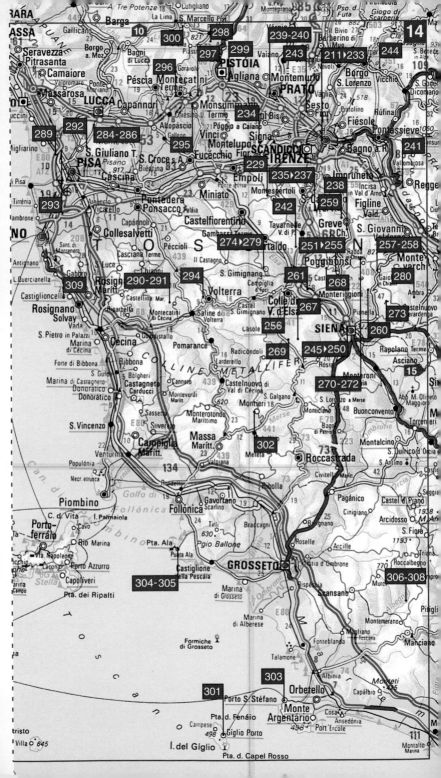

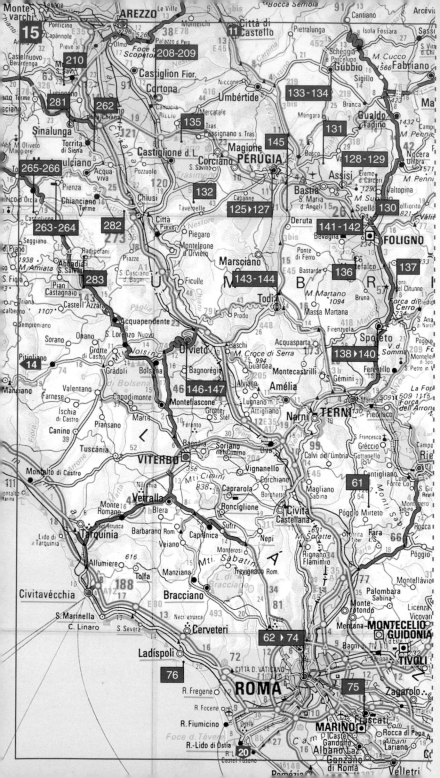

17

Abruzzi

◀ **16**

Split

ilvi

Montesilvano Marina ◀ **7**

PESCARA

Francavilla
al Mare

CHIETI

Bucchiánico

◎ Ortona
103

A 14

Marina S. Vito

S. Francesco   S. Vito Chietino
Orsogna   Fossacésia
                 Fossacésia Marina
Lanciano   Torino di Sangro Marina
99
                 78
uardiagrele
22
                 Casal-   P. d. F
                 bordino
ibedicente
                 Vasto ◎   Marina di Vasto
Cásoli
Mart.   **le. Trémiti** ☨ I. Cap
ama d'Peligni   **Atessa** Cupello ◎   ☨ I. S. Ni
                                  17   I. S. Domino
Bomba   Casa   Gissi   **16** Petacciato
         lánguida   Marina
Torricella   **S. Salvo**   **16**
Peligna   Furci
Villa   ◎ **Térmoli**
S. Maria   S. Bruno   **22**
                            Montenero
Monfázzoli   di Bisáccia   Marina
                                                 di Chiéuti   Torr
                   Carúnchi   Mafalda   Campo-
etta   Torrebruna   marino
Pescopennataro   Palata   **Guglionesi** S. Martino
                                              in Pénsilis   ◎ **Lésina**
Castiglione   S.   Montefalcone nel Sánnio Ururi   Chiéuti
Capracotta   Messer M. Castel-   Serra-
gerardi   **650**   Cannto-Castel- Guardia-   capriola
             mauro   fiera   Larino   Montório
Agnone   Civita   **82** in Frentani   Rotello   S. Páolo   Apricena
Vasto   campomarano   di Civitáte
            Trivento   Lícito Casa-   S. Ma
Caroville   S. Blase   **82** calenda   **21**
            Pesco-   **S. SEVERO**
Bagnoli   Petrella

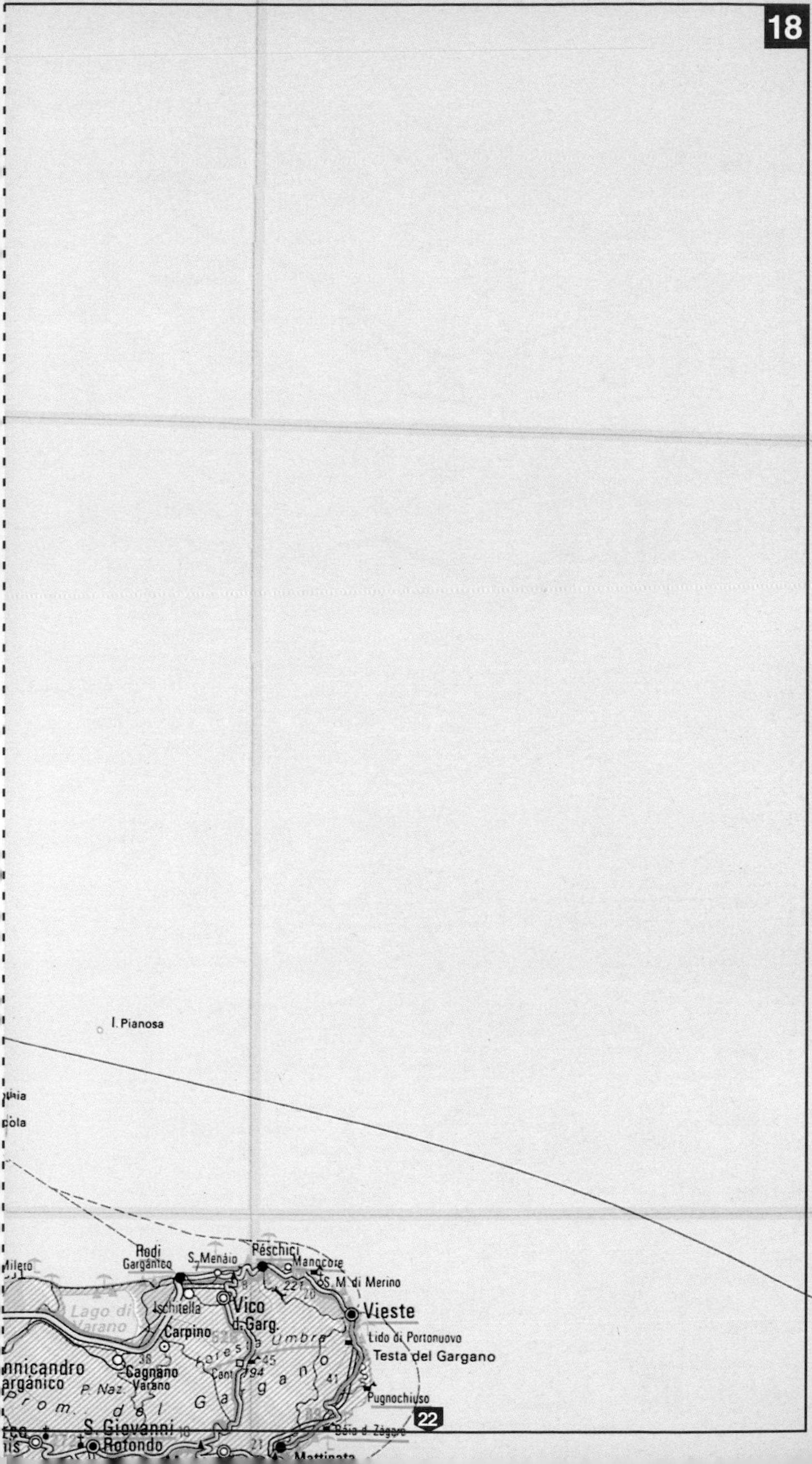

I. Pianosa

ÿhia

cola

Rodi
Garganteo
S. Menàio
Peschici
Mancoure
S. M. di Merino
227.0

Vico
d. Garg.
Ischitella
Vieste
Carpino
Lido di Portonuovo
Testa del Gargano

Lago di
Varano

nnicandro
argànico
Cagnano
Varano
P. Naz
594
41
Pugnachiuso

rom
del
Ga
Bàia d. Zàgare

S. Giovanni
Rotondo
Mattinata

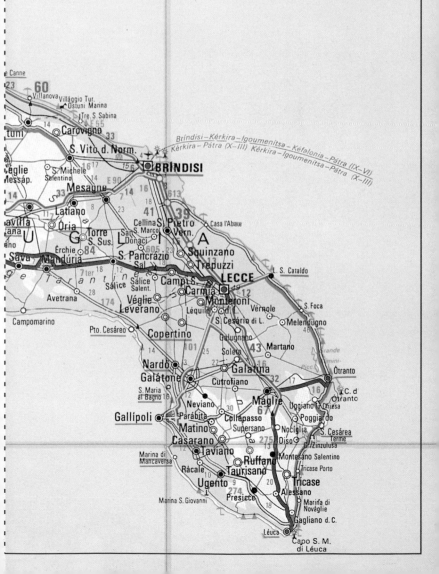

e Canne

60

Villanova
Villággio Tur.
Tre. S. Sabina

14   Carovigno   **33**

S. Vito d. Norm.

tuni

Brindisi–Kérkira–Igoumenitsa–Kéfalonia–Pátra (IX–III)
Kérkira–Pátra (X–III) Kérkira–Igoumenitsa–Pátra (IX–VI)
Kérkira–Igoumenitsa–Pátra (X–III)

églie
Messáp.

S. Michele
Salentino

BRÍNDISI

Mesagne

E90

14

7

18

613

aville
tana

U

Latiano

Ória

G

Torre
S. Sus.

San
S. Marco

Cellina S. Pietro
Vern.

Casa l'Abate

Érchie

84

S. Pancrázio
Sal.

San
Dónaci

605

Squinzano

39

A

ano

14

Sava   Mandúria

7 ter 18

12

Sálice
Salent.

23

Trepuzzi

L. S. Cataldo

Campi S.

Sálice

Camp S.

LECCE

Avetrana   28

174

Véglie

Carmia

12

Léquile

Monteroni

Vérnole

S. Foca

Leverano

cid

Campomarino

Pto. Cesáreo

Copertino

S. Cesário di L.

Melendugno

14

101

Galugnano

43

Martano

25

Soleto

22

Nardó   **3**

Galátone

Galatina

32

17

Ótranto

S. Maria
al Bagno

Cutrofiano

16

C. d
Ótranto

Gallípoli

Neviano

30

67

Máglie

Uggiano l. Chiesa

Parábita

Poggiardo

Matino

10

Collápasso

Supersano

Nocíglia

S. Cesárea
Terme

Marina di
Mancaversa

Casarano

Taviano

Diso

275

Gr. Zinzulusa

Rácale

Ruffano

Montesano Salentino

Tricase Porto

Taurisano

20

Tricase

Ugento

9

Alessano

Marina S. Giovanni

Presicce

274.

18

Mariña di
Nováglie

Gagliano d. C.

Léuca

Capo S. M.
di Léuca

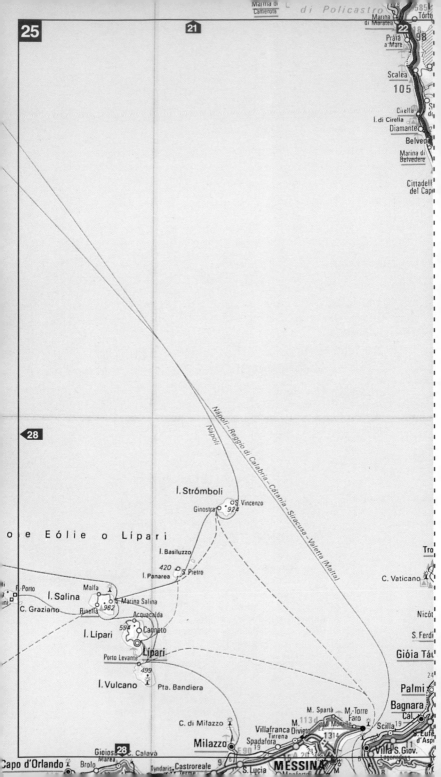

191-192

190

S   I   C   I

PALERMO

I. di Ústica   238 Ústica

Capo Gallo
Ísola delle
Fémmine   Mondello
Punta Ráisi A29 14
S. Vito   Terrasini   P. Acqua   C. Zaffarano
lo Capo   Capaci   d. Corsari
Capo S. Vito   Carini   Torretta   23   Solunto
Castelluzzo   Monte   Sferracavallo   Bagheria
              Terrasini   Lepre   Monreale
Érice   Altofonte   G. di Términi Imerese   Cefalù
TRAPANI Castellammare Balestrate   Villabate   14   Términi   Collesano
Grosso   Valdérice d. Golfo 14   Partinico   13 Piana   Misilmeri   Imerese 49   di Rocca
Pacèco   Nápola   Buseto Palizz   Pla. d. Páglia d.Albanesi Bolognetta E90 Trabia Cácccamo   14 Cerda   Gratteri   Pzo C.
        31 13 12 Bruca 9   Alcamo Giuseppe   856   Marineo Villafrati Pla. Ciminna Montemaggiore 30   17   Pla.   197
              Salemi Calatafimi S. Cipirello   477   di   Belsito M Caltavuturo   di Mare
LA   Camporeale   M   Mezzojuso   Alia Collesano
74   Calamita Vita 104   Roccamena z   a Campofelice di Fit Lercara   Villaadormo   82
          S. Ninfa Gibellina Corleone   Pla. Imbriaca   Friddi   Pla. Scavo   1876
Pizzolato   Partanna Salaparuta Contessa-Entellina   Prizzi   Vallelunga Pratameno Resuttano
          S. Margherita   Bisacquino   Pla. Móla   Pratameno
Mazara   di   Sambuca   Palazzo   Cammarata   Villalba   97 822 Pla.
del Vallo E931 16 di Sicília   S. Carlo   Adriano   Bivona   S. Stéfano Quisq. Maranópoli 121 Reca
      Campobello   Menfi   Búrgio   Alessándria   Mussomeli   S. Caterina Vill.
      di Mazara   Caltabellotta   Cianciana   d. Rocca S. Biágio Plátani Casteltérmini
Torretta   Marinella Porto   Ribera   76
Granitola   Palo   94   Milena   S. Cataldo   98
Pta. Granitola   Sciacca   Cattólica   S. Elisabetta Montedoro
C. S. Marco   Eraclea   118   Aragona Grotte Racalmuto Serradifalco   Bai
          Secca Grande Eraclea Minoa   Montallegro   Raffadali   Casteltérmini 640 Délia   90
                  Siculiana   Naro Canicattì Sommatino
                Siculiana Marina   Porto   AGRIGENTO   Campobello di Licata Ravan
                  Empédocle   S. Leone   Palma di
                        Marina di Palma   Montechiaro 80
                                      Licata

188-189

I. di Lampedusa
199
Lampedusa

Hotel Barbieri ★★★

Via San Nicola, 30
87042 Altomonte (Cosenza)
Tel. (0981) 94 80 72 - Fax (0981) 94 80 73
Sig. Barbieri

Rooms 30 with air-conditioning, telephone, shower, WC and TV. **Price** Single 70,000L, double 125,000L. **Meals** Breakfast included, served 6:30-10:00; half board 110,000L, full board 120,000L (per pers., 3 days min.). **Restaurant** Service 12:30-15:00, 19:30-23:00; menus 65-75,000L. Specialties: Pasta fatta in casa, funghi, salumi tipici. **Credit cards** All major. **Pets** Dogs allowed. **Facilities** Swimming pool in casa Barbieri, tennis (5,000L), parking. **Nearby** Altomonte (with Cathedral tomb of Filippo Sangineto XIV[e] and "Saint Ladislas" attributed to Simone Martini), excursions to Monte Pollino from Castrovillari, old Calabrian villages (Stilo, Sibari and Paola as well as Altomonte). **Open** All year.

Behind the unprepossing facade of this hotel hides one of the best restaurants in Calabria. You can savor excellent regional dishes while enjoying a marvelous view of the town of Altomonte, a vista framed by a fifteenth-century monastery and splendid houses. Italian-style breakfast is a real delight. You can, if you like, have it by the shores of Lago del Fareto: the first bite of your day will be delicious if you have the warm ricotta cheese on lightly toasted bread, topped with home-made berry confiture, also available in the gift shop next door. Rooms are spacious, pleasant and unpretentiously decorated (some have small balconies with great views). The hotel has a family atmosphere.

How to get there *(Map 26): 50 km north of Cosenza via A3, Altomonte exit.*

Grand Hotel San Michele ★★★★

87022 Cetraro (Cosenza)
Tel. (0982) 91 012
Fax (0982) 91 430
Sig.ra Siniscalchi

Rooms 73 with air-conditioning, telephone, bath or shower, WC and TV.
Price Single 100-200,000L, double 170-300,000L, suite 220-350,000L.
Meals Breakfast 15,000L, served 7:30-10:00; half board 145-255,000L, full board
160-270,000L (per pers., 3 days min.). **Restaurant** Service 13:00-14:30, 19:30-
21:30, menu 40-60,000L, also à la carte. Specialties: Regional cooking.
Credit cards All major. **Pets** Dogs allowed. **Facilities** Swimming pool, tennis, golf
(30,000L) and private beach with restaurant service in summer. **Nearby** Old
Calabrian villages (Stilo, Sibari, Paola, Altomonte). **Open** All year (except Nov.).

This enchanting turn-of-the-century villa, in a small beach
resort on the Tyrrhenian Sea was built at the beginning of
the century by the owner's father. Today it is a luxury hotel
with many facilities and excellent service–it's one of the few
places in Calabria with visible charm and personality. In addition
to the well-decorated villa, there are several small houses on the
124-acre estate you can rent. Fresh produce for the hotel
kitchen is grown on the property.

How to get there *(Map 26): 55 km northwest of Cosenza via A3,
Lagonegro-North exit, towards Praia, then SS18 direction south.*

Locanda delle Donne Monache ★★★★

Via Carlo Mazzei, 4
85046 Maratea (Potenza)
Tel. (0973) 87 74 87 – Fax (0973) 87 76 87
Sig. Raffaele Bruno

Rooms 30 and 6 suites with air-conditioning, telephone, bath and cable TV.
Price Single 135-200,000L, double 200-300,000L. **Meals** Breakfast included
(buffet), served 7:30-10:00; half board 140-330,000L (per pers.).
Restaurant Service 12:30-14:30, 20:00-23:00; à la carte. Specialties: Italian and
regional cuisine. **Credit cards** All major. **Pets** Dogs not allowed **Facilities** Swimming
pool, private beach, parking. **Nearby** Sanctuario Monte San Biagio, Rivello, S.
Lorenzo in Padula, Monte Pollino. **Open** Season begins week before Easter.

This charming hotel between the mountains and the sea, is in
Maratea, a village nestled in a cove on the Tyrrhenian coast.
Once an old monastery in the center of the village, it has been
completely refurbished and decorated with sobriety and elegance,
except for the slightly Baroque-like lobby. The rooms, which have
kept a monastic air, are very comfortable, with canopy beds and
simple, tasteful furniture in the best tradition of modern Italian
design. In front of the house there is a secluded garden with a nice
swimming pool. The hotel's private beach is even better; a boat at
your disposal can take you out to view the Gulf of Policastro. Those
who prefer to go hiking and horseback riding will want to head for
the back country: the Basicilate is mostly mountains and hills, with
beautiful wildlife preserves.

How to get there *(Map 22): 176 km southeast of Salerno via A3,
Lagonegro-North Maratea exit, S585 and Maratea.*

Hotel Santavenere ★★★★★

Fiumicello di Santa Venere
85040 Maratea (Potenza)
Tel. (0973) 87 69 10 – Fax (0973) 87 76 54
Sig. Olivieri

Rooms 44 with telephone, bath, WC and TV. **Price** Single 190-252,000L, double
334-451,000L. **Meals** Breakfast included, served 7:00-10:00; half board 327-
360,000 L (per pers.). **Restaurant** Service 13:00-14:30, 20:00-21:30; menu:
111,000L, also à la carte. Specialties: Seafood and regional cuisine. **Credit cards**
All major. **Pets** Dogs not allowed. **Facilities** Swimming pool, tennis, private beach.
Nearby Maratea, Sanctuario Monte San Biagio, Rivello, S. Lorenzo in Padula,
Monte Pollino. **Open** Apr. – Oct.

The lush green landscape and circular pool out front give you
a foretaste of just how charming a stay at the Hotel
Santavenere can be. You can take in the extraordinary view
from most of the rooms in the hotel, including the restaurant
with its enormous windows. An enfilade of salons with low,
vaulted ceilings creates a beautiful architectural element. The
pastel decor adds to the relaxing atmosphere of this beachfront
hotel. The terraces and the beach will invite you to enjoy the
dolce farniente so prized by Italians. The restaurant menu
specialises in fresh fish. As you'll realize from the first welcome,
your well-being and peace of mind are priorities at this hotel.

How to get there *(Map 22): 166 km southeast of Salerno via A3,
Lagonegro-North Maratea exit, then S585 and Maratea, then S18 (5 km
via the coast).*

Grand Hotel Telese ★★★★

Via Cerreto, 1
82037 Telese Terme (Benevento)
Tel. (0824) 94 05 00 – Fax (0824) 94 05 04
Sig. Montagna

Rooms 110 with telephone, bath or shower, WC, TV and minibar. **Price** Single 120,000L, double 205,000L, suite 386,000L. **Meals** Breakfast included, served 7:00-9:30; half board 110-140,000L, full board 130-150,000L. (per pers., 3 days min.). **Restaurant** Service 12:30-14:30, 19:30-21:30; à la carte. Specialties: Risotto con brocoli, agnello. **Credit cards** Amex, Visa, Eurocard, MasterCard. **Pets** Small dogs allowed. **Facilities** Swimming pool, tennis (8,000L), parking. **Nearby** Telesia, Faicchio, Cerreto Sannita, Benevento. **Open** All year.

The Grand Hotel Telese built at the turn of the century has preserved the old-fashioned charm typical of the spas of this resort town. Ouside, its neoclassical facade is chic. Inside, you will be impressed by the grand staircase, the beautiful ground-floor rooms with painted ceilings and the second-floor—Louis XV lounge. All the guest rooms are luxurious. The restaurant is in the cellar between the billiard and chess rooms. All in all, it would be a perfect hotel, except for its proximity to a highway, which sometimes disturbs the prevaling tranquility.

How to get there *(Map 21): 65 km north of Napoli via A1, Caserta-South exit, then S265 towards Maddaloni to Telese.*

Hotel Della Baia ★★★★

Via dell' Erica
Baia Domizia – 81030 Cellole (Caserta)
Tel. (0823) 72 13 44 – Fax (0823) 72 15 56
Sig.ra Sello

Rooms 56 with telephone, bath or shower and WC. **Price** Single 80-100,000L, double 120-150,000L. **Meals** Breakfast 15,000L, served 7:30-9:30; half board 125-150,000L, full board 135-160,000L (per pers.). **Restaurant** Service 12:30-14:15, 19:30-21:00; menu: 50-60,000L, also à la carte. Specialties: Tonnarelli freddi con crema di trota affumicata, coquilles Saint-Jacques farcite di gamberi. **Credit cards** All major. **Pets** Small dogs allowed only in the rooms. **Facilities** Tennis (20,000L), parking. **Nearby** Gaeta, Caserta, Napoli, Pompeii. **Open** May 11 – Sept. 29.

The spacious front lawn of this beautiful white house stretches down to a sandy beach. You'll be warmly welcomed by the three sisters who run the inn. They share a passion for refinement that is obvious in the decor and the fine cuisine of Paolo Granzioli, one of Italy's renowned chefs. Comfort, quiet luxury and serenity are found here–you'll be treated royally.

How to get there (Map 21): 67 km northwest of Napoli. Via A1 (Rome-Napoli), Cassino exit, towards Formia and Napoli to the stoplight of Cellole, then on the right.

Hotel Miramare ★★★★

Via Nazario Sauro, 24
80132 Napoli
Tel. (081) 764 7589 – Fax (081) 764 0775 – Sig. Rosolino

Rooms 31, with air-conditioning, telephone, bath or shower, WC, TV and minibar. **Price** Single 195-230,000L, double 250-350,000L. **Meals** Breakfast included, served 8:30-10:30; half board +50,000L (per pers.). **Restaurant** Service 19:30-22:30; closed Sun., Aug., late Dec. – early Jan.; menus 45-60,000L, also à la carte. Specialties: Seafood, arrosto di vitello al forno. **Credit cards** All major. **Pets** Dogs allowed. **Nearby** Napoli (Capodimonte National Gallery and Museum, Villa Floridiana, Certosa di San Martino), Pompeii, Ercolano, Cuma, Pozzuoli sulphur springs, Vesuvius, Capri, Ischia, Amalfi coast. **Open** All year.

The Hotel Miramare sits on a beach, next to the port of Santa Lucia with the Bay of Naples and a view of the mist-wreathed Vesuvius forming a backdrop–as if in a picture painted with the sunny palette of a Neapolitan watercolor. The owner has restored this old turn-of-the-century master's house, carefully preserving its Liberty style (the Italian version of art nouveau). The comfortable rooms are decorated with modern elegance in monochromatic shades of blue and gray, with 20's-style lamps and furniture. In summer, meals are served on the terrace overlooking the Bay. The service here is courteous and friendly, however, the hotel is in a crowded, touristy neighborhood, full of the strains of mandolines and the traffic of trattorias–but that's the tradeoff for a room with a view. The hotel does have a few rooms in the rear, which are quieter.

How to get there *(Map 21): Along the bay, between Castel dell'Ovo, the port of Santa Lucia and the Palazzo Reale.*

Villa Brunella ★★★★

Isola di Capri
Via Tragara, 24
80073 Capri (Napoli)
Tel. (081) 837 01 22 - Fax (081) 837 04 30 - Sig. Ruggiero

Rooms 11 and 10 suites with air conditioning, telephone, bath, WC, cable TV and minibar. **Price** Double 340,000L, suite 400,000L. **Meals** Breakfast included, served 8:30-12:00; half board 165,000L (per pers.). **Restaurant** Service 12:30-15:30, 19:30-23:00; menus: 37-42,000L, also à la carte. Specialties: Ravioli alla caprese, frutti di mare, linguine al cartoccio. **Credit cards** Amex, Visa, Eurocard, MasterCard. **Pets** Dogs not allowed. **Facilities** Swimming pool. **Nearby** Capri (Certosa di San Giacomo, Villa Jovis, Punta Tragara, Blue Grotto, Villa Malaparte) Monte Solaro, Napoli, Pompeii, Herculaneum, Cuma, Pozzuoli sulphur springs, Vesuvius, Ischia, Amalfi coast. **Open** Mar. 19 – Nov. 6.

This hotel, near the road that leads to Villa Tiberio, has a nice family atmosphere. Its terraces, which are on several levels and are protected from the wind by berry bushes, jut excitingly out over the sea. It's a marvelous place to enjoy the relaxing lunchtime buffet. The rooms are spacious and comfortable. The ones facing the sea are nicer than those facing the courtyard. The suites have individual terraces. There is no elevator, and it is necessary to climb stairs to even get to the rooms on the ground-floor due to Capri's hilly terrain.

How to get there *(Map 21): Ferry services from Napoli (40 min-70 min), from Sorrento (35 min); in Capri, from Piazzetta towards Villa Tiberio, via Camerelle and via Tragara.*

Europa Palace Hotel ★★★★

Isola di Capri
80071 Anacapri (Napoli)
Tel. (081) 837 38 00 – Fax (081) 837 31 91
A. Cacace and A. Mantegazza

Rooms 93 with air-conditioning, telephone, bath, WC, minibar and TV, (4 with private swimming pool). **Price** Single 180-250,000 L, double 280-480,000L, suite 600-780,000L (with private swimming pool). **Meals** Breakfast included, served 7:00-12:00; half board +50,000L (per pers.). **Restaurant** Service 12:00, 19:30; menus 50-55,000L, also à la carte. Specialties: Tagliolini al limone, ravioli caprese, risotto al melone, spigola del golfo farcita al salmone, torta di mandorla, torta di limone emandorle. **Credit cards** All major. **Pets** Dogs not allowed. **Facilities** Swimming pool. **Nearby** Anacapri (Villa San Michele, Monte Solaro), Capri (Certosa di San Giacomo, Villa Jovis, Punta Tragara, Blue Grotto, Villa Malaparte), Napoli, Pompeii, Herculaneum, Cuma, Pozzuoli sulphur springs, Vesuvius, Ischia, Amalfi coast. **Open** Apr. – Oct.

This modern hotel, incomparable charm, with is full of extraordinary facilities. A privileged clientele enjoys the luxurious comfort of its rooms, gardens and fountains. The height of luxury: suites with private swimming pools. A well-equipped health club tops off the list of services offered. On summer evenings, you can dine very pleasantly on the terraces where excellent cuisine is offered, especially the seafood specialties. The service is impeccable.

How to get there (Map 21): Ferry services from Napoli (40 min-70 min), from Sorrento (35 min); in Capri, at the port, take a taxi or the private bus of the hotel.

Hotel Luna ★★★★

Isola di Capri
Via G. Matteotti, 3
80073 Capri (Napoli)
Tel. (081) 837 04 33 – Fax (081) 837 74 59 – Sig. Vuotto

Rooms 18 with air conditioning, telephone, bath, WC, cable TV, safe and minibar.
Price Single 170-210,000L, double 230-450,000L. **Meals** Breakfast included,
served 7:30-11:30; half board 160-275,000L (per pers.). **Restaurant** Service
12:30-14:30, 19:30-21:30; menus: 50,000L, also à la carte. Specialties: Italian
and Neapolitan cooking. **Credit cards** All major. **Pets** Dogs not allowed.
Facilities Swimming pool. **Nearby** Capri (Certosa di San Giacomo, Villa Jovis,
Punta Tragara, Blue Grotto, Villa Malaparte), Anacapri (Villa San Michele, Monte
Solaro), Napoli, Pompeii, Herculaneum, Cuma, Pozzuoli sulphur springs, Vesuvius,
Ischia, Amalfi coast. **Open** Apr. 1 – Oct. 31.

This is a delightful hotel in an exceptional location. The
rooms are large and freshly decorated in a classical style.
They are a touch overdone, but very comfortable. Irresistible
attractions for visitors are the terraces jutting out over the sea,
the large floral garden and the pool close to the Carthusian
monastery. Though only a few minutes from the center of
Capri, it is a perfect place to get away from it all.

How to get there *(Map 21): Ferry services from Napoli (40 min-70 min),
from Sorrento (35 min); in Capri, from the Piazzetta towards Giardini di
Augusto via Vittorio Emanuele and via F. Serena.*

Hotel Punta Tragara ★★★★

Isola di Capri
Via Tragara, 57
80073 Capri (Napoli)
Tel. (081) 837 08 44 - Fax (081) 837 77 90 - Sig. Ceglia

Rooms 47 with air-conditioning, telephone, bath or shower, WC, cable TV and minibar. **Children** Under 12 not allowed. **Price** Double 310-430,000L, suite 400-540,000L. **Meals** Breakfast included, served 7:00-11:00; half board +60,000L, full board +100,000L (per pers.). **Restaurant** Service 13:00-15:30, 20:00-22:30; menu 75,000L, also à la carte. Specialties: Mediterranean cuisine. **Credit cards** All major. **Pets** Dogs not allowed. **Facilities** 2 swimming pools. **Nearby** Capri (Certosa di San Giacomo, Villa Jovis, Punta Tragara, Blue Grotto, Villa Malaparte), Anacapri (Villa San Michele, Monte Solaro), Napoli, Pompeii, Herculaneum, Cuma, Pozzuoli sulphur springs, Vesuvius, Ischia, Amalfi coast. **Open** Apr. – Oct.

The last place you might except to find a project designed by Le Corbusier is on Capri, but this group of ochre-colored brick houses–built into a stone cliff, hanging over the sea–bears the signature of the celebrated 20th-century architect. Today, it is a luxury hotel with more suites than rooms. The entire hotel is sumptuously decorated with antique furniture, paintings, rugs and old tapestries. Its two restaurants are very pleasant; La Bussola has a terrace for outside dining and a marvelous view. The tropical garden overflowing with giant bougainvilleas and other exotic plants, contains two beautiful salt-water pools continually heated to 94°. You can expect a luxury hotel-style welcome and service.

How to get there *(Map 21): Ferry services from Napoli (40 min-70 min), from Sorrento (35 min); in Capri, from the Piazzetta, towards the Villa Tiberio, via Camerelle and via Tragara.*

Hotel Villa Sarah ★★★

Isola di Capri
Via Tiberio, 3/A - 80073 Capri (Napoli)
Tel. (081) 837 06 09/837 78 17 - Fax (081) 837 72 15
Sig. de Martino Domenico

Rooms 20 with, telephone, bath or shower, WC and cable TV. **Price** Single 130-140,000L, double 210-250,000L. **Meals** Breakfast inclded, served 8:00-10:00; half board 155-265,000L (per pers.). **Restaurant** See p.397. **Credit cards** Amex, Visa, Eurocard and MasterCard. **Pets** Dogs not allowed. **Facilities** Solarium. **Nearby** Capri (Certosa di San Giacomo, Villa Jovis, Punta Tragara, Blue Grotto, Villa Malaparte), Anacapri (Villa San Michele, Monte Solaro), Napoli, Pompeii, Herculaneum, Cuma, Pozzuoli sulphur springs, Vesuvius, Ischia, Amalfi coast. **Open** Easter –Oct.

This villa, built by an English lord in the middle of vineyards, looks out over the bay of Capri. The owner recently turned the management of the hotel over to his son. Let's hope he continues to give the same refined welcome and preserves the discreet family atmosphere. The comfort of the rooms is variable, but decent nonetheless. Breakfast is served on the terrace with homemade preserves and juices fresh-squeezed from the fruit in the orchard. You can tan quietly in the light of the large solarium. A most desirable accomodation in a resort town where prices can be fairly steep.

How to get there *(Map 21): Ferry services from Napoli (40 min-70 min), from Sorrento (35 min); in Capri, from the Piazzetta towards the Villa Tiberio, via Camerelle and via Tragara.*

Pensione Quattro Stagioni ★

Isola di Capri
80073 Marina Piccola (Napoli)
Tel. (081) 837 00 41
Sig. and Sig.ra Cecchini

Rooms 12 (6 with bath or shower, 4 with WC). **Price** 140-160,000L. **Meals** Breakfast included, served 8:00-10:00; half board 110-130,000L (per pers.). **Restaurant** Service 20:00; menu. Specialties: Pasta alle zucchine, pollo caprese. **Credit cards** Visa, Eurocard, MasterCard. **Pets** Dogs not allowed. **Nearby** Capri (Certosa di San Giacomo, Villa Jovis, Punta Tragara, Blue Grotto, Villa Malaparte), Anacapri (Villa San Michele, Monte Solaro) Napoli, Pompeii, Herculaneum, Cuma, Pozzuoli sulphur springs, Vesuvius, Ischia, Amalfi coast. **Open** Mar. 15 – Oct.

This is one of the few family-run inns in Capri. The proximity to the beach and the serenity and the friendliness of the owners are among top features of this *pensione*. Then add the beautifully kept garden and the terrace overlooking the sea and you have a nice, inexpensive place to stay. Half of the rooms lack private bath, so be sure to specify one when making reservations. The cuisine is pleasant.

How to get there *(Map 21): Ferry services from Napoli (40 min-70 min), from Sorrento (35 min).*

Park Hotel Miramare ★★★★

Isola d'Ischia
80070 Sant'Angelo (Napoli)
Tel. (081) 99 92 19 – Fax (081) 99 93 25
Sig.ra Calise

Rooms 50 with bath or shower, WC, TV, minibar and fan. **Price** Single 155,000L, double 430,000L. **Meals** Breakfast 18,000L, served 7:30-10:00; half board 200,000L (per 1 pers.), 190,000 (per 1 pers., in double). **Restaurant** Service 13:00-14:00, 19:30-21:00; menu and carte 75,000L. Specialties: Regional cooking. **Credit cards** Diners, Visa, Eurocard, MasterCard. **Pets** Dogs allowed. **Facilities** Thermal baths «Giardini Aphrodite». **Nearby** Ischia (Boat or car tour of the island, Castello, Mont Epomeo (788m) from Serrara-Fontana (1h), Beach of Citara in Forio, Lacco Ameno), Lido S. Montano, Capri, Napoli, Pompeii, Herculaneum, Cuma, Pozzuoli sulphur springs, the Amalfitan coast to Salerno, Paestum. **Open** Apr. – Sept.

The short ferry ride to the island of Ischia is delightful. On the way, you will cross the sumptuous Gulf of Naples below the majestic silhouette of Vesuvius, and sail along the Procida peninsula. The Hotel Miramare is in Sant Angelo, one of the few unspoiled places on the island. Directly overhanging the sea, it is just a few steps from the small port and the pretty piazzetta. The hotel has a pleasant atmosphere of longstanding tradition. The rooms are comfortable and warmly decorated, some with balconies with a spectacular panoramic view. A restaurant on the terrace will entice you with classic island seafood. A few steps away, a private flower-lined path leads to the marvelous Aphrodite-Apollo Thermal Garden, which has twelve pools of varying temperatures that are built into the cliff in a series of descending terraces.

How to get there *(Map 21): south of Napoli via A3, Castellammare di Stabia exit, then towards S 145. Ferry service from Napoli (70 min) and from Pozzuoli (40 min).*

Pensione Casa Sofia

Isola d'Ischia
80070 Sant'Angelo (Napoli)
Via Sant'Angelo,29 B
Tel. (081) 99 93 10 - Fax (081) 99 93 10 - Sig.ra Bremer-Barricelli

Rooms 8 with shower and WC. **Price** With half board 80,000L (per 1 pers.), 50,000L (per 1 pers. in double). **Meals** Breakfast included, served from 8:00. **Restaurant** Service 18:30 (19:30 in summer), menu. Specialties: Regional cooking. **Credit cards** Not accepted. **Pets** Small dogs allowed. **Facilities** Thermal baths. **Nearby** Ischia (Boat or car tour of the island, Castello, Mont Epomeo (788m) from Serrara-Fontana (1h), Beach of Citara in Forio, Lacco Ameno), Lido S. Montano, Capri, Napoli, Pompeii, Herculaneum, Cuma, Pozzuoli sulphur springs, the Amalfitan coast to Salerno, Paestum. **Open** Mar. 16 – early Nov.

Sig.ra Bremer-Barricelli's large beautiful house, which has a splendid view of the sea, is the ideal place for a quiet family vacation. The rooms are all charming and nicely decorated. Copious breakfasts are served on a terrace overlooking the entire Bay of Sant' Angelo. The old fishing village of Sant'Angelo is the only one on the island of Ischia where you can still find the unspoiled atmosphere of the old days. Next to Casa Sophia you can unwind in the thermal pools of the Garden of Aphrodite (groups of no fewer than ten at a time are admitted). If your travels take you to Ischia, don't miss this invigorating place.

How to get there *(Map 21): south of Napoli via A3, Castellammare di Stabia exit, then towards S 145. Ferry service from Napoli (70 min) and from Pozzuoli (40 min).*

Hotel La Villarosa ★★★★

Isola d'Ischia
Via Giacinto Gigante, 5
80077 Porto d'Ischia (Napoli)
Tel. (081) 99 13 16 – Fax (081) 99 24 25 – Sig. Pepe

Rooms 33 (10 with air conditioning) and 4 suites with telephone, bath, WC and minibar (20 with cable TV). **Price** Single 110-130,000L, double 180-200,000L, suite +50,000L. **Meals** Breakfast 10,000L, served 7:00-10:00; half board 120-160,000L, full board 140-170,000L (per pers.). **Restaurant** For residents, service 13:00-14:00, 19:30-21:00; menus 40-60,000L. **Credit cards** Amex, Visa, Eurocard, MasterCard. **Pets** Small dogs allowed. **Facilities** Swimming pool, thermal baths, hydrotherapy. **Nearby** Ischia (Boat or car tour of the island, Castello, Mont Epomeo (788 m) from Serrara-Fontana (1 h), Beach of Citara in Forio, Lacco Ameno), Lido S. Montano, Capri, Napoli, Pompeii, Herculaneum, Cuma, Pozzuoli sulphur springs, the Amalfitan coast to Salerno, Paestum. **Open** Mar. 22 – Oct.

L a Villarosa is a hard place to say goodbye to. You will see this as soon as you arrive. This enchanting hotel is set in the middle of a lush tropical garden. Good taste and the best of everything prevail: simplicity, discretion and refinement are evident down to the last detail. An elegant salon opens onto a garden with a springfed swimming pool. The rooms, some with a terrace or a flowering balcony, all have the discreet charm of an old–fashioned country house. You can enjoy your meals in the rooftop restaurant or, in summer, on the marvelous wisteria–covered terrace. The hotel spa is discreetly located in the basement.

How to get there *(Map 21): Ferry services from Napoli-Molo Beverello (75 min by ferry, 40 min by hydrofoil).*

La Bagattella Hotel ★★★

Isola d'Ischia
Spiaggia di San Francesco – Via Tommaso Cigliano
80075 Forio d'Ischia (Napoli)
Tel. (081) 98 60 72 – Fax (081) 98 96 37 – Sig.ra Lauro

Rooms 25 and 26 mini-apart. with telephone, bath, WC. **Price** With half board 130-155,000L, full board 155-1785,000L (per pers.). **Meals** Breakfast included, served 7:30-9:30. **Restaurant** For the residents, service 13:00-14:00, 19:00-20:30; menus, also à la carte. Specialties: Seafood. **Credit cards** Amex, Visa, Eurocard, MasterCard. **Pets** Dogs not allowed. **Facilities** 2 swimming pools (1 indoor), hydrotherapy, parking. **Nearby** Ischia (Boat or car tour of the island, Castello, Mont Epomeo (788 m) from Serrara-Fontana (1 h), Beach of Citara in Forio, Lacco Ameno), Lido S. Montano, Capri, Napoli, Pompeii, Herculaneum, Cuma, Pozzuoli sulphur springs, the Amalfitan coast to Salerno, Paestum. **Open** Apr. – Oct.

La Bagatella looks like an oversize Moorish wedding cake dropped into a tropical garden ablaze with oleander bushes and bouganvilleas. The fresh–looking rooms are very luxurious. Some are slightly overdone but are nonetheless pleasant and some have flowering balconies. A modern wing has been added, with simple, functional rooms and efficiency apartments. The new wing and the restaurant open onto a garden with a springfed swimming pool, surrounded by hibiscus bushes and palm trees. There is also a beautiful sand beach just five minutes away on foot.

How to get there *(Map 21): Ferry services from Napoli-Molo Beverello (75 min by ferry, 20 min by hydrofoil); 10 km from Porto d'Ischia.*

Albergo Terme San Montano ★★★★★

Isola d'Ischia
80076 Lacco Ameno (Napoli)
Tel. (081) 99 40 33 – Fax (081) 98 02 42
Sig. Precisano

Rooms 65 and 2 suites with telephone, bath, WC, TV and minibar. **Price** Single 160-240,000L, double 260-500,000L, suite +100,000L. **Meals** Breakfast included, served 7:00-11:00; half board 180-280,000L, full board 220-320,000L. **Restaurant** Service 13:00-15:00, 20:00-22:00, à la carte. **Credit cards** All major **Pets** Small dogs allowed only in the room. **Facilities** Swimming pool, tennis, private beach, water-skiing, sauna, private bus, parking. **Nearby** Ischia (Boat or car tour of the island, Castello, Mont Epomeo (788 m) from Serrara-Fontana (1 h), Beach of Citara in Forio, Lacco Ameno), Lido S. Montano, Capri, Napoli, Pompeii, Herculaneum, Cuma, Pozzuoli sulphur springs, the Amalfitan coast to Salerno, Paestum. **Open** 1 week before Easter – Oct. 20.

This hotel enjoys one of the most beautiful locations on Ischia. It sits on the top of a hill, overlooking the countryside on one side and the sea on the other, with a great view of the Vivara and Procida Islands, and the slightly hazy outline of Vesuvius in the distance. The San Montano tends to be austerely modern in both its appearance and personality, but the great luxury and comfort of the place more than compensate. The rooms, all with superb view, are decorated in a nautical style. Some have a balcony, others a private garden. On the terraced hillside grounds are two swimming pools and a tennis court. A shuttle bus will take you to the private beach. The prices are high, but well worth it.

How to get there *(Map 21): Ferry services from Napoli-Molo Beverello (75 min by ferry, 20 min by hydrofoil). 6 km from Porto d'Ischia.*

Palazzo Belmonte

84072 Santa Maria di Castellabate (Napoli)
Tel. (0974) 96 02 11 – Fax (0974) 96 11 50
Sig.ra Wilkinson

Suites 21 with telephone, bath, WC and mini-kitchen. **Price** Suite 280-340,000L (2 pers.), 460-620,000L (3 pers.), 600-720,000L (4 pers.) 860-1,040 000L (6 pers.). **Meals** Breakfast included **Restaurant** Service 12:30-14:30, 19:30-22:00, à la carte. Specialties: Regional and Italian cuisine. **Credit cards** All major. **Pets** Dogs not allowed. **Facilities** Swimming pool, private beach, parking. **Nearby** Sorrento, the bay of Sorrento, Napoli, Pompeii, Paestum, Capri, Padula Vietri. **Open** May – Oct.

Several months a year, the prince of Belmonte opens up his palace to the outside world. This beautiful historical monument was built in the 17th century in the small fishing village and is still used by his family as a hunting lodge to receive royal visitors from Spain and Italy. The prince and his family live in one wing and there are suites for guests in another part of the palazzo. They are unpretentiously but elegantly decorated in light colors and have nice bamboo furniture. Certain guest rooms open onto a pretty courtyard full of fragrant Chilian jasmine; others overlook a garden fragrant pine trees, magnolias, hibiscus and oleanders; and still others have a terrace on the sea with views of the island of Capri when the weather is clear. The regional specialties served in the restaurant are made with fresh produce from the palace's vegetable garden. The swimming pool and private beach at the edge of a pine forest may make you want to take it easy, but the enticements of Naples, Pompeii and the Amalfi coast are so close by!

How to get there *(Map 21): 90 km south of Napoli via A3, Battipàglia exit, then towards Paestum, Agropoli and Castellabate.*

Grand Hotel Excelsior Vittoria ★★★★

Piazza Tasso, 34
80067 Sorrento (Napoli)
Tel. (081) 807 10 44 – Fax (081) 877 12 06
Sig. Fiorentino

Rooms 106 (some with air-conditioning) telephone, bath or shower, WC., TV, safe and minibar. **Price** Single 286,000L, double 355-510,000L, suite 650-1 080,000L. **Meals** Breakfast included, served 7:00-10:00; half board 346-385,000L. **Restaurant** Service 12:30-14:30, 19:30-22:00; menu 70,000L, also à la carte. Specialties: Italian and Neapolitan cuisine. **Credit cards** All major. **Pets** Dogs allowed (fee). **Facilities** Swimming pool, parking. **Nearby** Bay of Sorrento, Napoli, Paestum, Capri. **Open** All year.

Overlooking the Gulf of Naples from the top of a rocky crag, this palace-hotel is one of the most prestigious in Sorrento. The garden, with a terrace facing the open sea, is an enchanting mixture of fragrant flowers, rose bushes and vines. A highlight is the winter garden overflowing with dwarf palm trees and turquoise flowers. The interior of the palace still has its original frescoes, stucco trimming and ceilings painted in Liberty style. The salons and rooms are all spacious and comfortable and furnished with beautiful antiques. In summer, meals are served on the panoramic terrace, and on Sundays you can join in a *buffet dansant*. Many illustrious personages have stayed here, including Goethe, Wagner and Verdi. The most requested room is the one Caruso lived in at the end of his life, a stay immortalized in a renown song often sung by Luciano Pavarotti.

How to get there *(Map 21): 48 km south of Napoli via A3 to Castellammare di Stabia, then S145.*

Grand Hotel Cocumella ★★★★★

Via Cocumella, 7
80067 Sorrento (Salerno)
Tel. (081) 878 29 33 – Fax (081) 878 37 12
Sig.ra. Gaia del Papa

Rooms 60 with air-conditioning, telephone, bath, WC, cable TV and minibar **Price** Single 260-320,000L, double 420-520,000L, suite 550-700,000L. **Meals** Breakfast included (buffet), served 7:30-10:30; half board 225,000L, full board 266,000L. **Restaurant** Service 12:45-14:30, 19:30-22:30; menus 50-80,000L, also à la carte. Specialties: Mediterranean and regional cooking. **Credit cards** All major. **Pets** Dogs allowed in the rooms only. **Facilities** Swimming pool, sauna, health center, parking. **Nearby** Bay of Sorrento, Napoli, Paestum, Capri. **Open** All year.

Some thirty miles (50 km) from Naples along the Amalfi coast, you can still occasionally find a little piece of paradise. The Hotel Cocumella is one of them. Time seems to go by slowly here, perhaps due to the sun, salty sea air and the pungent fragrance of flowers. You will enjoy sunbathing, reading in the shade of the cloister in the afternoon, drinking tea and fresh squeezed orange juice on white linen tablecloths and savoring marvelous spaghetti in the cool dining room. If you like, you can also spend a day at sea in the hotel sailboat, which will take you to Capri and bring you back in the evening. Take note, however, that the hotel organizes concerts and professional shows. Check these dates when making your reservation if you prefer to avoid sharing your idyll with such activities.

How to get there *(Map 21): 48 km south of Napoli via A3 to Castellammare di Stabia, then S145.*

Hotel Bellevue Syrene ★★★

Piazza della Vittoria, 5
80067 Sorrento (Napoli)
Tel. (081) 878 10 24 – Fax (081) 878 39 63
Sig. Russo

Rooms 59 with telephone, bath or shower and WC. **Price** Single 170-220,000L, double 220-350,000L, suite 470-600,000L. **Meals** Breakfast included (buffet), served 7:00-10:00, half board 135-170,000L. **Restaurant** Service 19:30-20:45; menu 70,000L, also à la carte. Specialties: Spaghetti con cozze, gnocchi. **Credit cards** All major. **Pets** Dogs allowed in the rooms only. **Facilities** Private beach, parking. **Nearby** Bay of Sorrento, Napoli, Paestum, Capri. **Open** All year.

The hotel is in a venerable 18th-century building just above the sea on the site of an ancient Roman villa where Virgil and Tiberius once lived. There is a large, well-decorated dining room next to a billiard room and bar whose frescoes and mosaics recall a rich historical past. To get to the private beach, you can take the elevator, but be sure to explore the stairway and vaulted passage which are, like the columns in the garden, vestiges of the original Roman villa. Some rooms are more interesting than others: ask for room 4, one of the few with a balcony overlooking the sea.

How to get there (Map 21): 48 km south of Napoli via A3 to Castellammare di Stabia, then S145.

Hotel Capo La Gala ★★★★

Via Luigi Serio, 7
Vico Equense (Napoli)
Tel. (081) 801 57 58 - Fax (081) 879 87 47
Sig.ra Savarese

Rooms 18 (9 with air conditioning) with telephone, bath or shower, WC, TV and minibar. **Price** Single 165,000L, double 240,000L, suite 450-600,000L. **Meals** Breakfast included (buffet), served 8:00-10:30; half board 170-215,000L, full board 220-265,000L. **Restaurant** Service 13:00-15:00, 20:00-22:00; menu 60,000L, also à la carte. Specialties: Seafood, frutti di mare. **Credit cards** All major. **Pets** Dogs allowed in the rooms only. **Facilities** Swimming pool, sauna (+1,500L), health center, parking (+20,000L). **Nearby** Gulf of Salerno and Amalfitan coast, Napoli, Paestum, Capri. **Open** Apr. – Oct.

Designed around a series of terraces and small stairways cut into the stone hillside, the Capo La Gala blends so well into its surrounding that it seems more a part of the sea than of the land. The rooms, few in number, are all identical. Each one, distinguished by the name of a wind instead of a number, has a balcony facing the sea. You will find a homey atmosphere here, and will enjoy relaxing beside the sulphur–water swimming pool. The restaurant serves mainly seafood and fresh vegetables.

How to get there (Map 21): 39 km south of Napoli via A3 to Castellammare di Stabia, then S145, towards Sorrento.

Hotel Cappuccini Convento ★★★★

84011 Amalfi (Salerno)
Tel. (089) 87 18 77
Fax (089) 87 18 86
Sig. Aielli

Rooms 54 with telephone, bath or shower, WC and TV. **Price** Single 100-120,000L, double 140-160,000L. **Meals** Breakfast 20,000L, served 7:30-10:30; half board 140-180,000L, full board 120,000L. (per pers., 3 days min.). **Restaurant** Service 13:00-14:30, 19:30-21:00; menus, also à la carte. Specialties: Seafood, regional cooking. **Credit cards** All major. **Pets** Dogs allowed. **Facilities** Private beach, parking. **Nearby** Amalfi (Duomo, "Cloisters of Paradise," Emerald Grotto), Gulf of Salerno and Amalfitan coast (Positano, Ravello, Salerno), Paestum, Capri, Napoli, Pompeii, Herculaneum, Cuma, Pozzuolo sulphur spring, Ischia. **Open** All year.

The Cappuccini Convento, formerly a 7th-century convent, is built into the side of a mountain and accessible only by elevator. Beyond the wisteria bushes and the bougainvilleas is a great view of Amalfi and the sea. The atmosphere is unusual: monks' cells have been converted into pleasant, comfortable rooms. Excellent seafood and shellfish dishes are served in the vaulted dining room. The quiet salons are delightful to relax in after walks on the winding, blossom-perfumed paths nearby. The downside is that the salons and cloister are often rented out for receptions.

How to get there *(Map 21): 25 km west of Salerno via A3, Vietri sul Mare exit, then S163 along the coast.*

Hotel Luna Convento ★★★★

Via P. Comite, 19
84011 Amalfi (Salerno)
Tel. (089) 871 002 - Fax (089) 87 13 33
Sig. Milone

Rooms 48 with telephone, bath or shower, WC and TV. **Price** Single 130-150,000L, double 200-240,000L, suite 250-280,000L. **Meals** Breakfast 20,000L, served 7:30-10:00; half board 140-180,000L, full board 120,000L. (per pers., 3 days min.). **Restaurant** Service 12:30-14:30, 19:30-21:30; menus 60,000L, also à la carte. Specialties: Cannelloni del convento, crespoline, risotto pescatore, gamberoni alla griglia. **Credit cards** All major. **Pets** Dogs not allowed. **Facilities** Swimming pool, private beach, parking. **Nearby** Amalfi (Duomo, "Cloisters of Paradise," Emerald Grotto), Gulf of Salerno and Amalfitan coast (Positano, Ravello, Salerno), Paestum, Capri, Napoli, Pompeii, Herculaneum, Cuma, Pozzuolo sulphur springs, Ischia. **Open** All year.

This former 13th-century convent once welcomed St. Francis of Assisi, as well as, more recently, composer Richard Wagner and playwright Henrik Ibsen. All of the rooms have nice furniture, but avoid the ones on the street side. Breakfast is served in the Byzantine-style cloister. There is a swimming pool and private beach backed up by rocks. The family which runs the hotel will give you a courteous welcome. This is a great address, and has been for generations.

How to get there (Map 21): 25 km west of Salerno via A3, Vietri sul Mare exit, then S163 along the coast.

Hotel Santa Caterina ★★★★

84011 Amalfi (Salerno)
Tel. (089) 87 10 12
Fax (089) 87 13 51

Rooms 68 with air conditioning, telephone, bath or shower, WC, TV and minibar.
Price Single 270-330,000L, double 370-520,000L, suite 650-1 000,000L. **Meals**
Breakfast included, served 7:30-10:00, half board +75,000L, full board +140,000L.
(per pers., 2 days min.). **Restaurant** Service 13:00-15:00, 20:00-22:00, menus
65,000L, also à la carte. Specialties: Linguine al limone, limoni farciti Santa
Caterina, crespoline all'amalfitana, penne alla saracena. **Credit cards** All major.
Pets Dogs not allowed. **Facilities** Swimming pool, private beach, parking (25,000L).
Nearby Amalfi (Duomo, "Cloisters of Paradise," Emerald Grotto), Gulf of Salerno and
Amalfitan coast (Positano, Ravello, Salerno), Paestum, Capri, Napoli, Pompeii,
Herculaneum, Cuma, Pozzuolo sulphur springs, Ischia. **Open** All year.

For three generations now, the Hotel Santa Caterina has belonged to a family which understands and enjoys the art of hospitality. The furniture, mostly antiques, has been meticulously selected, giving each room a particular flavor. The bathrooms, are very modern–some even have a whirlpool bath. An elevator will take you down to the sea or the salt-water swimming pool. Ask to stay in the "chalet," a small house tucked away among the lemon trees in the garden.

How to get there *(Map 21): 25 km west of Salerno via A3, Vietri sul Mare exit, then S163 along the coast.*

Hotel Belvedere ★★★★

84010 Conca dei Marini (Salerno)
Tel. (089) 83 12 82 – Fax (089) 83 14 39
Sig. Lucibello

Rooms 36 with telephone, bath or shower and WC. **Price** Single 95-125,000L, double 150-200,000L, suite 230-280,000L. **Meals** Breakfast 15,000L, served 7:00-10:00; half board 155-200,000L, full board 180-230,000L. (per pers., 3 days min.). **Restaurant** Service 12:30-14:00, 19:30-21:00; menu 45,000L, also à la carte. Specialties: Crespolini, timballo di maccheroni. **Credit cards** All major. **Pets** Dogs not allowed. **Facilities** Swimming pool, private beach, parking, private car from Salerno railway station 100,000L, from Napoli aereoporto 150,000L. **Nearby** Amalfi (Duomo, "Cloisters of Paradise," Emerald Grotto), Gulf of Salerno and Amalfitan coast (Positano, Ravello, Salerno), Paestum, Capri, Napoli, Pompeii, Herculaneum, Cuma, Pozzuolo sulphur springs, Ischia. **Open** Apr. – Oct.

You may be impressed by the classical facade of the Belvedere, or by the fact that it is built into a cliff over the sea, but what is truly extraordinary is its view of the entire Amalfi coast with its steep hillsides and beautiful lemon tree orchards. The rooms are modern and very comfortable, with either a balcony or terrace overlooking the sea. An interior elevator will take you down to the pool on the rocks and to the walkway to the sea. The Belvedere is a singularly professional hotel, the cuisine excellent, and the service impeccable yet friendly, and the atmosphere of warm, unimposing hospitality.

How to get there (Map 21): 65 km southeast of Napoli via A3, Castellammare di Stabia exit, then N336, towards Amalfi.

Hotel San Pietro ★★★★★

84017 Positano (Salerno)
Tel. (089) 87 54 55 – Fax (089) 81 14 49
Sig. Attanasio

Rooms 60 with air-conditioning, telephone, bath or shower, WC, minibar and TV. **Price** Standard 500-520,000L, medium 580-600,000L, luxury (3 pers.) 660-680,000L. **Meals** Breakfast included, served 7:00-11:30; half board +80,000L, full board +140,000L. (per pers., 3 days min.). **Restaurant** Service 13:00-15:00, 20:00-21:30; à la carte. Specialties: Italian and Neapolitan cooking. **Credit cards** All major. **Pets** Dogs not allowed. **Facilities** Swimming pool, private beach, tennis, windsurfing, parking. **Nearby** Gulf of Salerno and Amalfitan coast (Positano, Amalfi, Ravello, Salerno), Paestum, Capri, Napoli, Pompeii, Herculaneum, Cuma, Pozzuolo sulphur springs, Ischia. **Open** Apr. – Oct.

From the sea, the San Pietro looks like a froth of vegetation cascading from terrace to terrace down the side of Mount Lattari. The luxurious hotel is a fantasia of architecture environmentally integrated, with the fabulous view, with bouganvilleas and vines almost climbing right into the salons. The rooms, with Hollywood-style bath, are as sumptuous as they are comfortable. The balconies are overlaid with ceramic tiles. An elevator cut into the rough stone hillside will take you down to the bottom of the 286-foot-high cliff to a private beach. You can have lunch at the snack bar there, or play tennis on the court in a nearby cove. The hotel restaurant serves excellent Italian cuisine, and the staff will give you a remarkable welcome. For security reasons, children under twelve are not allowed.

How to get there *(Map 21): 57 km south of Napoli via A3, Castellammare di Stabia exit, towards Sorrento, Positano.*

Le Sirenuse ★★★★

Via C. Colombo, 30
84010 Positano (Salerno)
Tel. (089) 87 50 66 – Fax (089) 81 17 98
Sig. Sersale

Rooms 60 with air-conditioning, telephone, bath or shower, WC, TV and minibar.
Price Single 250-480,000L, double 400-640,000L, suite 650-800,000L.
Meals Breakfast included, served 7:00-11:00; half board +75,000L, full board
+125,000L. (per pers., 3 days min.). **Restaurant** Service 13:00-14:30, 20:00-
22:00; à la carte. Specialties: Pasta, seafood. **Credit cards** All major. **Pets** Dogs
allowed in the rooms only. **Facilities** Heated swimming pool, parking. **Nearby** Gulf
of Salerno and Amalfitan coast (Positano, Amalfi, Ravello, Salerno), Paestum,
Capri, Napoli, Pompeii, Herculaneum, Cuma, Pozzuolo sulphur springs, Ischia.
Open All year.

Behind the red–ochre facade of Le Sirenuse you'll find one of
the best hotels on the Amalfi coast. This former 18th-
century palace looks out over the bay of Positano. It has been
modified and expanded over the years, and today the hotel
appears to be an odd but charming series of angles, often
extended by terraces. The rooms are extremely comfortable and
decorated with lovely Venetian and Neapolitan furniture.
Certain rooms in the oldest part still have their original ceramic
tile floors. You can have lunch and dinner at tables set around
the pool. The new chef offers innovative cuisine based on
traditional Neapolitan recipes. The staff is friendly and efficient.

How to get there *(Map 21): 57 km south of Napoli via A3,
Castellammare di Stabia exit, towards Sorrento, Positano.*

Hotel Poseidon ★★★★

Via Pasitea, 148
84017 Positano (Salerno)
Tel. (089) 81 11 11 – Fax (089) 87 58 33
Famiglia Aonzo

Rooms 45 and 3 suites with air-conditioning, telephone, bath or shower, WC, TV and minibar. **Price** Double 180-320,000L, suite 350-520,000L. **Meals** Breakfast included, served 8:00-11:00; half board 185-215,000L (per pers., 3 days min.). **Restaurant** Service 13:00-14:30, 20:00-22:00; à la carte. **Credit cards** All major. **Pets** Dogs allowed in the rooms only. **Facilities** Swimming pool, health center (20-80,000L), parking (30,000L). **Nearby** Sorrento, Gulf of Salerno and Amalfitan coast (Positano, Amalfi, Ravello, Salerno), Paestum, Capri, Napoli, Pompeii, Herculaneum, Cuma, Pozzuolo sulphur springs, Ischia. **Open** Easter – Nov.

In the fifties the Aonzo family decided to build a little vacation house. Today it has become a four-star hotel whose friendly atmosphere that will make you feel right at home. Like the rest of the village, the house is built into the hill overlooking the bay. The rooms are elegant and spacious, and have private terraces. You will find the same simple elegance in the salons. The large panoramic terrace is, in fact, a large outdoor living area. In summer, a restaurant is set up under the bougainvillea, just next to the pool and solarium. The hotel also has a "well-being center," which will help you get back into shape after a late evening out in Positano.

How to get there *(Map 21): 57 km south of Napoli via A3, Castellammare di Stabia exit, towards Sorrento, Positano.*

Hotel Villa Franca ★★★★

Viale Pasitea, 318
84017 Positano (Salerno)
Tel. (089) 87 56 55 - Fax (089) 87 57 35
Sig. Russo

Rooms 28 with air conditioning, telephone, bath or shower, WC, TV and minibar.
Price Single 240-260,000L, double 300-320,000L, suite 360-380,000L.
Meals Breakfast included, served 7:30-11:00; half board +50,000L (per pers., 3
days min.). **Restaurant** Service 13:00-15:00, 19:00-22:00, menu 70,000L, also à
la carte. Specialties: Linguine all'astice, agnolotti in salsa di spinaci, gnocchi alla
mozzarella, risotto ai frutti di mare, scampi gratinati al forno. **Credit cards** All
major. **Pets** Small dogs allowed. **Facilities** Swimming pool, parking (25,000L).
Nearby Sorrento, Gulf of Salerno Amalfitan coast (Positano, Amalfi, Ravello,
Salerno), Paestum, Capri, Napoli, Pompeii, Herculaneum, Cuma, Pozzuolo sulphur
springs, Ischia. **Open** Mar. 18 – Oct. 31.

The mere mention of the name Positano is enough to make
people dream of holiday hotels. A case in point is the Villa
Franca, has that perfect kind of beauty that people come to the
Amalfi coast to find. It is light and airy, and has large picture
windows, superb Mediterranean-style rooms, and large terraces
opening onto the blue of the sky and the sea. The decor,
ceramics and vegetation blend many beautiful shades of blue,
green and orange. You will spend your days on the terraces,
which rise in a series of steps to the swimming pool on the roof,
where, suspended between the sky and the sea, you will
experience an intense sensation of the good life.

How to get there *(Map 21): 57 km south of Napoli via A3,
Castellammare di Stabia exit, towards Sorrento, Positano.*

Hotel Palazzo Murat ★★★★

Via dei Mulini, 23
84017 Positano (Salerno)
Tel. (089) 875 177 – Fax (089) 81 14 19
Famiglia Attanasio

Rooms 28 with telephone, bath, WC, TV and minibar. **Price** Single 175-195,000L, double 225-295,000L. **Meals** Breakfast included, served 8:00-11:00; half board +75,000L, full board +125,000L. (per pers., 3 days min.). **Restaurant** See p. 399. **Credit cards** All major. **Pets** Dogs allowed. **Nearby** Gulf of Salerno and Amalfitan coast (Positano, Amalfi, Ravello, Salerno), Paestum, Capri, Napoli, Pompeii, Herculaneum, Cuma, Pozzuolo (sulphur springs), Ischia. **Open** Easter – Oct., Dec. 26 – Jan. 10.

The palazzo was built to be the summer residence of Joachim Murat, Marshal of France and king of Naples. It has now been converted into a hotel. Many of the original Baroque-style features remain, such as the charming patio where chamber music concerts are sometimes given. The most pleasant rooms are in the old part (prices are higher there, too), particularly Rooms 5 and 24, each of which has a balcony with a view on Positano Bay. You cannot drive directly to the hotel, but you can park your car in the parking lot at the Piazza dei Mulini, about one hundred and fifty feet away. Some rooms are air conditioned.

How to get there *(Map 21): 57 km south of Napoli via A3, Castellammare di Stabia exit, towards Sorrento, Positano.*

Albergo Casa Albertina

Via Tavolozza, 3
84017 Positano (Salerno)
Tel. (089) 87 51 43 – Fax (089) 81 15 40
Sig. L. Cinque

Rooms 21 with air conditioning, telephone, bath or shower, WC and minibar.
Price Half board in single 120-150,000L, in double 130-160,000L, in suite 160-180,000L (per pers.). **Meals** Breakfast included, served 7:30-12:00.
Restaurant Service 20:00-21:30; à la carte. Specialties: Risotto alla pescatore, penne all'impazzata, zuppa di pesce, pesce alla griglia. **Credit cards** All major.
Pets Dogs allowed. **Facilities** Parking (20-25,000L). **Nearby** Gulf of Salerno and Amalfitan coast (Positano, Amalfi, Ravello, Salerno), Paestum, Capri, Napoli, Pompeii, Herculaneum, Cuma, Pozzuolo sulphur springs, Ischia. **Open** All year.

Take a few steps up a steep little street and you will discover the simple but charming Albergo Casa Albertina. This old village house is run by the son of a fisherman, a former employee of the nearby Sirenuse. Apart from the marvelous 18th-century wooden doors, most of the hotel has a rakish 60's-style decor. However, the dishes, chairs and knick-knacks crafted by local artisans give the place an atmosphere typical of the region. Most of the rooms have a sea-view balcony–it's the perfect place to have breakfast. The service is particularly warm and friendly. You cannot reach the hotel by car, but porter service is available.

How to get there (Map 21): 57 km south of Napoli via A3, Castellammare di Stabia exit, towards Sorrento, Positano.

Grand Hotel Tritone ★★★★

Via Campo, 5
84010 Praiano (Salerno)
Tel. (089) 87 43 33 – Fax (089) 87 43 74
Sig. Gagliano

Rooms 62 (49 with air-conditioning), telephone, bath or shower, WC (15 with minibar). **Price** Single 140-200,000L, double 210-320,000L, suite 300-400,000L. **Meals** Breakfast 18,000L, served 7:00-10:00; half board 150-210,000L, full board 180-240,000L. **Restaurant** Service 13:00-14:30, 19:30-21:30; menu 60,000L, also à la carte. Specialties: Risotto, seafood. **Credit cards** All major. **Pets** Dogs allowed. **Facilities** 2 swimming pools, private beach, parking. **Nearby** Gulf of Salerno and Amalfitan coast (Positano, Amalfi, Ravello, Salerno), Paestum, Capri, Napoli, Pompeii, Herculaneum, Cuma, Pozzuolo sulphur springs, Ischia. **Open** Apr. 15 – Oct.

This hotel, magnificently sited on a series of terraces dramatically descending to the sea, has long attracted politicians, sports and show business celebrities such as Madonna. You, too, will enjoy it all: the private beach (accessible by elevator), the two salt water swimming pools, the impeccable service and the hotel's grotto-level restaurant.

How to get there (Map 21): 65 km southeast of Napoli via A3, Castellammare di Stabia exit, towards Sorrento, Positano.

Hotel Caruso Belvedere ★★★★

Via San Giovanni del Toro, 52
84010 Ravello (Salerno)
Tel. (089) 85 71 11 – Fax (089) 85 73 72
Sig.ra Caruso

Rooms 24 with telephone, bath or shower and WC. **Price** With half board 230-325,000L, full board 320-416,000L (per 2 pers.). **Meals** Breakfast included, served 7:00-10:00. **Restaurant** Service 12:30-14:30, 19:30-21:00; closed 15 days in Feb.; menu 42,000L, also à la carte. Specialties: Crespolini al formaggio, spaghetti alla contadina, soufflé al limone e cioccolata. **Credit cards** All major. **Pets** Dogs allowed (fee). **Nearby** Ravello (Villa Rufolo and Villa Cimbrone), Gulf of Salerno and Amalfitan coast (Positano, Amalfi, Ravello, Salerno), Paestum, Capri, Napoli, Pompeii, Herculaneum, Cuma, Pozzuolo sulphur springs, Ischia. **Open** All year.

This 12th-century palace on the breathtaking Gulf of Salerno still bears the marks of elegance left by prestigious guests, including Greta Garbo and members of the Italian royal family. Today, Gino Caruso's polished management attracts a mostly English and American clientele. You will delight in the comfort and tranquility here, the great service and the refined cuisine.

How to get there (Map 21): 65 km southeast of Napoli via A3, Salerno exit, towards Vietri sul Mare and Ravello.

Villa Cimbrone ★★★

Santa Chiara, 26
84010 Ravello (Salerno)
Tel. (089) 85 74 59 – Fax (089) 85 77 77
Famiglia Vuilleumier

Rooms 18 with telephone, (10 with bath or shower), WC. **Price** Single 270,000L, double 300,000L, suite 350-400,000L. **Meals** Breakfast 18,000L, served 8:00-10:30. **Restaurant** See p. 398. **Credit cards** Amex, Visa, Eurocard, MasterCard. **Pets** Dogs not allowed. **Nearby** Ravello (Villa Rufolo and Villa Cimbrone), Gulf of Salerno and Amalfitan coast (Positano, Amalfi, Ravello, Salerno), Paestum, Capri, Napoli, Pompeii, Herculaneum, Cuma, Pozzuolo sulphur springs, Ischia. **Open** All year except 2 weeks before Easter.

Incorporating a beautiful 8th-century cloister, this celebrated residence once belonged to an old English family. The gazebo in the garden offers a spectacular panoramic view of the sea, as does every room in the house. Some still have the original mosaics or fireplaces, while others have trompe-l'oeil frescoes. Recent renovations have considerably improved the overall comfort-level.

How to get there *(Map 21): 65 km southeast of Napoli via A3, Salerno exit, towards Vietri sul Mare and Ravello.*

Hotel Palumbo – Palazzo Gonfalone ★★★★★

Via San Giovanni del Toro, 28
84010 Ravello (Salerno)
Tel. (089) 85 72 44 – Fax (089) 85 81 33
Sig. Vuilleumier

Rooms 21 with telephone, bath or shower, WC, TV, safe and minibar. **Price** Half board in the palazzo 320-365,000L, in the annex 215-240,000L, full board in the palazzo 370-425,000L, in the annex 275-280,000L. **Meals** Breakfast included, served 7:30-10:30. **Restaurant** Service 12:30-14:30, 20:00-21:30; menu 90,000L, also à la carte. Specialties: Crespelle Palumbo, ravioli alla menta, filetto al Gonfalone. **Credit cards** All major. **Pets** Small dogs allowed. **Facilities** Parking (20,000L). **Nearby** Ravello (Villa Rufolo and Villa Cimbrone), Gulf of Salerno and Amalfitan coast (Positano, Amalfi, Ravello, Salerno), Paestum, Capri, Napoli, Pompeii, Herculaneum, Cuma, Pozzuolo sulphur springs, Ischia. **Open** All year.

Elegance reigns in this 12th-century palace, which has kept its original architecture intact. The owners have decorated the rooms with delicate refinement. A savory dinner complemented by wine from the hotel's own vineyard and served by candlelight on the terrace with a view of the Amalfi Bay and will make your stay unforgettable despite the somewhat stiff service. A modern annex has been built on the grounds. The prices are low considering the five-star comfort, the beautiful gardens and the excellent restaurant.

How to get there (Map 21): 65 km southeast of Napoli via A3, Salerno exit, towards Vietri sul Mare and Ravello.

Hotel Corona d'Oro ★★★★

Via Oberdan, 12
40126 Bologna
Tel. (051) 23 64 56 – Fax (051) 26 26 79
Sig. Orsi

Rooms 35 with air-conditioning, telephone, bath or shower, WC, cable TV, minibar and elevator. **Price** Single 190-290,000L, double 275-420,000L. **Meals** Breakfast included, served 7:00-12:00. **Restaurant** See pp. 399-400. **Credit cards** All major. **Pets** Dogs allowed. **Nearby** Bologna (Piazza Maggiore and Piazza del Nettuno, Churches of S. Petronio, S. Domenico, S. Francesco, National Picture Gallery), Madonna di San Lucca, San Michele in Bosco, "Giro sulle colline" (car tour around Bologna), Road of the castles (Bazzano, Monteveglio, S. Maria), Golf Course (18-hole) in Chiesa Nova di Monte San Pietro. **Open** All year.

The blend of styles in this small, four-star hotel right in the historical center of Bologna gives it a pleasant, informal atmosphere. Although the building dates from the 8th century, it has been modified several times; You can now admire a Madonna and Child from the 15th century as well as the Liberty-style stucco decoration circa 1900. The hotel continues to improve on what has been its reputation up to now: comfort, service, and quiet.

How to get there (Map 10): Via A14, Bologna-Arcoveggio exit, towards Stazione Centrale, then enter the town by the Porta Galliera and via dell'Indipendenza to the Metropolitana, then left towards the Palazzo Ancivescovile and, on the left, take the via Oberdan.

Hotel Commercianti ★★★

Via de' Pignattari, 11
40124 Bologna
Tel. (051) 23 30 52 – Fax (051) 22 47 33
Sig. Orsi

Rooms 3 with air-conditioning, telephone, shower, WC, cable TV, safe and minibar. **Price** Single 130-175,000L, double 200-275,000L. **Meals** Breakfast included, served 7:00-11:30. **Restaurant** See pp. 399-400. **Credit cards** All major. **Pets** Small dogs allowed. **Facilities** Parking (25,000L). **Nearby** Bologna (Piazza Maggiore and Piazza del Nettuno, Churches of S. Petronio, S. Domenico, S. Francesco, National Picture Gallery), Madonna di San Lucca, San Michele in Bosco, "Giro sulle colline" (car tour around Bologna), Road of the castles (Bazzano, Monteveglio, S. Maria), Golf Course (18-hole) in Chiesa Nova di Monte San Pietro. **Open** All year.

The most convenient feature of this hotel is its location: right next to the San Petronio cathedral in a special traffic-free zone (which, however, hotel guests can enter with car to use the hotel garage). The Commercianti was originally the town hall in the 12th century, and a lot of the original architecture is still intact. The decor is functional and contemporary with air-conditioning and comfortable bathrooms. The nicest rooms in the old tower have a remarkable view of the rooftop stained-glass windows and of the cathedral. The other rooms look out on the Piazza Maggiore.

How to get there *(Map 10): via A14, Bologna-Arcoveggio exit. On the "Tangenziale," number 7 exit towards center; via Marconi, via Testoni, then signs for the Hotel Commercianti.*

Hotel Orologio ★★★

40123 Bologna
Via IV November, 10
Tel. (0532) 231 253– Fax (0532) 260 552
Sig.ra Orsi

Rooms 32 with air-conditioning, telephone, Bath or shower, WC, cable TV, safe and minibar. **Price** Single 130-175,000L, double 200-275,000L. **Meals** Breakfast included, served 7:00-11:00. **Restaurant** See pp. 399-400. **Credit cards** All major. **Pets** Dogs allowed. **Facilities** Parking (25,000L). **Nearby** Bologna (Piazza Maggiore and Piazza del Nettuno, Churches of S. Petronio, S. Domenico, S. Francesco, National Picture Gallery), Madonna di San Lucca, San Michele in Bosco, "Giro sulle colline" (car tour around Bologna), Road of the castles (Bazzano, Monteveglio, S. Maria), Golf Course (18-hole) in Chiesa Nova di Monte San Pietro. **Open** All year.

This small well-located hotel is next to the Piazza Maggiore in Bologna, one of the most visited towns in Italy, where it can be especially difficult to find a place to stay in professional exhibit season. This town is also a great place for tourism and gastronomy. The Hotel Orlogio has been entirely renovated and now offers comfortable, more personalized rooms, most of which have a nice view on the oldest vestiges of the town. The professionalism of the Orsi family, which runs some of the finest establishments in town, is evident in the quality of the service. Don't lose this address.

How to get there *(Map 10): via A14, Bologna-Arcoveggio exit. On the "Tangenziale," number 7 exit towards center; via Marconi, via Testoni, then signs for the Hotel Orologio.*

Albergo Annunziata ★★★★

Piazza della Reppublica, 45
44100 Ferrara
Tel. (0532) 20 11 11 - Fax (0532) 20 32 33
Sig. Govoni Corrado

Rooms 24 with telephone, bath or shower, WC, TV and minibar. **Price** Single 190,000L, double 300,000L, suite 400,000L. **Meals** Breakfast included, served 7:00-10:30. **Restaurant** See pp. 400-401. **Credit cards** All major. **Pets** Dogs not allowed. **Facilities** Parking. **Nearby** Ferrara (Duomo, Palace of Ludovic the Moor, Diamond Palace, Casa Romei, spectacle of the traditional Palio in May), Abbey of Pomposa, Comacchio, Abbey of S. Barto, Cento and Pieve di Cento. **Open** All year (except Dec. 20-Jan. 10 and Aug. 10-20).

As soon as all the school children on class trips have left, Ferrara's Piazza di Castello Estense emanates a serene charm, a sense of time and spare that seems to transport you back through centuries. Just across from the landmark castle is the Albergo Annunziata, an elegant haven of peace, a Palazzetto whose rooms done in gray and green, open either onto gardens or rooftops. And even if the decor is perturbed by butterfly-motif shower curtains, or the old New York–style fire escape, the Annunziata remains a fine in-town address with charming service.

How to get there *(Map 11): 47 km northeast of Bologna via A13, Ferrara-North exit; in the old city.*

Canalgrande Hotel ★★★★

Corso Canalgrande, 6
41100 Modena
Tel. (059) 21 71 60 – Fax (059) 22 16 74

Rooms 79 with air-conditioning, telephone, bath or shower, WC, TV and minibar.
Price Single 180,000L, double 262,000L, for 3 pers. 318,000L, suite 401,000L.
Meals Breakfast included, served 7:00-10:30. **Restaurant** Service 12:30-13:45,
19:30-21:45; closed Tuesday; menus 35-45,000L, also à la carte. Specialties:
Paste modenesi, verdure ai ferri, dolci casalinghi. **Credit cards** All major. **Pets**
Dogs allowed. **Facilities** Garage (15,000L). **Nearby** Modena (Duomo, Estense
Gallery and Library), Roman churches of San Cesario sul Panano and of Pieve
Trebbio near Monteorsello, Abbey of Nonantola, Golf Course (27-hole) in
Colombaro di Formigine. **Open** All year.

The Canalgrande is located right in the center of town, and
has a large garden with a charming fountain surrounded by
enormous several-hundred-year-old trees. Formerly a patrician
villa, it is today a hotel with Neoclassical architecture. The foyer
and the series of salons around the entry are handsomely done in
stucco. Contemporary armchairs and beautiful old paintings give
the place a cosy atmosphere. The guest rooms and bathrooms
are comfortable. Be sure to check out La Secchia Rapita, the
restaurant in the cellar, with its beautiful vaulted brick ceiling.

How to get there *(Map 10): 39 km northwest of Bologna via A1,
Modena-South exit , then S9 (via Emilia-East) to Corso Canalgrande and
to the left (near by the church).*

Villa Gaidello Club

Via Gaidello, 18
41013 Castelfranco Emilia (Modena)
Tel. (059) 92 68 06 – Fax (059) 92 66 20
Sig.ra Bini

Apartments 3 with bath or shower, WC, TV and minibar. **Price** 130-270,000L. **Meals** Breakfast 8,000L, served 8:00-10:00. **Restaurant** Service 13:00, 20:00; closed Thusday; menus 35-45,000L, also à la carte. Specialties: Paste modenesi, verdure ai ferri, dolci casalinghi. **Credit cards** All major. **Pets** Dogs not allowed. **Facilities** Lake in the park, parking **Nearby** Church in Castelfranco, Modena, Roman churchs of San Cesario sul Panano and of Pieve Trebbio near by Monteorsello, Abbey of Nonantola, Bologna, Golf Course (27-hole) in Colombaro di Formigine. **Open** All year (except Aug., Sunday evening, Monday).

Located in the heart of Emilia, the Gaidello Club is a beautiful farm. That has been fully restored and now looks more like a country house than a hotel. There are only three apartments, which are large and tastefully decorated with country-style furniture. The excellent cuisine is based on fresh local produce. Meals are served on an enclosed air-conditioned porch. The Italian-style breakfast is copious, and the service is friendly and personal. There is a small fishing lake, a solarium, and exceptional peace and quiet. With only three accomodations, reservations must be confirmed.

How to get there *(Map 10): 13 km southeast of Modena - 26 km northwest of Bologna via S9 (the hotel is in the country, 1 km from the city).*

I Girasoli

Misano Monte 47046 Misano Adriatico (Forli)
Via Ca' Rastelli,13
Tel. (0541) 61 07 24 – Fax (0541) 69 23 54
Sig. Leardini

Rooms 7 with air conditioning, telephone, shower, TV, minibar and Safe. **Price** Double 190,000L, for 3 pers. 240,000L. **Meals** Breakfast included, served 7:00-13:30. **Restaurant** Service 12:30-14:30, 19:30-24:00, closed Monday, tuesday, Wenesday in winter; menu 40,000L. Specialties: Regional cooking. **Credit cards** All major. **Pets** Dogs not allowed. **Facilities** Heated swimming pool, tennis (12,000L), bikes, parking. **Nearby** Riviera del sole (Rimini, Riccione, Pesado), Conca Valley (rocca de Malatesta), Ravenna. **Open** Mar. 1 – Jan. 6.

The hotel is located on the hills of Riccione, several kilometers from the Felliniesque Rimini. This part of the coast has all of the charms and drawbacks of popular resorts of the Adriatic coast. Away from the effervescence of the beaches, I Girazsoli is the ideal place to get away from it all. This old villa has been transformed into a hotel, its original structure still intact. With seven large rooms, pleasantly decorated with period furniture, it has kept a certain intimacy. If you are tired of swimming in the sea, the hotel offers a variety of facilities including a pool, a tennis court and a *bacci* court. This is a nice place to unwind from your Adriatic adventures.

How to get there *(Map 11): 20km of Rimini; via A14, Riccione exit, towards Morciano. After motorway bridge, second road on your right.*

Hotel Al Vecchio Convento ★★★

Via Roma, 7
47010 Portico di Romagna (Forli)
Tel. (0543) 96 70 53 - Fax (0543) 96 71 57
Sig.ra Raggi

Rooms 14 with telephone (9 with bath or shower and TV.). **Price** Single 80,000L, double 100,000L. **Meals** Breakfast 12,500L, served at any time; half board 100,000L (per pers. 3 days min.). **Restaurant** Service 12:30-14:00, 19:30-22:00, closed Wenesday except in summer; menus 35-55,000L, also à la carte. Specialties: Funghi tartufi, cacciagione. **Credit cards** All major. **Pets** Dogs not allowed. **Facilities** Parking. **Nearby** Church of Polenta, Biblioteca Malatestiana in Cesena, Abbey of Madona del Monte near Cesena, Ravenna. **Open** All year.

A l Vecchio Convento is now open to travelers. It is located in Portico di Romagna, a town on the border between Tuscany and Emilia–Romagna. On the same street is another famous venerable palace, which once belonged to Beatrice Portinari, Dante's muse. The interior of the Vecchio Convento, which has been tastefully restored and is most comfortable. The salon and the dining room look out over the countryside and are decorated with antique furniture, as are the guest rooms. You will appreciate the friendly welcome, the warm atmosphere, and the delicious traditional cuisine, especially the breakfasts with homemade preserves. If you like horseback riding, you can ride through the Aquacheta Valley which Dante described in "The Divine Comedy".

How to get there *(Map 11): 97 km southeast of Bologna via A14, Forli exit - S67 (towards Firenze).*

Hotel Della Porta ★★★

Via Andrea Costa, 85
47038 Santarcangelo di Romagna (Forli)
Tel. (0541) 62 21 52 – Fax (0541) 62 21 68
Sig. G. Ghiselli

Rooms 20 and 2 suites with air-conditioning, telephone, bath, WC, TV and minibar. **Price** Single 90,000L, double 120,000L, suite 240,000L. **Meals** Breakfast included, served 7:00-10:30. **Restaurant** See p. 403. **Credit cards** All major. **Pets** Dogs allowed. **Facilities** Sauna (15,000L), parking. **Nearby** Santarcangelo (museum, Rocco Malatestiana, San Michele), Verruchio, Longiano, Rimini, San Marino, Amalia Golf Course (9-hole). **Open** All year.

The Hotel Della Porta is in Santarcangelo, several miles from Rimini, in Montefeltro, between Romagna and the Marches. This region was the cradle of the famous Malatesta family, and is dotted with splendid Renaissance monuments, along with traces of the forbidden romance of Francesca and Paolo, which Dante immortalized in his "Divine Comedy." It consists of two houses in the old village. The spacious salon-reception area serves as a tourist information office. It is illuminated by a sizeable skylight, and decorated in contemporary style. The guest rooms are large and very comfortable and have a more traditional decor. A nice touch is that each one has a work or living area. Our favorite rooms are in the adjoining house, with its antique furniture and ornate frescoes of flowers on the ceiling. There is no restaurant, but the hotel will help make arrangements with the best ones in the village.

How to get there *(Map 11): 15 km west of Rimini; via A14 Rimini-North exit, then towards Santarcangelo.*

Hotel Verdi ★★★★

43100 Parma
Viale Pasini, 18
Tel. (0521) 29 35 39 – Fax (0521) 29 35 59
Sig Dondi

Rooms 20 with air-conditioning, telephone, bath or shower, WC, TV, minibar and elevator. **Price** Single 175,000L, double 255,000L, suite 285,000L. **Meals** Breakfast 15,000L, served 7:00-12:00; half board +35,000L (per pers., 3 days min.). **Restaurant** «Santa Croce». Service 12:00-14:00, 20:00-22:00; closed Sat. lunch and Sun.; menu and carte 50-60,000L. Specialties: Regional cooking. **Credit cards** All major. **Pets** Dogs not allowed. **Facilities** Parking, garage. **Nearby** Parma (Duomo, Baptistery, Abbey of St. John, National Gallery, Farnese Theater, Arturo Toscanini's Birthplace), House of Verdi in Roncole, Verdi Theater in Busseto, Villa Verdi in Sant'Agata, Mantova, Sabbioneta. **Open** All year except 2 weeks in Aug.

The Hotel Verdi is located is near the gardens of the Ducal Palace in Parma. This recently restored hotel was originally a small Liberty-style palace, and is today a charming, friendly place to stay for those visiting Parma. The only drawback is the road beside the hotel, which can be noisy. Parma is a town somewhat off the beaten track, which shines like a little Mannerist jewel in the heartland of northern Italy. Its churches and palaces feature splendid works by famous painters (Le Corrège and Le Parmesan). The town is also a haven for fans of fine Italian cuisine. Don't miss the famous Santa Croce restaurant right near the hotel, famous for its *culatello*, and homemade tortellini and lasagna.

How to get there *(Map 10): 13 km southeast of Modena - 96 km northwest of Bologna via S9.*

Palazzo Calvi

43011 Samboseto di Busseto (Parma)
Tel. (0524) 90 211 – Fax (0524) 90 213
Sig. Morsia

Rooms 8 with air-conditioning, telephone, shower, WC, TV and minibar.
Price Single 140,000L, double 180,000L, suite 240,000L. **Meals** Breakfast
included, served to 10:30. **Restaurant** Service 12:00-14:30, 20:00-22:30; closed
Tues. lunch and Mon.; also à la carte 65-75,000L. Specialties: Regional cooking.
Credit cards All major. **Pets** Dogs not allowed. **Facilities** Parking. **Nearby** Parma,
Verdi pilgrimage tour: Arturo Toscanini's Birthplace in Parma, House of Verdi in
Roncole, Verdi Theater in Busseto, Villa Verdi in Sant'Agata; La Rocca golf course
(9-hole) in Sala Barganza. **Open** All year - Closed Mon.

A few miles from Roncole, the birthplace of Guiseppe Verdi, is
this marvelous place for fine dining. The Palazzo Calvi is an
18th-century patrician villa where you can still find the solemn
elegance of the old days in its *settecento* furniture and in its
meticulously well-kept gardens. Even though there are a few
beautiful rooms available at this luxurious inn, it is above all a
restaurant, so famous that it has become something of a shrine for
lovers of Parmesan cuisine. Be sure to try the *culatello* (natives
consident the best ham in the world) and the *tortellini alla parmegiana*.
If you are staying in Parma, don't miss this epicurian adventure.

How to get there *(Map 10): 40 km northwest of Parma via A1, Fidenza
exit - Salsomaggiore Terme and S359 to Soragna, towards Samboseto,
Busseto.*

Locanda del Lupo ★★★★

Via Garibaldi, 64
43009 Soragna (Parma)
Tel. (0524) 69 04 44 – Fax (0524) 69 350
Sig. E. Dioni

Rooms 46 with air-conditioning, telephone, bath or shower, WC and TV. **Price** Single 120,000L, double 200,000L, suite 270,000 L. **Meals** Breakfast included, served 7:30-10:30; half board 140-160,000L (per pers.). **Restaurant** Service 12:00-14:00, 19:30-22:00; menus, also à la carte. Specialties: Salami tipici, formaggi di Parma, tortelli di ricotta. **Credit cards** All major. **Pets** Dogs allowed in the rooms only. **Facilities** Parking. **Nearby** Parma; Verdi pilgrimage tour: Arturo Toscanini's birthplace in Parma, House of Verdi in Roncole, Verdi Theater in Busseto, Villa Verdi in Sant'Agata; La Rocca golf course (9-hole) in Sala Barganza. **Open** All year (except Aug. 1-25).

For years, Locanda del Lupo was famous locally for its fine cuisine, and appreciated as well by Parisian gastronomic critics. It has now expanded operatious to become a hotel. The rooms and salons are simply decorated but refined and comfortable. The main attraction, however, remains the restaurant where early recipes from the archives of Prince Meli Lupi, a former resident, are brilliantly prepared and served. The wine cellar is well stocked. You may count on a warm welcome here.

How to get there *(Map 10): 33 km northwest of Parma via A1, Fidenza exit.*

Bisanzio Hotel ★★★★

Via Salara, 30
48100 Ravenna
Tel. (0544) 21 71 11 - Fax (0544) 32 539
Sig.ra Fabbri

Rooms 38 with air-conditioning, telephone, bath or shower, WC, cable TV, safe and minibar. **Price** Single 135,000L, double 158-198,000L. **Meals** Breakfast included (buffet), served 7:00-10:00. **Restaurant** See p.401. **Credit cards** All major. **Pets** Dogs allowed. **Facilities** Parking. **Nearby** Ravenna (The Neoiam Baptistery, Archiepiscopal Museum and Church of St. Andrea, Church of San Vitale, Basilica of St. Apollinare Nuovo, Dante's Tomb), Basilica of St. Apollinare in Classe (about 4 miles south of the city, bus no. 4), The Adriatic coast, Adriatic Golf Course (18-hole). **Open** All year (except Dec. – Jan.).

Don't get the wrong impression from the fading facade of this Hotel. Walk inside and you will find yourself in a warm salon-reception area facing onto a small garden with pretty furniture. The rooms are small but tastefully decorated and furnished, with well-designed modern bathrooms. This hotel combines provincial charm with professionalism. The Bisanzio is ideally located in the center of Ravenna, just behind the San Vitale cathedral with its famous mosaics. You can easily visit the old town on foot from here. Ask for a room on the garden, as the Via Salara side can get pretty busy.

How to get there *(Map 11): 74 km east of Bologna, via A14, Ravenna exit - from Rimini, Cervia Cesena exit.*

Relais Torre Pratesi ★★★★

Cavina 48013 Brisighella (Ravenna)
Via Cavina, 11
Tel. (0546) 845 45 – Fax (0546) 845 58
Sig.ra and Sig. Raccagni

Rooms 3 and 4 suites with air-conditioning, telephone, bath or shower, WC, TV, minibar and safe. **Price** Double 180,000L, suite 220,000L. **Meals** Breakfast included, served to 14:00; half board 130-150,000L (per pers.). **Restaurant** Service 20:00-22:00; closed Tues.; menu and carte 50,000L. Specialties: Regional cooking. **Credit cards** All major. **Pets** Dogs not allowed. **Facilities** Golf Club la Torre, Manneggio Villa Corte, thermal baths «Riolo Terme». **Nearby** Faenza, Brisighella, Church of San Pietro in Sylvis, Ravenna. **Open** All year.

This massive hotel towers deep in the lush Romagnian countryside, which is famous for its wine, oil and truffles. It was built in 1510, and a farm was added in the 19th century. Renovated with careful attention to artistic detail, the rooms have the spacious dimensions of days gone by. The elegant simplicity of the furniture highlights the materials, stone and wood. The modern conveniences do not at all detract from the beautiful restoration work. Home–style cuisine allows you to savor products fresh from your hosts' farm. This place is magical–it's a great way to experience the beautiful, well-preserved Lamona valley, which extends all the way to Florence.

How to get there *(Map 11): 28 km south pf Faenza, via A14, Faenza exit, then S302 (Brisighella-Firenze) to Fognano, then towards Valletta during 4 km.*

Hotel Posta ★★★★

Piazza del Monte, 2
42100 Reggio Nell'Emilia
Tel. (0522) 43 29 44 – Fax (0522) 45 26 02
C. Salomon

Rooms 43 with telephone, bath or shower, WC, TV and minibar. **Price** Single 190,000L, double 250,000L, suite 290,000L. **Meals** Breakfast included, served 7:00-10:30. **Restaurant** See p. 402. **Credit cards** All major. **Pets** Dogs allowed. **Facilities** Parking (15,000L). **Nearby** Reggio (Galeria Parmeggiani), Parma, Matilde di Canossa Golf Course (18-hole). **Open** All year (except Aug.).

This former palace is in an ideal location in the heart of the historic town center, on Cesare Battisti Square. The austere medieval facade conceals the rococo interior which is embellished with old stucco ornaments from the walls of a famous local bakery frequented by the notables of the town. The rooms are highly original and offer all the comforts you would expect from a four-star hotel.

How to get there *(Map 10): 27 km southeast of Parma via A1, Reggio Nell'Emilia exit.*

Albergo Casa Matilda ★★★★

42030 Puianello (Reggio Emilia)
Via A. Negri, 11
Tel. (0522) 88 90 06 – Fax (522) 88 90 06
Family Bertolini

Rooms 7 with telephone, bath, WC, minibar and TV. **Price** Single 185,000L, double 240,000L, suite 280,000L. **Meals** Breakfast included, served from 7:30. **Credit cards** Not allowed. **Pets** Dogs not allowed. **Nearby** Parma, Verdi pilgrimage tour: Arturo Toscanini's Birthplace in Parma, House of Verdi in Roncole, Verdi Theater in Busseto, Villa Verdi in Sant'Agata; La Rocca golf course (9-hole) in Sala Barganza. **Open** All year.

If you would like to get away from it all in a country setting, where fine dining is time-honored tradition, Casa Matilde is a destination to consider. This friendly inn, in the shady hills of the Parmesan Appenin, is in the middle of a small park full of flowers. The spacious rooms are individually decorated. The large beautiful salons have been carefully laid out to ensure that you have all of the comforts of home. The surroundings are perfect for long romantic walks. Your hostess will be happy to answer any questions you might have. She knows all about this *queen-valkyrie* named Matilda and the mysteries of the region.

How to get there *(Map 10): 35 km southwest of Parma; 10 km of Reggio Emilia. Via A1, Reggio Emilia exit, then towards Puianello-Quattro Castella.*

Castello di Balsorano

Piazza Piccolomini, 10
Balsorano (L'Aquila)
Tel. (0863) 95 12 36 – Fax (0775) 86 85 11
Sig. Coretti and Sig. Troiani

Rooms 15 with bath or shower and WC. **Price** Double 110,000L, suite 130,000L.
Meals Breakfast incl., half board 95,000L, full board 130,000L. (per pers., 3 days
min.). **Restaurant** Service 12:00-14:30, 19:30-22:00; closed Mon. except for
guests; also à la carte. Specialties: Seafood, salvagina. **Credit cards** Amex, Visa,
Eurocard and MasterCard. **Pets** Small dogs allowed. **Facilities** Parking.
Nearby Abbey of Casamari, National Park of Abbruzzi, Medieval cities of Ferentino
and Alatri. **Open** All year.

This castle on the top of Balsorano Hill overlooks the Sora
River valley. The rooms are simply furnished, with low
beds and dark woodwork, giving this former manor a Medieval
feeling. Some of them are connected by old secret passages,
adding a touch of mystery. The owners of Castello di Balsorano
are dedicated to preserving an atmosphere of quiet and
tranquility. They offer fine regional cuisine based on fresh local
products.

How to get there *(Map 16): 113 km east of Rome via A1, Frosinone
exit, then SS214 to Sora and S82 to Balsorano.*

Hotel Castello Miramare ★★★★

Via Pagnano
04023 Formia (Latina)
Tel. (0771) 70 01 38 – Fax (0771) 70 01 39
Sig.ra Celletti

Rooms 10 with air conditioning, telephone, bath or shower, WC, TV, safe and minibar. **Price** Single 100-110,000L, double 130-150,000L. **Meals** Breakfast 16,000L, served 7:30-12:00; half board 130-160,000L, full board 150-180,000L. (per pers., 3 days min.). **Restaurant** Service 12:30-15:00, 19:30-21:30; menu 65,000L, also à la carte. Specialties: Tonnarelli all'aragosta e funghi, cocktail di astice alla catalana. **Credit cards** All major **Pets** Small dogs allowed. **Facilities** Parking. **Nearby** Cicero's Tomb, Church of San Pietro in Minturno, Abbey of Montecassino, Island of Ponza. **Open** All year.

This 19th-century manor has retained a rich atmosphere of elegance. The magnificent grounds overlook Formia, the departure point for the islands of Ponza, Ischia, and Capri. The rooms, with a view of the Gulf of Gaeta, are decorated with comfortable Spanish-style furniture. The cuisine features refined dishes such as seafood risotto and lobster. The service is friendly.

How to get there *(Map 20): 76 km southeast of Latina via A2, Cassino exit, then S630 towards Formia and SS7.*

Grande Albergo Miramare ★★★★

Via Appia L. Napoli, 44
04023 Formia (Latina)
Tel. (0771) 26 71 81 - Fax (0771) 26 71 88
Sig. Celletti

Rooms 15 with telephone., bath or shower, WC and TV. **Price** Single 90-100,000L, double 120-140,000L. **Meals** Breakfast 16,000L; half board 130-150,000L, full board 150-180,000L. (per pers., 3 days min.). **Restaurant** Service 12:00-14:30, 19:30-22:00; closed Mon. except for guests; also à la carte. Specialties: Seafood, salvagina. **Credit cards** Amex, Visa, Eurocard and MasterCard. **Pets** Small dogs allowed. **Facilities** Swimming pool, parking. **Nearby** Cicero's Tomb, Church of San Pietro in Minturno, Abbey of Montecassino, Island of Ponza. **Open** All year.

It was here that Elena de Montenegro, the queen of Italy, spent her summers among the bouganvillea and jasmine flowers, and the orange and pine trees. Her former residence, a sumptuous white mansion, is now a grand hotel which still has a somewhat royal ambience. The rooms are both simple and luxurious, with 19th-century furniture and private terraces. The days go by very peacefully here. You can take a swim in the early morning while the sea is calm, breakfast on your own private terrace, relax in a lounge chair by the pool in the afternoon, walk in the garden, then spend the evening at the convivial piano-bar on a terrace overlooking the sea. The excellent cuisine is based on grilled seafood and shellfish. Try the *spaghetti al mare*.

How to get there *(Map 20): 76 km southeast of Latina via A2, Cassino exit, then S630 towards Formia and SS7.*

Hotel Cernia

Isola di Ponza
Via Panoramica
Chiaia di Luna 04027 Ponza (Latina)
Tel. (0771) 804 12/80 99 51 – Fax (0771) 80 99 54 – Sig. Greca

Rooms 60 (40 with air conditioning), telephone, bath or shower, WC, TV and minibar. **Price** Single 140-190,000L, double 210-330,000L. **Meals** Breakfast incl., served 8:30-10:30. **Restaurant** Service 13:00-14:30, 20:00-21:30; menus 60-70,000L, also à la carte. Specialties: Seafood, italian and regional cuisine. **Credit cards** All major. **Pets** Dogs allowed. **Facilities** Swimming pool, tennis, private bus. **Nearby** Beach of Chaia di Luna. **Open** April 1-Oct.

Buried in a dense and fragrant garden, the Cernia is just a five minute walk from the beautiful Chiaia di Luna beach, and near the port where you will find the most famous restaurant on the island, Gennarino a Mare. The hotel is vast and the rooms numerous. Certain rooms–201, 202, 203 and 204–have a large terrace and a rewarding view of the sea. The straw window-shades, wicker furniture, rocking chairs and white couches create a friendly vacation atmosphere in the salon enfilade. The beach isn't far away, but a swim in the large hotel swimming pool set in the shade can also be nice on a hot summer day.

How to get there *(Map 20): Ferry services from Rome, Napoli, Anzio, San Felice Circeo, Terracina, Formia (1:30/2:00) - cars are permitted in summer if you stay 15 days minimum on the island.*

Hotel Le Dune

04016 Sabaudia (Latina)
Lungomare
Tel. (0773) 511 511 – Fax (0773) 55 643
Sig. Zanotti

Rooms 78 with air conditioning, telephone, bath or shower, WC, TV and 10 with minibar. **Price** Single 130-165,000L, double 190-270,000L, suite 450-550,000L. **Meals** Breakfast (buffet) 20,000L, served 7:30-12:00; half board 165-230,000L, full board 190-265,000L (per pers., 3 days min.). **Restaurant** Service 13:00-14:30, 19:30-22:00; menus and carte 50-70,000L. Specialties: Pesce - risotto alla crema di scampi, ravioli con ripieno di scamorza e melanzane, spigola al cartoccio. **Credit cards** All major. **Pets** Dogs not allowed. **Facilities** Swimming pool, tennis (16,000L), sauna, parking. **Nearby** Beach. **Open** Apr. – Oct.

This hotel is in Sarabuda, a vacation spot for the Roman intelligentsia. Some 60 miles from Rome, it has all of the advantages of a beach resort, located in a national park on a peninsula extending all the way into the shade of the majestic Circeo promontory. The spacious comfortable rooms are all on the sea, just in front of the hotel, past the pool and the private beach. When the morning mist lifts, you can see the island of Ponza from your balcony. The restaurant features "elaborate" and (sometimes happy) seafood cuisine. If you would like a break from the hustle and bustle of Rome, don't hesitate to come here and enjoy the sea air, but if its peace and quiet you are looking for, you'd better come in June or September.

How to get there *(Map 20): 20 km south of Latina, on the sea front 2 km of Sabaudia.*

Hotel Punta Rossa ★★★★

Via delle Batteria
04017 San Felice Circeo (Latina)
Tel. (0773) 54 80 85 – Fax (0773) 54 80 75
Sig. and Sig.ra Battaglia

Rooms 36 and 4 suites and 20 mini-apartments with air-conditioning, telephone, bath or shower, WC, TV, video and minibar. **Price** Double 220-450,000L, suite 420-520,000L. **Meals** Breakfast incl., served 8:00-11:00; half board in high season 255,000L (per pers.). **Restaurant** Service 13:00-14:30, 20:00-22:30; menu 65,000L. Specialties: Tonnarelli seafood, frutti di mare. **Credit cards** All major. **Pets** Dogs allowed. **Facilities** Swimming pool, sauna (+ 20,000L), private beach, health center, parking. **Nearby** Terracina, Abbey of Fossanova, Temple of Jupiter Anxur, National park of Circeo. **Open** All year.

The seven-and-a-half acres of the Hotel Punta Rossa lie within a protected site on the San Felice Circeo peninsula, truly unique location. The architecture is slightly dated, but the hotel is otherwise fully up-to-date. It looks like a miniature village set into the contours of a hill abounding with lush vegetation. The rooms are vast in size, simply decorated, and very comfortable. They all face the sea, and most of them have landscaped terraces. Several mini-apartments, suitable for four to six people are tucked away in the garden; there can be rented by the week. The hotel has a health-and-beauty center, a nice salt-water swimming pool, a private beach, and a small port at the end of a path that winds through the rocks and plantings. The restaurant is excellent.

How to get there *(Map 20): 106 km southeast of Rome via A1, exit N148, towards Latina then Terracina.*

Parkhotel Fiorelle ★★★

Via Fiorelle, 12
04029 Sperlonga (Latina)
Tel. (0771) 540 92 – Fax (0771) 540 92
Sig. Di Mille

Rooms 33 with telephone, bath or shower, WC and safe. **Price** Single 110-120,000L, double 140,000L. **Meals** Breakfast 10,000L, served 8:00-9:30; half board 85-120,000L, full board 95-130,000L (per pers., 3 days min.). **Restaurant** Service 13:00-14:00, 19:30-22:00; closed Friday, menu 35,000L, also à la carte. Specialties: Seafood, regional cooking. **Credit cards** Not accepted. **Pets** Dogs allowed. **Facilities** Swimming pool, private beach, parking. **Nearby** In Sperlonga: National Archeological Museum and Tiberius, Grotto; Terracina (Duomo and Piazza del Municipio), Abbey of Fossanova. **Open** Easter – Oct. 1.

The regulars who come to the Fiorelle to unwind year after year tend to keep their distance from newcomers. This works out very well within the overall peaceful ambiance which the owners carefully cultivate for all their guests. No one from outside the hotel is admitted to the bar, the pool, or the private beach. The garden, an important part of the pleasant experience of the hotel, is well kept and has flowers blooming year-round. Meals are prepared with fresh vegetables from the garden, and menus are submitted to the guests the day before for selection.

How to get there (Map 20): 57 km southeast of Latina via S148 to Terracina, then S213 to Sperlonga.

Hotel Borgo Paraelios ★★★★★

02040 Poggio Mirteto Scalo (Rieti)
Valle Collicchia
Tel. (0765) 26 267 – Fax (0765) 26 268
Sig. Salabe

Rooms 13 and 2 suites with air-conditioning, telephone, bath or shower, WC and TV. **Price** single 350,000L, double 450,000L. **Meals** Breakfast 25-35,000L, served 8:00-10:30; half board 690,000L. (per 2 pers., wine not incl.). **Restaurant** Service 13:00-15:00, 20:00-22:30; menus 100-130,000L, also à la carte. Specialties: Italian cooking. **Credit cards** All major **Pets** Dogs allowed (+suppl.). **Facilities** 2 swimming pools (1 indoor), tennis, sauna, parking, private bus to the station or airport, parking. **Nearby** Roma, Colle dei Tetti golf course (9-hole). **Open** All year.

The Borgo Paraelios is amazing: there are few rooms but many salons of all sizes. It is, above all, a haven of elegance in the Roman countryside. The sumptuous decor of this splendid house compares favorably with the luxury level typically found in palaces. There are very beautiful furnishings and paintings in every room, including the garden-level rooms. Try your best billiard shots under the stony gaze of Roman emperors carved of marble. This place is quiet, luxurious, exquisite.

How to get there *(Map 15): 40 km north of Rome via A1, Fiano Romano exit - until S4 to Passo Corese, S313, Poggio Mirteto, towards Cantalupo Terni.*

Hotel Lord Byron ★★★★★

Via G. de Notaris, 5
00197 Rome
Tel. (06) 322 04 04 – Fax (06) 322 04 05
Sig. Ottaviani and A. Savona

Rooms 37 with air-conditioning, telephone, bath, WC, TV, safe and minibar.
Price Double 360-530,000L, suite 800-1 000,000L. **Meals** Breakfast incl., served
from 7:00. **Restaurant** Service 12:30-15:00, 20:00-22:30, closed Sunday and 2
weeks in Aug., à la carte. **Credit cards** All major. **Pets** Small dogs allowed (fee).
Facilities Parking. **Nearby** Tivoli (Villa d'Este, Villa Adriana), Castelli Romani
(Castel Gandolfo, Frascati, Grottaferrata), Anzio and Nettuno, Palestrina, Anagni,
Etruscan zone (Cerveteri, Tarquinia), golf course (9-18-hole) in Rome. **Open** All
year.

The Lord Byron is located in the heart of the Parioli
district–the most fashinable in Rome–facing the Villa
Borghese gardens. Amadeo Ottaviani, the owner, has given it a
high-style look. Thick luxurious carpeting, capacious white
armchairs bearing the initials of the hotel, lacquered white
ceilings, sumptuous bouquets and many other details reflect his
taste for perfection. The Relais du Jardin restaurant is popular
with Romans, who come for the fine dining and the lovely
decor. Spend some time at the bar; your compassion might turn
out to be a countess.

How to get there *(Map 15): Near the Galleria Nazionale d'Arte
Moderna - and the Villa Borghese gardens.*

Hotel Forum ★★★★

Via Tor de Conti, 25
00184 Rome
Tel. (06) 679 24 46 – Fax (06) 678 64 79
Sig. Troiani

Rooms 80 with air-conditioning, telephone, bath or shower, WC and TV. **Price** Single 300,000L, double 450,000L, suite 650,000L. **Meals** Breakfast incl., served 7:00-10:30. **Restaurant** Service 12:30-15:00, 19:30-23:00; closed Sunday; à la carte 100,000L. Specialties: Pappardelle alla forum, risottino alle erbette, seafood. **Credit cards** All major. **Pets** Dogs not allowed. **Facilities** Garage (+40,000L). **Nearby** Tivoli (Villa d'Este, Villa Adriana), Castelli Romani (Castel Gandolfo, Frascati, Grottaferrata), Anzio and Nettuno, Palestrina, Anagni, Etruscan zone (Cerveteri, Tarquinia), golf course (9-18-hole) in Rome. **Open** All year.

This former palace, a popular meeting place for political and financial VIPs, has a unique location, being close to the Coliseum and the Trajan Forum. The service is elegant and remarkably efficient. In summer you can dine in the terraced gardens while watching the spectacular Roman sunsets. The rooms have simple, functional furniture and modern conveniences. Several areas are in need of renovation, but let's hope they don't touch its lovely old-luxury–hotel atmosphere.

How to get there *(Map 15): Behind the Forum of Augustus - Piazza Venezia, via dei Fori Imperiali.*

Hotel Giulio Cesare

Via degli Scipioni, 287
00192 Rome
Tel. (06) 321 07 51 - Fax (06) 321 17 36
Sig. Pandolfi

Rooms 90 with air-conditioning, telephone, bath or shower, WC, TV and minibar. **Price** Single 280,000L, double 380,000L. **Meals** Breakfast incl., served 7:00-10:30. **Restaurant** See pp. 403-406. **Credit cards** All major. **Pets** Dogs not allowed. **Facilities** Parking. **Nearby** Tivoli (Villa d'Este, Villa Adriana), Castelli Romani (Castel Gandolfo, Frascati, Grottaferrata), Anzio and Nettuno, Palestrina, Anagni, Etruscan zone (Cerveteri, Tarquinia), golf course (9-18-hole) in Rome. **Open** All year.

An atmosphere of elegance pervades this large hotel, the former residence of Countess Solari. Antique furniture, rugs, and tapestries give the rooms a feeling of well-being and comfort. Breakfast is served in the garden as soon as the weather permits. You may want to spend some time there, as it is one of the most charming parts of this lovely hotel.

How to get there (*Map 15*): *Near the Piazza del Popolo.*

Hotel d'Inghilterra ★★★★

Via Bocca di Leone, 14
00187 Rome
Tel. (06) 69 981 – Fax (06) 699 222 43
Sig. Richard

Rooms 90 and 12 suites with air-conditioning, telephone, bath or shower, WC, TV and minibar. **Price** Single 310-375,000L, double 410-480,000L, suite 600-860,000L. **Meals** Breakfast 24,500L, served 7:30-10:30. **Restaurant** Service 12:30-15:30, 19:30-22:30; menus 60-80,000L, also à la carte. Specialties: New italian cuisine. **Credit cards** All major. **Pets** Dogs not allowed. **Nearby** Tivoli (Villa d'Este, Villa Adriana), Castelli Romani (Castel Gandolfo, Frascati, Grottaferrata), Anzio and Nettuno, Palestrina, Anagni, Etruscan zone (Cerveteri, Tarquinia), golf course (9-18-hole) in Rome. **Open** All year.

Anatole France, Franz Liszt, and Felix Mendelssohn have all stayed at the Hotel d'Inghilterra, a first-class grand hotel and a favorite among celebrities all over the world. It is on a pedestrian cul-de-sac near the Piazza di Spagna, and has recently been carefully restored. The lobby is superb, done in black and white marble, with stucco columns decorated with white palm trees. The salon is decorated with both antique and contemporary furniture, oriental rugs, and marvelous Neapolitan gouache paintings. The rooms are all excellent, but if you want to have the rare pleasure of breakfast overlooking the rooftops of Rome, ask for ones with a terrace on the top floor. Room service is available for light meals. The service is impeccable.

How to get there *(Map 15): Near the Piazza di Spagna.*

Hotel Raphaël ★★★★

Largo Febo, 2
00186 Rome
Tel. (06) 68 28 31 – Fax (06) 68 78 993
Sig. Vannoni

Rooms 60 with air-conditioning, telephone, bath or shower and WC (10 with balcony). **Price** Single 315,000L, double 450,000L, suite 575,000L. **Meals** Breakfast incl., served 7:00-11:00. **Restaurant** See pp. 403-406. **Credit cards** All major. **Pets** Dogs not allowed. **Nearby** Tivoli (Villa d'Este, Villa Adriana), Castelli Romani (Castel Gandolfo, Frascati, Grottaferrata), Anzio and Nettuno, Palestrina, Anagni, Etruscan zone (Cerveteri, Tarquinia), golf course (9-18-hole) in Rome. **Open** All year.

This small hotel, lushly covered with Virginia creeper vines, is located right next to the Piazza Navona. The rooms and salons decorated with antique furniture and knick-knacks give this place its very pleasant atmosphere, so popular with the Italian intellegensia. The rooms are comfortable, though some of them don't have renovated bathrooms, much to the regret of certain guests. Conversely, the "luxury" rooms have been superbly redecorated and furnished and by a Venetian artist. Lunch and dinner are served in the Café Picasso, except on weekends when snack bar service is available. In the summer, the hotel organizes dinners for hotel guests on the marvelous terrace by reservation only.

How to get there *(Map 15): Near the Piazza Navona.*

Hotel Sole Al Pantheon ★★★★

Piazza della Rotonda, 63
00186 Rome
Tel. (06) 678 04 41 – Fax (06) 699 406 89
Sig. Giraudini

Rooms 26 with air-conditioning, telephone, bath or shower, WC, TV and minibar.
Price Single 340,000L, double 470,000L, suite 560-650,000L. **Meals** Breakfast
incl., served 7:00-11:00. **Restaurant** See pp. 403-406. **Credit cards** All major.
Pets Dogs not allowed. **Facilities** Parking (+35,000L). **Nearby** Tivoli (Villa d'Este,
Villa Adriana), Castelli Romani (Castel Gandolfo, Frascati, Grottaferrata), Anzio
and Nettuno, Palestrina, Anagni, Etruscan zone (Cerveteri, Tarquinia), golf course
(9-18-hole) in Rome. **Open** All year.

This hotel, picturesquely located on the Piazza della Rotonda
facing the Pantheon, has recently been completely
renovated, with special care taken to preserving its old world
charm. There are only twenty-six rooms, all very comfortable
(request a quiet back room). Each one bears the name of a
celebrity who stayed there, among them Jean-Paul Sartre, who
was a regular. The bathrooms are particularly well-equipped. A
whirlpool bath can be a real delight after a day out and about in
Rome. In addition to the list of restaurants we recommend at
the end of this guidebook, try the little trattorias on the square,
where on summer evenings you can dine very pleasantly just
across from the Pantheon, Imperial Rome's best-preserved
monument.

How to get there *(Map 15): In front of the Pantheon.*

Hotel Carriage ★★★

Via delle Carrozze, 36
00187 Rome
Tel. (06) 699 01 24 – Fax (06) 678 82 79
Sig. Del Sole

Rooms 24 with air-conditioning, telephone, bath or shower, WC, TV and minibar. **Price** Single 215,000L, double 270,000L, triple 330,000L, suite 440,000L. **Meals** Breakfast incl., served 7:00-11:00. **Restaurant** See pp. 403-406. **Credit cards** All major. **Pets** Dogs not allowed. **Nearby** Tivoli (Villa d'Este, Villa Adriana), Castelli Romani (Castel Gandolfo, Frascati, Grottaferrata), Anzio and Nettuno, Palestrina, Anagni, Etruscan zone (Cerveteri, Tarquinia), golf course (9-18-hole) in Rome. **Open** All year.

The Carriage is a small hotel in the heart of a quarter where many of the capital's luxury boutiques are located, near the Piazza di Spagna. The entry, the salon, and the ground-floor breakfast room all have an elegant 18th-century decor. The rooms are comfortable, and air conditioned, which means you won't hear street noise. If you make your reservation in time, ask for Rooms 501 or 601, which are on a terrace with a beautiful view of the rooftops of the Eternal City. Even if you don't get these rooms, you can still have breakfast on the terrace. The suites accommodate up to four people.

How to get there *(Map 15): Near the Piazza di Spagna.*

Hotel Gregoriana ★★★

Via Gregoriana, 18
00187 Rome
Tel. (06) 679 42 69 - Fax (06) 678 42 58
Sig. Panier-Bagat

Rooms 19 with air-conditioning, telephone, bath or shower, WC, TV and minibar. **Price** Single 180,000L, double 280,000L. **Meals** Breakfast incl., served 7:00-11:00. **Restaurant** See pp. 403-406. **Credit cards** Not accepted **Pets** Dogs allowed (fee). **Nearby** Tivoli (Villa d'Este, Villa Adriana), Castelli Romani (Castel Gandolfo, Frascati, Grottaferrata), Anzio and Nettuno, Palestrina, Anagni, Etruscan zone (Cerveteri, Tarquinia), golf course (9-18-hole) in Rome. **Open** All year.

The Gregoriana is located on an legendary Roman street, just off the top of the Spanish Steps. In the 19th century many famous artists and writers favored this address; today, it is home to the finest couture salons. Luckily, you can stay at the Gregoriana for remarkably reasonable rates. The Art Deco-style rooms are very comfortable, and the service is friendly, but its location in one of the nicest neighborhoods in Rome makes the Gregoriana a favorite choice for visitors to the Italian capital.

How to get there *(Map 15): From Piazza di Spagna ascend the Spanish Steps.*

Hotel Locarno ★★★

Via della Penna, 22
00186 Rome
Tel. (06) 36 10 841 – Fax (06) 32 15 249
Sig.ra Celli

Rooms 38 with air-conditioning, telephone, bath or shower, WC, cable TV., safe and minibar. **Price** single 170,000L, double 250,000L, suite 320,000L. **Meals** Breakfast incl., served 7:00-11:30. **Restaurant** See pp. 403-406. **Credit cards** All major. **Pets** Dogs not allowed. **Facilities** Bikes. **Nearby** Tivoli (Villa d'Este, Villa Adriana), Castelli Romani (Castel Gandolfo, Frascati, Grottaferrata), Anzio and Nettuno, Palestrina, Anagni, Etruscan zone (Cerveteri, Tarquinia), golf course (9-18-hole) in Rome. **Open** All year.

Just next to the Piazza del Popolo, the Lucarno has very pretty rooms. We recommend the recently renovated ones, with old-fashioned furniture and examples of hand-crafted porcelain. In the summer you can have breakfast on the ground-floor patio under big, white, sun umbrellas. The bar service is great. In winter, a roaring fire in the fireplace warms the living room. Prices are reasonable, and its location near the heart of the city makes this a very pleasant place to stay. There is also a charming terrace where you can take in a beautiful view of Rome. The service is always cordial.

How to get there *(Map 15): Next to the Piazza del Popolo.*

Teatro di Pompeo ★★★

00186 Roma
Largo del Pallaro, 8
Tel. (06) 687 28 12 – Fax (06) 688 055 31
Sig. Mignoni

Rooms 12 with air-conditioning, telephone, bath or shower, WC, TV, safe, minibar and elevator. **Price** Single 190,000L, double 250,000L. **Meals** Breakfast incl., served 7:00-10:00. **Restaurant** See pp. 403-406. **Credit cards** All major. **Pets** Dogs allowed. **Nearby** Tivoli (Villa d'Este, Villa Adriana), Castelli Romani (Castel Gandolfo, Frascati, Grottaferrata), Anzio and Nettuno, Palestrina, Anagni, Etruscan zone (Cerveteri, Tarquinia), golf course (9-18-hole) in Rome. **Open** All year.

If you are looking for a quiet but centrally located hotel for your Roman vacation, this is the place. Located right in the heart of Rome, with its back to the Campo dei Fiori and close to the Piazza Navona, the hotel is on a quiet little square. All of the rooms, under the roof, have sloping ceilings, and half of them open onto the square. Though the decor is simple, the size of the hotel makes it a warm friendly place, with the charm of an old-fashioned pensione (plus modern conveniences). The adjoining restaurant "Costanza" is independent of the hotel and serves fine cuisine. The arched ruins of the old theatre of Pompeii , inaugurated in the year 55 B.C. provide the decor. The service is discreet but efficient.

How to get there (Map 15): near Piazza Campo dei Fiori and the church of S. Andrea della Valle.

Hotel Sant'Anselmo ★★★

00153 Roma
Piazza Sant' Anselmo, 2
Tel. (06) 575 08 45/574 35 47 – Fax (06) 578 36
Sig. Piroli

Rooms 45 with telephone, bath or shower, WC and TV. **Price** Single 100-140,000L, double 150-190,000L. **Meals** Breakfast incl., served 7:00-10:30. **Restaurant** See pp. 403-406. **Credit cards** All major. **Pets** Dogs not allowed. **Facilities** Parking. **Nearby** Tivoli (Villa d'Este, Villa Adriana), Castelli Romani (Castel Gandolfo, Frascati, Grottaferrata), Anzio and Nettuno, Palestrina, Anagni, Etruscan zone (Cerveteri, Tarquinia), golf course (9-18-hole) in Rome. **Open** All year.

Already prized in antiquity for its quiet (the Romans built their thermal baths here) Aventino Hill is a haven of tranquility from the summer heat of Rome even today. There are three old patrician houses there, submerged in verdant shaded alleyways, which are hotels. The S. Anselmo and the Villa S. Pio are right next door to each other, and the Aventino is nearby. There is one reservation number for all three hotels; ask for the first or second one. The rooms are small but charming. The upper rooms overlooking the whole south side of the town are the nicest ones. Breakfast is simple, but served in a cool interior garden. This is one of the rare places in Rome with quiet, elegance, and reasonable prices.

How to get there *(Map 15): near Termal of Cracalla.*

72

Hotel Villa del Parco ★★★

Via Nomentana, 110
00161 Rome
Tel. (06) 442 377 73 - Fax (06) 442 375 72
Famiglia Bernardini

Rooms 25 with air-conditioning, telephone, bath or shower, WC, TV and minibar (2 rooms with wheelchair access). **Price** single 135-165,000L, double 190-215,000L, triple 245,000L, suite 300,000L. **Meals** Breakfast incl., served 7:00 10:30. **Restaurant** See pp. 403-406. **Credit cards** All major. **Pets** Dogs allowed. **Facilities** Parking. **Nearby** Tivoli (Villa d'Este, Villa Adriana), Castelli Romani (Castel Gandolfo, Frascati, Grottaferrata), Anzio and Nettuno, Palestrina, Anagni, Etruscan zone (Cerveteri, Tarquinia), golf course (9-18-hole) in Rome. **Open** All year.

This beautiful turn-of-the-century house, with its gracefully fading pink facade, is located in a quiet residential quarter, a twenty-minute walk from the Via Veneto, just outside of the historic district. The shade trees in the little garden and the park nearby keep it cool in the summertime. You will like the series of small salons (several in the basement remind one of similar rooms you might find in London), the small bar tucked into an alcove, and the tables under the trees where you can have tea and light snacks. This will quickly become your Rome home-away-from-home. Prices vary greatly, and the cheapest rooms are sometimes the most charming. Our favorites are 5, 7, 12, and 22.

How to get there *(Map 15): North of Rome, next to the Porta Bologna.*

Pensione Scalinata di Spagna ★★★

Piazza Trinita dei Monti, 17
00187 Rome
Tel. (06) 69 94 08 96 – Fax (06) 69 94 05 98
Sig. Bellia

Rooms 15 with telephone, bath or shower, WC, TV, safe and minibar. **Price** Single 350,000L, double 380,000L, triple 450,000L, suite (4-5 pers.) 650,000L. **Meals** Breakfast incl., served 7:30-11:00. **Restaurant** See pp. 403-406. **Credit cards** All major. **Pets** Dogs allowed. **Nearby** Tivoli (Villa d'Este, Villa Adriana), Castelli Romani (Castel Gandolfo, Frascati, Grottaferrata), Anzio and Nettuno, Palestrina, Anagni, Etruscan zone (Cerveteri, Tarquinia), golf course (9-18-hole) in Rome. **Open** All year.

Many connaisseurs say this is one of the nicest hotels in Rome. It is extraordinarily well located, right at the top of the Spanish Steps, across from the prestigious Hotel Hassler-Medici, and close to the Pincio Gardens, the Villa Medici. There is a great view of the city from the terrace. This elegant and comfortable residence combines delicate charm with a pleasant family atmosphere. Note that the hotel is extremely popular: there are reports you have to reserve more than a year in advance for certain weeks!

How to get there (Map 15): Up the stairs of the Piazza di Spagna.

Hotel Villa Fiorio ★★★★

Viale Dusmet, 28
00046 Grottaferrata
Frascati (Rome)
Tel. (06) 945 92 76/941 04 50 - Fax (06) 941 34 82

Rooms 17 with telephone, bath or shower, WC and TV. **Price** Single 170,000L, double 200,000L, suite 230,000L. **Meals** Breakfast incl., served 7:30-10:30. **Restaurant** Service 13:00-14:00, 20:00-22:00; menus 50-70,000L. Specialties: Regional cooking. **Credit cards** All major. **Pets** Dogs not allowed. **Nearby** Rome, Tivoli (Villa d'Este, Villa Adriana), Castelli Romani (Castel Gandolfo, Frascati, Grottaferrata), Anzio and Nettuno, Palestrina, Anagni, Etruscan zone (Cerveteri, Tarquinia), golf course (9-18-hole) in Rome. **Open** All year.

The Villa Fiorio was built at the turn of the century as a private vacation residence on one of the hills near the Eternal City. Wealthy Romans used to come to Frascati in summer to get away from the heat. Today this region of the Castelli Romani is famous for its vineyards, white wine and magnificent palazzi. The charming salons of the Villa Fiorio still have their original frescoes. The guest rooms are spacious and quiet, and look out onto the garden. They look quaint with their old fashioned furniture, but the bathrooms could be a little more up-to-date. The grounds and swimming pool are pleasant. We like this place because it is cool in the summer, an easy commute to Rome, set in a rich historical environment, and close to little trattorias, which are part of the charm of this region.

How to get there (Map 15): 21 km southeast of Rome. Via A2, exit Rome, S511 towards Grottaferrata, via Tuscolana for Frascati.

La Posta Vecchia ★★★★

00055 Palo Laziale (Rome)
Tel. (06) 99 49 501
Fax (06) 99 49 507
Sig. Scio

Rooms 17 with telephone, bath, WC and TV. **Price** Standard 640,000L, superior 840,000L, suite 1,340-2,140,000L. **Meals** Breakfast incl., served 8:00-10:00. **Restaurant** Service 13:00-15:00, 20:00-22:00; closed Tuesday; menu 120,000L, also à la carte. Specialties: Seafood. **Credit cards** All major. **Pets** Dogs not allowed. **Facilities** Swimming pool, parking. **Nearby** Rome, Tivoli (Villa d'Este, Villa Adriana), Castelli Romani (Castel Gandolfo, Frascati, Grottaferrata), Anzio and Nettuno, Palestrina, Anagni, Etruscan zone (Cerveteri, Tarquinia), golf course (9-18-hole) in Rome. **Open** All year.

Of all of the beautiful country inns we have seen, La Posta Vecchia is undoubtedly the most amazing. This ancient Roman villa overlooks the sea, and you can still see the ancient foundations *en reticolato*; there is even a mini-museum devoted to mosaics. The house fomerly belonged to billionaire J. Paul Getty, and has the splendor and magnificence of a billionaire's taste in furniture, paintings, tapestries, and overall decor. You must have a reservation, and show some sort of ID to get past the eagle-eyed doormen. Paradise has its price, which is high, but here it seems perfectly justified.

How to get there (Map 15): 37 km north of Rome.

Villa La Floridiana ★★★★

Via Casilina, km 63,700
03012 Anagni (Frosinone)
Tel. (0775) 767 845 – Fax (0775) 767 845/6
Sig.ra Camerini

Rooms 9 with telephone, bath or shower, WC and TV. **Price** Single 100,000L, double 130,000L, suite 150,000L. **Meals** Breakfast 10,000L, served 7:00-10:00; half board 110,000L, full board 140,000L (per pers.). **Restaurant** Service 12:00-15:00, 19:30-22:00; closed Sun. evening and Mon. noon; menu 50,000L. Specialties: Traditional cooking. **Credit cards** All major **Pets** Dogs allowed. **Facilities** Parking. **Nearby** In Anagni: cathedral, Palazzo Boniffacio VIII, Palazzo Comunale; Rome, Tivoli (Villa d'Este, Villa Adriana), Castelli Romani (Castel Gandolfo, Frascati, Grottaferrata), Anzio and Nettuno, Palestrina, Anagni, Etruscan zone (Cerveteri, Tarquinia), golf course (9-18-hole) in Rome. **Open** All year (except Aug).

Villa La Floridiana is located about thirty miles south of Rome in Anagni, a beautiful medieval village on the slopes of Mount Ernici, former summer residence of emperors and popes (three were born here!). This recently opened hotel exudes an old country-house charm, with its rough pink facade, green shutters, and large shady terrace. The interior is simply decorated with pretty regional furniture, floral and gingham fabrics, giving the place a cheerful atmosphere. The rooms are spacious and comfortable, the service friendly and attentive. The hotel can provide you with information about when to visit the historical monuments, which are off the usual tourist track. Most of the attractions don't keep very formal hours.

How to get there *(Map 20): 50 km southeast of Rome. Via A2, Anagni exit.*

Villa Vignola ★★★★

Corso Vannucci, 97
Vignola 66054 Vasto (Chieti)
Tel. (0873) 31 00 50 – Fax (0873) 31 00 60
Sig. Mazzetti

Rooms 5 with air-conditioning, telephone, bath or shower, WC, TV and minibar. **Price** Single 160,000L, double 280,000L. **Meals** Breakfast incl., served 7:30-10:30. **Restaurant** Service 12:30-14:30, 19:30-22:30; menu 65,000L. Specialties: Traditional cooking, seafood. **Credit cards** All major. **Pets** Dogs allowed (fee). **Facilities** Parking. **Nearby** Vasto. **Open** All year.

The Villa Vignola is a very intimate place, scaled for a limited clientele, as there are only five rooms and about ten tables. You can see the sea from the rooms and the terraces through a multitude of trees growing close to the beach. The place has the air of a private vacation house on the beach. The cozy salon, the small number of rooms, and their intimate, elegant decor certainly have a lot to do with this effect. This is a great place to come for a rest.

How to get there *(Map 17): 74 km south of Pescara via A14, Vasto exit, then towards Porto di Vasto (6 km north of Vasto).*

Hotel Cenobio dei Dogi ★★★★

Via Nicolo Cueno, 34
15032 Camogli (Genova)
Tel. (0185) 77 00 41 – Fax (0185) 77 27 96
Sig. Bungaro

Rooms 109 with air-conditioning, telephone, bath or shower, WC, TV and minibar.
Price Single 100-200,000L, double 240-480,000L, suite 450-520,000L.
Meals Breakfast included, served 7:30-10:10; half board 210-250,000L, full
board 260-300,000L (per pers., 3 days min.). **Restaurant** Service 12:45-14:15,
20:00-21:30; à la carte. Specialties: Seafood. **Credit cards** Amex, Visa, Eurocard,
MasterCard. **Pets** Dogs allowed. (+15,000 L). **Facilities** Swimming pool, tennis
(+20,000L), private beach, parking. **Nearby** Ruta and Portofino Vetta (Monte di
Portofino); Hamlets of San Rocco, San Nicolò, Punta Chiappa and the Abbey of S.
Fruttuoso by foot or boat; Portofino, Rapallo and the Riviera di Levante; Rapallo
golf course (18-hole). **Open** All year.

At the far end of the village of Camogli, with its beautiful pastel
houses painted in trompe-l'œil and its flowering terraces on
the sea, you will find the Hotel Cenebio dei Dogi. It is between
the hills and the sea, on grounds with trees that are hundreds of
years old. Formerly the residence of doges, this hotel, with elegant
and slightly overripe architecture, is one of the few unspoiled sites
on the Ligurian coast. The rooms are spacious and comfortable
and look out on the deep blue water of the Gulf of Paradis. This
hotel has everything needed for a pleasant stay, including a tennis
court, a heated sea-water swimming pool, a small private beach
and fine seafood cuisine. The service is efficient.

How to get there *(Map 9): 26 km east of Genova via A12, Recco exit,*
then S333 to Recco, Camogli, along the coast.

Albergo da Giovanni

Casale Portale, 23
15032 San Fruttuoso – Camogli (Genova)
Tel. (0185) 77 00 47
Famiglia Bozzo

Rooms 7 with shower (indoor). **Price** Single 60,000L, double 90,000L. **Meals** Half board 100,000L, full board 130,000L. **Restaurant** Service 13:00-14:30, 20:00-21:15; menu, also à la carte. Specialties: Seafood. **Credit cards** Not accepted. **Pets** Dogs not allowed. **Nearby** Abbey of S. Fruttuoso, Camogli, Portofino. **Open** June – Sept. (open weekends Oct. – May).

The Albergo da Giovanni is in San Fruttuoso, a magical, forgotten-by-time town dating from Roman antiquity, which most people stop off and visit during boat trips from Camogli and Portofino. The city is set on a small inlet surrounded by woods that border the sea, and has a cathedral, an abbey, a bell-tower and the Andréa Doria tower. Previously regarded as a day-trip destination, San Fruttuoso now welcomes adventurous overnighters, thanks to this beach house. The comfort is basic and the service nonexistent, but the restaurant is great and serves dishes made with fish fresh from the sea. The most magical part is being able to stay behind in this wonderfully evocative place and wave goodbye as the last boat of the day sails away.

How to get there *(Map 9): 26 km east of Genova via A12, Recco exit, then S333 to Recco then Camogli along the coast. Ferry services from Camogli to San Fruttuoso. (Information: 39-185-77 10 66.).*

Albergo Splendido ★★★★★

Viale Baratta, 13
16034 Portofino (Genova)
Tel. (0185) 26 95 51 - Fax (0185) 26 96 14
Sig. Saccani

Rooms 64 with air-conditioning, telephone, bath or shower, WC, TV and minibar.
Price With half board 450-660,000L (1 pers.), 990-1,240 000L (2 pers.), 1,600-
2,050 000L (suite), with full board +96,000L. **Meals** Breakfast included, served
7:30-10:00. **Restaurant** Service 13:00-14:30, 20:00-21:45; menu, also à la carte.
Specialties: Italian cooking. **Credit cards** All major. **Pets** Dogs allowed in the
rooms. **Facilities** Swimming pool, tennis (+40,000L), sauna, health center,
private beach (10 mn by foot), parking (+30,000L). **Nearby** Abbey of S. Fruttuoso
by foot or boat, Rapallo and the Riviera di Levante, golf course of Rapallo (18-
hole). **Open** Mar. 22 – Jan. 2.

Elizabeth Taylor, Humphrey Bogart and the Duke of Windsor
have all stayed here. It's one of the world's most famous hotels,
set atop a hill overlooking picture-postcard Portofino. The rooms
are luxurious and have marble bathrooms. The newer rooms are
the most comfortable. The older ones, with balconies in the trees,
are very nice, too, but have smaller bathrooms. In addition to a
heated pool, a tennis court and a restaurant with a beautiful vista,
you will have a sauna and a beauty salon at your disposal. Having
cocktails on the terrace is a grand event. You'll luxuriate in the
impeccable service.

How to get there *(Map 9): 36 km east of Genova via A12, Rapallo exit,
S227 along the coast to Portofino.*

Hotel Nazionale ★★★★

Via Roma, 8
16038 Portofino (Genova)
Tel. (0185) 26 95 75 - Fax (0185) 26 95 78
Sig. Briola

Rooms 12 with telephone, bath or shower, WC, TV and minibar. **Price** Double 255,000L, suite 450-500,000L. **Meals** Breakfast 25,000L, served 7:30-12:00. **Restaurant** See p. 408. **Credit cards** Visa, Eurocard, MasterCard. **Pets** Dogs allowed. **Facilities** Swimming pool, tennis (+26,750L), sauna, health center, private beach (10 mn by foot), parking (+25,000L). **Nearby** Abbey of S. Fruttuoso di Camogli by foot or boat, Rapallo and the Riviera di Levante, Rapallo golf course (18-hole). **Open** March 15 – Nov. 30.

The Hotel Nazionale is in the very hub of Portofino, the chic epicenter of Italian yachting. Brightly-hued, with green shuters typical of Portofino-style architecture, it's one of the most famous buildings near the harbor. Its location, right on the port, will allow you to experience the daytime hustle and bustle of this Italian version of Saint Tropez–enjoyable by day, less so at night. Service is slow and rates pretty high and rooms a tad démodé, but they're very comfortable, but location is great.

How to get there *(Map 9): 36 km east of Genova via A12, Rapallo exit, S227 along the coast to Portofino. (Parking is 300 meters from the hotel).*

Imperiale Palace Hotel ★★★★

Via Pagana, 19
16038 Santa Margherita Ligure (Genova)
Tel. (0185) 28 89 91- Fax (0185) 28 42 23
Sig. Lenci

Rooms 102 with air-conditioning, telephone, bath or shower, WC, TV and minibar.
Price Single 210-285,000L, double 350-515,000L. **Meals** Breakfast included,
served 7:30-10:30. **Restaurant** Service 13:00-14:30, 20:00-22:30; menu 90,000L,
also à la carte. Specialties: Italian cooking. **Credit cards** All major. **Pets** Dogs
allowed in the rooms. **Facilities** Swimming pool, private beach, garage, parking.
Nearby Abbey of S. Fruttuoso by foot or boat, Rapallo and the Riviera di Levante,
Rapallo golf course (18-hole). **Open** Apr. – Nov.

The splendors of the past await you at the Imperiale Hotel.
Originally the property of a rich Corsican family in 1889, it
became a hotel around 1910. Since then it has hosted important
historic events–the treaty of Rapallo between Russia and
Germany–and many noted movie stars. Rooms are spacious,
classically decorated, and luxurious. The ones in the front have a
wonderful view of the sea. The salons and dining rooms are
superb. In summer, you can enjoy lunch on the terrace just over
the hotel's private beach, and in the evening, candlelight dinners
and dancing on the large terrace. A truly palatial experience.

How to get there *(Map 9): 30 km east of Genova via A12, Rapallo exit,*
then S227 along the coast.

Grand Hotel dei Castelli ★★★★

Penisola, 26
16039 Sestri Levante (Genova)
Tel. (0185) 48 72 20 – Fax (0185) 447 67
Sig. Zanotto

Rooms 30 (15 with air-conditioning), telephone, bath or shower, WC, TV and minibar. **Price** Single 180-240,000L, double 255-320,000L, suite 400-500,000L. **Meals** Breakfast 20,000L, served 7:30-10:00; half board 230-265,000L (per pers. 3 days min.). **Restaurant** Service 12:30-14:30, 20:30-23:00; menu 60,000L, also à la carte. Specialties: Insalata di polpa di granchio con punte di asparagi, trofiette al pesto leggero con vongole e zucchine, tagliata di tonno rosso con misticanza di insalatine. **Credit cards** All major. **Pets** Dogs allowed. **Facilities** Private beach (34,000L), parking. **Nearby** Sestri Levante (Baia del Silenzio, The coast road from Sestri Levante to Monterosso al Mare), The Cinque Terre by boat or by train, Rapallo golf course (18-hole). **Open** May – Oct.

On the peninsula separating the Baia del Silencio from the Baia del Favole, three castles–Castello dei Cipressi, Castello dei Lecci, and Castello delle Agavi–raise their lacy medieval towers against the sky. They are surrounded by a superb estate of more than 160,000 square meters descending to the sea in a series of panoramic terraces; an elevator can quickly deliver you to the beach. The Grand Hotel is in one of the castles. The decor is very warm and welcoming, with beautiful woodwork in the reception area, Moorish columns, mosaics and a superb veranda fronting the sea. The staff is extremely cordial and friendly. The restaurant is in one of the other castles, which has an equally beautiful view of the sea.

How to get there (Map 9): 50 km east of Genova via A12, Sestri Levante exit.

Grand Hotel Villa Balbi ★★★★

Viale Rimembranza, 1
16039 Sestri Levante (La Spezia)
Tel. (0185) 42 941 - Fax (0185) 48 24 59 - Sig. Rossignotti

Rooms 92 with air-conditioning (on request), telephone, bath or shower, WC, TV and minibar. **Price** Single 130-160,000L, double 220-300,000L, suite 300-400,000L. **Meals** Breakfast 18,000L, served 7:30-10:30; half board 165-230,000L, full board 195-260,000L (per pers. 3 days min.). **Restaurant** Service 12:30-14:00, 19:30-21:00; menu 65-75,000L, also à la carte. Specialties: Italian cuisine. **Credit cards** All major. **Pets** Dogs not allowed. **Facilities** Heated swimming pool, private beach, parking (+15,000L). **Nearby** Sestri Levante (Baia del Silenzio, coast road from Sestri Levante to Monterosso al Mare), the Cinque Terre by boat or by train, Rapallo golf course (18-hole). **Open** May – Nov.

Villa Balbi looks like something out of a 17th-century Baroque dream. The crimson patina of the facade gleams among the palm trees, and the large front door, crowned by a balcony and a pediment, gives it an overly formal look. Not surprisingly, queens, such as Elisabetta Farnèse, and doges have stayed here. The cool dark interiors are bathed in a gentle light, and are accented with sparkling frescoes and gleaming marble. The guest rooms are furnished with carefully preserved antiques. As for comfort, it has kept pace with the changing standards of luxury down through the centuries. There is a heated salt-water swimming pool on the grounds and a comfortable living room with plush armchairs and bow windows reflecting the many shades of green of the garden. The service is palace-style: discreet, elegant and efficient.

How to get there (Map 9): 50 km east of Genova via A12, Sestri Levante exit.

Hotel Helvetia ★★★

Via Cappuccini, 43
16039 Sestri Levante (Genova)
Tel. (0185) 41 175 – Fax (0185) 457 216
Sig. Pernigotti

Rooms 28 with air-conditioning (on request), telephone, bath or shower, WC, cable TV and minibar. **Price** Single 160,000L, double 210,000L, suite 230,000L. **Meals** Breakfast included (buffet), served 7:30-10:30. **Restaurant** See p. 409. **Credit cards** Visa, Eurocard, MasterCard. **Pets** Dogs allowed (+10,000L). **Facilities** Private beach, bikes, parking (+10,000L). **Nearby** Sestri Levante (Baia del Silenzio, coast road from Sestri Levante to Monterosso al Mare), Cinque Terre by boat or by train, Rapallo golf course (18-hole). **Open** Mar. – Oct.

The Hotel Helvetia, with a beautiful terrace on the Baia del Silenzio and a private beach, meets the quality and service standards of a grand hotel. Lorenzo Pernigotti, the owner, is a man who loves his work. You can see this in the elegant yet family-oriented atmosphere that he has created. The rooms have everything you need to feel right at home. Breakfasts are excellent, consisting of a copious buffet with fresh fruit, fruit juice, croissants and cheeses. Not only will you receive warm a welcome, but you'll get a little surprise when you leave. A private shuttle bus takes you back and forth to the garage.

How to get there *(Map 9): 50 km east of Genova via A12, Sestri Levante exit.*

Royal Hotel ★★★★★

Corso Imperatrice, 80
18038 San Remo (Imperia)
Tel. (0184) 53 91 – Fax (0184) 61 445
Sig. Boccardo

Rooms 147 with air-conditioning, telephone, bath or shower, WC, TV and minibar. **Price** Single 165-292,000L, double 292-474,000L, suite 470-980,000L. **Meals** Breakfast included, served 7:30-10:15; half board 206-350,000L, full board 243-395,000L (per pers. 3 days min.). **Restaurant** Service 12:30-14:15, 19:30-22:00; menu 90,000L, also à la carte. Specialties: Risotto ravioli di nasello salsa all'astrice-angello Royal-branzino ai carciofi. **Credit cards** All major. **Pets** Dogs allowed (+20,000L). **Facilities** Swimming pool, tennis (22,000L), fitness, parking (+11,000L). **Nearby** On the Riviera di Ponente, the "Giardino Hanbury" in Mortala Inferiore, San Remo, Genoa, San Remo golf course (18-hole). **Open** Dec. 20 – Sept.

A large garden full of palm trees ferns, and other subtropical plants protects this large, splendid hotel from the commotion of San Remo. It is one of the last oases of quiet and luxury on this part of the Ligurian coast, a golden cage millionaires from times past never felt like flying from. This prestigious hotel has welcomed the aristocratic families of Europe since 1872, a study in total refinement with large colonnaded salons facing the sea, vast, luxurious rooms and bathrooms of pink or white marble. Expect excellent service.

How to get there *(Map 8): 56 km east of Nice (France) via A10, San Remo exit.*

Hotel Punta Est ★★★★

Via Aurelia, 1
17024 Finale Ligure (Savona)
Tel. (019) 60 06 11 - Fax (019) 60 06 11
Sig. Podesta

Rooms 40 with telephone, bath or shower and WC (25 with TV, minibar).
Price Single 200,000L, double 300,000L, suite 400,000L. **Meals** Breakfast
20,000L, served 8:00-10:00 (15:00 in room); half board and full board 170-
260,000L (per pers. 3 days min.). **Restaurant** Service 13:00-14:00, 20:00-21:00;
menu 50-75,000L, also à la carte. Specialties: Branzino al sale. **Credit cards**
Amex, Visa, Eurocard, MasterCard. **Pets** Dogs not allowed. **Facilities** Swimming
pool, tennis (half-court), parking. **Nearby** Abbey of Finale Pia, prehistoric caves
near by Toirano, coast road from Finale Ligure to Savona (Noli, Spotorno), Golf
Garlenda Course (18-hole). **Open** May – Sept.

The Hotel Punta Est is perched on a little promontory
overhanging the beach. It consists of two buildings–an
18th-century villa and a modern addition–set in the middle of a
trellised garden with large pine trees, palms, bougainvillea and
hibiscus. The rooms are comfortably furnished and all have a
view of the sea. The private swimming pool and reserved spaces
on the beach across from the hotel allow you to escape the
summer crowds. The large, panoramic terrace with piano bar is
a nice place to spend an evening.

How to get there *(Map 8): 30 km south of Savona via A10, Finale
Ligure exit.*

La Meridiana ★★★★

Via ai Castelli, 11
17033 Garlenda (Savona)
Tel. (0182) 58 02 71 – Fax (0182) 58 01 50
Sig. and Sig.ra Segre

Rooms 32 with telephone, bath or shower, WC, cable TV and minibar. **Price** Double 280-360,000L, apart. 360-450,000L. **Meals** Breakfast 25,000L; half board 225-240,000L (per pers. 3 days min.). **Restaurant** In summer, lunch at the swimming pool; dinner 20:00-22:00; menu 90,000L, also à la carte. **Credit cards** All major. **Pets** Small dogs allowed in rooms (+30,000L). **Facilities** Swimming pool, bike, sauna (20,000L), parking (+11,000L). **Nearby** The Riviera di Ponente to Genoa, Garlenda golf course (18-hole). **Open** Mar. – Dec.

The road to the Meridiana is not always pleasant, but once you have arrived, you will have no regrets. The atmosphere is one of a large country house, opening on the countryside, with beautiful grounds and a swimming pool. You will find the same airy comfort in the rooms. The hotel restaurant, Il Rosmario, is one of the better ones in the area. Mr. Segre, the dynamic owner, sees to it that only the best local products are used in the fine cuisine. A plus for many is the golf course right next door. This is a great place for a get away; ask about the special weekend package and golf rates.

How to get there *(Map 8): 100 km east to Nice (France) via A10, Albenga exit, then S453 towards Garlenda.*

Hotel Porto Roca ★★★★

Via Corone, 1
19016 Monterosso Al Mare (La Spezia)
Tel. (0187) 81 75 02 – Fax (0187) 81 76 92
Sig.ra Guerina Arpe

Rooms 43 with telephone, bath or shower, WC, TV and minibar **Price** Single 195,000L, double 210-295,000L. **Meals** Breakfast included, served 7:30-10:00; half board 140-195,000L, full board 165-220,000L (per pers. 3 days min.). **Restaurant** Service 12:30-13:30, 19:30-21:00; menu 60-70,000L, also à la carte. Specialties: Sfogliatelle Porto Roca, straccetti "paradiso", branzino al sale, crostate di frutta fresca. **Credit cards** Amex, Visa, Eurocard, MasterCard. **Pets** Dogs allowed (+15-20,000L). **Facilities** Private beach in summer, parking in the village. **Nearby** The Riviera di Levante, the Cinque Terre by boat or by rail, Marigola golf course (9-hole) in Lerici. **Open** Apr. 20 – Nov.

Monterosso is every bit as charming as the other villages in the Cinque Terre, but it's the only one to have a hotel like the Porto Roca, which overlooks the Bay of Porticciolo and Monterosso Beach. The congenial decor is a mixture of different styles, from medieval to modern. If you'd like to work on your tan, you have a choice of the beach or the hotel terrace overlooking the cliffs. In summer, leave your car in the village parking lot, which is secured day and night; a minibus will take your bags to the hotel.

How to get there *(Map 9): 32 km northwest of La Spezia via S370, along the coast.*

Albergo San Vigilio ★★★

24100 Bergamo Alta
Via San Vigilio, 15
Tel. (035) 25 31 79 – Fax (035) 40 20 81
Sig.ra Franceschi

Rooms 7 with telephone, bath or shower and WC. **Price** Double 150,000L.
Meals Breakfast 15,000L, served 7:30-10:30. **Restaurant** Service 12:30-14:30,
19:30-22:00; closed Sun. evening, Mon., Jan.; menu 50-70,000L, also à la carte.
Specialties: Italian and Lombard cooking. **Credit cards** All major. **Pets** Dogs not
allowed. **Nearby** In Bergamo alta: Piazza Vecchia, Church of Santa Maria
Maggiore, Colleoni Chapel; in Bergamo bassa: Accademia Carrara; Lake Garda, La
Rossera golf course (9-hole) in Chiuduno. **Open** All year.

This small inn is in Bergamo, a Lombardy towns known far
and wide for its rich artistic and historical heritage. The San
Vigilio is famous for its restaurant but also offers quiet,
comfortable rooms. The pleasant dining room is on a covered
terrace overlooking the valley. Reasonable prices, great cuisine
and a superb location will certainly make your stay here a
pleasant one.

How to get there (Map 3): 47 km northeast of Milano - Airport di Orio
al Serio, 4 km.

I Due Roccoli ★★★

via Silvio Bonomelli, 54
25049 Colline di Iseo (Brescia)
Tel. (030) 982 18 53 - Fax (030) 982 18 77
Sig. Agoni

Rooms 13 with telephone, bath or shower, WC., TV, safe and minibar **Price** Single 110-135,000L, double 160-190,000L, suite 200-240,000L. **Meals** Breakfast 15,000L, served 7:30-10:00. **Restaurant** Service 12:00-14:00, 19:30-22:00; menu 45-65,000L, also à la carte. Specialties: Agotino di ricotta, code di gamberi, pesce del lago. **Credit cards** All major. **Pets** Small dogs allowed. **Nearby** Lake Iseo, Bergamo, Brescia, Lake Garda, Lake Como, Franciacorta golf course (18-hole). **Open** Mar. 11 – Oct. 31.

I Due Roccoli is in Iseo, a place which is, as a little boy once said, "a little bit pretty and a little bit ugly." The unspoiled beauty of the lake is undeniable, and the old houses, with their red or yellow gently time-worn walls, are lovely. The new ones are much less poetic. In the hills around the lake, you will find farmhouses built of old stone as well as the I Due Roccoli inn. Hidden in the trees, it is made up of a fine patrician villa, the main body of an old farmhouse, and a series of newer but well-integrated rooms. They are pleasantly decorated with flowered cotton fabrics in a pastel color scheme. Some open onto the grounds while others have a superb view of the lake and the mountains of Franciacorta. The service is full of sparkle and cordiality.

How to get there *(Map 4): 25 km north of Brescia (via A4 Milano/Venezia, Rovato exit), towards Lago Iseo, then Polaveno (4 km of Iseo).*

Cappuccini ★★★

via Cappucini, 54
Cologne Franciacorta (Brescia)
Tel. (030) 755 72 54 – Fax (030) 715 72 57
Sig. and Sig.ra Pelizzari

Rooms 7 with air-conditioning, telephone, bath or shower, WC, cable TV, safe and minibar **Price** Single 160,000L, double 240,000L, suite 300,000L. **Meals** Breakfast included, served 9:30-11:00. **Restaurant** Service 12:30-14:30, 19:30-22:00; menu 55-80,000L, also à la carte. Specialties: Manzo all' olio, stracotto con polenta, seafood. **Credit cards** All major. **Pets** Dogs not allowed. **Nearby** Lake Iseo, Bergamo, Brescia, Lake Garda, Lake Como, Franciacorta golf course (18-hole). **Open** All year (except Jan. 1 – 20 and Aug. 1 – 20).

With its gently, rolling hills and valleys, the landscapes of Franciacorta have a simple and poetic beauty only recently discovered by tourists. Standing on a hill, the Convento dei Cappuccini, built in 1569, will very quickly impress you with its serene beauty. It has been rigorously restored, and the austerity which gives grandeur to monastic architecture has been left intact. The long vaulted hallways, the exposed beams, the all-white rooms and the dark wood furniture all enhance this atmosphere. The deliberate simplicity is not achieved at the expense of comfort, however, which is elegant rather than monastic. The restaurant, lit by candles, offers fine cuisine. The delightful fragrance of Acacia, the regional wine, floats over this place where good food and spirituality make for an excellent mix.

How to get there (Map 4): 27 km west of Brescia, towards Bergamo.

L'Albereta ★★★★

Via Vittorio Emanuele, 11
Erbusco (Brescia)
Tel. (030) 776 05 50
Fax (030) 776 05 73

Rooms 44 with air-conditining, telephone, bath, WC, TV and minibar. **Price** Single 180-220,000L, double 260-320,000L, suite 370-420,000L. **Meals** Breakfast 20-45,000L, served 7:30-10:30; half board 210,000L, full board 240,000L (per pers.,3 days min.). **Restaurant** "Gualtieri Marchesi" Service 12:30-14:00, 19:30-22:00; closed Sunday evening, Mon.; menu 80-150,000L, also à la carte. Specialties: Italian "nouvelle cuisine". **Credit cards** All major. **Pets** Dogs allowed. **Facilities** Swimming pool, tennis, sauna, parking, garage. **Nearby** Lake Iseo, Bergamo, Brescia, Lake Garda, Lake Como, Franciacorta golf course (18-hole). **Open** All year (except 20 days in Jan.).

Gualtiero Marchesi is the dean of a school of Italian cuisine that teaches evolution within tradition. He created the Albereta, based on his refined taste and his masterful blueprints, without modifying the harmony of its original plan. The rooms in the tower are large and richly furnished, with canopy beds, heavy drapes and other decorative elements skillfully blending the authentic and the imported. The impression that lingers is one of well-assimilated luxury. And where is the charm in all this? To find it, all you have to do is have dinner in the beautiful dining room, decorated with frescoes, or take a swim in the pool or laze in the Roman baths redone by Marchesi, which you must not miss.

How to get there *(Map 4): 20 km west of Brescia, via A4 (Milano/Venezia) Rovato.*

La Mongolfiera di Bellavista ★★★★

Bellavista 25030 Erbusco (Brescia)
Tel. (030) 726 84 51
Fax (030) 776 03 86

Rooms 6 with telephone, bath or shower, WC, TV and minibar. **Price** Single 150,000L, double 195,000L, suite 250,000L. **Meals** Breakfast included, served 7:30-10:00; half board 270,000L, full board 345,000L (per 2 pers.). **Restaurant** Service 12:00-14:00, 19:30-22:00; menu, also à la carte. Specialties: Regional cooking. **Credit cards** All major. **Pets** Dogs not allowed. **Facilities** Parking. **Nearby** Lake Iseo, Bergamo, Brescia, Lake Garda, Lake Como, Franciacorta golf course (18-hole). **Open** All year (except Jan. 3 – 16 and Aug. 8 – 24).

What is a hotel of charm? It is often a pretty house in an attractive setting. But what other ingredients are needed? Large rooms and comfortable baths. Here, at the Mongolfiera, it is also the coolness of floor tiles, the blended fragrance of acacias, jasmine and honeysuckle, afternoon naps in the shade of the spreading chestnut trees and sunsets over the fields and vineyards of Bellavista. It is also breakfast with the smell of just-made coffee and bread before going fishing, visiting historical sites or trying out the golf course next to the hotel. In short, the Mongolfiera is the archetypical hotel of charm. We have just receved word that tere may be plans to close the hotel, so be sure to contact them before going there.

How to get there (*Map 4*): *20 km west of Brescia (via A4 Milano/Venezia, Rovato exit), Erbusco, then towards Torbiato.*

Hotel Villa del Sogno ★★★★

Lago di Garda
Via Zanardelli, 107
25083 Fasano di Gardone Riviera (Brescia)
Tel. (0365) 29 01 81 - Fax (0365) 29 02 30 - Famiglia Calderan

Rooms 34 with telephone, bath or shower, WC and TV. **Price** Single 185-225,000L, double 300-380,000L, suite 420-500,000L. **Meals** Breakfast included, served 7:30-10:00; half board 190-230,000L, full board 210-260,000L (per pers.,3 days min.). **Restaurant** Service 12:30-14:30, 19:30-21:30; menu 80,000L, also à la carte. Specialties: Trota del Garda, ossibuchi alla gardesana, spaghetti alla trota. **Credit cards** All major. **Pets** Dogs not allowed. **Facilities** Swimming pool, tennis, sauna, parking **Nearby** Lake Garda, Villa Martinengo in Barbarno, botanical garden of Gardone di Sotto, The Vittoriale (D'Annunzio estate), Belvedere San Michele; Verona, Bogliaco golf course (9-hole), Solan golf course. **Open** Apr. – Oct. 20.

A symphony of ochres and soft yellow illuminates the facade of this romantic turn-of-the-century villa with a dreamy, dazzling terrace and luxuriant gardens. Slightly elevated, it looks out over Lake Garda. This elegant hotel is decorated with antique furniture and old paintings from different periods so the occasional odd piece or detail in no way compromises the ensemble of the decor. The rooms are spacious and some located below the main terrace have private terraces. The cuisine is simple and the bar pleasant. In the yard near the lake is a swimming pool and a tennis court.

How to get there *(Map 4): 130 km east of Milano - 36 km northeast of Brescia via S45 bis the left bank (Fasano, 2 km).*

Grand Hotel Fasano ★★★★

Lago di Garda
Corso Zanardelli, 160
25083 Fasano di Gardone Riviera (Brescia)
Tel. (0365) 290 220 – Fax (0365) 210 54/290 221 – Sig.ra Mayr

Rooms 8/ with telephone, bath or shower, WC and TV; elevator, wheelchair access. **Price** Double 220-440,000L, suite 400-480,000L. **Meals** Breakfast included, served 7:30-10:30; half board +15,000L (per pers.). **Restaurant** Service 12:30-14:30, 19:30-21:30; menu 59,000L, also à la carte. Specialties: Italian cuisine. **Credit cards** Not accepted. **Pets** Dogs allowed (+10,000L). **Facilities** Swimming pool, tennis (25,000L), parking (10,000L). **Nearby** Lake Garda, Villa Martinengo in Barbarno, botanical garden of Gardone di Sotto, The Vittoriale (D'Annunzio estate), Belvedere San Michele; Verona, Soiano-hole golf course (9-18-hole). **Open** Easter – Nov.

The Grand Hotel Fasano used to be a hunting lodge belonging to the imperial family of Austria, which perhaps explains, apart from the origins of the owner, the number of German tourists who come here. The hotel is comfortable, if a little over-decorated. The rooms are all pleasant, but ask for one in the older part. The garden, right on the lake, consists of beautiful plantings of palm trees, flower, and greenery.

How to get there *(Map 4): 130 km east of Milano - 36 km northeast of Brescia via S45 bis, on the left bank (Fasano Gardone, 1 km).*

Villa Fiordaliso ★★★★

Lago di Garda
Corso Zanardelli, 132
25083 Gardone Riviera (Brescia)
Tel. (0365) 20 158 - Fax (0365) 29 00 11 - Sig. Tosetti

Rooms 6 with telephone, bath, WC., TV and minibar. **Price** Double 300-700,000L.
Meals Breakfast included, served 8:00-10:00. **Restaurant** Service 12:30-14:00,
19:30-22:00, closed Mon. and Tues. lunch; menus 68-98,000L, also à la carte.
Specialties: Season-cuisine. **Credit cards** All major. **Pets** Dogs not allowed.
Facilities Private embarcadère, parking. **Nearby** Lake Garda, Villa Martinengo in
Barbarno, botanical garden of Gardone di Sotto, The Vittoriale (D'Annunzio
estate), Belvedere San Michele, Verona, Bogliaco golf course (9-hole). **Open** Dec.
21 – Jan. 7, Feb. 12 – Oct. 31.

Once home to Gabriele d'Annunzio, Italy's most celebrated
20th-century poet, the Villa Fiordaliso, faces the shores of
Lake Garda. Architectural eclecticism reigns in this residence,
with Renaissance porches hard by 19th-century windows.
Restoration work has left intact all the charm of d'Annunzio's
historic house. The guest rooms are comfortable and some have
a terrace on the lake. One pink suite has a sumptuous bathroom
done in Carrera marble. The restaurant is a great place for a
meal, even if you don't stay at the hotel.

*How to get there (Map 4): 130 km east of Milano - 5 km northeast of
Brescia via S45 on the left bank (1 km of Gardone Riviera).*

Hotel Baia d'Oro ★★★

Lago di Garda
Via Gamberera, 13
25084 Gargnano (Brescia)
Tel. (0365) 71 171 - Fax (0365) 72 568 - Sig. Terzi

Rooms 12 with telephone, bath, WC, TV and minibar. **Price** Single 85,000L,
double 130,000L. **Meals** Breakfast 20,000L, served 8:00-10:30; half board
150,000L. **Restaurant** Service 12:30-14:00, 19:30-21:30; à la carte. Specialties:
Pasta fatta in casa, pesce del lago e di mare. **Credit cards** Amex, Visa, Eurocard
and MasterCard. **Pets** Dogs allowed. **Facilities** Garage (15,000L). **Nearby** Lake
Garda, Villa Feltrinelli, Lake Idro, Church of Madonna di Monte Castello, Pieve di
Tremosine, Verona, Bogliaco golf course (9-hole). **Open** Apr. – Oct.

The colored facade of the Baia d'Oro, formerly a smallish
house belonging to a fisherman, makes it easy to spot on the
edge of Lake Garda. A private wharf keeps a *motoscaffo* at the
disposal of the guests. On the picturesque lakeside terrace, you
can enjoy lunch or dinner based on some of the best cuisine of
the region–the hotel even recommends guests choose the half-
board option so as not to miss out on the local treats. The rooms
are comfortable and most have a small balcony, where you can
have a pleasant breakfast while taking in the superb view. On
the dining room walls are complimentary letters with famous
signatures, notably one from Winston Churchill.

How to get there *(Map 4): 46 km northwest of Brescia via S45 bis, on
the left bank.*

Villa Giulia ★★★

Lago di Garda
25084 Gargnano (Brescia)
Tel. (0365) 71 022 – Fax (0365) 72 774
Sig. and Sig.ra Bombardelli

Rooms 17 with telephone, bath or shower, WC, cable TV, minibar and safe. **Price** Single 120-140,000L, double 230-280,000L. **Meals** Breakfast included, served 8:00-10:00; half board 145-170,000L. **Restaurant** Service 12:30-13:30, 19:30-20:30; à la carte. Specialties: Regional cooking. **Credit cards** Not accepted. **Pets** Small dogs allowed (10,000L). **Facilities** Swimming pool, sauna, private beach, parking. **Nearby** Lake Garda, Villa Feltrinelli, Lake Idro, Church of Madonna di Monte Castello, Pieve di Tremosine, Verona, Bogliaco golf course (9-hole). **Open** 1 week before Easter – Oct. 10.

Success is often a question of passion and perseverance, two qualities which helped Rina Bombardelli turn the family *pensione* into a hotel of considerable charm. This Gothic-style villa, right on Lake Garda, has a great view of the lake and the Baldo mountains, which appear green or snowy white according to the season. The atmosphere is very cozy. The salon-bar is divided into distinctly different areas by wing and club chairs. The dining room, similarly divided, is lit by two beautiful Murano crystal chandeliers. In summer, the restaurant is set up on the veranda. The well-furnished rooms have a view of either the garden or the lake. Off to one side there is a swimming pool and a solarium on the lawn.

How to get there *(Map 4): 46 km northwest of Brescia via S45 bis, on the left bank.*

Hotel Laurin

Lago di Garda
25087 Salo (Brescia)
Viale Landi, 9
Tel. (0365) 220 22 – Fax (0365) 223 82 – Sig. Rossi

Rooms 36 (18 with air-conditioning) with telephone, bath or shower, WC, TV and minibar. **Price** Single 150,000L, double 300,000L, suite 380,000L. **Meals** Breakfast included, served 8:00-10:00; half board 170-250,000L (per pers., 3 days min.). **Restaurant** Service 12:30-14:30, 20:00-21:30; menus, à la carte. Specialties: Fish. **Credit cards** All major. **Pets** Small dogs allowed. **Facilities** Swimming pool, parking. **Nearby** Villa Martinengo in Barbarano, Garden of Gardone di Sotto, Vittoriale degli Italiani, Belvedere San Michele, Verona, Bogliaco golf course (9-hole). **Open** Feb. – Nov.

A popular vacation spot in the last century, Lake Garda has kept beautiful vestiges of this era. Salo, one of the rare villages to have kept the luster of the old days, is also etched painfully into the history of Italy, having been the last bastion of Mussolini's supporters. The Hotel Laurin is an admirably preserved Liberty–style villa, one of the precious jewels of the area. The salons are decorated with frescoes of voluptuous romantic subjects. The rooms have parquet floors and delicate furniture adding to the elegant harmonious atmosphere. Most of them have an enchanting view of the lake. The staff will welcome you warmly. Be sure to take a walk along the banks up to the village and visit the very unusual "Vittoriale," the palace–museum of the poet Gabriele d'Annunzio.

How to get there *(Map 4): 130 km east of Milano - 35 km northeast of Brescia via S45 on the left bank (1 km of Gardone Riviera).*

Villa Cortine Palace Hotel *****

Lago di Garda
Via Grotte, 12
25019 Sirmione (Brescia)
Tel. (030) 99 05 890 – Fax (030) 91 63 90 – Sig. Cappelletto

Rooms 55 with telephone, bath, WC, TV and minibar. **Price** Single 200-300,000L, double 350-500,000L, suite 650-900,000L. **Meals** Breakfast included, served 7:30-10:30. **Restaurant** Service 12:30-14:15, 19:30-21:15; menus 80-90,000L, also à la carte. Specialties: Italian cooking. **Credit cards** All major. **Pets** Dogs allowed (+40,000L). **Facilities** Swimming pool, tennis (15,000L), private beach, parking. **Nearby** Lake Garda, Grotte di Catullo and Castle of Scaliger in Sirmione, Brescia, Verona, Soiano golf course (9-18-hole). **Open** Apr. – Oct. 25.

This neoclassical villa, built at the turn of the century on Lake Garda, is a true symbol of luxury, although the modern annex detracts a bit from the overall harmony. Palm trees, fountains and tropical plants embellish the grounds of this romantic dreamscape. As for swimming, the pool is just as nice as the private beach on the lake. Vast rooms with period furniture add yet another touch of elegance. The impeccably behaved staff and the luxury cars lined up in the parking lot conjure up the dolce vita of days gone by.

How to get there *(Map 4): 127 km east of Milano - 40 km east of Brescia via A4, Sirmione exit - San Martino di Battaglia.*

Grand Hotel Villa Serbelloni ★★★★★

Lago di Como
Via Roma, 1
22021 Bellagio (Como)
Tel. (031) 95 02 16 - Fax (031) 95 15 29 - Sig. Spinelli

Rooms 85 (42 with air-conditioning) with telephone, bath, WC, TV and minibar.
Price Single 286-313,000L, double 419-456,000L. **Meals** Breakfast included,
served 7:30-10:30; half board +77,000L, full board +147,000L (per pers., 3 days
min.). **Restaurant** Service 12:30-14:30, 20:00-22:00; menu 95,000L, also à la
carte. Specialties: Pasta della casa, pesce del lago. **Credit cards** All major. **Pets**
Dogs allowed. **Facilities** Swimming pool, tennis (15,000 L), sauna, fitness and
beauty, squash, private garage (20,000L), parking. **Nearby** Milano, Lake Como
(Villa Melzi, Erba to Bellagio by the Vallassina), Bellagio to Como, Villa Trotti,
Grotta verde in Lezzeno, Careno, Villa Pliniana in Riva di Faggetto, Grandola golf
course (18-hole). **Open** Apr. – Oct.

The quintessence of romanticism, this sited palace on the banks
of Lake Como is the premier address for visitors to Bellagio,
often called "Italy's prettiest town." The immense, lavishly
decorated salons have coffered ceilings, wall murals, oriental rugs,
overstuffed couches and, of course, vistas of the lake. Although all
rooms are very comfortable, we prefer those in the original villa,
with their small salons, ceiling murals and columns. As soon as it
gets warm, the restaurant moves outside to its summer quarters on
the large terrace, which overlooks the lake. For the health-
conscious, the hotel has opened a health and beauty center with the
future possibility of spa-style cuisine. Guests—who have included
John F. Kennedy and Winston Churchill—delight in visiting the
many historic villas on the lake.

How to get there (Map 3): 31 km north of Como via S583; on the right bank.

Hotel Florence ★★★

Lago di Como
Piazza Mazzimi
22021 Bellagio (Como)
Tel. (031) 950 342 – Fax (031) 951 722 – Sig. and Sig.ra Ketzlar

Rooms 36 with telephone, bath or shower, WC, cable TV, hairdrayer and minibar. **Price** Double 190,000L, suite 250,000L. **Meals** Breakfast included, served 7:30-10:15; half board 140-155,000L (per pers.). **Restaurant** Service 12:30-14:30, 19:30-21:30; à la carte. Specialties: Terrina di lavarello, lasagnette ai pesci di lago, lasagnette verdi alle verdure, pesce persico ai pomodori confits. **Credit cards** Visa, Eurocard, MasterCard. **Pets** Dogs allowed in rooms. **Facilities** Swimming pool, tennis (15,000 L), sauna, fitness and beauty, private garage (20,000L), parking. **Nearby** Milano, Lake Como (Villa Melzi, Erba to Bellagio by the Vallassina), Bellagio to Como, Villa Trotti, Grotta verde in Lezzeno, Careno, Villa Pliniana in Riva di Faggetto, Grandola golf course (18-hole). **Open** Apr. 20 – Oct. 20.

Under the arcades that line Bellagio's harbor, just next to the entrance of Serbelloni Hotel, you may notice people having refreshments on a pretty terrace in front of the Hotel Florence. Here, a warm welcome awaits you. You can listen to jazz at the American-style bar. The dining room and guest rooms are upstairs, and look out onto the lively port of Lake Como. They have been nicely furnished. The dining room has a fireplace and a very cordial atmosphere. For sheer luxury, head for the Serbelloni next door; for plenty of charm, the Hotel Florence fits the bill—and the price is right.

How to get there *(Map 3): 31 km north of Como via S583; on the right bank.*

Grand Hotel Villa d'Este ★★★★★

Lago di Como
Via Regina, 40 - 22012 Cernobbio (Como)
Tel. (031) 348 1 - Fax (031) 348 844
Sig. Marco Sorbellini

Rooms 156 with air-conditioning, telephone, bath, WC, cable TV, safe and minibar. **Price** Single 375,000L, double 775,000L, suite 1,105 000L. **Meals** Breakfast included **Restaurant** Service 12:00-14:30, 21:30-22:00; à la carte. Specialties: International cooking. **Credit cards** All major. **Pets** Dogs allowed. **Facilities** 2 swimming pools, sauna, turkish bath, tennis, garage, parking. **Nearby** Milano, Lake Como (Ossuccio and gardens of the Villa Arconati in Punta di Balbia), Villa Carlotta in Tremezzo, Mennagio, Lugano, boat for Bellagio in Tremezzo, Villa d'Este golf course (18-hole) in Montorfano. **Open** Mar. – Nov.

Some rank this grand palace, built by a prince of the church in 1658, as the most beautiful hotel in the world. It's no wonder—everything about it is sumptuous. It is situated on the main part of Lake Como, in a magnificent Italian garden filled with rare and varied plantings and a sycamore tree more than 600 years old. The 16th-century gravel-mosaic pathway provides a nice view of a colossal statue of Hercules. The interiors are equally splendid. Beautiful 18th-century furniture embellishes the long pillared arcade of the entry, which is highlighted by a grand stairway. The rooms, accessed by a silk-lined elevator, live up to the image of luxury and comfort that have established the reputation of this hotel. The activity and entertainment programs are so varied and full that you will never need to leave the premises. The service is remarkably unpretentious and most pleasant.

How to get there (Map 3): 5 km north of Como via S340, on the left bank.

San Giorgio Hotel ★★★

Lago di Como
Via Regina, 81 - Tremezzo 22016 Lenno (Como)
Tel. (0344) 40 415 - Fax (0344) 41 591
Sig.ra Cappelletti

Rooms 26 with telephone, bath or shower and WC. **Price** With half board 99-132,000L. (per pers., 3 days min.). **Meals** Breakfast 18,000L, served 8:00-11:00. **Restaurant** Only for residents; Service 12:30-13:30, 19:30-20:30; menu. **Credit cards** Amex, Visa, Eurocard, MasterCard. **Pets** Dogs not allowed. **Facilities** Tennis (18,000L), parking. **Nearby** Milano (Lake Como, Villa Carlotta in Tremezzo, Mennagio, Lugano), boat for Bellagio in Tremezzo, golf course (18-hole) in Grandola e Uniti. **Open** Apr. – Sept.

The San Giorgio is a gracious hotel, run as a family affair. It's located in the heart of the Bay of Tremezzina–the dreamiest part of Lake Como. The main building, next to the small old house, was built by the current owner's grandfather. The dining room and the grand salon, which still have the family furniture, 19th-century chairs and couches and a mahogany roll-top desk, open onto a garden-level porch. The rooms are all large and have functional bathrooms, balconies and a view of the bay and the mountains. The grounds, formerly an olive grove, dip gently downward to the lake. They bloom with wisteria and magnolia flowers in the spring, and in the fall are full of the fragrance of exotic plants. The hotel is only a few miles from the wharves of Tremezzo, Cadenabbia and Menaggio–perfect for sailing buffs eager to explore the Italian lakes.

How to get there *(Map 3): 27 km north Como via S340, on the left bank.*

Grand Hotel Victoria ★★★★

Lago di Como
22017 Menaggio (Como)
Tel. (0344) 32 003 – Fax (0344) 32 992
Sig. Proserpio

Rooms 53 with telephone, bath or shower, WC, cable TV and elevator. **Price** Single 135-165,000L, double 200-240,000L, suite 330,000L. **Meals** Breakfast 23,000L (buffet), served 7:30-11:00; half board +45,000L (per pers.). **Restaurant** Service 12:30-14:00, 19:30-22:00; menu 55,000L, also à la carte. Specialties: Italian cooking. **Credit cards** All major. **Pets** Dogs allowed. **Facilities** Swimming pool, parking. **Nearby** Milano (Lake Como, Villa Carlotta in Tremezzo, Mennagio, Lugano, boat for Bellagio in Tremezzo), golf course (18-hole) in Grandola e Uniti. **Open** All year.

Set on magnificent grounds with enormous trees facing Lake Como, the Grand Hotel Victoria is a late 1880s-style palace. The vast salons have parquet floors, stucco ceilings and a quiet and harmonious atmosphere. As soon as the weather allows, meals are served on the terrace facing the lake under a big striped tent. The most recently refurnished rooms gained in comfort what they may have lost of their former personality.

How to get there (Map 3): 35 km north of Como via S340, on the left bank.

Hotel Stella d'Italia ★★★

Lago di Lugano
Piazza Roma, 1
San Mamete 22010 Valsolda (Como)
Tel. (0344) 68 139 - Fax (0344) 68 729 - Sig. Ortelli

Rooms 35 with telephone, bath or shower and WC. **Price** Single 70,000L, double 115-135,000L. **Meals** Breakfast 15,000L, served 7:30-10:00; half board 105-115,000L (per pers., 3 days min.). **Restaurant** Service 12:30-14:00, 19:30-21:00; menu 35,000L, also à la carte. Specialties: Seafood, pasta. **Credit cards** All major. **Pets** Small dogs allowed. **Facilities** Private beach, garage (10,000L). **Nearby** Lake Lugano, Villa Favorita, Lake Como (Lugano-Mennagio, Villa Carlotta in Tremezzo). **Open** Apr. – Oct.

On the shores of Lake Lugano, San Mamete is a pretty little village, home to the Stella d'Italia, which has been run by the Ortelli family for three generations. Many readers have written to us about the beautiful interiors adorned with Madame Ortelli's interesting collection of paintings, artistic lighting and comfortable furniture. The rooms have been renovated and the nicest ones, in the front, have large door-windows facing on the lake. The lakeside garden is marvelous and here you can dine pleasantly under a large trellis smothered with Virginia creeper and roses. There is a small beach where you can sunbathe and go for a swim in the lake. The panorama and surroundings are superb, the prices moderate and the service friendly.

How to get there *(Map 3): 42 km north of Como via A9, Lugano-south exit, then S340, on the north bank.*

Villa Giulia Al Terrazo

Lago di Como
22049 Valmadrera (Lecco)
Via Parè, 69
Tel. (0341) 58 31 06 - Fax (0341) 20 11 18

Rooms 12 with telephone, shower, WC, TV and 10 with monibar. **Price** Single 99-120,000L, double 160,000L, suite 190,000L. **Meals** Breakfast 15,000L (buffet), served 7:00-10:30; half board 150,000L, full board 180,000L (per pers., 3 days min.). **Restaurant** Service 12:30, 19:30; closed 15 days in Aug.; menus 60-90,000L, also à la carte. Specialties: Carpaccio di storione con melone e caviale, prosciutto d'amatra con finocchio e acquadelle, gratin di pragole al limone, parfait al caffè con riso. **Credit cards** All major. **Pets** Dogs allowed. **Facilities** Parking. **Nearby** Lecco (Villa Manzoni), villa Monastero Mornico gardens, Lecco to Erba (basilicata San Pietro al Monte). **Open** All year.

Trying to find a hotel in Milan (unless you stay in a palace) is doomed to failure if the trip has not been planned a long time in advance. This is why one of our readers told us about the Villa Giulia, about 30 miles from Milan, easily accessible by highway. It is in a late 18th century villa on the shores of Lake Como, (known locally as Lago di Lecco), and is famous mostly for its restaurant. You can enjoy fine cuisine on the large terrace overlooking the lake. Several pretty comfortable rooms will allow you to prolong your visit and enjoy the quality of the service and the kindness of the staff. This is a good standby hotel, but is also an ideal place to stay for those interested in exploring the Italian lakes.

How to get there *(Map 3): 56 km north of Milano via motorway towards Lecco.*

Villa Simplicitas e Solferino **

22028 San Fedele d'Intelvi (Como)
Tel. (031) 83 11 32
Sig. Castelli

Rooms 10 with telephone, shower and WC. **Price** With half board 115-150,000L, full board 150,000L (per pers., 3 days min.). **Meals** Breakfast included. **Restaurant** Service 12:30-14:30, 20:30-22:00; closed Wed.; menus 40-50,000L. Specialties: Italian and regional cuisine. **Credit cards** All major. **Pets** Dogs allowed (fee). **Facilities** Parking. **Nearby** Lake Como, Val d'Intelvi, Lugano **Open** Apr. – Oct.

In a beautiful landscape typical of this region of lakes, mountains and lush vegetation, the Villa Simplicitas is surrounded by pastures and centenarian chestnut trees. The interior has an early 19th-century country-house atmosphere down to the smallest detail—wing chairs, Thonet chairs, pedestal tables with runners and framed engravings. Everything is polished and genuine. The charming rooms are full of trompe-l'œil effects and walnut furniture. The cuisine is very good and is made with fruit and vegetables fresh from the garden. Meals are served in fall in a small dining room in front of a fireplace and in summer in a large room that opens onto the countryside.

How to get there (Map 3): 30 km north of Como via S340, on the left bank to Argegno, then left towards San Fedele Intelvi.

Albergo San Lorenzo ★★★★

Piazza Concordia, 14
46100 Mantova
Tel. (0376) 22 05 00 – Fax (0376) 32 71 94
Sig. Tosi

Rooms 39 with air-conditioning, telephone, bath or shower, WC, cable TV, minibar and elevator. **Price** Single 220,000L, double 260,000L, suite 300,000L. **Meals** Breakfast included, served 7:00-11:00; half board 95-105,000L (per pers., 3 days min.). **Restaurant** See p. 412. **Credit cards** All major. **Pets** Dogs not allowed. **Facilities** Garage (22,000L). **Nearby** Mantova (Churches of Sant'Andrea and San Sebastiano (Leon Alberti), Appartamento dei nani (Dwarfs' Apartment), Appartamento del Paradiso, Camera degli Sposi (Mantegna), Casa di Andrea Mantegna), Sabbioneta, Parma, Verona. **Open** All year.

The Albergo San Lorenzo is the ideally place for visiting the wealthy town of Mantua (Mantova). It is in the middle of a pedestrian area close to the Duomo and the Palazzo Ducale. Decorated with antique furniture and a rococo decor, it is spacious and comfortable. Breakfast is served on a pretty rooftop terrace. The staff is very discreet and the absence of a restaurant makes this a very restful place. Mantua offers the considerable advantage of being off the beaten tourist track, even though it is undeniably beautiful.

How to get there (Map 10): 62 km northeast of Parma via S343. 45 km southwest of Verona.

Il Leone ★★★

Piazza IV Martiri, 2
Pomponesco (Mantova)
Tel. (0375) 86 077 – Fax (0375) 86770
Famiglia Mori

Rooms 8 with air-conditioning in the double room, telephone, shower, WC, TV and minibar. **Price** Single 95,000L, double 130,000L. **Meals** Breakfast 10,000L, served 8:00-10:00; half board 140,000L, full board 150,000L (per pers., 3 days min.). **Restaurant** Service 12:00-14:00, 20:00-22:00; closed Sun. evening, Mon.; à la carte. Specialties: Salumeria, ravioli al zucca, tartufi, risotto, zabaione e semi-freddo. **Credit cards** All major. **Pets** Small dogs allowed. **Facilities** Swimming pool. **Nearby** Church in Viadana, Church in Villa Pasquali, Sabbioneta, Mantova, Parma. **Open** Jan. 27 – Dec. 26.

Behind the austere facade of this house in the village of Pomponesco—formerly the fiefdom of the celebrated Gonzagua family—you will find a swimming pool and a lovely patio. The salons are impressive: they have superb furniture and high ceilings, and one is decorated with magnificent frescoes. The rooms are large and comfortable. Ask for one by the pool. Breakfasts are copious, the cuisine is perfect and the risotto unforgettable. The wine cellar is well stocked with Italian and international wines.

How to get there *(Map 10): 32 km northwest of Parma via S62 to Viadana, then on the right towards Pomponesco.*

Four Seasons Hotel ★★★★★

Via Gesù, 8
20121 Milano
Tel. (02) 77 088 - Fax (02) 77 08 5000
Sig. V. Finizzola

Rooms 70 and 28 suites with air-conditioning, telephone, bath, WC, cable TV and minibar. **Price** Single 590-650,000L, double 660-790,000L, suite 820-4,000 000L. **Meals** Breakfast 30,000L, served 7:00-11:30. **Restaurants** "La Veranda"; service 11:30-23:00; menu: 60,000L, also à la carte. "Il teatro"; service 19:30-23:00; closed Sun. and Aug. 1 – 20; menu 90,000L. Specialties: Regional cooking. **Credit cards** All major. **Pets** Dogs allowed in rooms. **Facilities** Garage (25,000L). **Nearby** Milano (Duomo, Galleria Vittore Emmanuele, Teatro alla Scala, Pinacoteca di Brera, Castello Sforzesco), Lake Como, Certosa di Pavia, golf course (9-18-hole) at Parco di Monza. **Open** All year.

A superb oasis in the lively triangle of culture and fashion formed by the junction of the Via Montenapoleone, Via della Spiga, and Sant' Andrea, the Four Seasons is in a former Fransiscan monastery built in the 15th century, complete with cloister and intact frescoes. Discreetly luxurious, the hotel features simple, elegant rooms accented with Fortuny fabrics in faded colors, sycamore wood furniture and marble baths. Everything is comfortable, softly lit and very quiet. Room service is available around the clock, so if you prefer to have dinner in your room after your evening at La Scala, all you need do is ring. Otherwise, you can enjoy fine savory cuisine at one of two restaurants before having one last drink at the *Foyer*, the hotel bar.

How to get there *(Map 3): In the center of the town.*

Excelsior Hotel Gallia ★★★★

Piazza Duca d'Aosta, 9
20124 Milano
Tel. (02) 6785 - Fax (02) 66 713 239
Sig. Occhiolini

Rooms 239 with air-conditioning, telephone, bath, WC, cable TV and minibar. **Price** Single 335-390,000L, double 390-440,000L, suite 850-1,300,000L. **Meals** Breakfast 22-35,000L, served 7:00-10:30. **Restaurant** Service 12:30-14:30, 19.30-22.30; menu: 70,000L, also à la carte. Specialties: Italian cooking. **Credit cards** All major. **Pets** Small dogs allowed. **Facilities** Sauna, fitness, garage (15,000L). **Nearby** Milano (Duomo, Galleria Vittore Emmanuele, Teatro alla Scala, Pinacoteca di Brera, Castello Sforzesco), Lake Como, Certosa di Pavia, golf course (9-18-hole) at Parco di Monza. **Open** All year.

Just across from the train station, the Excelsior Gallia is one of the great institutions of Milan. It was built in the 305 and its interior announces comfort and luxury. The elegant, comfortable rooms have 30s, 50s, and contemporary decor. You will find excellent cuisine (one of the best restaurant in Milan) and perfect service here. Night owls can sip a nightcap while listening to the piano music in *The Baboon*. This classic grand hotel is a great find.

How to get there *(Map 3): In front of the station.*

Hotel Diana Majestic ★★★★

Viale Piave, 42
20129 Milano
Tel. (02) 29 51 34 04 – Fax (02) 20 10 72

Rooms 94 with air-conditioning, telephone, bath, WC, TV and minibar.
Price Single 308,000L, double 424,000L. **Meals** Breakfast 25-40,000L, served
7:00-10:30. **Restaurant** See pp. 409-411. **Credit cards** All major. **Pets** Small dogs
allowed. **Facilities** Parking. **Nearby** Milano (Duomo, Galleria Vittore Emmanuele,
Teatro alla Scala, Pinacoteca di Brera, Castello Sforzesco), Lake Como, Certosa di
Pavia, golf course (9-and 18-hole) at Parco di Monza. **Open** All year.

This hotel is at the end of Corso Venezia. The Cigna hotel
group acquired and meticulously restored the Art Deco
architecture to its former splendor. On the ground floor there is a
small lobby with 1930s leather armchairs. This leads to a large
round lounge, with wicker furniture, that opens onto the garden,
which once went all the way to la Porta Venezia. In April an
enormous wisteria blooms in a delightful flowering arbor. The
statue of the huntress Diana hovers over the garden, recalling the
days of the Diana Baths, Italy's first public swimming pool for
women, where it once was displayed. Unfortunately, there is no
restaurant in this superb setting. The rooms still have their original
decor, which has been modified slightly to make them more
comfortable. The Diana remains one of the most the charming
hotels in Milan.

How to get there (Map 3): *Near the Corso Venezia.*

Hotel de la Ville ★★★★

Via Hoepli, 6
20121 Milano
Tel. (02) 86 76 51 – Fax (02) 86 66 09
Sig. Nardiotti

Rooms 104 with telephone, bath, WC, cable TV and minibar. **Price** Single 280-320,000L, double 350-410,000L, suite 500-650,000L. **Meals** Breakfast included **Restaurant** See pp. 409-411. **Credit cards** All major. **Pets** Small dogs allowed. **Facilities** Snack. **Nearby** Milano (Duomo, Galleria Vittore Emmanuele, Teatro alla Scala, Pinacoteca di Brera, Castello Sforzesco), Lake Como, Certosa di Pavia, golf course (9-18-hole) at Parco di Monza. **Open** All year (except Aug.).

The elegant Hotel de la Ville is ideal for active vacationers, as it is close to stores, the Duomo and La Scala. The walls and chairs of the salons and the smoking room are monochromatic shades of pink and blue. The very comfortable rooms are carefully decorated with beautiful fabrics on the walls, matching the bedspreads and curtains. The most spacious suites also enjoy the privilege of a view of the spires of the Duomo. There is no restaurant in the hotel, but, you can dine very pleasantly at *Le Canova* nearby.

How to get there *(Map 3): Between piazza S. Babila and piazza della Scala.*

Albergo del Sole ★★★★

Via Trabattoni, 22
20076 Maleo
Tel. (0377) 58 142 – Fax (0377) 45 80 58
Sig. Colombani

Rooms 8 with telephone, bath or shower, WC, TV and minibar **Price** Single 180,000L, double 270,000L, suite 300,000L. **Meals** Breakfast included, served 7:00-10:30; full board 280,000L (per pers., 3 days min.). **Restaurant** Service 12:15-14:15, 20:15-21:45; closed Sun. and Mon.; menu 80,000L, also à la carte. Specialties: spaghetti con pomodori, olive e capperi, fegato di vitello all'uva, seafood. **Credit cards** All major. **Pets** Dogs allowed. **Nearby** Milano, Cremona, Piacenza, Certosa di Pavia. **Open** All year (except Jan., Aug.).

For many years people who appreciated fine dining came to Maleo to enjoy the delicious Lombardian cuisine of Franco Colomani, but after dinner it wasn't always easy to find a place to stay. To answer this demand Franco opened this inn. The rooms are simple, elegant and very comfortable. This is a great place to stop off for a meal or spend a pleasant weekend if you are visiting the Pavia or Crémona monasteries.

How to get there (Map 9): 60 km south of Milano via A1 Casalfusterlengo exit, towards Codogno, then Maleo at 5 km.

Albergo Ristorante Il Sole di Ranco ★★★★

Lago Maggiore
Piazza Venezia, 5
21020 Ranco (Varese)
Tel. (0331) 97 65 07 – Fax (0331) 97 66 20
Sig. and Sig.ra Brovelli

Apart. 8 with air conditioning, telephone, bath or shower, WC., TV, safe and minibar. **Price** Single 210,000L, double 290,000L, suite 350,000L. **Meals** Breakfast included, served 7:30-11:00; half board 260-290,000L (per pers., 3 days min.). **Restaurant** Service 12:30-14:00, 19:45-21:30; menus 100-120,000L, also à la carte. Specialties: Regional cooking. **Credit cards** All major. **Pets** Dogs not allowed. **Facilities** Parking. **Nearby** Milano, Lake Maggiore: Stresa, Borromean islands (Isola Bella, Isola dei Pescatori, Isola Madre); Villa Bozzolo, Villa Taranto. **Open** All year (except Jan.).

For three generations, Il Sole has been famous for its fine restaurant. Eight duplex suites have been added, each with a balcony or terrace on Lake Maggiore. The comfortable furniture is a fine example of the talent of Italian designers. The warm shades of colors used in the fabrics give the rooms a cozy feel. The cuisine is, of course, masterful; the restaurant is still reputed to be among the best in Italy. Carluccio Brovelli, with the help of his son, David, is the family cook, and his wife, Itala, makes wonderful preserves and other homemade specialties, which you can buy at the gift shop. You will find all this–plus beautiful grounds, a delightful terrace and excellent service at Il Sole.

How to get there *(Map 3): 67 km northwest of Milano via A8, Sesto Calende exit; then S33 and S629 towards Laveno, on the right bank; 30 km from the airport Mimano-Malpensa.*

Hotel Fortino Napoleonico ★★★★

Via Poggio
60020 Portonovo (Ancona)
Tel. (071) 80 14 50 / 80 14 70 – Fax (071) 80 14 54
Sig. Roscioni

Rooms 30 with air-conditioning, telephone, bath or shower, WC, TV and minibar. **Price** Double 220-250,000L, suite 350,000L. **Meals** Breakfast included, served about 7:30; half board 180,000L, full board 210,000L (per pers., 3 days min.). **Restaurant** Service 13:00-14:30, 20:00-22:00; menus 60-70,000L, also à la carte. Specialties: Seafood. **Credit cards** All major. **Pets** Dogs allowed. **Facilities** Swimming pool, tennis (15,000L), gym, private beach, parking. **Nearby** Portonovo (Abbey Santa Maria di Portonovo), Ancona, Conero golf course (27-hole) in Sirolo. **Open** All year.

The "Fort Napoleon," erected on Bay of Portonovo in 1808, is now an extraordinary hotel. The road that winds around this former military edifice has been transformed into flowering terraces with laurel and other fragrant plants and the old arms room has metamorphosed into multiple salons and dining rooms filled with Empire-style furniture. Carefully selected antique furniture and contemporary materials coexist in perfect harmony in the guest rooms. The seafood-based cuisine is innovative and excellent.

How to get there *(Map 12): 10 km south of Ancona via A14, Ancona-South exit, towards Camerano.*

Hotel Emilia ★★★★

Poggio di Portonovo, 149
60020 Portonovo (Ancona)
Tel. (071) 80 11 45 – Fax (071) 80 13 30
Sig. Fiorini

Rooms 27, 3 suites and 1 apartment with air-conditioning, telephone, bath or shower, WC, TV and minibar. **Price** Double 70-180,000L, suite 200-300,000L. **Meals** Breakfast included; half board 120-180,000L, full board 150-220,000L (per pers., 3 days min.). **Restaurant** Service 12:45-14:00, 20:00-22:00; menus 30-70,000L, also à la carte. Specialties: Seafood, pasta fatta in casa e verdure. **Credit cards** All major. **Pets** Dogs not allowed. **Facilities** Swimming pool, tennis, parking. **Nearby** Portonovo (Abbey Santa Maria di Portonovo), Ancona, Conero golf course (27-hole) in Sirolo. **Open** All year.

A beautiful green lawn extends from the foot of the hotel to the cliff overhanging the ocean. The twittering of the swallows living on the rooftops will wake you in the morning. The pleasant rooms look out over the sea. This family estate, named after a woman who actively campaigned for the preservation of the region, has an atmosphere of deep tranquility. Today, father and son, continuing the family tradition manage the hotel and restaurant.

How to get there *(Map 12): 10 km south of Ancona via A14, Ancona-South exit, towards Camerano.*

Hotel Monte Conero ★★★

Badia di San Pietro
60020 Sirolo (Ancona)
Tel. (071) 93 30 592 – Fax (071) 93 30 365

Rooms 48 with telephone, bath or shower and WC. **Price** With half board 90,000L (1 pers.), 125-135,000L (2 pers., 2 days min.). **Meals** Breakfast 7,000L, served 8:00-9:45. **Restaurant** Service 13:00-14:30, 20:00-22:00, closed Sun. evening, Mon., Jan.; menu 60,000L, also à la carte. Specialties: Seafood. **Credit cards** All major. **Pets** Small dogs allowed. **Facilities** Swimming pool, tennis (15,000L), parking. **Nearby** Abbey of San Pietro, Abbey Santa Maria di Portonovo, Ancona, Golf Conero Course (27-hole) in Sirolo. **Open** Mar. 15 – Nov. 15.

At the summit of the regional park bearing the same name, this 12th century Carmaldosian abbey overlooks the sea and the village of Sirolo. Around the abbey the owners have built a comfortable, modern hotel with a panoramic restaurant. The simple rooms are well equipped and face the sea. The rooms over the restaurant have a private terrace. Since the beaches of Sirolo are only two-and-a-half miles away, the Monte Conero is filled with Italian tourists in the summer and at such times, seems like a typical tourist resort. Summer, therefore, is not the best season to visit this beautiful place. There is a large, inviting pool on the grounds, as well as a golf course two-and-a-half miles away.

how to get there *(Map 12): 26 km southeast of Ancona via the coast to Fonte d'Olio, towards Sirolo, then towards Badia di San Pietro.*

Hotel Vittoria ★★★★★

Piazzale della Libertà, 2
61100 Pesaro
Tel. (0721) 34 343 – Fax (0721) 65 204
Sig. A. Marcucci Pinoli

Rooms 30 with air-conditioning, telephone, bath or shower, WC, TV, elevator.
Price Single 120-160,000L, double 190-250,000L, apartment 300-420,000L.
Meals Breakfast 20,000L (buffet), served 7:30-10:30. **Restaurant** Service 13:00-
15:00, 20:00-22:00; menu 30-40,000L, also à la carte. Specialties: Seafood.
Credit cards All major. **Pets** Dogs allowed. **Facilities** Swimming pool, sauna,
garage. **Nearby** Pesaro: Piazza del popolo (Palazo Ducale), house of Rossini; Villa
Caprile, Villa Imperiale, Gradara, Urbino, Civici museum. **Open** All year.

Meeting place for the stars of the Rossini Opera Festival in
August, the Hotel Vittoria is on the sea and is one of the
best hotels in town. The salon still has its original 1900 stucco
finish; it opens onto a restaurant on a large Scandinavian-style
porch. In summer, the large windows are opened and you can
dine outside with a view of the sea. The rooms are simple,
elegant and provide every comfort; the same is true for the
bathrooms. The owners have several similar estates in the area,
so if you like variety you can enjoy a meal in one these.

How to get there (Map 12): Between Bologna and Rome via A14.

Villa Pigna ★★★

Via Assisi, 33
63040 Folignano (Ascoli Piceno)
Tel. (0736) 491 868 – Fax (0736) 491 868

Rooms 54 with air-conditioning, telephone, bath or shower, WC, TV, minibar, elevator. **Price** Single 160,000L, double 170,000L, apartment 200,000L. **Meals** Breakfast included, served 7:30-10:00. **Restaurant** Service 13:00-15:00, 20:00-22:00; menus 30-45,000L, also à la carte. Specialties: Regional cooking. **Credit cards** All major. **Pets** Small dogs allowed. **Facilities** Parking. **Nearby** Piazza del Popolo in Ascoli Piceno, Colle San Marco. **Open** All year.

The Villa Pigna is in Folignano, a farming village only 5 miles (8 km) from Ascoli Piceno. This beautiful Liberty-style house on pretty grounds is the perfect place from which to explore Ascoli, a small village with grandiose architecture. Its palaces and churches are really worth seeing. The hotel lobby opens onto a pretty blue and white salon. You will find these colors throughout the house: The rooms, for example, are light and comfortable and have white furniture in an all-blue decor. The cuisine features regional specialties including wine produced especially for the hotel.

How to get there *(Map 16): 120 km south of Ancona via A14, Ascoli Piceno exit.*

Hotel Bonconte ★★★★

61029 Urbino
Via della Mura, 28
Tel. (0722) 24 63 – Fax (0722) 47 82
Sig. A. M. Pinoli

Rooms 23 with air conditioning, telephone, bath or shower, WC, cable TV and minibar. **Price** Single 130,000L, double 200,000L, suite 330,000L. **Meals** Breakfast 20,000L, served 7:30-10:30. **Restaurant** Service 20:00-22:30, closed Tuesday; menu 25,000L. Specialties: Antipasti vegetali, passatelli in brodo, ravioli agli asparagi, agnello, filetto G. Cesare. **Credit card** All major. **Pets** Dogs allowed (8-10,000L). **Facilities** Parking. **Nearby** Urbino (Palazzo Ducal, Galleria delle Marche, San Giovanni Battista), Urbania, Sant'Angelo in Vado, Castles and villages of Montefeltro: Sassocoruaro, Macereta, Feltria - Pesado ("Victoria Club" beach). **Open** All year.

The Hotel Boconte is in the historic town of Urbino. This old duchy seems unchanged since the days of splendor of its prince of light, Federico de Montefeltro. He wanted it to be a model for a new society where the refinement of manners would reflect the elegance of thought and taste, as described by Castiglione in *The Perfect Courtisan (Il Cortegiano)*. The hotel is on the outskirts of this pink village, close to the Ducal Palace. It has a splendid view of the magical hills of Umbria which illuminate the backgrounds of the paintings of Piero della Francesca. This will make you forget the small size but comfortable rooms.

How to get there *(Map 11): 36 km southwest of Pesaro via A14, Pesado-Urbino exit, then S423*

Locanda della Posta ★★★★

Corso Vanucci, 97
06100 Perugia
Tel (075) 57 28 925 - Fax (075) 57 22 413
Sig. Bernardini

Rooms 40 with air-conditioning, telephone, bath or shower, WC, TV, minibar, elevator. **Price** Single 150-187,000L, double 200-295,000L, suite 300-350,000L. **Meals** Breakfast included, served 7:30-10:00. **Restaurant** See p. 413. **Credit cards** All major. **Pets** Dogs allowed. **Nearby** Perugia (Corso Vanucci, Duomo, Palazzo dei Priori, Fontana Maggiore), Torgiano (home to the Lungarotti winery and wine museum), Gubbio, Assisi, Bettona, Spello, Spoleto, Ellera golf course (18-hole) in Perugia. **Open** All year.

The Locanda della Posta is an old palace which has been entirely restored. On the Corso Vanucci, one of the most beautiful and famous avenues—which can get pretty noisy—you will have a chance to feel the pulse of the town and enjoy the Peruginian pace of life. The rooms are extremely comfortable. The decor is subtle, elegant and very pleasant. The salons still have their original frescoes. The service is friendly. Be sure to spend some time visiting this historic city, on whose walls you can actually see traces of the Etruscan, Roman and Renaissance periods.

How to get there (Map 15): In the old city.

Hôtel Brufani ★★★★★

Piazza Italia, 12
06100 Perugia
Tel (075) 57 32 541 – Fax (075) 57 20 210
Sig. Carturan

Rooms 24 with air-conditioning, telephone, bath or shower, WC, TV, minibar,
elevator. **Price** Single 236,500-308,000L, double 380-440,000L, suite 440-660,000L.
Meals Breakfast 27,500L, served 7:00-11:00. **Restaurant** Service 12:00-15:00,
19:30-22:00, closed Sun.; menu 35-50,000L, also à la carte. Specialties: Umbricelli
al tartufo, spaghetti alla Brufani, torello alla perugina, trota alla filignate.
Credit cards All major. **Pets** Dogs allowed in rooms. **Facilities** Garage (25,000L).
Nearby Perugia (Corso Vanucci, Duomo, Palazzo dei Priori, Fontana Maggiore),
Torgiano (home to the Lungarotti winery and wine museum), Gubbio, Assisi, Bettona,
Spello, Spoleto, Ellera golf course (18-hole) in Perugia. **Open** All year.

The hotel entryway will impress you: leaving behind the raucous
atmosphere of the typical Italian square, you enter the luxurious
warmth of a vast circular room with plush velvet couches and white
walls inset with statues in classical poses, illuminated by a large picture
window. Despite the haughty, grand hotel-style lobby, the bell
captain is attentive and will only be too happy to let you inspect the
rooms, to choose the one you like best. The corner rooms are the
nicest and most spacious, with remarkable views of Assisi and Todi;
our favorite is Room 314. The rooms are all the same price, so be
sure to ask when making reservations. The small, friendly restaurant
offers straightforwardly simple cuisine. The prices are geared to the
business clientele who regularly frequent this hotel.

How to get there (Map 15): In the old city.

Castello dell'Oscano
Villa Ada - La Macina

Cenerente 06134 Perugia
Tel (075) 69 01 25 - Fax (075) 69 06 66 - Sig. Bussolati

Rooms 22 with telephone, shower, WC, TV and minibar. **Price** Double 170-
310,000L. **Meals** Breakfast included, served 7:00-10:00. **Restaurant** Only for
residents, Service 20:30; closed Thus.; menu 50,000L. **Credit cards** All major.
Pets Dogs allowed. **Facilities** Parking. **Nearby** Perugia (Corso Vanucci, Duomo,
Palazzo dei Priori, Fontana Maggiore), Torgiano (home to the Lungarotti winery
and wine museum), Gubbio, Assisi, Bettona, Spello, Spoleto, Ellera golf course
(18-hole) in Perugia. **Open** All year (except Jan. 15 – Feb. 15).

In the wooded hills of Umbria, the Castello dell'Oscano, the
Villa Ada and La Macina vie for your attention. The castle, the
most noble of the three, is absolutely enchanting. The rooms have
antique furniture and an exquisite atmosphere of old-time
elegance. The beautiful wooden staircase, the stained glass
windows, the library filled with carefully bound books and the
comfortable salons make the Castello a truly prestigious place. The
Villa Ada and La Macina (functioning agricultural estates where
you can rent apartments) offer the same degree of professionalism,
but with simplicity, in the facilities and services (with accordingly
lower prices). You have access to the castle salons and swimming
pool.

How to get there *(Map 15): 8 km of Perugia, towards Firenze, Madonna
alta exit; stade Renato Curi; railway bridge; south Marco; Cenerente.*

Hotel Subasio ★★★★

Frate Elia, 2
06081 Assisi (Perugia)
Tel (075) 81 22 06 – Fax (075) 81 66 91
Sig. Elise

Rooms 70 with air-conditioning, telephone, bath or shower, WC, TV, minibar, elevator. **Price** Single 150,000L, double 240,000L, suite 320,000L. **Meals** Breakfast 15,000L, served 7:00-10:00; half board 150,000L, full board 170,000L (per pers., 3 days min.). **Restaurant** Service 12:00-14:00, 19:00-21:00; menu 40,000L, also à la carte. Specialties: Pollo in porchetta, spaghetti alla Subasio. **Credit cards** All major. **Pets** Dogs allowed. **Facilities** Parking. **Nearby** Assisi (Basilica S. Francesco, Santa Chiara, Duomo, Ermitage Eremo delle Carceri, Basilica San Damiano), Perugia, Spello, Spoleto, Ellera golf course (18-hole) in Perugia. **Open** All year.

The Subasio, a historic hotel which has entertained many illustrious guests, may seem a little outdated at first, but it is being renovated. It is a very comfortble hotel in an exceptional location–near the Saint François Basilica. Perhaps you won't like the emphatic decor of the rooms, but you absolutely must have a meal in the old vaulted dining room or on the beautiful terrace covered with linden trees, overlooking the Umbrian Valley. The Subasio, mindful of Saint François, is part of the pilgrimage to Assisi.

How to get there *(Map 15): 25 km east of Perugia via S75 then S147 to Assisi; near the Basilica of San Francesco.*

Hotel Umbra ★★★

Via degli Archi, 6
06081 Assisi (Perugia)
Tel (075) 81 22 40 – Fax (075) 81 36 53
Sig. Laudenzi

Rooms 25 (16 with air conditioning), with telephone, bath or shower, WC and 24 with TV, minibar. **Price** Single 90-100,000L, double 120-140,000L, suite 140-160,000L. **Meals** Breakfast 15,000L, served 8:00-10:00. **Restaurant** Service 12:30-14:00, 20:00-21:15; closed Thus.; à la carte. Specialties: Delizia di cappelletti, crespelle all' Umbra, friccò, piccione alla ghiotta, zabaione al cioccolato. **Credit cards** All major. **Pets** Dogs not allowed. **Nearby** Assisi (Basilica S. Francesco, Santa Chiara, Duomo, Ermitage Eremo delle Carceri, Basilica San Damiano), Perugia, Spello, Spoleto, Ellera golf course (18-hole) in Perugia. **Open** All year (except Jan. 16 – Mar. 14).

A little street off the Piazza del Commune will lead you right to the beautiful terrace of this hotel. Even though it is right in the center of Assisi, the hotel has a very pretty view and is absolutely quiet because the town center is closed to automobile traffic. You will have no trouble finding a secluded spot on one of the many terraces and in summer you can enjoy Umbrian cuisine—specialties made with truffles and mushrooms from the Norcian forests—under the *pergola*. The traditional dishes served here are accompanied by flavorful wines from local vineyards.

How to get there *(Map 15): 25 km east of Perugia via S75, then S147 to Assisi; in the old city.*

Le Silve di Armenzano ★★★★

Armenzano 06081 Assisi (Perugia)
Tel (075) 801 90 00
Fax (075) 801 90 05
Sig.ra Taddia

Rooms 15 with telephone, bath or shower, WC, TV and minibar. **Price** Single 135,000L, double 270,000L. **Meals** Breakfast included, served 8:00-10:00; half board 175,000L, full board 215,000L (per pers., 3 days min.). **Restaurant** Menus 50-65,000L, also à la carte. Specialties: Regional cooking. **Credit cards** All major. **Pets** Dogs not allowed. **Facilities** Swimming pool, tennis, sauna, parking. **Nearby** In Assisi: Basilica S. Francesco, Santa Chiara, Duomo, Ermitage Eremo delle Carceri, Basilica San Damiano; Perugia, Spello, Spoleto, Ellera golf course (18-hole) in Perugia. **Open** All year (except Jan. 15 – Feb. 20).

The quiet and solitude of the mountains await you at the Armenzano. Only seven-and-a-half miles from Assisi, this restored medieval hamlet has been transformed into a hotel. Set in a wild and grandiose landscape, the Silve has retained its rustic charm, while offering comfortable, tastefully furnished rooms, a swimming pool and tennis court. The Silve also has facilities for horseback riding and mountain motorbiking. The owners of this private estate try to outdo the professionals. A glance through the guest book, will reveal all the nice things guests have written about the service and the cuisine enjoyed during their visits.

How to get there *(Map 15): 32 km east of Perugia to Assisi via S75 - when you leave Assisi, turn on the right towards Armenzano (12 km).*

Castel San Gregorio

Via San Gregorio, 16 a
San Gregorio 06081 Assisi (Perugia)
Tel (075) 803 80 09 – Fax (075) 803 89 04
Sig. Bianchi

Rooms 12 with telephone, bath or shower and WC. **Price** Single 75,000L, double 115-230,000L. **Meals** Breakfast 15,000L, served 8:00-10:00; half board 105-130,000L, full board 135-160,000L (per pers., 3 days min.). **Restaurant** Service 13:00-13:30, 20:00-21:00, closed Mon.; menu 40,000L. Specialties: Tartufo, agnello. **Credit cards** All major. **Pets** Small dogs allowed. **Facilities** Parking. **Nearby** In Assisi: Basilica S. Francesco, Santa Chiara, Duomo, Ermitage Eremo delle Carceri, Basilica San Damiano; Perugia, Spello, Spoleto, Ellera golf course (18-hole) in Perugia. **Open** All year (closed Mon.).

About six miles from Assisi, the Castel overlooks the old medieval town of San Gregorio. It is set on grounds with magnificent trees, including impeccably trimmed boxwoods. The terrace enjoys a nice view of the *piano degli Angeli* and the green hills of the surrounding area. You can have your meals on another terrace, sheltered from the wind. The hotel has a very beautiful living room with antique furniture, and comfortable rooms which are simply and tastefully furnished. Add to this the very friendly service and great regional cuisine and you will understand why the Castel attracts so many English and French visitors in love with Italy.

How to get there *(Map 15): 13 km northwest of Assisi via S147, then towards Petrignano d'Assisi.*

Villa di Monte Solare

Colle San Paolo - Tavernelle di Panicale
Via Montali, 7
06136 Fontignano (Perugia)
Tel (075) 83 23 76 / 83 55 818 - Fax (075) 83 554 62
Sig. and Sig.ra Strunk

Rooms 10 and 5 suites with shower and WC. **Price** With half board 130-150,000L (per pers., 3 days min.). **Meals** Breakfast included, served 8:00-10:30. **Restaurant** Service 13:00, 20:00; menu. Specialties: Umbrian cooking. **Credit cards** Diners, Visa, Eurocard and MasterCard. **Pets** Dogs not allowed. **Facilities** 2 Swimming pools, tennis, riding, parking. **Nearby** Perugia, Assisi, Bettona, Church of Madonna dei Miracoli in Castel Rigone near by Passignano, Lake Trasimeno, Ellera golf course (18-hole) in Perugia. **Open** All year.

The road is long to Monte Solare and unpaved, but driveable, and so pretty with its Umbrian landscapes planted with vineyards and olive orchards, devoted since antiquity to the sun-god-Apollo. A beautiful, 18th-century patrician house has been restored with careful attention to preserving its cachet, with original *cotto* floor, period furniture, and breakfast room frescoes. The rooms each with private bath have a lot of charm. The suites in the nearby 17th-century farmhouse are very comfortable and have salons, and are priced the same as a double room in the main house. The Italian-style garden has been replanted and a swimming pool is being built. The one-hundred-and-thirty-eight acre (56 ha) farm produces olive oil, wine, and produce that are used in the fine cuisine served here.

How to get there *(Map 15): 25 km southwest of Perugia, via SS220 towards Città delle Pieve; before Tavernelle, take the road on the right for Colle San Paolo to Monte Solare.*

Hotel Bosone Palace ★★★

Via XX Settembre, 22
06024 Gùbbio (Perugia)
Tel (075) 92 20 688 – Fax (075) 92 20 552 – Sig. Menichetti

Rooms 30 with telephone, bath or shower, WC, TV and minibar. **Price** Single 105,000L, double 140,000L, suite 240-295,000L. **Meals** Breakfast 9,000L, served 7:30-10:30; half board 105,000L, full board 135,000L (per pers., 3 days min.). **Restaurant** "Taverna del Lupo" Service 12:30-13:30, 19:30-21:30; menus 45-55,000L, also à la carte. Specialties: Umbrian cooking. **Credit cards** All major. **Pets** Dogs allowed. **Nearby** In Gùbbio: S. Francesco, Piazza della Signoria, Palazzo dei Consoli (museum), Duomo, Palazzo Ducale, Via dei Consoli; Festival of the Candles ("Ceri") every May 15.; Perugia, Spello, Spoleto, Ellera golf course (18-hole) in Perugia. **Open** All year.

This hotel, formerly the Palazzo Raffaelli, used to belong to a noble family, contemporaries of Dante. It is situated in the heights of Gubbio in close to the Duomo and the Palazzo Ducale. Gubbio was once a major religious center for Umbrians, called *Iguvium*. Some time later, Saint François of Assisi stayed here. Today it is one of the towns in Italy which has best preserved its medieval character, with stairs and streets which seem to go directly ascend Mount Ingino. The hotel in itself is not exceptional, although the rooms are comfortable and decorated in an old-fashioned style; their small windows open onto the soft light of Umbria. The lobby is quaint, and the staff is just friendly enough. The prices, and especially its location, are what make this a really interesting place to stay. It is the best way to experience Gubbio intimately. In the evening, when the tour groups have left for the day, you can explore the town just like you might have a thousand years ago.

How to get there *(Map 15): 41 km northwest of Perugia.*

Villa Montegranelli Hotel ★★★

Monteluiano
06024 Gùbbio (Perugia)
Tel (075) 92 20 185 – Fax (075) 92 73 372
Sig. Mongelli

Rooms 21 with telephone, bath or shower, WC, TV and minibar. **Price** Single 128,000L, double 160,000L, suite 230,000L. **Meals** Breakfast 12,000L, served 7:30-10:30; half board 138,000L, full board 170,000L (per pers., 3 days min.). **Restaurant** Service 12:30-14:30, 19:00-22:30; menus 50-65,000L, also à la carte. Specialties: Caciotti fusa al coccio con tartufo, ghiotta di fegatelli, tozzetti con vino santo, crespella con crema di gelato alla vaniglia e salsa calda di frutti di bosco. **Credit cards** All major. **Pets** Dogs allowed. **Facilities** Garage and parking. **Nearby** In Gùbbio: S. Francesco, Piazza della Signoria, Palazzo dei Consoli (museum), Duomo, Palazzo Ducale, Via dei Consoli; Festival of the Candles ("Ceri") every May 15.; Perugia, Spello, Spoleto, Ellera golf course (18-hole) in Perugia. **Open** All year.

Montegranelli is a large villa on one of the hills facing Gubbio, less than three miles from its historic center. It bears the name of its first owner, Count Guidi di Romena e Montegranelli, who had it built in the 18th century. Salons with original frescoes are bathed in a beautiful light, which seems to pour in from all directions, making this villa a very pleasant place to stay. The guest rooms enjoy this same luminosity. They are painted white, with have large windows and pretty bathrooms. The staff is courteous and efficient. Centenarian cypress trees and a small chapel complete the beautiful decor, which is characteristic of the region. They Frequently play host to seminars, so ask about them when making reservations.

How to get there *(Map 15): 35 km northwest of Perugia, 4 km of Gùbbio.*

Hotel da Sauro ★★★

Lago Trasimeno
06060 Isola Maggiore (Perugia)
Tel (075) 82 61 68 – Fax (075) 82 51 30
Sig. Sauro

Rooms 10 with telephone, bath or shower and WC. **Price** Double 80,000L, apart. for 2-4 pers. 120-150,000L. **Meals** Breakfast included, served 7:00-10:00; half board 68,000L, full board 70,000L (per pers., 3 days min.). **Restaurant** Service 12:00-14:00, 19:00-20:30; menus 20-30,000L, also à la carte. Specialties: Regional cooking, seafood. **Credit cards** Diners, Visa, Eurocard and MasterCard. **Pets** Dogs allowed. **Facilities** Garage and parking. **Nearby** In Isola Maggiore: Church of Salvatore; Perugia, Spello, Assisi, Città del Castello. **Open** All year (except Nov. 8 – 30 and Jan. 10 – Feb. 28).

The Hotel Sauro is located in an exceptional place. Lake Trasimeno offers numerous possibilities for water sports and quiet beaches, without being too far from the historic centers of the region. The boat ride to the Isola Maggiore makes for a pleasant outing. The island has an authentic, well preserved atmosphere, as yet uninvaded by tourists. Blue nets lay to dry in the sun on the front of fishermen's houses, lacemakers work on doorsteps, and the small church will beseesh your generosity so the priest can have the roof redone. The Hotel Sauro is a very simple albergo, with good cuisine featuring fresh fish from the island fishmarket, a cordial staff, and reasonable prices. This is a highly recommendable hotel.

How to get there *(Map 15): 20 km west of Perugia. Ferry services from Passignano and Tuoro (Navaccia) to l'Isola Maggiore (15 mn).*

Hotel Villa Pambuffetti ★★★★

Via della Vittoria, 20
06036 Montefalco (Perugia)
Tel (0742) 379 417 – Fax (0742) 379 245
Sig.ra Angelucci

Rooms 15 with air-conditioning, telephone, bath or shower, WC, TV, safe and minibar. **Price** Single 150,000L, double 240,000L, suite 320,000L. **Meals** Breakfast included, half board 175-215,000L (per pers.). **Restaurant** Service 20:00-21:00, closed Mon.; menus 50,000L. Specialties: Regional cuisine. **Credit cards** All major. **Pets** Dogs not allowed. **Facilities** Swimming pool, parking. **Nearby** In Montefalco: Pinacoteca di San Francesco, church of S. Agostino, Palazzo Comunale (view); Bevagna, Assisi, Perugia, Bettona, Spello, Spoleto, Todi, Orvieto. **Open** All year.

The Villa Pambuffetti, a former country house now maintained as a combination private residence and guest house, has always belonged to the same family. It is in the middle of beautiful grounds which overlook the valley. The house has been reorganized to create spacious rooms each meticulously decorated with antique furniture, and all different. The most amazing one is is located in the little tower and has six windows from which create a panoramic view of the entire valley. The restaurant serves regional specialties and has an excellent wine list, including the notable Sagranito, a specialty of Montefalco. This is an elegant address in the D'Annunzio's fabled "town of silence."

How to get there *(Map 15): 41 km southeast of Perugia to Foligno, then to Montefalco.*

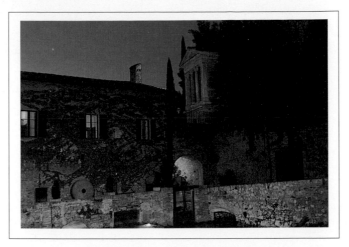

Albergo Vecchio Molino ★★★★

Via del Tempio, 34
06042 Pissignano - Campello sul Clitunno (Perugia)
Tel (0743) 52 11 22 - Fax (0743) 27 50 97

Rooms 13 with air-conditioning, telephone, bath, WC, TV and minibar.
Price Single 126,000L, double 163,000L. **Meals** Breakfast 16,000L, served 7:30-
11:30. **Restaurant** In Spoleto and Campello sul Clitunno see p. 414.
Credit cards All major. **Pets** Dogs not allowed. **Facilities** Parking. **Nearby** Fonti
del Clitunno, Tempietto del Clitunno, Ponte delle Torri, Church of S. Pietro,
Basilica of S. Salvatore, Church of S. Ponziano, Monteluco and Convento of
S. Francesco, Trevi, Spoleto, Spello, Orvieto, Soiano golf course (9-hole).
Open April – Oct.

The small Christian temple just above the Vecchio Molino is
a reminder of the cultural and artistic past of the cheery
Clitunno Valley. This 15th-century mill is now a very pleasant
hotel. Inside you can see the original equipment, and watch the
river flow by. The decor is very simple, almost entirely white,
which enhances the antique lines of the building. The rooms are
large and superbly decorated. Each one is different, and some
have a salon. On every floor are spots to read and relax. Only a
few miles from Spoleto, this is one of the favorite hotels of the
culture-seeking clientele which attends the Festival of Two
Worlds run by Gian Carlo Menotti.

How to get there *(Map 15): 50 km southeast of Perugia via SS75 to
Foligno, then S3.*

Hotel Gattapone ★★★★

Via del Ponte, 6
06049 Spoleto (Perugia)
Tel (0743) 223 447 – Fax (0743) 223 448
Sig. Hanke

Rooms 14 with telephone, bath or shower, WC, TV and minibar. **Price** Single 140,000L, double 170,000L, suite 270,000L. **Meals** Breakfast 15,000L, served 7:30-10:30. **Restaurant** See p. 414. **Credit cards** All major. **Pets** Dogs allowed. **Nearby** In Spoleto: Ponte delle Torrri, Duomo, Arch of Drusus, Roman theater, Festival of Two Worlds from mid-June to mid-July; Monteluco and the Convento di San Francesco, Fonti del Clitunno, Tempietto del Clitunno, Trevi, Spello, Soiano golf course (9-hole). **Open** All year.

Just outside the village of Spoleto, the Hotel Gattapone is the secret address of music fans who attend the celebrated festival. Built into a cliff overlooking the entire Tessino Valley, facing the Roman aqueduct beloved by Lucrecia Borgia, the duchess of Spoleto, the Gattapone is perfectly integrated into the landscape. Its interior decor is a model of comfort and harmony. The rooms are superb, modern, and have in commun a panoramic view on the countryside, which gives them an atmosphere of quiet serenity. Professor Hanke, the owner, has a real sense of hospitality, and makes sure his guests feel at home.

How to get there *(Map 15): 65 km southeast of Perugia via SS3 bis, towards Terni to Acquasparta, then S418 to Spoleto.*

Palazzo Dragoni

Via del Duomo, 13
06049 Spoleto (Perugia)
Tel (0743) 22 22 20 - Fax (0743) 22 22 25

Rooms 15 with telephone, bath or shower, WC, TV and minibar. **Price** Single 200,000L, double 250,000L, suite 270,000L. **Meals** Breakfast 15,000L, served 7:30-10:30. **Restaurant** See p. 414. **Credit card** Diners. **Pets** Dogs allowed. **Nearby** In Spoleto: Ponte delle Torrri, Duomo, Arch of Drusus, Roman theater, Festival of Two Worlds from mid-June to mid-July; Monteluco and the Convento di San Francesco, Fonti del Clitunno, Tempietto del Clitunno, Trevi, Spello, Soiano golf course (9-hole). **Open** All year on request.

Located in the historic center of Spoleto near the Duomo, this monumental palazzo is an important part of the stunning and particularly daring architecture of the old town. It was built on the edge of a cliff overlooking the valley. From here, Spoleto appears as a town of depth and beauty. This historical palace is now a private residence, which Umbrian regional authorities have allowed to open for an informed clientele. It is hard to list its charms without giving a guided tour. Let's just say that you will be dazzled by the gallery, the dining room, and the almost bare salons, decorated with only a few pieces of important beautiful furniture. The rooms, or rather the suites, have been impeccably decorated. Another plus: the palace closes when it hosts receptions, so as not to mix two types of clientele.

How to get there *(Map 15): 65 km southeast of Perugia via SS3 bis, towards Terni to Acquasparta, then S418 to Spoleto.*

Hotel Eremo delle Grazie

Monteluco
04960 Spoleto (Perugia)
Tel (0743) 49 624 – Fax (0743) 49 650
Professore Lalli

Rooms 11 with telephone, bath or shower and WC. **Price** Single 130,000L, double 350,000L, suite 450,000L. **Meals** Breakfast included, served 7:30-10:30. **Restaurant** On request, closed Mon.; à la carte. **Credit cards** All major. **Pets** Dogs allowed. **Facilities** Swimming pool. **Nearby** In Spoleto: Ponte delle Torrri, Duomo, Arch of Drusus, Roman theater, Festival of Two Worlds from mid-June to mid-July; Monteluco and the Convento di San Francesco, Fonti del Clitunno, Tempietto del Clitunno, Trevi, Spello, Soiano golf course (9-hole). **Open** All year.

Eremo delle Grazie is another one of the group of period residences, palaces, and monasteries which Umbria has authorized to open to a clientele seeking originality and authenticity. Submerged in the dark green of the sacred woods of Monteluco, the Eremo had for centuries been a center for spiritual life for *Anachorites,* hermits who having chosen a life of poverty and prayer, lived scattered among the hills. Today it is a hotel with a strange sort of beauty, where the small monks' cells are richly decorated but still monastic-looking guest rooms. Why not spend a night in Fra Gelsumino's room, or in Fra Ginepro's for that matter? This age-old property is a bit expensive, but there is certainly no other place like it anywhere in the world, and dinner on the terrace overlooking the green oak forest and the whole valley makes it well worth the price.

How to get there *(Map 15): 65 km southeast of Perugia via SS3 bis, towards Terni to Acquasparta, then S418 to Spoleto - 8 km southeast of Spoleto.*

Hotel Palazzo Bocci ★★★★

via Cavour, 17
06038 Spello (Perugia)
Tel (0742) 30 10 21 - Fax (0742) 30 14 64
Sig. Fabrizio Buono

Rooms 14 with air-conditioning, telephone, bath or shower, WC, cable TV, safe and minibar; elevator. **Price** Single 105-130,000L, double 180-220,000L, suite 240-320,000L. **Meals** Breakfast included, served 7:30-10.00; half board +40,000L, full board +80,000L. **Restaurant** "Il Molino", service 12:30-15:00, 19:30-22:00; closed Tues.; menus: 40-60,000L, also à la carte. Specialities: Pinturicchio, tagliatelle alla molinara, oca alla fratina, funghi porcini, tartufo. **Credit cards** All major. **Pets** Dogs not allowed. **Facilities** Parking. **Nearby** In Spello: Church of Santa Maria Maggiore (cappella Baglioni), Palazzo Comunale, Ponte Venere, Belvedere, Church Tonda (2 km); Assisi, Perugia, Trevi, Bevagna, Montefalco, Spoleto, Fonti del Clitunno, Tempietto del Clitunno. **Open** All year.

It comes as no surprise that a palace as beautiful as the Palazzo Bocci lies hidden in the side streets of this superb little town in the heart of Umbria. It looks like something Visconti might have dreamed up, with its salons with arched ceilings and walls covered with panoramic murals and frescos. The successive restorations in the 18th and 19th centuries have given it its current look–a rich, "upper class" decor which has survived thanks to modern facilities carefully integrated into the decor. The rooms are spacious and have very comfortable bathrooms with whirlpools. You will be welcomed by a friendly young girl with the efficiency of a professional. The hanging garden is marvelous, as are the breakfasts served there on warm summer mornings.

How to get there *(Map 15): 31 km southeast of Perugia.*

Hotel La Bastiglia ★★★

Piazza Vallegloria, 7
06038 Spello (Perugia)
Tel (0742) 65 12 77 – Fax (0742) 65 12 77
Sig. L. Fancelli

Rooms 15 and 7 suites with air-conditioning, telephone, bath or shower, WC, TV and minibar. **Price** Double 100,000L, suite 130,000L. **Meals** Breakfast 10,000L, served 8:00-10:00. **Restaurant** Service 13:00-14:30, 20:00-21:30, closed Wed. and Jan.; menu: 40,000L, also à la carte. Specialties: Umbrian cooking. **Credit cards** All major. **Pets** Dogs not allowed. **Facilities** Parking. **Nearby** In Spello: Church of Santa Maria Maggiore (cappella Baglioni), Palazzo Comunale, Ponte Venere, Belvedere, Church Tonda (2 km); Assisi, Perugia, Trevi, Bevagna, Montefalco, Spoleto, Fonti del Clitunno, Tempietto del Clitunno. **Open** All year.

This charming little hotel is in the historical center of Spello, an ancient Roman town on the slopes of Mount Subasio. Formerly an old mill, it still has certain elements of its original architecture, such as the arches in the reception rooms. There is a superb terrace off of the salon with a lovely view of the olive trees and the valley. The dining room is very inviting with its white tablecloths, exposed beams and rustic furniture. The cuisine features old Umbrian specialties prepared with carefully selected regional products. The rooms are light, airy, and comfortable. Ask for the ones on the upper floors on the terrace side, which have a view of the countryside. (The suites have a private garden and a separate entry.) The service is charming, and the prices are reasonable. You just might want to prolong your visit to Umbria.

How to get there *(Map 15): 31 km southeast of Perugia.*

Hotel Fonte Cesia ★★★★

Via Lorenzo Leonj, 3
06059 Todi (Perugia)
Tel (075) 894 37 37 – Fax (075) 894 46 77
Sig. Felice

Rooms 32 and 5 suites with air-conditioning, telephone, bath or shower, WC, cable TV and minibar. **Price** Single 140,000L, double 220,000L, suite 155-310,000L. **Meals** Breakfast included, served 8:00-10:00; half board 195-205,000L, full board 225-235,000L (per pers, 3 days min.). **Restaurant** Service 13:00-14:30, 20:00-21:30; menu, also à la carte. Specialties: Umbrian cuisine. **Credit cards** All major. **Pets** Dogs not allowed on request. **Facilities** Parking. **Nearby** In Todi: Church of Santa Maria della Consolazione (1km), Orvieto, Perugia, Assisi, Spoleto, Gubbio, ad Ellera golf course (9-hole) in Perugia. **Open** All year.

The Hotel Fonte Cesia has recently opened its doors in a setting charged with history, the ancient Etruscan town of Todi, home of Jacopone da Todi, poet and author of the famous "Stabat Maler". You can still find traces of the flourishing medieval period in its small winding streets. The hotel is in a beautiful 17th century palace, a harmonious blend of tradition, elegance, and modern comfort. The well-preserved architecture is the most beautiful decorative element, notably its superb vaulted ceilings in small bricks. It is an intimate, tasteful decorated hotel with comfortable well-furnished rooms, some of which have a trompe-l'œil decor. The Umbrian delicacies served in the restaurant will convince you, if you still need convincing, that this is a great place for fine living.

How to get there *(Map 15): 45 km south of Perugia, via SS3bis, Todi exit.*

Hotel Bramante ★★★★

Via Orvietana, 48
06059 Todi (Perugia)
Tel (075) 894 83 81/82 83 – Fax (075) 894 80 74
Sig. Montori

Rooms 43 and 7 suites with air-conditioning, telephone, bath or shower, WC, TV and minibar. **Price** Single 150,000L, double 200,000L. **Meals** Breakfast 15,000L, served 8:00-10:00; half board 160,000L, full board 190,000L (per pers. 3 days min.). **Restaurant** Service 13:00-14:30, 20:00-21:30; closed Mon.; menu: 45,000L, also à la carte, Specialties: Old Umbrian recipes. **Credit cards** All major. **Pets** Dogs allowed. **Facilities** Swimming pool, tennis, parking. **Nearby** In Todi: Church of Santa Maria della Consolazione (1 km); Orvieto, Perugia, Spoleto. **Open** All year.

This former 14th-century convent is located in Todi, one of the most beautiful towns in Umbria, with its austere edifices and cypress tress, and peaceful, green hills and pure, clean air. It is near Santa Maria della Consolazione, a beautiful Renaissance church designed by Bramante. The rooms and salons, often painted white, are light and airy. The owner is as conscientious about taking care of the hotel as he is about serving the needs of his guests.

How to get there (Map 15): 45 km south of Perugia via SS3 bis exit Todi; 1 km from the city center.

Albergo Le Tre Vaselle ★★★★★

Via G. Garibaldi, 48
06089 Torgiano (Perugia)
Tel (075) 98 80 447 - Fax (075) 98 80 214
Sig. Margheritini

Rooms 48 and 12 suites with telephone, bath or shower, WC, TV and minibar. **Price** Single 190-220,000L, double 290-330,000L, suite 400,000L. **Meals** Breakfast included, served 7:30-10:00; half board +65,000L, full board +130,000L (per pers. 3 days min.). **Restaurant** Service 12:30-14:30, 20:00-22:00; menus: 65-75,000L, also à la carte. Specialties: Quaglie su letto di insalatina di campo e chicchi d'uva, fondente di coniglio nostrano alle erbe aromatiche, umbricelli al tartufo nero di norcia. **Credit cards** All major. **Pets** Dogs not allowed. **Facilities** Swimming pool, health fitness club, parking. **Nearby** In Torgiano: wine museum (home to the famous Lungarotti winery); Perugia, Gubbio, Assisi, Bettona, Spello, Spoleto, Ellera golf course (18-hole) in Perugia. **Open** All year.

The elegant Albergo Le Tre Vaselle, a 16th-century residence formerly belonging to the Baglioni family, has been transformed into a hotel. It is located in the village of Torgiano, in a beautiful part of Umbria with rolling hills and valleys. The rooms are beautiful and the decor is simple and refined. The atmosphere and the service complement the setting. The cuisine and the wines are excellent. The particular charm of this place is largely due to the discreet but attentive presence of the director, Giovanni Margheritini.

How to get there (Map 15): 16 km from Perugiavia, SS3 bis towardsTodi.

Villa Ciconia ★★★★

Ciconia 05019 Orvieto Scalo (Terni)
Via dei Tigli, 69
Tel. (0763) 92 982 – Fax (0763) 90 677
Sig. Falcone

Rooms 10 with telephone, bath or shower, WC, TV and minibar. **Price** Single 110,000L, double 160-180,000L. **Meals** Breakfast 10,000L, served 7:30-10:30; half board +30,000L, full board +70,000L (per pers.). **Restaurant** Service 13:00-15:00, 20:00-22:00; closed Monday; menus: 45-55,000L, also à la carte. Specialties: Piatti al tartuffo, porcini, trota al cartoccio, carni alla griglia, carpaccio. **Credit cards** All major. **Pets** Small dogs allowed. **Facilities** Parking. **Nearby** In Orvieto: Duomo, Palazzo del Popolo; Medieval hamlet of Baschi, Bolsena (Church Santa Cristina), Lake Bolsena, Etruscan country from San Lorenzo Nuovo to Chiusi (grotta di Castro, Pitigliano, Sorano, Sovana, Chiusi); Todi, golf course (9-hole) in Viterbo. **Open** All year except 15 days in Feb.

At the gates of Orvieto, below its majestic Duomo (a must-see for the delicate sculpted decorations on the four pilasters) you will find the Villa Ciconia. Don't hesitate to stop off at this 16th century manor, sheltered by its sizable grounds crossed by a peaceful stream. The staff will welcome you in spacious salons, and large beautiful rooms with canopy beds and antique family furniture, which give this place a exceptionally harmonious atmosphere. The restaurant is in two vast rooms decorated with frescos and magnificent woodwork. You will delight in the delicacy of Umbrian cuisine, based on truffles and trout fresh from the neighboring river.

How to get there *(Map 15): 86 km south of Perugia via SS3 bis to Todi exit, then S448 towards Orvieto; Orvieto Scalo, drive under the motorway towards Todi-Perugia and left towards Arezzo.*

Hotel Ristorante La Badia ★★★★

La Badia
05019 Orvieto (Terni)
Tel (0763) 90 359 - Fax (0763) 92 796
Sig.ra Fiumi

Rooms 17 and 7 suites with telephone, bath or shower and WC (10 with TV).
Price Single 165-190,000L, double 230-260,000L, suite 370-450,000L.
Meals Breakfast 18,000L, served 7:30-10:00; half board required in high season
215,000L, full board 282,000L (per pers.). **Restaurant** Service 12:30-14:30,
19:30-21:30; closed Wed.; menus: 65,000L, also à la carte. Specialties: Panicetti,
coccinillo, scaloppe Badia. **Credit cards** Amex, Visa, Eurocard and MasterCard.
Pets Dogs not allowed. **Facilities** Swimming pool, 2 tennis courts, parking.
Nearby In Orvieto: Duomo, Palazzo del Popolo; Medieval hamlet of Baschi, Bolsena
(Church Santa Cristina), Lake Bolsena, Etruscan country from San Lorenzo Nuovo
to Chiusi (grotta di Castro, Pitigliano, Sorano, Sovana, Chiusi); Todi, golf course
(9-hole) in Viterbo. **Open** March – Dec.

This superb hotel, on four-and-a-half acre grounds several miles from Orvieto, was formerly an old 7th-century Romano-Lombardian abbey where Saints Severo and Martirio lived, and was long inhabited by Benedictine monks. The rooms are furnished in the rustic style of the region. There are several salons and an intimate bar with a piano. The hotel also has two tennis courts and a pool next to which you can have breakfast or a cocktail. This place is beautiful and refined.

How to get there (Map 15): 5 km south of Orvieto.

Villa Sassi-El Toula ★★★★

Strada Traforo del Pino, 47
10132 Torino Sassi
Tel. (011) 89 80 556 – Fax (011) 89 80 095
Sig.ra Aonzo

Rooms 17 with telephone, bath or shower and WC. **Price** Single 270,000L, double 400,000L. **Meals** Breakfast 20,000L, served 7:00-10:30; half board 270-320,000L, full board 350-400,000L (per pers., 3 days min.). **Restaurant** Service 12:30-14:30, 20:00-22:30; closed Sun.; à la carte. Specialties: Local and Italian dishes. **Credit cards** All major. **Pets** Dogs not allowed. **Facilities** Parking. **Nearby** In Torino: Palazzo Madama, Museo Egizio (Egyptian Museum) and Galleria Sabauda (16th- and 17th-century Dutch and Flemish paintings), Mole Antonelliana, Sanctuario della Consolata, Galleria d'Arte Moderna; Basilica de Superga, Villa Reale in Stupinigi, Cathedral in Chieri, Church of Sant'Antonio di Ranverso, Abbey Sacra di San Michele, I Roveri golf course in La Mandria. **Open** All year (except Aug.).

Five minutes away from the hustle and bustle of the town center, in the beautiful Piedmontais hills, this spot is perfect for romantic types looking for a quiet place to get away from it all. Centenarian trees on a fifty-four-and-a-half acre estate shelter the Villa Sassi-El Toula from noise. The Count Cavour was a regular here in the last century. This discreetly luxurious hotel has rooms with period furniture, two suites, and meticulous and silent service. The restaurant, run by the "el Toula" chain, serves excellent cuisine and is much in demand.

How to get there *(Map 8): Torino-west exit; towards Pino Torinese or Chieri.*

Hotel Victoria ★★★

Via Nino Costa, 4
10123 Torino
Tel. (011) 56 11 909 – Fax (011) 56 11 806 – Sig. Vallinotto

Rooms 100 with air-conditioning, telephone, bath or shower, WC, TV and minibar; elevator. **Price** Single 130-160,000L, double 160-190,000L, suite 250,000L. **Meals** Breakfast 20,000L (buffet), served 7:30-11:00; half board 270-320,000L. **Restaurant** See p. 414-416. **Credit cards** All major. **Pets** Dogs not allowed. **Nearby** In Torino: Palazzo Madama, Museo Egizio (Egyptian Museum) and Galleria Sabauda (16th- and 17th-century Dutch and Flemish paintings), Mole Antonelliana, Sanctuario della Consolata, Galleria d'Arte Moderna; Basilica de Superga, Villa Reale in Stupinigi, Cathedral in Chieri, Church of Sant'Antonio di Ranverso, Abbey Sacra di San Michele, I Roveri golf course in La Mandria. **Open** All year.

The Hotel Victoria, hidden in the middle of this secret town, is a place to experience. This recently built, modern building is in the heart of the shopping district, near the Piazza San Carlo, the Duomo, and the train station. The decor is an innovative blend of function, fantasy and humor. The rooms are all very pretty; you will have trouble choosing between the Egyptian room, the more romantic ones with their Art Nouveau prints, or the ones with a New Orleans motif. They are all very quiet, overlooking either a pedestrian street or the chamber of commerce garden. The breakfast room has all the charm of a winter garden, and the very cozy salon offers a peaceful view of a patio full of green plants. This three-star hotel offers four-star comfort. You will like the Victoria for the quiet, the nice decor, and the reasonable prices.

How to get there *(Map 8): Near Piazza San Carlo and train station.*

Castello San Giuseppe ★★★★

Castello San Giuseppe
10010 Chiaverano d'Ivrea (Torino)
Tel. (0125) 42 43 70 – Fax (0125) 64 12 78
Sig. Naghiero

Rooms 16 with telephone, bath or shower, WC and TV. **Price** Single 125,000L, double 175,000L, suite 190,000L. **Meals** Breakfast included, served 7:30-10:00; half board 135,000L (per pers., 3 days min.). **Restaurant** Service 20:00-23:30; closed Sun.; menu: 50,000L, also à la carte. **Credit cards** All major. **Pets** Small dogs allowed. **Facilities** Parking. **Nearby** Lake Sirio de campagna, Lake S. Michele, National Park Gran Paradiso, Torino. **Open** All year.

This amazing monastery with its "In the Name of the Rose" atmosphere is perched on the top of a hill, protected by walls. The landscape, which you will cross on a narrow road, is the sort you would like to see forever protected. The interior of this well-restored castle is a series of pretty surprises, with its polished furniture, waxed terra cotta floors, and vast rooms–some of which still have beautiful original vaulted ceilings. The nicest rooms are the corner ones. You will want to spend some time here–infact, you may find yourself rushing back from small forays into town to relax in the lounge chairs in the garden (abounding in araucaria, olive, cedar, and magnolia trees).

How to get there *(Map 2): 40 km north of Torino via A5, Ivrea exit, towards Lake Sirio.*

Il Capricorno ★★★★

10050 Sauze-d'Oulx (Torino)
Le Clotes
Tel. (0122) 850 273 - Fax (0122) 850 273
Sig. and Sig.ra Sacchi

Rooms 7 with telephone, bath, WC and TV. **Price** Single 180,000L, double 180-240,000L. **Meals** Breakfast included, served 8:00-10:30; half board 180,000L (per pers., 3 days min.). **Restaurant** Service 12:30-14:30, 19:30-21:00; à la carte. Specialties: Antipasti di Mariarosa, scottata rucola e Parmigiano, tacchino su zucchini, gnocchi alla menta, ravioli alla crema di zucchini, portofoglio alla Capricorno, maltagliati al ragù di verdure. **Credit cards** Visa, Eurocard and MasterCard. **Pets** Dogs not allowed. **Facilities** Parking in summer. **Nearby** Skiing (from the hotel), Bardonecchia, Sestriere, Briançon (France), golf course (18-hole) in Sestriere. **Open** Nov. – May 1, June 8 – Sept. 15.

Sauze d'Oulx is a ski resort town located at an altitude of 4875 feet (1500 meters), near the Franco-Italian border at Clavière Montgenèvre. Il Capricorno is even higher, deep in the mountains, at 5850 feet (1800 meters). This pretty chalet has only seven rooms, all with small but very functional bathrooms. The small number of boarders allows Mariarosa, the owner, to pamper her guests. Her cuisine is absolutely delicious. Il Capricorno, in a location well adapted for both hikers and skiers, is as pleasant in summer as it is in winter, as it is only a few miles from Bardonecchia and Sestrière, and 18 miles (30 km) from Briançon. Reservations are a must.

How to get there *(Map 7): 81 km west of Torino via A70.*

Hotel Principi di Piemonte ★★★★

10058 Sestriere (Torino)
Via Sauze di Cesana
Tel. (0122) 7941 – Fax (0122) 70270
Sig. Clemente

Rooms 94 with telephone, bath or shower, WC, TV and minibar. **Price** Single 90-150,000L, double 180-280,000L. **Meals** Breakfast 15,000L, served 7:30-11:30; half board 160-180,000L, full board 180-200,000L (per pers., 7 days min.). **Restaurant** Service 12:30-14:00, 19:30-21:00; menus: 45-55,000L, also à la carte. Specialties: Piedmontais cuisine. **Credit cards** All major. **Pets** Small dogs allowed. **Facilities** Sauna, beauty shops, garage (20,000L), parking. **Nearby** Skiing (from the hotel), Bardonecchia, Briançon (France), golf course (18-hole) in Sestrire. **Open** Dec. 20 – April 15 and June 17 – Aug. 23.

Surrounded by the famous towers of this ski resort, the Principi di Piemonte used to be considered the traditional grand hotel of Sestriere. The towers have now become clubs and the Principi has undergone transformations to adapt to a new clientele. The rooms are extremely comfortable and the suites are plush. In addition to the salons and dining rooms, there is a discothèque, stores, and a hairdresser. You will find everything you need to have a nice, active sports vacation and to spend enjoyable evenings here. Prices are lower in summer. Those who remember the way it was a few years ago may feel slightly nostalgic for a certain atmosphere which once reigned in this hotel inspired by Suvretta de Saint-Moritz.

How to get there (Map 7): 93 km west of Torino via E70.

Locanda del Sant' Uffizio ★★★★

14030 Cioccaro di Penango (Asti)
Tel. (0141) 91 62 92
Fax (0141) 91 60 68
Sig. Beppe

Rooms 35 with telephone, bath or shower, WC, TV and minibar. **Price** With half board 240-300,000L, full board 240-350,000L (per pers.). **Meals** Breakfast included, served 7:30-10:30. **Restaurant** Service 12:30-13:30, 19:30-21:00; menu: 100,000L, also à la carte. Specialties: Funghi tartufi, gnocchi de fonduta, cinghiale di bosco, lasagne con verdurini del orto, anatra stufata al miele e rhum. **Credit cards** Diners, Visa, Eurocad and MasterCard. **Pets** Small dogs allowed in rooms. **Facilities** Swimming pool, tennis, parking. **Nearby** Asti, Abbey of Vezzolano in Albrugnano, Sanctuario of Crea in Monferrato hills, golf course (18-hole) in Margara. **Open** All year (except Jan. 6 – 16, Aug. 9 – 20).

The Locanda del Sant' Uffizio is a former 15th-century convent nestled in the Monferrato hills, surrounded by vineyards. The small chapel, the marvelous and comfortable rooms, the absolute quiet, the beauty of the surrounding countryside and the red brick buildings make this, in our opinion, one of the most charming hotels in this book. Breakfast is served is a beautifully furnished room, and when the weather is warm, next to the swimming pool. The restaurant features exceptional regional cuisine accompanied by delicious wines including one produced right here. Meals are very generous. This place is not to be missed.

How to get there *(Map 8): 64 km east of Torino - 21 km north of Asti via S457 towards Moncalvo (3 km before Moncalvo).*

Hotel Pironi ★★★

Lago Maggiore
28052 Cannobio (Verbania)
Tel. (0323) 70 624/70 871 – Fax (0323) 721 84
Famiglia Albertella

Rooms 12 with telephone, bath or shower, WC, safe and minibar; elevator. **Price** Single 100-110,000L, double 145-170,000L. **Meals** Breakfast included (buffet). **Restaurant** See p.416. **Credit cards** Amex, Visa, Eurocad and MasterCard. **Pets** Small dogs allowed on request. **Nearby** Sanctuario della Pietà, Lake Maggiore: Stresa, Borromean islands, Verbania, Villa Taranto, Ascona; Locarno (Switzerland). **Open** March – Oct.

Cannobio is the last Italian village on this western bank of Lake Maggiore (called Lake Locarno in Switzerland), the most pleasant region on the lake. It is in an old building in the historic center of the small town. The arcades, the stairway, the porch, and the 15th-century frescos have all been meticulously restored. The house is also equipped with modern facilities. The rooms are on three floors, accessible by elevator, and are furnished in a pretty, rustic style complementing the exposed beams and framework of the house. Some of them look out on the lake, and two have terraces. The dining room, entirely painted with frescos, is a real gem. The hotel is located in a quiet pedestrian zone. The only drawback is getting to the hotel, but when you make your reservation they will tell you the best way to get here, and when you arrive, will come and carry your luggage if you need help. The service is nice, and the prices are unusually low for Italy.

How to get there *(Map 3): 117 km northwest of Milano via A8, towards Lake Maggiore .*

Castello di Frino ★★

Lago Maggiore
Via Cristoforo Colombo, 8
28052 Ghiffa (Novara)
Tel. (0323) 59 181- Fax (0323) 59 783
Sig.ra Laforet

Rooms 14 with telephone, bath. **Price** 85-110,000L. **Meals** Breakfast 60-75,000L, served 8:00-11:00; half board 110,000L, full board 130,000L (per pers.). **Restaurant** Service 12:00-15:00, 19:00-22:00; menus: 45-60,000L, also à la carte. Specialties: Persic del lago Maggiore, risotto ai funghi, crespelle alla valdostana. **Credit cards** Visa, Eurocard and MasterCard. **Pets** Small dogs allowed. **Facilities** Swimming pool, tennis. **Nearby** Stresa, Borromean islands, Locarno, Ascona, Pian golf course di Sole. **Open** April – Oct.

Castello di Frino is in Ghiffa, a resort town with a very mild climate, sheltered from the wind and overhanging the lushly vegetated banks of Lake Maggiore. The owners of this 17th-century castle have opened a few rooms to travelers, six in the original building, the others in an outbuilding next to the castle. They are all comfortable but the ones in the house are nicer—they are large and have antique furniture which can be a bit theatrical. The salon is more intimate. The garden on the lake has beautiful trees, and you can reserve a *restanque* at the pool. The attentive management will attend to your comfort and activities.

How to get there *(Map 3): 102 km northwest of Milano via A8, Arona, towards Lake Maggiore exit, Locarno.*

Parc Hotel Paradiso ★★

Lago Maggiore
20, via Marconi
28055 Ghiffa (Novara)
Tel. (0323) 59 548 – Fax (0323) 59 878- Sig. and Sig.ra Anchisi

Rooms 20 with tel, shower and WC. **Price** Double 140,000L. **Meals** Breakfast 21,000L, served 8:00-12:00; half board 115,000L (per pers.). **Restaurant** Service 12:00-14:15, 19:00-20:30; menus: 45,000L, also à la carte. Specialties: scalopina, piccata, vitello ai funghi, porcini. **Credit cards** Not accepted. **Pets** Dogs allowed. **Facilities** Swimming pool, parking. **Nearby** Stresa, Borromean islands, Locarno, Ascona, Pian di Sole golf course. **Open** March 15 –Oct. 15.

The still, blue lake, its shores crowded with mimosas, camelias, and palm trees, will captirate you. From the road, it is hard to see the villa–you can scarcely see a bit of pink wall through the foliage. This little paradise, set on grounds overhanging the cool water of the lake, has remained almost perfectly intact. You will fully enjoy the rooms, which are large, beautiful, quiet, and sunny, and the Art Nouveau salon painted with frescos. It is a wonder this *paradiso* is still so unknown.

How to get there (*Map 3*): *102 km northwest of Milano via A8, Arona exit, towards Lake Maggiore, Locarno.*

Hotel Verbano ★★★

Lago Maggiore
Isola dei Pescatori
Isole Borromee 28049 Stresa (Novara)
Tel. (0323) 30 408/32 534 – Fax (0323) 33 129 – Sig. Zacchera

Rooms 12 with telephone, bath or shower and WC. **Price** Single 120,000L, double 170,000L. **Meals** Breakfast included; half board 130,000L, full board 170,000L (per pers.). **Restaurant** Service 12:00-14:30, 19:00-21:30; menus 40-60,000L, also à la carte. Specialties: Fish from the lake. **Credit cards** All major. **Pets** Dogs allowed. **Facilities** Boat. **Nearby** Borromean islands: Isola Bella (Palazzo Borromeo and his gardens), Isola Madre (botanical garden); Lake Maggiore, Stresa, Isole Borromee golf course (18-hole) in Stresa. **Open** March – Jan. 6.

A small, red brick house reflected in the lake is as pretty as a doll house, with its beautiful terrace, pink tablecloths, and pergola. This was a place where maestro Toscanini loved to come with his followers. The rooms all have names of flowers or musicians. At dusk the lights come on and twinkle on the riverbanks and on the Borromean Islands–dinner on the terrace is magical. You will be perfectly enchanted by a room with a view of the lake, or one with a crackling fire in the fireplace. On weekends a pianist comes to play. All of this is enhanced by the kindness of the owner.

How to get there *(Map 3): Northwest of Milano via A8, towards Lake Maggiore; in Stresa or in Pallanza, ferry services for the Borromean Islands, stop at Isola dei Pescatori.*

Hotel Villa Crespi ★★★★

Lago d'Orta
28016 Orta San Giulio (Novara)
Via Generale Fava, 8
Tel. (0322) 91 19 02 – Fax (0322) 91 19 19 – Famiglia Bacchetta

Rooms 10 and 4 suites with air conditioning, telephone, bath, WC, TV, minibar and elevator. **Price** Single 180-230,000L, double 320-380,000L, suite 380-480,000L. **Meals** Breakfast incl, served 7:00-10:30; half board 210-240,000L, full board 250-280,000L (per pers., 3 days min.). **Restaurant** Service 12:00-14:30, 19:30-22:00; menus 70-90,000L. Specialties: Millefoglie di patate, spugnole e fegato grasso in salsa «caline», raviolini del Pun in cesto di parmigiano, carré di agnello in crosta di sale, gratin di frutta di stagione. **Credit cards** All major. **Pets** Small dogs allowed. **Facilities** Sauna (25,000L), parking. **Nearby** Orta San Giulio, Sacro Monte (view), Island of San Giulio, Fondation Calderana in Vacciago, golf course in Gignese. **Open** All year.

On the banks of the very romantic Lake Orta you will notice an unusual Moorish minaret, a luxurious homage to the Orient built by a cotton industrialist, Benigno Crespi. The villa (1880) stands in the middle of marvelous grounds shaded by pine trees. The salons and rooms are a successful blend of a somewhat heavy orientalism with more classical furniture. The rooms have a Romantic decor with imposing canopy beds and lovely velvet fabrics. The spacious marble bathrooms feature ultramodern facilities including "matrimonial" jacuzzis. This is a family-run hotel and it is the manager himself who does the cooking for the restaurant, locally famous for its traditional fine cuisine. This is a nice place in an ideal location for wandering down the narrow cobblestone streets of the peninsula.

How to get there *(Map 2): 20 km west of Stresa and of Lago Maggiore.*

Hotel San Rocco

Lago d'Orta
28016 Orta San Giulio (Novara)
Via Gippini, 11
Tel. (0322) 91 19 77 – Fax (0322) 91 19 64 – Sig. Bacchetta

Rooms 74 with telephone, bath, WC, TV, minibar and elevator. **Price** Single 160-220,000L, double 240-280,000L, suite 280-340,000L. **Meals** Breakfast included, served 7:00-10:00; half board +40,000L, full board +70,000L (per pers., 3 days min.). **Restaurant** Service 12:30-14:00, 20:00; menu 72,000L. Specialties: Bacetti san Rocco, boconcini tartufati, salmone marinato al timo, code di gamberi con frutti tropicali, zabaglione al frutti di bosco. **Credit cards** All major. **Pets** Small dogs allowed. **Facilities** Sauna (26,000L), hearth center, parking, garage (15,000L). **Nearby** Orta San Giulio, Sacro Monte (view), Island of San Giulio, Fondation Calderana in Vacciago, golf course in Gignese. **Open** All year.

The Hotel San Rocco is right on the lake across from the Romanesque landscape of the island of San Giulio. Built on the foundations of a 17th century monastery, the hotel has kept its original architectural structure, enclosed shell–like on the lake and on its cloister. Inside you will find all of the efficiency of a modern hotel. The rooms all have a beautiful view and are simply decorated but very comfortable. When the weather gets warm, you can have breakfast in the garden on the lake and relax in the pool. The hotel also provides a private boat to explore all of the nooks and crannies of the island with. The restaurant features delicate variations on traditional recipes.

How to get there *(Map 2): 20 km west of Stresa and Lago Maggiore.*

Hotel Giardinetto ★★★

Lago d'Orta
Via Provinciale, 1
28028 Pettenasco (Novara)
Tel. (0323) 89 118 – Fax (0323) 89 219 – Sig. and Sig.ra Primatesta

Rooms 52 with telephone, bath or shower and WC (30 with TV, 8 with minibar).
Price With half board 97-137,000L, full board +30,000L (per pers., 3 days min.). .
Meals Breakfast included (buffet), served 7:30-10:00. **Restaurant** Service 12:15-
14:30, 19:15-21:30; menus 40-45,000L, also à la carte. Specialties: Antipasto
"Grand Gourmet", ravioli verdi al pesce di lago e fili di pomodoro, tagliolini con
scampetti e fiori di zucchino, sella di coniglio, crema catalana con sorbetto al
limone. **Credit cards** All major. **Pets** Dogs allowed. **Facilities** Swimming pool,
private beach, sauna (25,000L), windsurfing, parking. **Nearby** Orta San Giulio,
Sacro Monte (view), Island of San Giulio, Fondation Calderana in Vacciago, golf
course in Gignese. **Open** April – Oct. 23.

The Hotel Giardinetto is on a very pleasant quiet island on Lago
Orta, one of the smallest lakes in Italy (8 miles (13 km) long
and 1 mile (1,5 km) wide), surrounded by verdant hills, which are
more visited than the island itself. The hotel is on the water, not
far from the prettiest part of the island. It is modern, functional,
and not very expensive, which are its main attributes; a comfortable
hotel with a nice family atmosphere. Ask for the rooms on the
lake. The staff is friendly and the service efficient.

How to get there *(Map 2): 20 km west of Stresa and of the Lake Maggiore.*

Castello di San Giorgio ★★★★

Via Cavalli d'Olivola, 3
15020 San Giorgio Monferrato (Alessandria)
Tel. (0142) 80 62 03 - Fax (0142) 80 65 05 - Sig. Grossi

Rooms 10 and 1 suite with telephone, bath, WC, TV and minibar. **Price** Single 130,000L, double 200,000L, suite 280,000L. **Meals** Breakfast 15-20,000L (buffet), served 8:00-10:00; half board 200,000L, full board 260,000L (per pers., 3 days min.). **Restaurant** Service 12:00-14:30, 19:30-21:30; closed Mon.; menu 85,000L, also à la carte. Specialties: Agnolotti alla monferrina, seafood, funghi, tartufi. **Credit cards** All major. **Pets** Dogs allowed. **Facilities** Parking. **Nearby** Marengo (Villa Marengo), Asti, Abbey of Vezzolano in Albugnano. **Open** All year (except Aug. 1 – 20, Jan. 1 – 10).

This hotel and remarkable restaurant are located in the outbuildings (the farmhouse and stables) of Monferrat Castle, an enormous dark brick edifice built in the 14th century for Gonzague de Mantoue. On magnificent grounds inside its original walls, the buildings have been superbly renovated and partly decorated with furnitue and old paintings from the castle. The luxurious rooms have been tastefully done, and have a very pretty view of the vast, quiet plain dotted with hills. Sig. Grossi is not only an excellent hotel director, he is also connaisseur of French cuisine. Mrs. Grossi does the cooking, and thanks to her considerable culinary talent, produces remarkable results. You will enjoy gourmet meals at San Giorgio, which, along with the setting and the service, really make it worth the detour.

How to get there (Map 8): 26 km northwest of Alessandria via A26, Casale-Sud exit, 6 km towards Alessandria - Asti, road on the right towards San Giorgio Monferrato.

Hotel Hermitage ★★★★

Place des guides – Maquignaz, 4
11021 Breuil–Cervinia (Aosta)
Tel. (0166) 94 89 98 – Fax (0166) 94 90 32

Rooms 36 with telephone, bath, WC, TV and minibar. **Price** Single 150-300,000L, double 300-400,000L, suite 400-800,000L. **Meals** Breakfast 35,000L (buffet), served 7:30-10:00; half board 200-360,000L, full board +60,000L (per pers., 3 days min.). **Restaurant** Service 13:00-14:30, 20:00-21:30; menus 50-70,000L, also à la carte. Specialties: French and Italian cuisine. **Credit cards** Amex, Visa, Eurocard and MasterCard. **Pets** Dogs not allowed. **Facilities** Swimming pool, sauna, health center, parking. **Nearby** Matterhorn (Monte Cervino in Italian), ski, cable car to Plateau Rosà (view), Cervino golf course (9-hole). **Open** All year.

The most beautiful thing about Cervinia is the sumptuous view of the Cervin, the Breithorn, and the Twins, whose peaks are so marvelously close together. The architectural styles of the 60's and 70's were not kind to this resort town, and the beauty of the site makes this ugliness stand out all the more. There is one hotel, however, which pays homage to the magic mountains: the Hermitage. It is made of high quality materials and decorated with antique furniture, carved wood wardrobes and doors. The rooms are superb, intimate, and some suites have kept their fireplaces. The staff is perfectly courteous and friendly. The cuisine combines the best of Italy and France, with quality ingredients and creative recipes.

How to get there *(Map 2): 50 km northeast of Aosta via A5 Chatillon exit, then S406.*

Les Neiges d'Antan ★★★

Frazione Cret Perrères
11021 Breuil–Cervinia (Aosta)
Tel. (0166) 94 87 75 – Fax (0166) 94 88 52
Sig. and Sig.ra Bich

Rooms 28 with telephone, bath, WC, safe and TV. **Price** Single 10,000L, double 200,000L, suite (4 pers.) 230-340,000L. **Meals** Breakfast included, served 7:30-10:00; half board 90,000L, full board 140,000L. **Restaurant** Service 12:30-14:00, 19:30-21:30; menu 50,000L, also à la carte. Specialties: Italian and local cuisine. **Credit cards** Visa, Eurocard and MasterCard. **Pets** Dogs allowed in rooms. **Facilities** Parking. **Nearby** Matterhorn (Monte Cervino in Italian), ski, cable car to Plateau Rosà (view), Cervino golf course (9-hole). **Open** All year (except Sept. 17 – Dec. 5, May 3 – June 29).

Isolated high up in the mountains, facing Matterhorn, the Neiges d'Antan is a charming hotel, the reflection of the soul and the passion of an entire family. The decor is simple but warm and personal. The bar has paneled walls covered with a collection of photos. You can find books, magazines and newspapers to read in the large, modern salon and music room. This is a place of simple luxury, reflected in the excellent cuisine carefully supervised by Sig.ra Bich, who also makes the jellies you will be served at breakfast, in the wine list selected by Sig. Bich and his son, the wine-waiter, and in the old, lace doily up on which you will place your wine glass. The rooms all have the same good taste and great comfort. This is a quality hotel, run by quality people.

How to get there *(Map 2): 49 km northeast of Aosta via A5, Saint-Vincent exit - Chatillon, then S406 - 4 km before Cervinia.*

Villa Anna Maria ★★★

5, rue Croues
11020 Champoluc (Aosta)
Tel. (0125) 30 71 28 – Fax (0125) 30 79 84
Sig. Miki and Sig. Origone

Rooms 20 with telephone, TV (14 with bath or shower, WC). **Price** With half board 120,000L, full board 130,000L. (per pers., 3 days min.). **Meals** Breakfast 10,000L, served 8:15-11:00. **Restaurant** Service 12:45-14:00, 19:45-21:00; closed Dec. 5 – April 30, June 20 – Sept. 15; menus 30-40,000L, also à la carte. Specialty: Fonduta with melted Fontina. **Credit cards** Visa, Eurocard and MasterCard. **Pets** Dogs not allowed. **Facilities** Garage (6,000L). **Nearby** Skiing, Hamlets in the Valle d'Ayas: Antagnod, Perrias, Saint-Jacques; Castle of Verrès, Church in Arnad. **Open** All year.

This incontestably charming chalet is one of our favorite properties. Hidden behind spruce trees, covered with flowers in the summer and buried in snow in the winter, the Villa Anna Maria is perfect for people seeking for quiet. The dining room has a rustic, natural atmosphere with its gleaming copper pots and lovely polished wood walls. The cuisine is simple and sophisticated. The rooms have low ceilings and are a little dark, as mountain refuges often are. The hosts extend a warm and genuine welcome.

How to get there *(Map 2): 63 km east of Aosta via A5, Saint-Vincent exit - Chatillon, then S506 (via Saint-Vincent) to Champoluc.*

Hotel Bellevue ★★★★

Via Gran Paradiso, 22
11012 Cogne (Aosta)
Tel. (0165) 74 825 – Fax (0165) 74 91 92
Sig. and Sig.ra Jeantet and Roullet

Rooms 24, 9 suites and 4 chalets with telephone, bath or shower and WC, TV and minibar. **Price** Double 224-390,000L, suite 344-422,000L. (per pers.) **Meals** Breakfast 25,000L, served 7:30-10:00; half board 120-260,000L, full board +25,000L (per pers., 3 days min.) **Restaurants** Service 12:30-13:30, 19:30-20:30; menus 50-80,000L, also à la carte. Specialties: Favò, carbonada con polenta, crème of Cogne. **Credit cards** All major. **Pets** Dogs allowed in some rooms (30,000L). **Facilities** Swimming pool (indoor), whirlpool, turkish bath, sauna, garage, parking. **Nearby** Alpine Garden of Valnontey, Gran Paradiso National Park. **Open** Dec. 22 – Oct.

The Hotel Bellevue is located in the heart of the Gran Paradiso National Park, very near the center of Cogne, yet isolated in a field which goes on as far as the eye can see. The service is warm and the white wood and pastel decor is simple. The personnel, dressed in traditional costume, add to the charm of the place. The cuisine is exquisite and made with fine regional products; the bread, pastries, and jellies are homemade, and the hotel has its own private supplier of cheeses. The hotel owns three restaurants, two of which are at the hotel: one is for boarders, and the other small one is a place where you can dine à la carte. The third, *La Brasserie du Bon Bec*, is in the center of the village, and serves mountain specialties. The rooms, which all have a superb view, are very elegantly decorated. The hotel now has modern entertainment facilities and offers music and movie evenings.

How to get there *(Map 2): 27 km south of Aosta via S26 to Sarre, then S507.*

Le Cristallo ★★★★

Via Roma, 142
11013 Courmayeur (Aosta)
Tel. (0165) 84 66 66
Fax (0165) 84 63 27

Rooms 39, with telephone, bath or shower, WC, TV and minibar. **Price** Double 150-260,000L. **Meals** Breakfast included **Restaurant** in hotel. **Credit cards** Visa, Eurocard and MasterCard. **Pets** Dogs not allowed. **Facilities** Sauna, parking. **Nearby** Skiing, Mont Blanc (Monte Bianco), Lake of Ruitor, Cable car to the Col du Géant and Aiguille du Midi, round-trip to Punta Hellbronner, Val Veny and Val Ferret, Chamonix (in France) by Mont Blanc tunnel, golf course (18-hole) in Chamonix. **Open** July – Sept. 10.

The Cristallo is on the main street of Courmayeur, which shares Mount Blanc with its neighbor Chamonix, and is one of the biggest mountain resorts in Italy. The outer architecture of the hotel is classic 60's "when concrete was king"-style, but don't let that stop you from going in, because once inside you will feel right at home in this very pleasant place. The tastefully rustic interior decor, unlike the exterior, is done mainly in wood. In the salon, sculpted Afghan furniture blends in with regional pieces, pottery, and art knick–knacks from places such as Sweden, Piedmont, and India. The rooms, whose colors vary according to the floor they are on, have pine wood wall-paneling. They are all comfortable and have a view of the mountains. There are plans to open a restaurant, which will make this nice hotel even more comfortable.

How to get there *(Map 1): 38 km east of Aosta via S26.*

La Grange ★★★

Strada La Brenva
Entrèves 11013 Courmayeur (Aosta)
Tel. (0165) 86 97 33 – Fax (0165) 86 97 44 – Sig. Berthod

Rooms 23 with telephone, bath, WC, TV, radio and minibar. **Price** Single 100-150,000L, double 150-200,000L, suite (3-4 pers.) 300-400,000L. **Meals** Breakfast included, served 8:00-10:30. **Restaurant** See. p. 394. **Credit cards** All major. **Pets** Dogs allowed (5,000L). **Facilities** Sauna (12,000L), parking. **Nearby** Skiing, Mont Blanc (Monte Bianco), Ruitor Lake, cable car to Col du Géant and Aiguille du Midi, round-trip to Punta Hellbronner; Val Veny and Val Ferret, Chamonix (in France) by Mont Blanc tunnel, golf course (18-hole) in Chamonix, golf course (9-hole) in Plainpincieux. **Open** Dec. – April, July – Sept.

Despite its success and its evident charm, this small hotel remains relatively secret. Hidden in what used to be the depths of the Val d'Aoste, at the foot of the Brenva and Mount Blanc glacier, it is today along the road to the tunnel connecting Courmayeur and Chamonix. Fortunately, Entrèves is a good distance from the road and has remained an authentic mountain village, avoiding what has happened elsewhere in the valley. The interior of this very well restored former barn has a warm atmosphere. Antique furniture, objects, and engravings decorate the salon and the delightful breakfast room. The rooms are just as comfortable, cozy and intimate. The only drawback, especially for a mountain hotel in the winter, is the lack of a hotel restaurant, but the owners do have arrangements with some of the restaurants in the village (between 25,000L and 35,000L).

How to get there (Map 1): *42 km west of Aosta via S26, Courmayeur, towards the Mont-Blanc tunnel.*

Meublé Emile Rey ★★

La Saxe
11013 Courmayeur (Aosta)
Tel. (0165) 84 40 44 – Fax (0165) 84 64 97
Sig. Bucci

Rooms 10 with telephone, bath or shower. **Price** Single 60-65,000L, double 100-110,000L. **Meals** Breakfast included **Restaurant** See p. 417. **Credit cards** Visa, Eurocard and MasterCard. **Pets** Dogs not allowed. **Facilities** Parking. **Nearby** Skiing, Mont Blanc (Monte Bianco), Lake of Ruitor, cable car to Col du Géant and Aiguille du Midi, round-trip to Punta Hellbronner; Val Veny and Val Ferret, Chamonix (in France) by Mont Blanc tunnel, golf course (18-hole) in Chamonix, golf course (9-hole) in Plainpincieux. **Open** All year (except May, Oct., Nov.).

Located above the little village of Saxe, where a green vista and a few rocks show the way to Mount Blanc, you will find this old 19th-century house which belonged to the legendary mountain guide, Emile Rey. This *locanda* bears traces of his exploits, which you can try to match: the climbs, long hikes may result in fatigue and aching muscles, but the pleasure of drinking cold spring water and the joy of finding pathways through the rocks and reaching summits make up for the pair. For those who like high mountains, this property is precious. You can come here in the winter to ski (Courmayeur is a half a mile away), and in the summer to walk in the pastures. There is no lack of comfort here. The rooms are nice, the hosts are kind, and the wood and stone are untouched. This is a place where you can savor the simple things in life.

How to get there *(Map 1): 42 km west of Aosta via S26, Courmayeur, towards Mont-Blanc tunnel.*

La Barme ★★

11012 Valnontey (Aosta)
Tel. (0165) 74 91 77
Sig. Herren

Rooms 9. **Price** Double 55-65,000L. **Meals** Breakfast included; half board 70-85,000L (per pers.) - week «blanche ou verte» 350,000L (per pers. in double room) half board 450,000L. **Restaurant** Service 20:30-21:30; menu. specialties: Local dishes. **Credit cards** Not accepted. **Pets** Dogs not allowed. **Facilities** Parking. **Nearby** Skiing, alpine garden of Valnontey, Gran Pardiso National Park. **Open** All year (except May, Nov.).

About a mile and a half from Cogne, La Barme is in Valnontey, the last village on the edge of the Gran Paradiso National Park, famous for its "Paradisia" garden which has some rare species of alpine flora. Here the mountains become less civilized, wild animals show no fear, and the houses are few and far between. "La Barme," in the local dialect, means "the den," a fittings name for this small, gray, stone inn. It looks like a typical mountain house–half barn or stable, half dwelling place. On the wooden stairs, slippers await cross-country skiers with tired feet. The rooms are very simple but cozy. This is a place where you will be able to fully enjoy the mountains and numerous excursions in the Cogne Valley and the Valsavarenche.

How to get there *(Map 2): 27 km south of Aosta via S26 to Sarre, then S507. 3 km from Cogne.*

Hotel Lo Scoiattolo ★★★

11020 Gressoney-la-Trinité (Aosta)
Tel. (0125) 366 313
Fax. (0125) 366 220
Sig.ra Bethaz

Rooms 14 with telephone, bath or shower, WC and TV. **Price** With half board 70-130,000L (per pers.). **Meals** Breakfast 15,000L, served 8:00-10:00 **Restaurant** For residents; service 13:00 and 19:00; menu, also à la carte. **Credit cards** Visa, Eurocard and MasterCard. **Pets** Dogs not allowed. **Facilities** Garage. **Nearby** Skiing, Mont Rosa. **Open** Dec. – April, June 25 – Sept.

Gressoney-la Trinité is the last in a string of villages in the Val d'Aoste at the foot of Mount Rose. Frequented mainly by Italian families and couples, this village has a very different atmosphere from the other more urbane resorts in the area, and the hotels here cater to the needs of their clientele. The nicest one is this small hotel run by Silvana and her two daughters. The rooms are large and well furnished. Every room is paneled in light wood, giving them a real mountain feel. Sig.ra Bethaz can sometimes be a little gruff, but she does see to it that everything in the hotel and the kitchen runs smoothly. This is a good hotel for an economical vacation.

How to get there *(Map 2): 100 km east of Aosta via A5, Pont-Saint-Martin exit, then S505.*

Hotel dei Trulli ★★★★★

Via Cadore, 28
70011 Alberobello (Bari)
Tel. (080) 932 35 55 - Fax (080) 932 35 60
Sig. Farace

Rooms 19 with telephone, bath or shower, WC, TV and minibar. **Price** Single 120-150,000L, double 200-250,000L. **Meals** Breakfast 30,000L, served 7:30-9:30; half board 150-180,000L, full board 180-220,000L. (per pers., 3 days min.). **Restaurant** Service 12:30-14:30; 19:30-22:30; menu 60,000L. Specialties: Orecchiette alla barese, purè di fave con cicoria, agnello Alberobellese. **Credit cards** All major. **Pets** Dogs allowed. **Facilities** Swimming pool, parking. **Nearby** Alberobello (Trulli district), Castel del Monte, Locorotondo, Martina Franca, Tàranto (Museo Nazionale: Greeck and Roman artifacts collection), Castellana Grotte. **Open** All year.

Alberobello is the world capital of *trulli*, cute little houses which, at first glance, might remind you of the ones the dwarves live in at Disneyland, but they are, in fact, authentic old houses, typical of the region. The hotel is entirely made up of recently built trulli, which imitate the local style; each one is freshly whitewashed and has an arbor, one or two rooms, and a small living room with a fireplace. They are all charming, comfortable, and air-conditioned. The restaurant is in the main building. The hotel swimming pool is not very attractive, but you will really appreciate it on hot summer days.

How to get there *(Map 23): 55 km southeast of Bari via S100 to Casamàssima, then S172 to Putignano and Alberobello.*

Il Melograno ★★★★★

Contrada Torricella, 345
70043 Monopoli (Bari)
Tel. (080) 690 90 30 – Fax (080) 74 79 08 – Sig. Guerra

Rooms 37 with air-conditioning, telephone, bath or shower, WC, cable TV and minibar. **Price** Single 205-300,000L, double 290-480,000L, suite 530-750,000L. **Meals** Breakfast included, served 7:30-11:30; half board 200-300,000L, full board 230-340,000L. (per pers., 3 days min.). **Restaurant** Service 12:30-14:30, 20:00-22:30, closed Jan. 1– March 22; menu 80,000L. Specialties: Salmone affumicato in casa, agnello al forno. **Credit cards** All major. **Pets** Dogs not allowed. **Facilities** Swimming pool, tennis, health-center with indoor swimming pool , parking. **Nearby** Ruins of Egnazia, Alberobello (Trulli district), Castel del Monte, Locorotondo, Martina Franca, Tàranto (Museo Nazionale: Greeck and Roman artifacts collection), Castellana Grotte. **Open** March 23 – Nov. 11.

Here, in the hot region of Apulia, is an oasis of coolness, greenery and taste. Il Melograno was originally a sharecropper's fortified farmhouse from the 16th century. It is surrounded by a maze of white buildings which blend in with bouganvilleas, and olive, lemon, and pomegranate trees. Formerly a vacation house, it has been transformed into a hotel but has kept its characteristic personal touch. The rooms are very elegant, with their antique furniture and paintings, beautiful fabrics and traditional *cotto* (ceramic tile) floors. The salons seem lost in the orange grove seen through a picture window. The dining room-veranda, where you'll dine under a white canopy next to an ancient olive tree, is on the other side of the garden. The hosts are very nice. Note that sometimes there are seminars which can disturb guests.

How to get there *(Map 23): 50 km south of Bari, 3 km from Monopoli towards Alberobello.*

Villa Cenci ★★★

(Via per Ceglie Messapica)
72014 Cisternino (Brindisi)
Tel. (080) 71 82 08 – Fax (080) 71 82 08
Sig.ra Bianco

Rooms 25 with telephone, bath or shower and WC. **Price** Single 62-80,000L, double 120-160,000L. **Meals** Breakfast 10,000L, served 8:30-10:30. **Restaurant** Service 13:00-14:30, 20:00-22:00; menu 30,000L. Specialties: Italian and regional cooking. **Credit cards** Visa, Eurocard and MasterCard. **Pets** Dogs allowed. **Facilities** Swimming pool, parking. **Nearby** Alberobello (Trulli district), Castel del Monte, Locorotondo, Martina Franca, Tàranto (Museo Nazionale: Greck and Roman artifacts collection), Castellana Grotte. **Open** April – Sept.

Far from the hordes of tourists in this very busy region, this agricultural estate will host you for a very modest price. The beautiful white house, isolated among the grapevines, offers its guests tranquility, which you will feel this as you walk along the paths lined with white laurels. It is surrounded by *trulli,* conic constructions typical of Apulia; those here have cool rooms with simple, tasteful decor. In the villa itself there are other more classical rooms, as well as several functionals small apartments. The hotel is frequented by numerous Italian and English regulars. From the swimming pool you can have a nice view of the countryside. The fruit and vegetables served at meals are fresh from the garden, and the wine is "home made."

How to get there *(Map 23): 74 km southeast of Bari via SS16, coast to Fasano, then S172 to Laureto (towards Cisternino).*

Hotel Sierra Silvana

72010 Selva di Fasano (Brindisi)
Tel. (080) 933 13 22
Fax (080) 933 12 07

Rooms 120 with air-conditioning, telephone, bath or shower and WC.
Price Double 130-170,000L. **Meals** Breakfast 11,000L, served 7:00-10:00; half
board 95-103,000L, full board 158-173,000L (per pers.). **Restaurant** Service
12:30-14:00, 19:30-21:00; menu 40,000L, also à la carte. Specialties: Italian and
regional cooking. **Credit cards** All major. **Pets** Dogs not allowed. **Facilities**
Swimming pool, parking. **Nearby** Ruins of Egnazia near by Monopoli, Alberobello
(Trulli district), Castel del Monte, Locorotondo, Martina Franca, Tàranto (Museo
Nazionale: Greck and Roman artifacts collection), Castellana Grotte, golf course
(18-hole) in Riva dei Tessali. **Open** March 25 – Nov. 5.

The Hotel Sierra Silvana is built around an imposing old *trulli*
(a conical structure common to the Apulia region). In many
primitive societies, social status was reflected in the size of the
dwelling. Someone important must have lived in this one,
because it is enormous, with enough space for four rooms. There
is a great demand for these simple and elegantly decorated rooms.
The other rooms are in more modern buildings, and are quiet
and comfortable; all have a balcony on the garden. The hotel is
well equipped for receptions, but the staff ensures that guests are
not disturbed. Located 30 miles (50 km) from Brindisi, this hotel
is an interesting stopover on your way to Greece.

How to get there (Map 23): 60 km southeast of Bari.

Hotel Villa Ducale ★★★★

Piazzetta Sant'Antonio
74015 Martina Franca (Taranto)
Tel. (080) 70 50 55 – Fax (080) 70 58 85
Sig. A. Sforza

Rooms 24 with telephone, bath or shower, WC and minibar. **Price** Single 95,000L, double 140,000L, suite 160,000L. **Meals** Breakfast included, served 7:30-11:30. **Restaurant** Service 12:30-14:30, 20:00-22:00; menu 40,000L, also à la carte. Specialties: Regional cooking **Credit cards** All major. **Pets** Dogs allowed. **Nearby** In Martina Franca: Piazza Roma (Palazzo Ducale), Ruins of Egnazia near by Monopoli, Alberobello (Trulli district), Castel del Monte, Locorotondo, Martina Franca, Tàranto (Museo Nazionale: Greck and Roman artifacts collection), Castellana Grotte, golf course (18-hole) in Riva dei Tessali. **Open** All year.

Like all of the hotels in town, the Villa Ducale has gone the modern road. The building itself is unappealing but wel located, close to the old town and next to a large public garden and a 16th-century convent. Once inside, however, you will forget all about the facade; the decor is very avant-garde, and the lobby, the bar and the rooms all have a designer look. The hotel is pretty incongruous but very comfortable. Ask for the corner rooms (105, 205, 305) which have two windows and are very light, though sometimes a little noisy despite the double-panes. Be sure to visit the splendid Ducal palace. The entire town has interesting architecture, though it is off the beaten tourist track and you will need to stay here awhile to appreciate it.

How to get there *(Map 23): 74 km southeast of Bari via S100, Locorotondo and Martina Franca.*

Hotel Hieracon ★★★

Isola di San Pietro
Corso Cavour, 62
09014 Carloforte (Cagliari)
Tel. (0781) 85 40 28 – Fax (0781) 85 48 93 – Sig. Ferrando

Rooms 18 and 7 suites with air-conditioning, telephone, shower, WC and TV. **Price** Single 75,000L, double 115,000L, triple 160,000L. **Meals** Breakfast 6,000L, served 8:30-10:30; half board 98,000L, full board 130,000L. (per pers., 3 days min.). **Restaurant** Service 12:30-14:00, 19:30-21:30; menus 25,000L. Specialties: Italian and regional cuisine. **Credit cards** Not accepted. **Pets** Small dogs allowed. **Nearby** Beach (2 km), boat rentals. **Open** All year.

The Hotel Hieracon is located in San Pietro, a pretty little island with a rocky coastline dotted with inlets and beaches. This lovely Art Nouveau-style building is right on the port. The interior is a blend of light tile work and pastel colors. We recommend the rooms on the second floor, which have nice turn-of-the-century furniture. The ones on the other floors are darker and less comfortable. Behind the hotel there is a large terraced garden set in the shade of a tall palm tree. Four small ground floor apartments open onto the garden. The restaurant is superb with its black flagstones and its curving mezzanine which looks like the bridge of an old pre-war ocean liner. Ths cuisine is good and features typical island dishes. Dr. Ferrando will make you feel at home.

How to get there (Map 19): 77 km west of Cagliarii via SS130 to Portoscuro; ferry service from Porto Vesme (40 min.).

Pensione Paola e Primo Maggio ★★

Isola di San Pietro
Tacca Rossa
09014 Carloforte (Cagliari)
Tel. (0781) 85 00 98 - Sig. Ferraro

Rooms 21 with shower and WC. **Price** Double 90,000L. **Meals** Breakfast 5,500L,
served 8:00-11:00; half board 90,000L, full board 100,000L. (per pers.).
Restaurant Service 13:00-14:30, 19:00-23:00, à la carte. Specialties: Seafood.
Credit cards Amex, Visa, Eurocard and MasterCard. **Pets** Dogs not allowed.
Nearby Beach (2 km), boat rentals. **Open** April 16 – Oct.

The Pensione Paola, about a mile and a half from Carloforte,
faces the sea and offers rooms—at very reasonable
prices—which all enjoy the beautiful maritime view. In the main
house, a restaurant with a large shady terrace serves fine, solid
cuisine featuring many dishes typical of the island. Rooms 7, 8,
and 9 are our favorites, as they are more modern and
comfortable than the others. Downstairs, there are two garden-
level rooms which are just as nice as the other three in a
bungalow nearby.

*How to get there (Map 19): 77 km west of Cagliari via SS130 to
Portoscuro; ferry services from Porto Vesme (40 min.) - 3 km north of
Carloforte.*

Club Ibisco Farm

Isola di Sant'Antioco
09017 Capo Sperone (Cagliari)
Tel. (0781) 80 90 18 / (0041) 91 52 59 39 – Fax (0781) 80 90 03
Sig.ra Naef

Rooms 8 with telephone, shower, WC, TV and minibar. **Price** Single 150-230,000L, double 250-400,000L, triple 350-600,000L, apartment 450-680,000L. **Meals** Breakfast included, served 8:30-10:00; half board 150-230,000L (per pers., 7 days min.). **Restaurant** Service 20:30; menus. Specialties: Regional cuisine, seafood. **Credit cards** Visa, Eurocard and MasterCard. **Pets** Dogs not allowed. **Facilities** Tennis (25,000L at night), riding, boating, parking. **Nearby** Beach (100 m), museum and Tophet in San Antioco, Calasetta. **Open** June 19 – Sept. 18.

The Club Ibisco Farm is a nicely restored old farm on a vast 247-acre estate, overlooking the ocean. The owners, who love this unspoiled island, spend several months a year in this beautiful, wild setting. You will have a superb 17-meter wooden motor-sailboat, horses, a soccer field, and a tennis court at your disposal. The absolutely delicious dinners are made from produce and wine from the estate, and the fresh fish is caught daily. Meals are served outside around a big common table made of wood. Among the different rooms, we prefer the suite for three people and the apartment for four, which are light and spacious. The others are quite comfortable and quiet.

How to get there (Map 19): 95 km west of Cagliari via SS136 to Sant'Antioco, then via coast towards Capo Sperone (1 km after Peonia Rosa); Cagliari airport (private bus to and from the hotel: 100,000L per pers.).

Is Morus Hotel ★★★★

09010 Santa Margherita di Pula (Cagliari)
Tel. (070) 92 11 71
Fax (070) 92 15 96
Sig. Orru

Rooms 83 with air-conditioning, telephone, bath or shower, WC, TV and minibar.
Price With half board 190-350,000L (per pers.). **Meals** Breakfast included, served
7:30-10:00. **Restaurant** Service 13:00-14:30, 20:00-21:30; menus: 50-70,000L.
Specialties: Italian and regional cuisine, seafood. **Credit cards** All major.
Pets Small dogs allowed. **Facilities** Swimming pool, tennis, miniature golf,
private bus for the Is Molas golf course (no green fee), private beach, parking.
Nearby Nora (ancient city: ruins of temples, amphitheater, Roman theater,
mosaic pavement); Is Molas golf course (18-hole) at S. Margherita di Pula.
Open April – Oct.

Just like the Costa Smeralda, the coast south of Cagliari has
been experiencing a boom in beach construction. The Is
Morus is in Santa Margherita di Pula, right next to the golf
course. It is a luxury hotel with a marvelous location, in the
middle of a pine forest and on the superb turquoise-blue sea.
Some of the rooms are in villas set in the cool shade of pine
trees, something very rare in this part of Sardenia. The other
rooms are in the main house, a low building with white walls,
which looks like a large Spanish villa.

How to get there *(Map 19): 37 km southwest of Cagliari via the coast*
(S195) to Santa Margherita (6,5 km from Pula).

Hotel Su Gologone ★★★★

Sorgente Su Gologone
08025 Oliena (Nuoro)
Tel. (0784) 28 75 12 – Fax (0784) 28 76 68
Sig. Palimodde

Rooms 65 with air-conditioning, telephone, bath or shower, WC and TV (20 with minibar). **Price** Single 100-110,000L, double 150-180,000L. **Meals** Breakfast included, served 7:30-9:30; half board 130-170,000L, full board 175-220,000L (per pers., 3 days min.). **Restaurant** Service 12:30-15:00, 20:00-23:00; menu: 50,000L, also à la carte. Specialties: Sardinian cuisine, seafood. **Credit cards** Amex, Visa, Eurocard and MasterCard. **Pets** Dogs allowed. **Facilities** Swimming pool, tennis (8,000L), riding, parking. **Nearby** Sorgente su Gologone, Chapel of San Lussurgiu at Oliena. **Open** April – Oct. and Dec.

The main attraction of Sardinia is its coast, but the beautiful inland part really deserves more than a quick detour. The Su Gologone has it all, located about 12 miles from the coast between Dorgali and Oliean, at the foot of superb rocky mountains, the Supramonten. The famous hotel restaurant, open since 1961, serves excellent regional cuisine. The architecture of the hotel, inspired by the houses in Oliena, is a great achievement. The interior has been decorated with uncommon taste, with old exposed beams complementing the beautiful antique furniture and the paintings by Biasi, a talented Sardinian painter. The rooms are all different and very pleasant. The spring-fed swimming pool is splendid. The hotel organizes numerous excursions on horseback or by Land Rover in the surrounding area. The staff is very friendly.

How to get there *(Map 19): 20 km southeast of Nuoro to Oliena, then towards Dorgali.*

Villa Las Tronas ★★★★

07041 Alghero (Sassari)
Lungomare Valencia, 1
Tel. (079) 98 18 18
Fax (079) 98 10 44

Rooms 29 with air-conditioning, telephone, bath or shower, WC, TV, safe and minibar. **Price** Single 170-190,000L, double 200-300,000L. **Meals** Breakfast 12-65,000L, served 7:30-9:30; half board 140-240,000L, full board 180-290,000L. **Restaurant** Service 13:00-14:30, 20:00-21:30; menu, also à la carte. Specialties: Sardinian cuisine, seafood. **Credit cards** All major. **Pets** Dogs not allowed. **Facilities** Swimming pool, private beach, bikes, parking. **Nearby** Cathedral in Alghero, Grotto of Neptune, heights of Capo Caccia, Porto Conte, Route 129 from Nuoro to Bosa. **Open** All year.

The Villa Las Tronas, surrounded by very well kept garden, is on a small peninsula overlooking the Gulf of Alghero. Once a vacation spot for Italian kings during their visits to Sardinia, this unusual Moorish-style building is today a hotel with a Baroque atmosphere created by vast rooms with painted ceilings and gleaming chandeliers, and numerous salons of different colors. The spacious, high-ceilinged rooms are all on the sea and have every modern comfort. Rooms 110, 112, 114, 116, 118, and 216 are the nicest ones, with a very large common terrace from which you can take in the superb panoramic view. You can enjoy the same view in the lovely dining room. There is a pretty swimming pool, with access to the sea. The style and presence of the personnel contribute to the elegant atmosphere of this hotel.

How to get there *(Map 19): 35 km southwest of Sassari via S291 to Alghero.*

Hotel Li Capanni ★★★

Cannigione
07020 Arzachena (Sassari)
Tel. (0789) 86 041 – Sig. Pagni

Rooms 23 and 2 suites with shower and WC. **Price** Double 75,000L (1 pers.).
Meals Breakfast included; half board from June to Sept. 115-205,000L (per pers.).
Restaurant For residents; service 13:00-14:00, 20:30-21:00; menus: 30-35,000L.
Specialties: Sardinian and Italian cuisine. **Credit cards** Not accepted. **Pets** Dogs
not allowed. **Facilities** Private beach, parking. **Nearby** Tombe di Giganti (giants'
tombs) and ancient city of Li Muri, San Pantaleo, Pevero golf course (18-hole) in
Porto Cervo. **Open** May 1 – Oct.

Go up a dirt road about one mile, and suddenly, as if by magic,
you will find yourself far from the throngs of the Costa
Smeralda (where the environment is nonetheless protected and
campgrounds restricted). The Hotel Li Capanni aspires to be more
of a club than a hotel, to highlight its uniqueness and preserve its
tranquility. It is on a very lovely site facing the archipelago of the
Maddalena Islands, overlooking the sea. The small ochre houses
are scattered here and there on ten-acre grounds which slope
gently down to the sea and a very pretty, private beach. The rooms
are simply decorated and comfortable. The dining room and salons
are grouped in the main building. The dining room overlooks the
bay and is very inviting with its small blue wood tables and chairs.
A cozy salon looks just like the living room of a private home. For
security reasons, the hotel does not accept children under 14.

How to get there *(Map 19): 32 km north of Olbia via S125 towards
Arzachena, then via the coast towards Palau to Cannigione; the hotel is 3,5
km after Cannigione.*

Hotel Don Diego ★★★★

Costa Dorata
07020 Porto San Paolo (Sassari)
Tel. (0789) 40 006
Fax (0789) 40 026

Rooms 50 and 6 suites with air-conditioning, telephone, shower, WC and TV.
Price Double 300-500,000L. **Meals** Breakfast 25,000L, served 8:00-10:00; half
board 200-300,000L (per pers.). **Restaurant** Service 13:00-14:30, 20:00-21:30;
menus 70-80,000L, also à la carte. Specialties: Sardinian cuisine, seafood.
Credit cards All major. **Pets** Dogs not allowed. **Facilities** Swimming pool (sea
water), tennis, beach, parking. **Nearby** Church San Simplicio in Olbia, Tavolara
Island. **Open** All year.

Located south of Olbia, the Hotel Don Diego is a series of
small villas facing the sea, scattered among beautiful
bouganvilleas and pine trees. Each one has a separate entry and
six to eight rooms, and there's a pleasant coolness inside. The
reception area, bar, restaurant, and salons are located in the
closest house to the water. You will also find a sea-water
swimming pool and a sand beach here. Just across from the hotel
is Tavolara Island, an impressive rocky spur jutting into the clear
blue water. The Don Diego is a great place for a family
vacation.

How to get there *(Map 19): 16 km southeast of Olbia via S125 until
just after Porto San Paolo, then turn left towards the Costa Dorata coast.*

Hotel Cala di Volpe ★★★★★

Porto Cervo
07020 Cala di Volpe (Sassari)
Tel. (0789) 96 083 – Fax (0789) 96 442
Sig. Paterlini

Rooms 123 with air-conditioning, telephone, bath, WC, TV, safe and minibar.
Price With half board 415,000L, 515,000L, 615,000L. **Restaurant** On request;
service 13:00-14:30, 20:00-22:00. Specialties: Italian cuisine, seafood.
Credit cards All major. **Pets** Dogs not allowed. **Facilities** Tennis (+5,000L),
swimming pool, putting-green, private beach, private port, parking. **Nearby** Costa
Smeralda, Tombe di Giganti (giants' tombs) and ancient city of Li Muri, San
Pantaleo, Pevero golf course (18-hole) in Porto Cervo. **Open** May 12 – Sept.

Thirty years ago, Prince Karim Agha Khan and a group of
international financiers decided to build luxury hotel
complexes in la Gallura, this beautiful wild region of rolling hills
and valleys, and called it Costa Smeralda. The buildings are a sort
of cocktail of Mediterranean architectural styles–Spanish,
Moorish, and Provençale. The most famous hotel in the region,
the Cala di Volpe faces an enchanting bay, and was designed by a
French architect, Jacques Couelle. He used a medieval village as a
model, inspired by its towers and terraces, arcades and granite
passageways. The interior is decorated in the same motif, but
with all the modern comfort you could want. The gigantic pool,
private port, and impeccable service make this a unique place.

How to get there (Map 19): *25 km north of Olbia via S125, then
towards Porto Cervo to Abbiadoni and take a right towards Capriccioli to
Cala di Volpe.*

Hotel Le Ginestre ★★★★

07020 Porto Cervo (Sassari)
Tel. (0789) 92 030
Fax (0789) 94 087
Sig. Costa

Rooms 78 with air-conditioning, telephone, bath or shower, WC, TV, safe and minibar. **Price** With half board 159-310,000L, full board +40,000L (per pers.). **Meals** Breakfast included, served 8:00-10:30. **Restaurant** Service 13:00-14:30, 20:00-22:00. Specialties: Seafood. **Credit cards** All major. **Pets** Dogs not allowed. **Facilities** Swimming pool, tennis (35,000L), private beach, parking. **Nearby** Costa Smeralda, Tombe di Giganti (giants' tombs) and ancient city of Li Muri, San Pantaleo, Pevero golf course (18-hole) in Porto Cervo. **Open** May – Sept. or Oct. 15.

There are luxury hotels on the Costa Smeralda which are more affordable than the Ginestre, but not all of them have its charm. The rooms are in a series of small villas at the edge of a pine forest, slightly overhanging the Gulf of Pevero. It looks like a small hamlet, with its tangle of little streets on grounds with fragrant bushes and trees with brightly colored flowers typical of the Mediterrranean region. As is common in this area, the Neo-Realist architecture recalls Tuscan villages with their faded ochre facades. The rooms have pretty furniture, and most of them have balconies. A little off to one side, under a large thatched suncreen, there is a pleasant restaurant. Because of the number of rooms, the hotel loses in intimacy what it gains in atmosphere.

How to get there *(Map 19): 30 km north of Olbia via S125, towards Porto Cervo.*

Hotel Romazzino ★★★★

Porto Cervo
07020 Romazzino (Sassari)
Tel. (0789) 96 020
Fax (0789) 96 258

Rooms 98 with air-conditioning, telephone, bath or shower, WC, TV, safe and minibar. **Price** With half board 880-1,342,000L, full board 935-1,408,000L (per pers.). **Meals** Breakfast included, served 7:30-10:30. **Restaurant** Service 13:00-14:30, 20:00-22:00; menu. Specialties: Italian cuisine. **Credit cards** All major. **Pets** Dogs not allowed. **Facilities** Swimming pool, tennis, private beach, parking. **Nearby** Costa Smeralda, Tombe di Giganti (giants' tombs) and ancient city of Li Muri, San Pantaleo, Pevero golf course (18-hole) in Porto Cervo. **Open** May 15 — Oct. 10.

Next door to "Medieval village," the Romazzino, with its white walls, vaulted windows, and pink tiles, looks like an Andeluvian–if not Mexican–village. It looks magical when you see it from the road as you arrive, its superb silhouette rising in front of the sea. The Romazzino is a quiet hotel–a great place for resting and enjoying the sea. The fine sand beach is superb. A delicious barbecue awaits you at lunchtime. The interior is all curves, and gives the impression of sumptuous caverns or imaginary palaces. The bar is unique with a floor inlayed with juniper trunks. All the rooms are perfect and have private terraces. This dreamy place is all about the pleasures of the sea.

How to get there *(Map 19): 25 km north of Olbia via S125, then towards Porto Cervo to Abbiadoni, then turn right towards Capriccioli to Cala di Volpe - Romazzino is after Capriccioli.*

El Faro ★★★★

Porto Conte
07041 Alghero (Sassari)
Tel. (079) 94 20 10 – Fax (079) 94 20 30
Sig. Bruno Sarno

Rooms 92 with air-conditioning, telephone, bath or shower, WC, TV and minibar.
Price Single 107-167,000L, double 190-280,000L. **Meals** Breakfast included,
served 7:30-10:00; half board 105-210,000L, full board 125-240,000L. (per pers.,
3 days min.). **Restaurant** Service 13:00-14:00, 20:00-21:30; menu 70,000L, also
à la carte. Specialties: Lobsters, seafood. **Credit cards** All major. **Pets** Dogs
allowed except in restaurant and on the beach. **Facilities** Swimming pool, tennis,
sauna (25,000L), parking. **Nearby** Cathedral in Alghero, Grotto of Neptune,
heights of Capo Caccia, Route 129 from Nuoro to Bosa. **Open** April – Oct.

This hotel is superbly located on a small peninsula next to an
old lighthouse, facing Cap Caccia with it famous Neptune
caverns. The view encompasses all of the splendid Gulf with its
banks almost totally unspoiled by construction. This large,
ninety-two room hotel is a special place, thanks to the quality of
the service and the simple, well-planned Mediterranean decor.
All the rooms have a balcony and a view of the sea, with white
walls brightened by engravings of nautical themes, wooden
furniture, and pretty bathrooms. Down below, between several
terraces, there is a superb semi-covered swimming pool
overlooking the waves, and a little further beyond, a beach
among the rocks. This is a luxury hotel which is still affordable.

How to get there *(Map 19): 41 km southwest of Sassari via S291 to
Alghero and S127 bis to Porto Conte.*

Villa Athena ★★★★

Via dei Templi
92100 Agrigento
Tel. (0922) 59 62 88 - Fax (0922) 40 21 80
Sig. d'Alessandro

Rooms 40 with air-conditioning, telephone, bath or shower, WC and TV.
Price Single 150,000L, double 250,000L. **Meals** Breakfast included, served 7:30-
10:00; half board 290,000L, full board 330,000L (per 2 pers., 3 days min.).
Restaurant Service 12:30-14:30, 19:30-20:00; menu 40,000L, also à la carte.
Specialties: Involtini di pesce spado, cavatelli Villa Athena, pesce fresco.
Credit cards All major. **Pets** Dogs not allowed. **Facilities** Swimming pool, parking.
Nearby In Agrigento: Valley of the Temples, birthhouse of Luigi Pirandello; Naro,
Palma di Montechiano. **Open** All year.

Be sure to stop off at Agrigento and visit the Valley of the
Temples, a epicenter of archaeology if ever there was one.
Once you are there, you will see that there is only one hotel
which has any charm: the Villa Athena. This old 18th–century
villa used to belong to a prince and has recently been very well
renovated. It enjoys an exceptional location, across from the
Concord Temple; the view is best from Room 205. The rooms
and bathrooms are functional and comfortable. A large salon
opens onto the terrace and the temple. The swimming pool is
very pleasant.

*How to get there (Map 27): 2 km south of Agrigento towards "Valle dei
Templi."*

Hotel Kaos ★★★★

Villagio Pirandello
92100 Agrigento
Tel. (0922) 59 86 22 - Fax (0922) 59 87 70
Sig. Ribecca

Rooms 105 with air-conditioning, telephone, bath or shower, WC, TV and minibar.
Price Single 150,000L, double 200,000L. **Meals** Breakfast included, served 7:30-
9:30; half board 140,000L, full board 180,000L. (per pers., 3 days min.).
Restaurant Service 12:30-14:30, 19:30-20:00; menu 34,000L, also à la carte.
Specialties: Sicilian and Italian cuisine. **Credit cards** All major. **Pets** Dogs not
allowed. **Facilities** Swimming pool, tennis, parking. **Nearby** In Agrigento: Valley of
the Temples, birthhouse of Luigi Pirandello; Naro, Palma di Montechiano.
Open All year.

Near the valley of the temples, which according to the
Greek poet, Pindar, makes Agrigento "the most beautiful
of mortal cities" there is another place which the guidebooks
sometimes forget to mention a moving place—the house where
the playwright Pirandello was born and raised, and his tomb
under a solitary pine tree at the end of a path. Sicilians consider
this pine tree to be a historic monument, and its health, recently
endangered by pollution, set off a big debate on how to preserve
it, some even suggesting it be mummified. The hotel Kaos is a
less poetic place even if it is just next door. It consists of an old
family mansion and its outbuildings. The hotel is a bit
overdecorated but is otherwise comfortable, offers very good
services, and extends a very friendly welcome.

How to get there *(Map 27) 2 km south of Agrigento towards "Valle dei
Templi." 4 km from Porta Aurea.*

Hotel Elimo Erice

Via Vittore Emanuele, 75
91 016 Erice (Trapani)
Tel. (0923) 86 93 77 / 86 94 86 – Fax (0923) 86 92 52 – Sig. Tilotta

Rooms 21 with telephone, bath or shower, WC and TV. **Price** Single 120,000L, double 190,000L. **Meals** Breakfast included, served 7:30-10:00; half board 130,000L, full board 190,000L (per pers., 3 days min.). **Restaurant** Service 12:30-14:30, 19:30-20:00; menu 30-60,000L, also à la carte. Specialties: Sicilian cuisine. **Credit cards** All major. **Pets** Dogs allowed. **Facilities** Parking. **Nearby** Trapani, Egadi islands and island of Pantelleria. **Open** All year.

At the western end of Sicily, Erice, which rises straight up from a rock, seems to keep watch over a peaceful and silent world. The historical center is a labyrinth of narrow little streets, Renaissance palaces and churches from the Middle Ages, all of which seem to fit together like pieces of a jigsaw puzzle. Life goes on behind these facades, in the inner courtyards which are characteristic of the houses in Erice. The hotel Elimo is in one of these old houses. Carefully restored and comfortably furnished, the hotel's decor, inspired by the colors and materials of ancient motifs, is nevertheless a bit common. This is, however, a very pleasant place to stay in this beautiful town of Erice, with its remarkable architectural heritage. Be sure to go for a walk along the fortified walls surrounding the town from which you will have stunning views of the coast. From the Castello di Venere, you can see Trapani and the islands, and on a clear day, Tunisia. Don't be surprised if you hear people speaking foreign languages–the town is the headquarters for the International Center of Scientific Culture "Ettore Majorana."

How to get there *(Map 27): 13 km north of Trapani.*

Grand Hotel Villa Igiea ★★★★★

Via Belmonte, 43
90142 Palermo
Tel. (091) 54 37 44 - Fax (091) 54 76 54 - Sig. Arabia

Rooms 117 with air-conditioning, telephone, bath, WC, TV and minibar.
Price Single 230,000L, double 350,000L, suite 600,000L. **Meals** Breakfast
included, served 7:00-10:00; half board 235,000L, full board 270,000L (per pers.,
3 days min.). **Restaurant** Service 12:30-15:00, 19:30-23:00; menu 80,000L, also
à la carte. Specialties: Pennette alla lido, spada al forno. **Credit cards** All major.
Pets Dogs allowed in rooms. **Facilities** Swimming pool, tennis, parking. **Nearby** In
Palermo: Palazzo dei Normanni (Norman Royal Palace), Cappella palatina
(Palatine Chapel), Church of San Giovanni degli Eremiti, S. Francesco d'Assisi,
Oratorio S. Lorenzo, Regional Archeological Museum, Palazzo Abatellis
(Annunciation by Antonello da Messina); Cathedral of Monreale (10 km), Mondello,
Villa Palagonia in Bagheria, Solonte, Piana degli Albanesi, Cefalù. **Open** All year.

A superb example of Art Nouveau–style, the Villa Igiea is
certainly the most beautiful hotel in the west of Sicily, and
its location allows it to escape from the hustle and bustle of
Palermo. It's hard to find fault with this grand hotel which has
kept its period furniture and decor while guaranteeing its guests
almost flawless service and comfort. The bar, the winter dining
room, the veranda and the rooms are so pleasant that the most
sophisticated Palermians come here every night. The swimming
pool and the terraced gardens overlook the bay where you can
go for a swim. In summary it is impossible to pass the Villa Igiea
by when you are in Palermo.

How to get there (Map 27): *Towards district of Acquasanta, by via dei
Cantieri Navali.*

Centrale Palace Hotel ★★★

Corso Vittorio Emanuele, 327
90134 Palermo
Tel. (091) 33 66 66 - Fax (091) 33 48 81
Sig. Romano

Rooms 61 with air-conditioning, telephone, bath or shower, WC and minibar.
Price Single 150,000L, double 220,000L, 320,000L. **Meals** Breakfast 20,000L,
served 7.00-11.00; half board 175,000L, full board 195,000L (per pers.).
Restaurant See p. 420-421. **Credit cards** All major. **Pets** Dogs allowed in room.
Facilities Swimming pool, tennis, parking. **Nearby** In Palermo: Palazzo dei
Normanni (Norman Royal Palace), Cappella palatina (Palatine Chapel), Church of
San Giovanni degli Eremiti, S. Francesco d'Assisi, Oratorio S. Lorenzo, Regional
Archeological Museum, Palazzo Abatellis (Annunciation by Antonello da Messina);
Cathedral of Monreale (10 km), Mondello, Villa Palagonia in Bagheria, Solonte -
Piana degli Albanesi, Cefalù. **Open** All year.

This is a little hotel–a rare thing in Palermo. Located in the
heart of the historical center, the Centrale Palace Hotel has
reopened its recently renovated rooms and should quickly regain
its former splendor. At the moment you will find comfortable
rooms with traditional decor, modern facilities, and air-
conditioning. The prices are still reasonable. This is a good place
to stay, and one that will certainly go places.

How to get there *(Map 27): The Corso Vittorio Emanuele begins at the
piazza Independenza.*

Villa Lucia

96100 Siracusa
Traversa Mondello, 1 - Contrada Isola
Tel. (0336) 88 85 37 or (0931) 721 007 - Fax (0931) 61 817
Sig.ra Maria Luisa Palermo

Rooms 7 and 6 apartments (2-4 pers.) with bath or shower, WC, 3 with TV and 5 with minibar. **Price** Single 190,000L, double 290,000L, apartment (2-5 pers.) 50,000 (per pers., 2 nights min.). **Meals** Breakfast included, served 7:30-10:00. **Restaurant** See p. 422. **Credit cards** Not accepted. **Pets** Dogs allowed in room (fee). **Facilities** Parking. **Nearby** In Siracusa: Archeological Museum, Ortygia island, Catacombs, Castle of Euryale, Fountain of Arethusa. **Open** All year.

This listing was given to us by one of our charming readers and colleagues. It is an old family house which the owner, the Marquise Maria Luisa Palermo, has progressively adapted to receive guests. A pine tree-lined path leads up to the villa, with its faded pink, roughcast facade. There is no ostentatious luxury here in this former family vacation residence, just antique furniture which has been collected over many years, travel souvenirs, and paintings of the family. The extremely pleasant grounds have dense Mediterranean vegetation. Take a walk along the sea; the view of the island of Ortygia is divine. Thanks to her extraordinary contacts, Maria Luisa also organizes visits to other sumptuous private Sicilian houses. She is a truly charming hostess, and this is a great property.

How to get there *(Map 28): 6 km from Siracusa. At the highway, exit Catania/Siracusa, then take SS115. When you leave the town, take the bridge on the river Ciane, first road on the left, go around the port, Contrada Isola.*

Museo Albergo L'Atelier sul Mare

Via Cesare Battisti, 4
98070 Castel di Tusa (Messina)
Tel. (0921) 34 295 – Fax (0921) 34 283
Sig. Antonio Presti

Rooms 40 with telephone, bath or shower and WC. **Price** Single 80-105,000L, double 120-160,000L. **Meals** Breakfast included, served 7:30-9:30; half board 95-115,000L, full board 120-140,000L (per pers., 3 days min.). **Restaurant** Service 13:00-15:00, 20:30-22:30; menu 30-40,000L, also à la carte. Specialties: Sicialian cuisine, seafood. **Credit cards** Amex, Visa, Eurocard and MasterCard. **Pets** Dogs allowed (fee). **Facilities** Swimming pool, parking. **Nearby** Halaesa, S. Stefano di Camastra (Terracotta poteries), Cefalù. **Open** All year.

The Museo Albergo is a Mediterranean-style building right on the water, set on several levels with large terraces. What is really interesting is the concept which the hotel and especially the rooms are based on: art as an integral part of daily life. Each room is an "event" designed by a contemporary artist. By staying here, you will inhabit a unique work of art. In the lobby and the salon, you will find a series of paintings and sculptures, which go on right down to the beach (if the local government hasn't removed them). The art may not be to everyone's taste, but this hotel does fulfill all the criteria of a good hotel: It has comfort, good service, and a fine restaurant where you will enjoy Sicilian specialties and the hotel's fine fish dishes. Visits to the rooms are limited to hotel guests.

How to get there *(Map 28): 90 km east of Palerme; via A20 to Cefalù then along the coast towards Messina.*

San Domenico Palace Hotel ★★★★★

Piazza San Domenico, 5
96039 Taormina (Messina)
Tel. (0942) 23 701 - Fax (0942) 62 55 06
Sig. Menta

Rooms 111 with telephone, bath or shower, WC, cable TV and minibar. **Price** Double 400-620,000L. **Meals** Breakfast included, served 8:00-10:00; half board 290-400,000L, full board 370-480,000L. (per pers., 3 days min.). **Restaurant** Service 12:00-14:30, 20:00-22:30, menu 100,000L, also à la carte. Specialties: Sicialian and Italian cuisine. **Credit cards** All major. **Pets** Dogs allowed in room. **Facilities** Swimming pool, parking (30,000L). **Nearby** In Taormina: Greek Theater; Castello San Pancrazio, Castelmola (panorama from Cafe S. Giorgio), Forza d'Agro, Alcantara, Capo Schiso, Mazzaro beach, Messina. **Open** All year.

The San Domenico Palace, formerly a monastery built in 1430, is no doubt the most beautiful hotel in Sicily. It is frequented by a rich international clientele and some top-notch tour operators. To get to the marvelous garden, meticulously kept and flowering year-round, you walk through a cloister and numerous, long hallways decorated with 17th- and 18th-century paintings, which lead to luxurious rooms resembling monk's cells from the outside. You will spend dreamlike days next to the swimming pool, from which you can enjoy the view of the Greek theater, the sea, and Mount Etna. A dinner by candlelight on the terrace will prove that the San Domenico also has the finest restaurant in Taormina.

How to get there *(Map 28): 52 km south of Messina via A18 Taormina-North exit; near the belvedere of the via Roma.*

Hotel Villa Sant'Andrea ★★★★

Via Nazionale, 137
98030 Mazzaro - Taormina (Messina)
Tel. (0942) 23 125 - Fax (0942) 24 838
Sig. Rizzo

Rooms 67 with air conditioning, telephone, bath or shower, WC and TV. **Price** Single 185-330,000L, double 145-250,000L. **Meals** Breakfast included (buffet), served 7:30-10:00; half board 190-295,000L, full board 220-325,000L. (per pers.). **Restaurant** Service 13:00-14:30, 20:00-22:30, menu 65,000L, also à la carte. Specialties: Tagliolini con scampi e pesto, spigoletta creazione «Oliviero», parfait alle mandorle. **Credit cards** All major. **Pets** Dogs not allowed. **Facilities** Privated beach, parking (20,000L). **Nearby** In Taormina: Greek Theater; Castello San Pancrazio, Castelmola (panorama from Cafe S. Giorgio), Forza d'Agro, Alcantara, Capo Schiso, Mazzaro beach, Messina. **Open** All year.

Take full advantage of your stay in Taormina without suffering from its shortcomings by staying at the Villa Sant'Andrea. Located right on the water, away from streets crowded with tourists yet only five minutes from the village by cable-car, this hotel has resisted the temptation of becoming, a meeting place for tourist buses, in like its neighbors in Mazzaro. Your tranquility is guaranteed in this villa dating from the 50's, where the rooms (most of which are on the sea), the restaurants, the private beach, and the bar on the terrace are laid out with as much taste as discretion.

How to get there (Map 28): *52 km south of Messina via A18, Taormina-North exit - the hotel is 5,5 km north of Taormina, along the coast.*

Hotel Villa Belvedere ★★★

Via Bagnoli Croci, 79
98039 Taormina (Messina)
Tel. (0942) 237 91 – Fax (0942) 62 58 30
Sig. Pecaut

Rooms 51 (some with air-cond.), telephone, bath or shower and WC. **Price** Single 79-144,000L, double 128-225,000L. **Meals** Breakfast included, served 7:00-12:00; snack from April to Oct., service 11:30-18:00. **Restaurant** See p. 421. **Credit cards** Visa, Eurocard and MasterCard. **Pets** Dogs allowed. **Facilities** Swimming pool, parking (6,000L). **Nearby** In Taormina: Greek Theater; Castello San Pancrazio, Castelmola (panorama from Cafe S. Giorgio), Forza d'Agro, Alcantara, Capo Schiso, Mazzaro beach, Messina. **Open** 1 week before Easter – Oct.

The discreet Hotel Belvedere stands very close to the enchanting public garden of Taormina. Unlike most of the hotels of Taotmina which suffer from frenetic delusions of grandeur, the Belvedere has remained simple, comfortable and charming. It is remarkably managed by its French director, and who runs it according to three rules which have made is so popular among its clientele of artists and regulars: cleanliness, comfort, and silence. Five new very pretty rooms have been opened, with large balconies with a view of the sea. You couldn't ask for more, but the view on the Bay of Taormina and a beautiful swimming pool under the giant palm trees give it additional allure which, fortunately, you won't see in the final bill.

How to get there : (Map 28) 52 km south of Messina via A 18, Taormina-North exit - the hotel is next to the belvedere of the via Roma.

Hotel Villa Ducale ★★★

Via Leonardo da Vinci, 60
96039 Taormina (Messina)
Tel. (0942) 28 153 – Fax (0942) 28 710
Sig. and Sig.ra Quartucci

Rooms 10 with air-conditioning, telephone, bath or shower, WC, TV, hairdrayer, safe and minibar. **Price** Single 130-180,000L, double 210-250,000L. **Meals** Breakfast included, served 8:00-12:00. **Restaurant** See p. 421. **Credit cards** Amex, Visa, Eurocard, MasterCard. **Pets** Small dogs allowed. **Facilities** Parking, sauna, tennis, gym, swimming pool. **Nearby** Greek Theater, Castello San Pancrazio, Castelmola (panorama from Cafe S. Giorgio), Forza d'Agro, Alcantara, Capo Schiso, Mazzaro beach, Messina. **Open** Feb. 21 – Jan. 9.

The patrician Villa Ducale is a very comfortable and elegant hotel, built by the great grandfather of the current owners at the beginning of the century. The rooms, carefully decorated and furnished with antiques, are all different, but all have an incredible view of the sea, Etna and the valley. The ones on the third floor have a pleasant terrace with a table and lounge chairs. A very interesting library provides reading material on Sicily and its history; you can also play chess there. Don't miss the delicious breakfasts–served on the terrace–of Viennese pastries, jelly and honey from Etna, fresh fruit juice and other local products. The staffis very friendly.

How to get there *(Map 28): 52 km south of Messina via A18, Taormina-North exit.*

Club il Gattopardo

Isola di Lampedusa (Agrigento)
Tel. (0922) 97 00 51 – Reservation (011) 88 091 – 0922) 971 645

Rooms 11 and 2 suites with telephone, bath and WC. **Price** With full board
850,000-2,300,000L (per pers. for 1 week with car and boat rental included).
Restaurant Service 13:00 and 20:30; menu, also à la carte. Specialties: Sicilian
cuisine, seafood. **Credit card** Amex. **Pets** Dogs not allowed. **Nearby** Lampedusa
island. **Open** June – mid-Oct.

Lampedusa, the largest of the Pelagien Islands, which are scattered
between the coasts of Sicily and Tunisia, was inhabited in the
Bronze Age, then deserted from antiquity until 1843. Roberto and his
French wife Annette opened this hotel-club because Roberto, who
loves scuba diving, wanted to become better acquainted with this still
unspoiled island. Here, the word "club" takes on an intimate
connotation, as Il Gattopardo has only thirteen rooms. In the purest
architectural tradition of the island, the ochre stone and white domes
blend perfectly with the coast and the sea nearby. The rooms are
decorated in a Mediterranean style and are very comfortable. Everything
is organized to take full advantage of the sea: You will have two boats
(fishing and motor) at your disposal, as well as three camels, which will
allow you to explore the island. In the evening, you can enjoy the chef's
cuisine, and in the morning, the delicious breakfasts prepared by
Annette. In May and June, sea turtles come to Lampedusa to lay their
eggs on the beaches at night. The best time to visit is in September and
October, when the water is warm and the sky full of birds migrating
towards Africa. Children under 18 are not accepted at this hotel.

How to get there *(Map 27): From Palermo by plane (30 min.).*
Lampedusa Airport, tel. (39 922) 97 02 99.

Hotel Carasco ★★★

Isole Eolie o Lipari
Porto delle Genti
98055 Lipari (Messina)
Tel. (090) 981 16 05 - Fax (090) 981 18 28
Sig. Marco del Bono

Rooms 98 with telephone, bath or shower and WC. **Price** With half board 85-170,000L, full board 100-185,000L (per pers.). **Meals** Breakfast included, served 7:30-9:30. **Restaurant** Service 12:30-14:00, 20:00-21:30; à la carte. Specialties: Sicilian cuisine. **Credit cards** All major. **Pets** Dogs not allowed. **Facilities** Swimming pool, parking. **Nearby** Aeolian museum in Lipari, Canneto, Acquacalda, Puntazze (view), Ovattropani, Piano Conte, Quattrocchi. **Open** Apr. – Oct.

The Hotel Carasco, run by an Anglo-Italian couple, offers all the comfort of a grand hotel. The rooms are very large and most of them have a terrace with a view of the sea. There is a beach right at the foot of the hotel. Lipari is the biggest and most visited island of the archipelago.

How to get there *(Map 28): Hydrofoil service from Messina all year; from Napoli, Reggio, Cefalù and Palermo June-Sept.; car ferry service from Messina, Napoli and Milazzo (50 min-2 hrs).*

Hotel Rocce Azzurre ★★★

Isole Eolie o Lipari
Porto delle Genti, 69
98055 Lipari (Messina)
Tel. (090) 981 15 82 - Fax (090) 981 24 56
Sig.ra Casamento

Rooms 33 with telephone, bath or shower and WC. **Price** 70-90,000L.
Meals Breakfast included, served 8:00-9:30; half board 90-150,000L, full board
110-180,000L (per pers.). **Restaurant** Service 12:30-14:00, 20:00-21:30, à la
carte. Specialties: Sicilian cuisine. **Credit cards** All major. **Pets** Dogs allowed.
Nearby Aeolian museum in Lipari, Canneto, Acquacalda, Puntazze (view),
Ovattropani, Piano Conte, Quattrocchi. **Open** Apr. 8 – Oct. 15.

At the far end of a vast, pebble beach you will find the Rocce
Azzurre. Rooms are simple but comfortable; make sure to
ask for one overlooking the sea. The entire hotel has been
tastefully furnished. The terrace, where meals are served, is filled
with beautiful flowers. Sicilian cuisine is a specialty of the house.
There is no swimming pool, but the hotel does have direct
access to the sea via a special pontoon.

How to get there *(Map 28): Hydrofoil service from Messina all year; from*
Napoli, Reggio, Cefalù and Palermo June-Sept.; car ferry service from
Messina, Napoli and Milazzo (50 min-2 hrs).

Hotel Villa Augustus ★★★

Isole Eolie o Lipari
Vico Ausonia, 16
98055 Lipari (Messina)
Tel. (090) 981 12 32 – Fax (090) 981 22 33
Sig. D'Albora

Rooms 35 with telephone, bath or shower and WC. **Price** Single 50-130,000L, double 70-190,000L, suite 250,000L. **Meals** Breakfast 10-20,000L, served 7:00-11:.30; half board 100-150,000L (per pers.). **Restaurant** See p. 422. **Credit cards** Visa, Eurocard, MasterCard. **Pets** Dogs allowed. **Facilities** Parking. **Nearby** Aeolian museum in Lipari, Canneto, Acquacalda, Puntazze (view), Ovattropani, Piano Conte, Quattrocchi. **Open** Mar. – Oct.

The Augustus is in an old family villa built in 1950, located on a side street in the historical center of Lipari. We like this hotel for its simplicity, its garden, and its relatively spacious and comfortable rooms. Each one has a balcony or a terrace and a view of either the sea or the Lipari castle. It is more of a boarding house than a luxury hotel, but is nonetheless one of the more pleasant hotels in town. Although there is no hotel restaurant, there are several fine restaurants in the area where you can have lunch or dinner.

How to get there *(Map 28): Hydrofoil service from Messina all year; from Napoli, Reggio, Cefalù and Palermo June-Sept.; car ferry service from Messina, Napoli and Milazzo (50 min-2 hrs).*

Hotel Villa Meligunis ★★★★

Isole Eolie o Lipari
Via Marte, 8
98055 Lipari (Messina)
Tel. (090) 98 12 426 - Fax (090) 98 80 149
Sig. D'Ambra

Rooms 32 with air-conditioning, telephone, bath or shower, WC, cable TV and minibar. **Price** Single 140-225,000L, double 180-300,000L, suite 50,000L. **Meals** Breakfast included, half board 125-195,000L, full board 150-230,000L (per pers.). **Restaurant** Service 12:30-14:00, 20:30-23:00; menus: 30-55,000L, also à la carte. Specialties: regional cooking, fish. **Credit cards** All major. **Pets** Small dogs allowed. **Nearby** Aeolian museum in Lipari, Canneto, Acquacalda, Puntazze (view), Ovattropani, Piano Conte, Quattrocchi. **Open** All year.

The Aeolian Islands are one of the few remaining Mediterranean paradises which are still relatively unspoiled. The director of the Villa Meligunis has opened this hotel in hopes of attracting people from northern Europe in winter. The name Meligunis is meaningful and appropriate: It is the ancient Greek name for Lipari and means "gentleness." You will find this in the climate, the wine and the color of the sea. The hotel is in an old house, to which more modern Mediterranean-style buildings have been added. There is a large terrace overlooking the sea. The rooms, which have every comfort, are spacious and simply decorated. The restaurant serves local cuisine and features mainly fish dishes.

How to get there *(Map 28): Hydrofoil service from Messina all year; from Napoli, Reggio, Cefalù and Palermo June-Sept.; car ferry service from Messina, Napoli and Milazzo (50 min-2 hrs).*

Hotel Raya ★★★★

Isole Eolie o Lipari
San Pietro – 98050 Isola Panarea (Messina)
Tel. (090) 98 30 13 – Fax (090) 98 31 03
Sig.ra Beltrami and Sig. Tilche

Rooms 32 with air-conditioning, telephone, bath or shower, WC, cable TV and minibar. **Price** With half board 135-230,000L, full board 265-440,000L. **Meals** Breakfast 25,000L, served 8:00-11:30. **Restaurant** Service 20:30-24:00; menu 50,000L. Specialties: Mediterranean cuisine, Sicilian pastries. **Credit cards** All major. **Pets** Small dogs allowed. **Nearby** Bronze Age village at Capo Milazzese, Basiluzzo. **Open** Apr. 25 – Oct. 15.

It is surprising on this little Sicilian island to find a very trendy hotel–considered a local institution. It was built twenty years ago and consists of a series of pink and white bungalows which extend from the heights of the village down to the sea. Its Mediterranean architecture is ideal for its clean and modern interior decorated with beautiful, primitive art objects from Polynesia, Africa and the Orient. The lounges and all rooms overlook the sea. Each one has a terrace with a view of the windy archipelago. There is an open-air restaurant and a bar which overlook the port. The guests are mostly regulars and the hotel staff is hip. Young children are not allowed.

How to get there *(Map 28): Hydrofoil service from Milazzo and Napoli. No cars allowed on the island.*

Hotel L'Ariana ★★

Isole Eolie o Lipari
Rinella di Leni - Rotabile, 11
98050 Isola Salina (Messina)
Tel. (090) 980 90 75 - Fax (090) 980 9250
Sig.ra Lopez

Rooms 15 with telephone, bath or shower, WC and minibar. **Price** With half board 80-140,000L, full board 100-160,000L (per pers. 3 days min.). **Meals** Breakfast included, served 8:00-10:00. **Restaurant** Service 13:00-14:30, 20:00-22:00; closed Nov.– Feb.; menu: 25-50,000L, also à la carte. Specialties: Seafood, malvasia, lasagne all'eoliana. **Credit cards** All major. **Pets** Dogs not allowed. **Nearby** Excursions to the Mt. Fossa delle Felci, Malfa, Leni and Rinella. **Open** All year.

The Ariana, in an old villa in the village of Rinella, is one of the most pleasant hotels on the island. In summer, meals are served on the terrace facing the sea. Certain rooms also have this beautiful view. The warm, simple atmosphere and the attractive setting are very enjoyable. Stay here for a week off-season and you can have an extra day for free.

How to get there *(Map 28): Hydrofoil service and car ferries from Milazzo and Napoli; (3.5 km south of Malfa).*

Hotel La Sciara Residence ★★★

Isole Eolie o Lipari
98050 Isola Stromboli (Messina)
Tel. (090) 98 60 05 / 98 61 21 – Fax (090) 98 62 84
Famiglia d'Eufemia and Sig.ra Raffaelli

Rooms 62 with air-conditioning, telephone, bath or shower and WC. **Price** With half board 100-215,000L, (per pers., 7 day min. in high season). **Meals** Breakfast included, served 7:30-10:00. **Restaurant** Service 13:00-14:30, 20:00-22:00; menu: 25-50,000L, also à la carte. Specialties: Seafood, malvasia, lasagne all'eoliana. **Credit cards** All major. **Pets** Small dogs allowed. **Facilities** Swimming pool, tennis, private beach. **Nearby** The volcano, Sciara del Fuoco, Strombolicchio, Ginostra. **Open** May 18 – Sept.

Stromboli is a place to see, even if it's just for the Hotel La Sciara. The garden is splendid and filled with flowers–mostly fuchsia, pink and orange bougainvillea–which testify to the exceptional quality of the fertile volcanic soil. The rooms are spacious, comfortable and filled with antique furniture and objects of diverse origin, selected by the owner. In addition to the hotel, there are five old restored houses you can stay in, each with several rooms, one or two bathrooms, and a kitchenette. They overlook the sea and offer some hotel services.

How to get there *(Map 28): Hydrofoil service from Milazzo and Napoli. No cars allowed on island.*

Les Sables Noirs ★★★★

Isole Eolie o Lipari
Porto Ponente - 98050 Isola Vulcano (Messina)
Tel. (090) 98 50 - Fax (090) 98 52 454
Sig. Elio Curatolo

Rooms 48 with air-conditioning, telephone, bath or shower, TV, minibar and 18 with WC. **Price** With half board 145-230,000L, full board 175-230,000L (per pers. 3 days min.). **Meals** Breakfast included, served 7:00-10:00. **Restaurant** Service 13:00-15:00, 20:00-23:00; menu: 65,000L, also à la carte. Specialties: Mediterranean cuisine, seafood. **Credit cards** All major. **Pets** Small dogs allowed. **Facilities** Swimming pool, tennis, bike, private beach, parking. **Nearby** Access to the volcano's crater. **Open** June – Sept.

The white houses of Porto Ponente are spread out along the black sand beaches at the foot of the Piana volcano. One of them is the Hotel La Scaria Residence. It has been recently renovated, and is now a comfortable luxury hotel with four-star service. You will find both heaven and hell on this Aeolian island dedicated to the Roman god–Vulcan and the farthest south in the Lipari archipelago. Hell is near the large 500-meter crater continually belching up ash, steam, smoke and gas. Heaven is the verdant surroundings of the volcano and the coast, with its mysterious hidden grottos, inlets, beaches and transparent turquoise water. The biggest tourist attraction is, however, the large crater, which puts on a show unique to the archipelago, the coasts of Sicily and Etna.

How to get there *(Map 28): Hydrofoil services from Milazzo and Napoli. Cars subject to restrictions.*

Albergo San Michele ★★★★

Via Guelfa, 15
52044 Cortona (Arezzo)
Tel. (0575) 60 43 48 – Fax (0575) 63 01 47
Dott. Alunno

Rooms 40 (15 with air-conditioning) with telephone, bath or shower, WC, TV and 10 with minibar. **Price** Single 110,000L, double 150,000L, suite 170,000L, triple 180,000L, for 4 pers. 210,000L. **Meals** Breakfast included, served 7:30-10:30. **Restaurant** See p. 429. **Credit cards** All major. **Pets** Dogs not allowed. **Facilities** Swimming pool in casa Barbieri, tennis (5,000L), parking, garage (20,000L). **Nearby** Cortona (Church of Madonna del Calcinaio, Museo dell' Accademia Etrusca), Arezzo, Val di Chiana (Farneta abbey, Lucignano, Sinalunga), Trasimeno lake, Perugia. **Open** Mar. – Dec.

The Albergo San Michele is in an old palace dating from the Renaissance era, a period which has left its mark elsewhere on the town, notably the Church of the Madonna del Calcino. It has been restored with intelligence and simplicity, and offers very comfortable, pleasantly decorated rooms. The nicest have sloping ceilings and the most spacious have a mezzanine. You can expect a friendly welcome here. This is an ideal place to stay if you are traveling in Tuscany, or want to explore often neglected parts of Umbria.

How to get there *(Map 15): 28 km south of Arezzo via SS71.*

Relais Il Falconiere ★★★★

San Martino a Bolena 52044 Cortona (Arezzo)
Tel. (0575) 61 26 79 – Fax (0575) 61 29 27
Silvia and Riccardo Baracchi

Rooms 12 with air conditioning, telephone, bath or shower, WC, TV, minibar, elevator. **Price** Double 240,000L, suite 400,000L. **Meals** Breakfast included, served 7:00-10:00; half board 160,000L (per pers., 3 days min.). **Restaurant** Service 13:00-14:00, 20:00-22:00; closed Wed.; also à la carte. Specialties: Filetto cinghiale, budino di panna e formaggio con salsa de pere, tortino di cipollotti con fonduta di raviggiolo, pici alla cortenese, zuppa di fava e orzo, gnocchi alla ricottarombo con crema di asparagi, sfogliatina di mele e pinolo con cioccolato caldo. **Credit cards** All major. **Pets** Dogs not allowed. **Facilities** Swimming pool, parking. **Nearby** Cortona (Church of Madonna del Calcinaio, Museo dell'Accademia Etrusca), Arezzo, Val di Chiana (Farneta abbey, Lucignano, Sinalunga), Trasimeno lake, Perugia. **Open** All year.

This magnificent 17th century villa stands on a hill covered with olive trees and vineyards, facing Cortona. This family house, transformed into a hotel now, has kept all of the charm and polished luxury of the old days. The spacious, quiet rooms have beautiful classical furniture. Comfort and refinement pervade the hotel, creating a feeling of real well-being. We suggest, apart from the three garden-level suites (with pool-jacuzzis), the pretty little attic room from which you can see the majestic contours of the Etruscan town. And should you be inspired by "The Annunciation" by Fra' Angelico in the Diocese museum, there is a private chapel painted with frescoes at your disposal in the hotel garden.

How to get there *(Map 15): 28 km south of Arezzo via SS71. 3 km north of Cortona.*

Castello di Gargonza ★

Gargonza
52048 Monte San Savino (Arezzo)
Tel. (0575) 84 70 21 – Fax (0575) 84 70 54
Sig. Fucini

Rooms 40 with telephone, bath or shower and WC. **Price** Single 160-230,000L, apartment 673-1,952,000L (for 1 week). **Meals** Breakfast included, served 8:00-10:00; half board 110-135,000L, (per pers., 3 nights min.). **Restaurant** Service 12:30-14:30, 19:30-21:30, closed Tues.; menus: 33-40,000L. Specialties: Ribollita, tagliatelle, arrosto in porchetta. **Credit cards** All major. **Pets** Dogs allowed (fee). **Nearby** Monte San Savino (Loggia dei Mercanti, Church and Palazzo of Monte San Savino), Convent of San Fracesco in La Verna and La Penna (1,283 m), Arezzo. **Open** Apr. – Jan. 9.

Count Guicciardini, who owns the castle, has restored this abandoned village on the top of a wooded hill about twelve miles (20 km) from Arezzo and set up residences there. The small stone houses are very comfortable and some have kitchens. You can also rent apartments by the week. The view of the surrounding countryside is magnificent.

How to get there (Map 15): 29 km southwest of Arezzo via S73 to Monte San Savino, then right towards Gargonza.

Hotel Helvetia & Bristol ★★★★★

Via dei Pescioni, 2
50123 Firenze
Tel. (055) 28 78 14 – Fax (055) 28 83 53
Sig. Ensoli

Rooms 52 with air-conditioning, telephone, bath or shower, WC and cable TV.
Price Single 325-363,000L, double 435-545,000L, suite 693-1,430,000L.
Meals Breakfast 31-50,000L, served 7:00-10:30. **Restaurant** Service 12:30-14:30,
19:30-22:00; menus: 80-120,000L. Specialties: Mediterranean cuisine and old
Tuscan recipes. **Credit cards** All major. **Pets** Dogs not allowed. **Nearby** Firenze
(Baptistery, Duomo, Academy Gallery, the Medici chapels, Uffizi Gallery, Piazza
della Signoria, Sta Maria del Carmine, Pitti Palace, Boboli Gardens), Fiesole,
Certosa di Galluzzo, Villas and gardens around Firenze (tel. Palais Pitti: 055 21 48
56), Vallombrosa abbey, dell'Ugolino golf course (18-hole) in Grassina. **Open** All
year.

The Helvetia & Bristol is incontestably one of the best hotels of
this category in Firenze: everything here is perfect and tasteful.
This large, beautiful residence, once the meeting place of the
Tuscan intellegentsia, has now regained its former prestige. The
main salon sets the tone, a blend of British-style comfort and Italian
luxury.* Pretty old Indian calico fabrics add color to the small, very
elegant dining room. The bar on the veranda has the charm of a
winter garden. The exquisite rooms have beautiful fabric-covered
walls, comfortable beds and marble bathrooms with whirlpools.
The personnel is like the hotel–high class but irresistibly friendly
and Italian.

How to get there *(Map 14): Next to Piazza della Repubblica, via
Strozzi, via dei Pescioni.*

211

Hotel Regency ★★★★★

50121 Firenze
Piazza Massimo d'Azeglio, 3
Tel. (055) 24 52 47 – Fax (055) 23 46 735
Sig. Panelli

Rooms 35 with telephone, bath or shower, WC, TV, safe and minibar. **Price** Single 295-370,000L, double 360-550,000L. **Meals** Breakfast included. **Restaurant** Service 12:30-14:30, 19:30-22:30, à la carte. Specialties: Tuscan and Italian cuisine. **Credit cards** All major. **Pets** Dogs not allowed. **Nearby** Firenze (Baptistery, Duomo, Academy Gallery, the Medici chapels, Uffizi Gallery, Piazza della Signoria, Sta Maria del Carmine, Pitti Palace, Boboli Gardens), Fiesole, Certosa di Galluzzo, Villas and gardens around Firenze (tel. Palais Pitti: 055 21 48 56), Vallombrosa abbey, dell'Ugolino golf course (18-hole) in Grassina. **Open** All year.

Modern comfort and old fashioned hospitality is the motto of the owner of the Hotel Regency, Amedo Ottaviani. On the Piazza d'Azeglio, the Regency is a villa which used to belong to Florentine nobles. The almost English comfort of the rooms and the salons characterizes this place, as does the excellent cuisine served in a paneled dining room and the large glass wall opening onto the gardens. You will fined great elegance here, down to the last details. One practical note: It is easy to park on the square and the streets nearby.

How to get there *(Map 14): Next to Santa Croce by the via Borgo Pinti.*

Grand Hotel Villa Cora ★★★★★

Viale Machiavelli, 18–20
50125 Firenze
Tel. (055) 22 98 451 – Fax (055) 22 90 86
Sig. Zaccardi

Rooms 48 with telephone, bath or shower, WC, TV and minibar. **Price** Single 280-380,000L, double 400-600,000L, suite 760-1,200,000L. **Meals** Breakfast 24,000L, served 7:00-11:00; half board 65,000L, full board 130,000L. **Restaurant** Service 12:00-15:00, 19:30-23:00, à la carte. Specialties: Tuscan and Italian cuisine. **Credit cards** All major. **Pets** Dogs not allowed. **Facilities** Swimming pool, parking. **Nearby** Firenze (Baptistery, Duomo, Academy Gallery, the Medici chapels, Uffizi Gallery, Piazza della Signoria, Sta Maria del Carmine, Pitti Palace, Boboli Gardens), Fiesole, Certosa di Galluzzo, Villas and gardens around Firenze (tel. Palais Pitti: 055 21 48 56), Vallombrosa abbey, dell'Ugolino golf course (18-hole) in Grassina. **Open** All year.

Built in a pure Neo-Classical style in 1865 by Baron Oppenheim, the Villa Cora has belonged to the Empress Eugenia, and also to Baron Van Meck, Tchaikovsky's patron. It is located in a residential quarter, five minutes from the center of town, in a very pretty garden. The lobby and the salons are sumptuous, but their elegant decor shuns all heaviness. Dining under the dome of what used to be the Arab salon will give you the amusing impression of having excellent Italian food in a Morrocan palace. The rooms are tastefully furnished and very comfortable. We prefer the more modest (and less expensive) ones on the top floor, which open onto a terrace overlooking Firenze and the surrounding gardens. You can use the hotel shuttle bus to go back and forth to the center of town.

How to get there *(Map 14): Towards Forte Belvedere, Porta Romana.*

Hotel Brunelleschi ★★★★

50122 Firenze
Piazza S. Elisabetta, 3
Tel. (055) 56 20 68 – Fax (055) 21 96 53
Sig. Litta

Rooms 96 with air-conditioning, telephone, bath or shower, WC, TV and minibar.
Price Single 320,000L, double 450,000L, suite 700,000L. **Meals** Breakfast
included, served 7:00-10:00; half board +75,000L, full board +120,000L.
Restaurant Service 12:00-14:00, 19:30-22:00; menus, also à la carte. Specialties
Florentine and international cuisine. **Credit cards** All major. **Pets** Dogs allowed.
Facilities Swimming pool, parking (50,000L). **Nearby** Firenze (Baptistery, Duomo,
Academy Gallery, the Medici chapels, Uffizi Gallery, Piazza della Signoria, Sta
Maria del Carmine, Pitti Palace, Boboli Gardens), Fiesole, Certosa di Galluzzo,
Villas and gardens around Firenze (tel. Palais Pitti: 055 21 48 56), Vallombrosa
abbey, dell'Ugolino golf course (18-hole) in Grassina. **Open** All year.

The hotel was designed by Italo Gamberini, a renowned Italian
architect, and set up in a 5th-century Byzantine tower and
several adjoining houses, in the Duomo quarter. The decor is
modern with some Art Nouveau details. There is a lot of ceruse
wood, which goes nicely with the bricks in the tower and
throughout the hotel. The quiet rooms all overlook pedestrian
streets. The prettiest ones are on the fourth floor and have a view of
the Duomo and the tower. The hotel terrace is the perfect place to
watch spectacular sunsets over Firenze. This hotel, with a famous
restaurant, feels like a grand hotel.

How to get there *(Map 14): Near the Duomo.*

Hotel J & J ★★★★

Via di Mezzo, 20
50121 Firenze
Tel. (055) 234 50 05 – Fax (055) 24 02 82
Sig. Cavagnari

Rooms 20 with air-conditioning, telephone, bath or shower, WC, cable TV and minibar. **Price** Single 270,000L, double 330-375,000L, suite 450-500,000L. **Meals** Breakfast included, served 7:30-10:30. **Restaurant** See pp.422-425. **Credit cards** All major. **Pets** Dogs allowed (fee). **Facilities** Public parking (25,000L). **Nearby** Firenze (Baptistery, Duomo, Academy Gallery, the Medici chapels, Uffizi Gallery, Piazza della Signoria, Sta Maria del Carmine, Pitti Palace, Boboli Gardens), Fiesole, Certosa di Galluzzo, Villas and gardens around Firenze (tel. Palais Pitti: 055 21 48 56), Vallombrosa abbey, dell'Ugolino golf course (18-hole) in Grassina. **Open** All year.

Nicely located in the old quarter of Santa Croce, very close to the Duomo and the center of town, this hotel is in a 16th-century palace. Vestiges of that era, such as the cloister, the vaulted ceilings, and the frescos, have been preserved and restored. The rooms have simple, contemporary decor. Some are very large and can accomodate three or four people, and all have living rooms. There can be surprises, such as the bathtub in Room 9, but the decoration is so well done that these flights of fancy do not at all detract from the atmosphere. The hotel has no elevator and the stairs to the upper floors are a bit narrow.

How to get there (*Map 14*): *Near Santa Croce by the via Borgo Pinti.*

Hotel Monna Lisa ★★★★

Via Borgo Pinti, 27
50121 Firenze
Tel. (055) 247 97 51 – Fax (055) 247 97 55
Sig. Cona

Rooms 30 with air-conditioning, telephone, bath or shower, WC, cable TV, safe and minibar. **Price** Single 190-250,000L, double 280-380,000L, suite 600,000L. **Meals** Breakfast included (buffet), served 7:30-10:00. **Restaurant** See pp. 422-425. **Credit cards** All major. **Pets** Dogs allowed. **Facilities** Parking (20,000L). **Nearby** Firenze (Baptistery, Duomo, Academy Gallery, the Medici chapels, Uffizi Gallery, Piazza della Signoria, Sta Maria del Carmine, Pitti Palace, Boboli Gardens), Fiesole, Certosa di Galluzzo, Villas and gardens around Firenze (tel. Palais Pitti: 055 21 48 56), Vallombrosa abbey, dell'Ugolino golf course (18-hole) in Grassina. **Open** All year.

This old palace conceals its treasures behind its tall facade. How nice it is staying in this small hotel with flowering gardens and elegant decor with period furniture, Florentine ceramic tile floors, frescoes and beautiful fabrics. Be careful, however, to clearly express your wishes when you make your reservation in high season, as you might find yourself in a less comfortable, out of the way room. Ask for the ones on the garden. The welcoming staff and the quiet add considerably to the charm of this luxury *pensione*, right in the middle of Firenze.

How to get there *(Map 14): Near the Duomo and Santa Croce by the via Borgo Pinti.*

Hotel Montebello Splendid ★★★★

Via Montebello, 60
50123 Firenze
Tel. (055) 239 8051 – Fax (055) 21 18 67
Sig. Lupi

Rooms 54 with air-conditioning, telephone, bath or shower, WC, TV, safe and minibar. **Price** Single 250-300,000L, double 330-410,000L, suite 560,000L. **Meals** Breakfast included, served 7:00-11:00; half board 48,000L, full board 85,000L (per pers., 3 days min.). **Restaurant** Service 13:00-15:00, 19:30-23:00, menus 50-90,000L, also à la carte. Specialties: Florentine and international cuisine. **Credit cards** All major. **Pets** Dogs allowed. **Nearby** Firenze (Baptistery, Duomo, Academy Gallery, the Medici chapels, Uffizi Gallery, Piazza della Signoria, Sta Maria del Carmine, Pitti Palace, Boboli Gardens), Fiesole, Certosa di Galluzzo, Villas and gardens around Firenze (tel. Palais Pitti: 055 21 48 56), Vallombrosa abbey, dell'Ugolino golf course (18-hole) in Grassina. **Open** All year.

This elegant hotel with refined, slightly Parisian decor is in an old 14th-century villa in the heart of Firenze. The reception area, salons and bar are imbued with a sophisticated atmosphere, with their marble mosaic columns and floors, stucco ceilings, large 1900-style couches and profusion of green plants. All the rooms are extremely comfortable and have marble bathrooms. The ones overlooking the garden are quieter. Breakfasts and meals are served in a nice garden-level greenhouse.

How to get there *(Map 14): In the village center Porta al Prato, near the teatro comunale.*

Torre di Bellosguardo ★★★★

Via Roti Michelozzi, 2
50124 Firenze
Tel. (055) 229 81 45 – Fax (055) 22 90 08
Sig. Franchetti

Rooms 16 with telephone, bath or shower and WC. **Price** Single 290,000L, double 390,000L, suite 490-590,000L. **Meals** Breakfast 25,000L, served 7:30-10:00. **Restaurant** Lunch by the swimming pool in summer (see pp. 422-425). **Credit cards** All major. **Pets** Dogs allowed. **Facilities** Swimming pool, parking. **Nearby** Firenze (Baptistery, Duomo, Academy Gallery, the Medici chapels, Uffizi Gallery, Piazza della Signoria, Sta Maria del Carmine, Pitti Palace, Boboli Gardens), Fiesole, Certosa di Galluzzo, Villas and gardens around Firenze (tel. Palais Pitti: 055 21 48 56), Vallombrosa abbey, dell'Ugolino golf course (18-hole) in Grassina. **Open** All year.

Torre di Bellosguardo is on a hill just outside the center of Firenze and has an exceptional view of the city. It is an extraordinarily quiet place with a majestic palace, a 7th-century tower, a lovely harmonious garden and a beautiful swimming pool down below. Today it is an elegant and comfortable hotel, with sixteen unusually large rooms, many salons and a spectacular sun room. Each room is unique and has period furniture, extraordinary woodwork, and frescoes. In the tower, there is a suite on two floors with a marvelous view. All rooms are superb and have comfortable bathrooms. This hotel offers an elegance which today seems reserved for the happy few.

How to get there (Map 14): Towards Forte Belvedere, Porta Romana.

Villa Belvedere ★★★★

Via Benedetto Castelli, 3
50124 Firenze
Tel. (055) 22 25 01 - Fax (055) 22 31 63
Sig. and Sig.ra Ceschi - Perotto

Rooms 26 with air-conditioning, telephone, bath or shower, WC, cable TV, safe and minibar. **Price** Single 180-220,000L, double 250-290,000L. **Meals** Breakfast included, served 7:15-10:00. **Restaurant** Snack service for lunch and dinner (see pp. 422-425). **Credit cards** All major. **Pets** Dogs not allowed. **Facilities** Swimming pool, tennis, parking (50,000L). **Nearby** Firenze (Baptistery, Duomo, Academy Gallery, the Medici chapels, Uffizi Gallery, Piazza della Signoria, Sta Maria del Carmine, Pitti Palace, Boboli Gardens), Fiesole, Certosa di Galluzzo, Villas and gardens around Firenze (tel. Palais Pitti: 055 21 48 56), Vallombrosa abbey, dell'Ugolino golf course (18-hole) in Grassina. **Open** Mar. – Nov.

The Villa Belvedere is in the heights of Firenze, surrounded by a large quiet garden with a swimming pool and a tennis court. You will appreciate this place if you are traveling with children. The modern veranda, which has been added to the house, detracts a bit from its charm. The rooms have been entirely renovated and are all spacious and comfortable. Most have a superb view of Firenze, the countryside or the Certosa. The ones in the front have large terraces and the nicest are on the top floor. There's no restaurant, but if you are too tired to go out, snacks are available. The Ceschi family extends the warmest of welcomes.

How to get there *(Map 14): Towards Forte Belvedere - Porta Romana.*

Villa Carlotta ★★★★

50125 Firenze
Via Michele di Lando, 3
Tel. (055) 233 61 34 – Fax (055) 233 61 47
Sig. Gheri

Rooms 27 with air-conditioning, telephone, bath or shower, WC, TV and minibar.
Price Single 125-250,000L, double 175-350,000L. **Meals** Breakfast included,
served 7:00-10:30; half board 150-225,000L, full board 180-265,000L.
Restaurant Service 12:30-14:30, 19:30-21:00, closed Sun., à la carte. Specialties:
Tuscan and Italian cuisine. **Credit cards** All major. **Pets** Dogs allowed.
Facilities Parking. **Nearby** Firenze (Baptistery, Duomo, Academy Gallery, the
Medici chapels, Uffizi Gallery, Piazza della Signoria, Sta Maria del Carmine, Pitti
Palace, Boboli Gardens), Fiesole, Certosa di Galluzzo, Villas and gardens around
Firenze (tel. Palais Pitti: 055 21 48 56), Vallombrosa abbey, dell'Ugolino golf
course (18-hole) in Grassina. **Open** All year.

Close to the Palazzo Pitti and the Boboli Gardens, the Villa
Carlotta is an old patrician villa which has retained its nice
proportions and harmony. Large bow windows in the salons
open onto an inviting garden. The rooms are carefully
decorated–without surprises–and offer all the amenities you
might want.

How to get there *(Map 14): Towards Forte Belvedere - Porta Romana.*

Hotel Hermitage ★★★

Piazza del Pesce – Vicolo Marzio, 1 (Ponte Vecchio)
50122 Firenze
Tel. (055) 28 72 16 – Fax (055) 21 22 08
Sig. Scarcelli

Rooms 29 with air-conditioning, telephone, bath or shower, WC and cable TV.
Price Single 180,000L, double 260,000L. **Meals** Breakfast included, served 7:30-
9:30. **Restaurant** See pp. 422-425. **Credit cards** Visa, Eurocard, MasterCard. **Pets**
Small dogs allowed. **Nearby** Firenze (Baptistery, Duomo, Academy Gallery, the
Medici chapels, Uffizi Gallery, Piazza della Signoria, Sta Maria del Carmine, Pitti
Palace, Boboli Gardens), Fiesole, Certosa di Galluzzo, Villas and gardens around
Firenze (tel. Palais Pitti: 055 21 48 56), Vallombrosa abbey, dell'Ugolino golf
course (18-hole) in Grassina. **Open** All year.

This small hotel takes up the entire building next to the Ponte
Vecchio. The rooms are comfortable; each one is done in a
slightly different antiquated style and all have double-pane
windows, which makes them pretty soundproof. The quietest
rooms are those on the courtyard, especially Rooms 13 and 14;
but now that the area has become a pedestrian zone, you may
sleep just as well on the streetside. What made us choose this hotel
was its good prices and its terrace with an unforgettable view of
the Ponte Vecchio and the Pitti Palace on one side and the dome
of the Duomo and the rooftops of the Signoria on the other. If
you are traveling alone, reserve the terrace-level room. It is hard
to park, but the hotel can direct you to the nearest garage.

How to get there *(Map 14): In the village center, next to Ponte Vecchio.*

Hotel Loggiato dei Serviti ★★★

Piazza della SS. Annunziata, 3
50122 Firenze
Tel. (055) 28 95 92 – Fax (055) 28 95 95
Sig. Budini Gattai

Rooms 25, and 4 apartments with air-conditioning, telephone, bath or shower, WC, TV and minibar. **Price** Single 180,000L, double 255,000L, suite 300-550,000L. **Meals** Breakfast included, served 7:15-10:00. **Credit cards** All major. **Pets** Dogs allowed (fee). **Nearby** Firenze (Baptistery, Duomo, Academy Gallery, the Medici chapels, Uffizi Gallery, Piazza della Signoria, Sta Maria del Carmine, Pitti Palace, Boboli Gardens), Fiesole, Certosa di Galluzzo, Villas and gardens around Firenze (tel. Palais Pitti: 055 21 48 56), Vallombrosa abbey, dell'Ugolino golf course (18-hole) in Grassina. **Open** All year.

One of our favorite's in Firenze, this hotel is on the Piazza della SS. Annunziata, just across from the Hospital of the Innocents. Like the hospital, it was designed by Brunelleschi, a brilliant architect of the Tuscan Rennaissance. The hotel decor is simple and elegant, respectful of the archictectural proportions of the period. The rooms are spare and charming; some open onto the square and have views of the equestrian statue of Ferdinand I of Médicis and the portico by Brunelleschi, embellished with medallions by Della Robbia. The other rooms open onto the Accamedia garden and are quieter. The ones on the top floor have a nice view of the Duomo. The square has been surprisingly protected from the hustle and bustle of tourists; no café terraces or souvenir shops disturb the peace and quiet at nightfall–only the sound of swallows playing under the portico arches can be heard.

How to get there *(Map 14): Near the Duomo.*

Pensione Annalena ★★★

Via Romana, 34
50125 Firenze
Tel. (055) 22 24 02
Fax (055) 22 24 03

Rooms 20 with telephone, bath or shower, WC and TV. **Price** Single 155,000L, double 240,000L. **Meals** Breakfast included, served 8:00-10:30. **Restaurant** See pp. 422-425. **Credit cards** All major. **Pets** Dogs allowed. **Facilities** Parking (20,000L). **Nearby** Firenze (Baptistery, Duomo, Academy Gallery, the Medici chapels, Uffizi Gallery, Piazza della Signoria, Sta Maria del Carmine, Pitti Palace, Boboli Gardens), Fiesole, Certosa di Galluzzo, Villas and gardens around Firenze (tel. Palais Pitti: 055 21 48 56), Vallombrosa abbey, dell'Ugolino golf course (18-hole) in Grassina. **Open** All year.

Nicely located near the Palazzo Pitti, this 15th-century palace is charged with history. Once the residence of the Orlandini and the Medici families, its become the property of the beautiful Annalena who, because of a tragic love, withdrew from the world and bequeathed her palace to the Dominicans. The old salon is now a vast foyer–where you can see fragments of wall frescoes–which opens onto several salons, a bar and a breakfast room. The rooms are decorated with old-fashioned furniture. Our favorites are those on the gallery overlooking the old palace gardens, which have become a nursery, and those opening onto the terrace.

How to get there (Map 14): Near Palazzo Pitti (Porta Romana).

Hotel Villa Azalee ★★★

Viale Fratelli Rosselli, 44
50123 Firenze
Tel. (055) 21 42 42/28 43 31 – Fax (055) 26 82 64
Sig.ra Brizzi

Rooms 24 with telephone, bath or shower, WC, TV and minibar. **Price** Single 145,000L, double 218,000L, triple 303,000L. **Meals** Breakfast included, served 7:30-12:00; half board 75,000L, full board 120,000L. **Restaurant** Service 12:00-14:00, 19:30-22:00, menus, also à la carte. Specialties: Florentine and international cuisine. **Credit cards** All major. **Pets** Small dogs allowed. **Facilities** Parking in the street or public parking (25,000L). **Nearby** Firenze (Baptistery, Duomo, Academy Gallery, the Medici chapels, Uffizi Gallery, Piazza della Signoria, Sta Maria del Carmine, Pitti Palace, Boboli Gardens), Fiesole, Certosa di Galluzzo, Villas and gardens around Firenze (tel. Palais Pitti: 055 21 48 56), Vallombrosa abbey, dell'Ugolino golf course (18-hole) in Grassina. **Open** All year.

The Villa Azalee is several yards from the Santa Maria Novella Station (the train station in Firenze) on a small road off the *viali des circonvallazione* (highway circling the town). The location may seem as if it would be noisy, but the restoration of the villa has ensured maximum quiet and comfort for guests. The rooms are not very big, but have been furnished with talent and style. They have modern furniture and amenities (such as air-conditioning), and beautiful decor, which recreates the atmosphere of a private Tuscan villa. Ask for the ones on the garden or the ones in the small outbuilding. Breakfast is served in the garden-level dining room.

How to get there *(Map 14): Near the railway station (stazione).*

224

Hotel Morandi Alla Crocetta ★★★

Via Laura, 50
50121 Firenze
Tel. (055) 234 47 47 – Fax (055) 281 807
Sig.ra Doyle Antuono

Rooms 10 with air-conditioning, telephone, shower, WC, TV and minibar.
Price Single 99,000L, double 179,000L, triple 209,000L. **Meals** Breakfast
16,000L, served 8:00-12:00. **Restaurant** See pp. 422-425. **Credit cards** All major.
Pets Small dogs allowed. **Nearby** Firenze (Baptistery, Duomo, Academy Gallery,
the Medici chapels, Uffizi Gallery, Piazza della Signoria, Sta Maria del Carmine,
Pitti Palace, Boboli Gardens), Fiesole, Certosa di Galluzzo, Villas and gardens
around Firenze (tel. Palais Pitti: 055 21 48 56), Vallombrosa abbey, dell'Ugolino
golf course (18-hole) in Grassina. **Open** All year.

The small, nice Hotel Morandi Alla Crocetta is run by the
equally nice Katherine Doyle who came to Firenze for the
first time many years ago when she was only 12. The *pensione*
occupies part of a monastery built during the Renaissance on a
small street near the Piazza della SS. Annunziata. The interior is
as comfortable as in Anglo-Saxon homes, and the rooms all have
bathrooms and air-conditioning. The decor is very tasteful; each
room has antique furniture and beautiful collector's items. Two
of them have a beautiful flower-covered terrace on a countryard.
The atmosphere of the hotel is quiet and serene.

How to get there *(Map 14): Near Piazza della SS. Annunziata.*

225

Hotel Pensione Pendini ★★★

Via Strozzi, 2
50123 Firenze
Tel. (055) 21 11 70 – Fax (055) 21 01 56
Sig.ri Abolaffio

Rooms 42 with air-conditioning, telephone, bath or shower, WC and TV.
Price Single 120-140,000L, double 170-200,000L. **Meals** Breakfast included,
served 7:30-10:00. **Restaurant** See pp. 422-425. **Credit cards** All major. **Pets**
Small dogs allowed. **Nearby** Firenze (Baptistery, Duomo, Academy Gallery, the
Medici chapels, Uffizi Gallery, Piazza della Signoria, Sta Maria del Carmine, Pitti
Palace, Boboli Gardens), Fiesole, Certosa di Galluzzo, Villas and gardens around
Firenze (tel. Palais Pitti: 055 21 48 56), Vallombrosa abbey, dell'Ugolino golf
course (18-hole) in Grassina. **Open** All year.

When you cross the large Piazza della Repubblica or stop
and have a drink on the terrace of the Gilli or the Giubbe
Rosse, you won't be able to keep from noticing the building
with the immense sign, which since 1879 has advertised the
pensione within. The entrance is on a side street and an elevator
will take you to the right floor. You will have an immediate
impression of comfort as you walk in, and you won't be
disappointed. All the rooms are large; avoid the ones on the
Piazza della Republica, which is outside of the pedestrian area.
This hotel is remarkable for its quality and low prices.

How to get there *(Map 14): Near Piazza della Repubblica, entrance via*
Strozzi.

Hotel Tornabuoni Beacci ★★★

50123 Firenze
Via dei Tornabuoni, 3
Tel. (055) 21 26 45/26 83 77 - Fax (055) 28 35 94
Sig.ra Beacci

Rooms 29 with air-conditioning, telephone, bath or shower, WC, TV and minibar. **Price** Single 80-160,000L, double 130-260,000L. **Meals** Breakfast included, served 7:00-10:30; half board 35,000L. **Restaurant** Service 12:00-14:00, 19:30-22:00, menus, also à la carte. Specialties: Florentine and international cuisine. **Credit cards** All major. **Pets** Dogs allowed (5,000L). **Nearby** Firenze (Baptistery, Duomo, Academy Gallery, the Medici chapels, Uffizi Gallery, Piazza della Signoria, Sta Maria del Carmine, Pitti Palace, Boboli Gardens), Fiesole, Certosa di Galluzzo, Villas and gardens around Firenze (tel. Palais Pitti: 055 21 48 56), Vallombrosa abbey, dell'Ugolino golf course (18-hole) in Grassina. **Open** All year.

This hotel, on the upper floors of a 14th-century palace, shares one of the elegant streets of Firenze with famous fashion designers and jewelers. It is one of Firenze's oldest hotels; Bismark, himself, once stayed here. Today, many Americans like come to enjoy the excellent cuisine, the vast rooms and the old family *pensione* atmosphere. If you have a large family or if you are traveling with friends, the hotel offers discounts for reservations of ten or more.

How to get there *(Map 14): Between the Church of the Trinity and the Church of Santa Maria Novella.*

Hotel Il Guelfo Bianco ★★★

Via Cavour, 57
50129 Firenze
Tel. (055) 28 83 30/1 – Fax (055) 29 52 03
Sig.ra. Barchiacchi and Sig. Cenni

Rooms 29 with air-conditioning, telephone, bath or shower, WC, cable TV, safe and minibar. **Price** Single 135-170,000L, double 170-240,000L. **Meals** Breakfast included, served 7:30-10:30. **Restaurant** See pp. 422-426. **Credit cards** Amex, Visa, Eurocard, MasterCard. **Pets** Dogs not allowed. **Facilities** Parking (50,000L). **Nearby** Firenze (Baptistery, Duomo, Academy Gallery, the Medici chapels, Uffizi Gallery, Piazza della Signoria, Sta Maria del Carmine, Pitti Palace, Boboli Gardens), Fiesole, Certosa di Galluzzo, Villas and gardens around Firenze (tel. Palais Pitti: 055 21 48 56), Vallombrosa abbey, dell'Ugolino golf course (18-hole) in Grassina. **Open** All year.

Here is some good news: There is a new place to stay in Firenze, a pretty little hotel, which is already very popular, right in the historic center of town. Its simple decor highlights the exposed beams, high ceilings and other vestiges of the past. And you will find the same simplicity in the comfortable rooms. Most of them are in the main building (six floors), but there are also eight others in an adjoining one. What is really special is the friendly staff's willingness to really do all they can to help make your stay comfortable and interesting. It is like visiting old Italian friends.

How to get there *(Map 14): Towards Ponte Vecchio.*

Villa San Michele ★★★★★

Via Doccia, 4
50014 Firenze – Fiesole
Tel. (055) 59 451 – Fax (055) 59 87 34
Sig. Saccani

Rooms 26 with telephone, bath or shower, WC, TV and minibar. **Price** With half board: Single 650,000L, double 990-1,240,000L, suite 1,750-2,200,000L. **Meals** Breakfast included (buffet), served 7:00-10:00. **Restaurant** Service 13:00-14:30, 20:00-21:45; menus 90-110,000L, also à la carte. Specialties: Tuscan and international cuisine. **Credit cards** All major. **Pets** Dogs allowed in room. **Facilities** Heated swimming pool, parking. **Nearby** Firenze (Baptistery, Duomo, Academy Gallery, the Medici chapels, Uffizi Gallery, Piazza della Signoria, Sta Maria del Carmine, Pitti Palace, Boboli Gardens), Fiesole, Certosa di Galluzzo, Villas and gardens around Firenze (tel. Palais Pitti: 055 21 48 56), Vallombrosa abbey, dell'Ugolino golf course (18-hole) in Grassina. **Open** Mar. 28 – Dec. 1.

What can we say about the Villa San Michele except that it is undoubtedly one of the most beautiful hotels in the world (and one of the most expensive). Located in the heights of Fiesole, in the middle of a fabulous garden, it is a former 16th-century monastery with a facade designed by Michelangelo. The grounds are scented with dreamy fragrances. The entire hotel is extremely elegant: each detail seems to have been meticulously studied. The salons and the dining room are in the old cloister, the superb loggia overlooks Firenze and the rooms are immense and luxurious with perfect bathrooms, which have wonderful concessions to modernity—whirlpools. The grounds are scented with dreamy fragrances. This place is magical.

How to get there (Map 14): 8 km north of Firenze

Pensione Bencistà ★★★

Via Benedetto da Maiano, 4
50014 Firenze – Fiesole
Tel. (055) 59 163 – Fax (055) 59 163
Simone Simoni

Rooms 43 with telephone, bath or shower and WC. **Price** With half board 100-120,000L, full board 115-135,000L. **Meals** Breakfast included, served 8:00-10:00. **Restaurant** Service 13:00-14:00, 19:30-20:30; menu. Specialties: Traditional Tuscan cuisine. **Credit cards** Not accepted. **Pets** Dogs allowed in room. **Facilities** Parking. **Nearby** Firenze (Baptistery, Duomo, Academy Gallery, the Medici chapels, Uffizi Gallery, Piazza della Signoria, Sta Maria del Carmine, Pitti Palace, Boboli Gardens), Fiesole, Certosa di Galluzzo, Villas and gardens around Firenze (tel. Palais Pitti: 055 21 48 56), Vallombrosa abbey, dell'Ugolino golf course (18-hole) in Grassina. **Open** All year.

On the hills of Fiesole, this genvire family *pensione* is a charming establishment for those who love Tuscany. It has been simply and carefully decorated with antique furniture and travel souvenirs. The library, filled with books in English, is the perfect place to spend some quiet moments. The terrace is in a natural setting, and the garden is full of flowers and trees of diverse species. The rooms, which are made more comfortable year after year, are delightful. The home-style cuisine adds to the relaxed family atmosphere. Open year-round the Christmas and New Year's Eve, are celebrated at the *pensione* according to Tuscan tradition.

How to get there *(Map 14): 8 km north of Firenze. Bus for Firenze 200 meters from the hotel.*

Il Trebbiolo

50060 Molin del Piano – Fiesole (Firenze)
Tel. (055) 830 00 98 – Fax (055) 830 05 83
Sig.ra Rossi

Rooms 9 with telephone, bath or shower, WC, TV and minibar. **Price** Single 140,000L, double 210,000L, suite 310,000L. **Meals** Breakfast 20,000L, served 8:00-10:00; half board 75,000L, full board 120,000L. **Restaurant** Service 12:00-14:00, 19:30-22:00; menus, also à la carte. Specialties: Florentine and international cuisine. **Credit cards** All major. **Pets** Dogs not allowed. **Facilities** Parking **Nearby** Fiesole, Firenze (Baptistery, Duomo, Academy Gallery, the Medici chapels, Uffizi Gallery, Piazza della Signoria, Sta Maria del Carmine, Pitti Palace, Boboli Gardens), Certosa di Galluzzo, Villas and gardens around Firenze (tel. Palais Pitti: 055 21 48 56), Vallombrosa abbey, dell'Ugolino golf course (18-hole) in Grassina. **Open** All year (except 3 weeks in Jan.).

Carla Rossi, director of the famous Seeber bookstore in Firenze, offers nine rooms on a ten-acre estate full of oak trees, several miles from Firenze. The estate is close to the beautiful Mugello Valley, where you can see the hills of Fiesole. The house's atmosphere is intimate: furniture, engravings and old tapestries personalize each room. There are, of course, many kinds of books in the library (art, botany, history, cuisine, etc.). The rooms, named after flowers, are comfortable. Chef, Angelo Angelini's cuisine, is very well prepared. Here you can enjoy the serenity of the Tuscan countryside, which what attracted the monks of the abbey of Vallombrosa and the monastery of Mont Senario a long time ago.

How to get there (Map 14): 10 km northeast of Firenze. In Fiesole towards Olmo (7 km).

Hotel Villa La Massa ★★★★★

Via La Massa, 6
50010 Firenze - Candeli
Tel. (055) 65 10 101 – Fax (055) 65 10 109
Sig. Grillini

Rooms 38 with telephone, bath and WC. **Price** Single 240-295,000L, double 260-450,000L, suite 650-750,000L. **Meals** Breakfast included, served 7:00-11:00; half board +65,000L. **Restaurant** Service 13:00-14:30, 20:00-22:00; menus: 65-80,000L, also à la carte. Specialties: Regional and international cuisine. **Credit cards** All major. **Pets** Small dogs allowed. **Facilities** Swimming pool, parking. **Nearby** Firenze (Baptistery, Duomo, Academy Gallery, the Medici chapels, Uffizi Gallery, Piazza della Signoria, Sta Maria del Carmine, Pitti Palace, Boboli Gardens), Fiesole, Certosa di Galluzzo, villas and gardens around Firenze (tel. Palais Pitti: 055 21 48 56), Vallombrosa abbey; dell'Ugolino golf course (18-hole) in Grassina. **Open** All year (except Jan. 16 – Mar. 16).

This superb 16th-century villa, made up of three buildings, seems to recreate the atmosphere of the Garden of the Fitzi Contini. The well-kept lawns, the grounds, the old chapel and the secret underground passageways all radiate luxury and beauty. The large rooms, with antique furniture, look out on the fields or the river. The tennis court and swimming pool add to the charm of this magical place. La Massa has one of the best restaurants in Firenze, *Il Verrochio*, as well as an excellent wine cellar. The prices are accordingly high.

How to get there *(Map 14): Towards Pontassieve-Candeli. Bus services.*

Hotel Villa Le Rondini ★★★

Via Bolognese Vecchia, 224
50139 Firenze - Trespiano
Tel. (055) 40 00 81 - Fax (055) 26 82 12
Sig.ra Reali

Rooms 43 (some with air conditioning), telephone, bath or shower, WC, TV and minibar. **Price** Single 140-170,000L, double 210-250,000L. **Meals** Breakfast included, served 7:30-10:00; half board 150-170,000L, full board 185-215,000L. **Restaurant** Service 12:30-14:30, 19:30-21:30; menus: 45-80,000L, also à la carte. Specialties: Italian and international cuisine with the farm produces. **Credit cards** All major. **Pets** Dogs allowed (6,000L). **Facilities** Swimming pool, tennis (15,000L), sauna, parking. **Nearby** Firenze (Baptistery, Duomo, Academy Gallery, the Medici chapels, Uffizi Gallery, Piazza della Signoria, Sta Maria del Carmine, Pitti Palace, Boboli Gardens), Fiesole, Certosa di Galluzzo, villas and gardens around Firenze (tel. Palais Pitti: 055 21 48 56), Vallombrosa abbcy; dcll'Ugolino golf course (18-hole) in Grassina. **Open** All year.

The Rondini is on a superb fifty-four-acre estate full of olive and cypress trees on one of the hills crowning Firenze. The reception area, salons, dining room and the other nicest rooms are in the 16th-century villa. Two other villas also have very comfortable rooms, but they are more modern and breakfast is not served. The hotel only about four miles (7 km) from the center of Firenze and there is a very convenient bus stop right in front of the estate. You will be able to spend pleasant afternoons poolside unwinding after your day in town.

How to get there *(Map 14): 7 km north of Firenze, towards Fortessa da Bano until the Piazza della Libertà, via Bolognese. Bus no. 25 in front of the hotel entrance.*

Hotel Paggeria Medicea ★★★★

Viale Papa Giovanni XXIII, 3
50040 Artimino – Carmignano (Firenze)
Tel. (055) 871 80 81 – Fax (055) 871 80 80
Sig. Gualtieri

Rooms 37 with air conditioning and 23 apartments with telephone, bath or shower, WC, TV and minibar. **Price** Single 130-145,000L, double 210-250,000L. **Meals** Breakfast included, served 7:30-10:30; half board 35,000L (per pers., 3 days min.). **Restaurant** Service 12:30-14:00, 19:30-21:00; closed Wed. and Fri. at noon; menu, also à la carte. Specialties: Crêpe alla fiorentina, ribollita, arrosti misti toscani. **Credit cards** All major. **Pets** Dogs allowed. **Facilities** Swimming pool, garage (50,000L). **Nearby** Artimino (church and Etruscan ancient city of Pian di Rosello, Villa dell'Artimino), Etruscan Tomb of Montefortini in Comeana, Médici Villa Gardens' in Poggio a Caiano, Prato, Pistoia, Firenze, dell'Ugolino golf course (18-hole) in Grassina. **Open** All year.

If you dream of a comfortable, quiet, Mediterranean villa in the hills of Tuscany, surrounded by grapevines, cypress and olive trees, then the Paggeria Medicea farm is the place for you. It was built by Cosimo Grand Duke of Tuscany who divided the farm with a wall to create a wildlife reserve for hunting. His son built the villa "La Ferdinanda," where you can now find the Etruscan museum. The Paggeria offers the services of a luxury hotel. The rooms are comfortable and well furnished. If you stay in the apartments, you can enjoy the hotel amenities (swimming pool and tennis). The restaurant is also in a building from the Medician era; typically Tuscan cuisine is served there along with wine from the property. You can, visit the wine cellars and buy wine and olive oil.

How to get there *(Map 14): 22 km north of Firenze via A1, Firenze-Signa exit; via A11, Prato exit.*

Salvadonica

Via Grevigiana, 82
Val di Pesa – 50024 Mercatale (Firenze)
Tel. (055) 821 80 39 – Fax (055) 821 80 43
Sig. Baccetti

Rooms 5 with telephone, bath or shower, WC and TV (by request). 10 apartments
with kitchenettes. **Price** Single 85,000L, double 130-140,000L, apartments (by
request). **Meals** Breakfast included, served 8:00-10:00. **Restaurant** See p. 427.
Credit cards All major. **Pets** Dogs not allowed. **Facilities** Swimming pool with
whirlpool, tennis, parking. **Nearby** Firenze, Certosa di Galluzzo, Impruneta
(terracotta), Siena, dell'Ugolino golf course (18-hole) in Grassina. **Open** Mar. – Oct.,
Dec. 26 – Jan. 10.

Two Tuscan farmhouses, dating from the 14th century, have
been made into this luxurious hotel in the Tuscan
countryside. Its restoration is an example of one of the more
successful in the region because the rustic feeling of the original
buildings has been maintained in the renovation. They used old
materials and decorated the place with beautiful polished farm
furniture, but also added modern conveniences. The hotel
consists mostly of small apartments, which you are advised to rent
by the week. The housework is done for you every day. You can
have breakfast around a communal table at the hotel and dine
pleasantly in San Casciano and the surrounding area in the
evening. You can buy wine and olive oil produced on the farm.

How to get there *(Map 14): 20 km from Firenze via A1, Firenze-*
Certosa exit, then highway towards Siena, San Casciano exit; in San
Casciano, go left towards Mercatale.

Castello di Montegufoni

50020 Montagnana (Firenze)
Tel. (0571) 67.11.31
Fax (0571) 67.15.14
Sig. Posarelli

Rooms 25 with shower, WC, public phone. Apartments for 2-6 pers.
Price 150,000L (800,000L week), for 4 pers. 200,000L (1,100,000L week), for 6
pers. 250,000L. **Meals** Breakfast (fresh bread) by request. **Restaurant** By request
in "La Tavena," Mon., Wed., Fri. **Credit cards** Not accepted. **Pets** Dogs not
allowed. **Facilities** 2 swimming pools, parking. **Nearby** Firenze, Certosa di
Galluzzo, Impruneta (terracotta), Siena, dell'Ugolino golf course (18-hole) in
Grassina. **Open** Mar. – Nov.

If you dream of palaces, frescos and Italian–style gardens with a
terraces in the Florentine countryside, this is the place for you.
Here, there are terraces with flowering lemon trees and sunny
courtyards. You can rent a nice apartment in the castle or in one
of the outbuildings for two to six people for a long stay. The
cherubs on the walls will watch over you in this residence,
whose richness lies in its past present beauty. This is one of the
most authentic places in this guide.

*How to get there (Map 14): 15 km west of Firenze, via highway towards
Livorno-Pisa, Ginestra exit; in Ginestra, follow the signs to Montespertoli,
turn right, go 4 km to Baccaiano, then turn left (1 km).*

Fattoria La Loggia

50020 Montefiridolfi
San Casciano (Firenze)
Tel. (055) 82 44 288 – Fax (055) 82 44 283
Sig. Baruffaldi

Rooms 8 apartments for 2-6 pers. with kitchen, living room, bath or shower and
WC. **Price** 200,000L (per 2 pers.), 250,000L (per 3 pers.), 350,000L (4 pers.),
450,000L (per 6 pers.). **Meals** Breakfast included, served 8:00-10:00. **Restaurant**
By request. Service 20:00–22:00; menus 45-45,000L. Specialties: Tuscan cuisine
with products from the farm. **Credit cards** All major. **Pets** Dogs not allowed.
Facilities Swimming pool, tennis, mountain bikes, riding, parking.
Nearby Firenze, Certosa di Galluzzo, Impruneta (terracotta), Siena, Volterra, San
Gimignano, dell'Ugolino golf course (18-hole) in Grassina. **Open** All year.

You may have to pinch yourself to make sure you're not
dreaming when you cross the Tuscan countryside to one of
these beautiful farmhouses perched on top of a hill among a few
cypress trees with a view of the little furrowed valleys. The
Fattoria is not a hotel, but a functioning agricultural estate with a
carefully restored Renaissance hamlet of small private houses,
which have been decorated with Tuscan-style refinement. Here,
you can move at your own pace, as you would in your own
country house. But everything will be ready when you
arrive–from your first breakfast to the bottle of champagne to
celebrate your first evening.

How to get there *(Map 14): 21 km south of Firenze via A1, Firenze-*
Certosa exit; then via SS Firenze-Siena, Bargino exit.

Villa Le Barone ★★★

Via S. Leolino, 19
50020 Panzano in Chianti (Firenze)
Tel. (055) 85 26 21 - Fax (055) 85 22 77
Sig.ra Buonamici

Rooms 27 with telephone, bath or shower and WC. **Price** With half board 190-220,000L (per pers.). **Meals** Breakfast included, served 8:00-10:00. **Restaurant** Service 13:00-14:00, 19:30-21:00, menu 60,000L, à la carte. Specialties: Tuscan cuisine. **Credit cards** All major. **Pets** Dogs not allowed. **Facilities** Swimming pool, tennis, parking. **Nearby** Greve valley via S222 (vineyards of Chianti Classico from Greve to Gaiole), Firenze, Siena, dell'Ugolino golf course (18-hole) in Grassina. **Open** Apr. – Oct.

This 16th-century residence was transformed into a hotel by the Marquise della Robbia, who wanted to preserve all of the charm of the house where she grew up. Ensconced in the lush vegetation of the large surrounding park, which overlooks vineyards and olive trees, this villa is a haven peaceful. The warm welcome and the friendly service will make you feel like you are a guest in a friend's home. Breakfast is served on the terrace in the summertime. The cuisine is light, regional and well-prepared.

How to get there *(Map 14): 33 km south of Firenze via S222 to Panzano in Chianti via Greve in Chianti.*

Villa Santa Cristina ★★★

50047 Prato (Firenze)
Via Poggio Secco, 58
Tel. (0574) 59 59 51 – Fax (0574) 57 26 23
Sig. Chiais

Rooms 23 with air conditioning, telephone, bath, WC, TV and minibar. **Price** Single 170,000L, double 230,000L. **Meals** Breakfast included, served 7:00-10:00. **Restaurant** Service 12:30-14:00, 19:30-22:00, closed Sun., menu 35,000L, à la carte. Specialties: Tuscan cuisine. **Credit cards** All major. **Pets** Dogs allowed. **Facilities** Swimming pool, parking. **Nearby** Prato (Duomo (Filippo Lippi frescoes), Palazzo Pretorio, Castello dell'Imperatore), Villa of Médici in Poggio a Caiano, Firenze, dell'Ugolino golf course (18-hole) in Grassina. **Open** All year.

Away from the hustle and bustle of Prato, the Villa Santa Cristina is an oasis of peace and quiet. On the side of a hill, in a beautiful garden with pine and olive trees, the villa looks out over the whole valley. The main house, which is nicer than the more recently built outbuildings, still has all of its original charm. The dining room and other rooms (15, 21,23 and 24 Rooms are our favorites) are decorated with frescos. Spacious and sunny, these rooms have balconies. Perhaps you will prefer the quiet of the poolside garden. The restaurant features good Tuscan cuisine. The passing trains are all that will distract you from the languorous charm of this beautiful place.

How to get there *(Map 14): 15 km west of Firenze, 45 km east of Lucca. A11, Prato-est exit. A1 Prato/Calenzano exit, then towards Prato and railways station.*

Villa Rucellai – Fattoria di Canneto

50047 Prato (Firenze)
Via di Canneto, 16
Tel. (0574) 46 03 92 – Fax (0574) 46 03 92
Famiglia Piqué-Rucellai

Rooms 12 with bath or shower and WC. **Price** Double 100-130,000 L.
Meals Breakfast 10,000L, served at 8:00. **Restaurant** See p.425. **Credit cards** All
major. **Pets** Dogs not allowed. **Facilities** Swimming pool, parking. **Nearby** Prato
(Duomo (Filippo Lippi frescoes), Palazzo Pretorio, Castello dell'Imperatore), Villa of
Médici in Poggio a Caiano, Firenze, dell'Ugolino golf course (18-hole) in Grassina.
Open All year.

How could you not fall in love with this admirable
Renaissance Tuscan villa, which has belonged to the
Rucellai family since the 18th century. The charming Sig.ra
Piqué-Rucellai will greet you on the terrace of her Italian garden
and offer you a glass of Italian wine produced by the Rucellai
vineyard. Today, part of the villa is a hotel where international
artists in town for the theater or the contemporary art museum
like to stay. This is understandable because the villa is so much
charming and beautiful; its salons and gardens often provide the
setting for splendorousfeasts. The lovely rooms have modern
bathrooms. The almost nonexistent service is made up for by the
hosts'friendly attention. There's no restaurant, but breakfast is
served around a charming table. One drawback is that nearby
trains may disturb your sleep in the summer.

How to get there *(Map 14): 15 km west of Firenze, 45 km east of Lucca. Via
A11, Prato-est exit. Via A1, Prato/Calenzano exit. Then towards Prato and
train station, go via Machiavelli, go left via Lambruschini; then on right "Villa
S. Leonardo" and "Trattoria la Fontana," follow the railway on your left for 4 km.*

Villa Rigacci ★★★★

Via Manzoni, 76
50066 Vaggio - Reggello (Firenze)
Tel. (055) 865 67 18/865 65 62 - Fax (055) 865 65 37
Sig. Pierazzi

Rooms 29 with air-conditioning, telephone, bath or shower, WC, TV and minibar.
Price Single 120,000L, double 160-220,000L. **Meals** Breakfast included, served
7:30-10:30. **Restaurant** Service 12:00-14:30, 20:00-22:00; menu: 60,000L, also à
la carte. Specialties: French and Italian cuisine. **Credit cards** All major. **Pets** Dogs
not allowed. **Facilities** Swimming pool, parking. **Nearby** Vallombrosa abbey,
Church of Montemignaio, Castello Pretorio in Poppi, Firenze, Siena. **Open** All year.

This 15th-century Tuscan country house, a half hour from
Firenze, is perfect if you are looking for a change of scenery.
The Pierazzi family is friendly and you can enjoy walking in the
surrounding countryside, sunbathing by the side of the pool,
resting in the shade under the large trees, or relaxing in front of
the salon's immense fireplace in winter. Informal lunches and
dinners will give you the opportunity to savor traditional Tuscan
and French cuisine under the direction of David Pierre
Lecompte. Extremely generous breakfasts are served in what was
once the stable. All the rooms are different, and all have been
carefully and elegantly furnished.

How to get there *(Map 14): 30 km southeast of Firenze via A1, Incisa
exit, number 24, towards Matassino and Vaggio.*

Il Paretaio

Via Ponzano, 26 – San Filippo
50021 Barberino Val d'Elsa (Firenze)
Tel. (055) 80 59 218 – Fax (055) 80 59 231
Sig.ra de Marchi

Rooms 6 with shower and WC. **Price** Double 120-140,000L. **Meals** Breakfast included; half board 95-115,000L (per pers., 2 days min.). Communal meals, service 20:00. Specialties: Traditional cuisine. **Credit cards** Not accepted. **Pets** Dogs allowed. **Facilities** Riding, swimming pool, parking. **Nearby** Siena, Monteriggioni, Colle di Val d'Elsa, Firenze, San Gimignano, Certaldo, Castellina in Chianti, Volterra. **Open** All year (except Jan. 10 – Feb. 15).

What a wonderful place the Paretaio is for people who like to ride horses! This beautiful estate, in the heart of the Tuscan countryside, is surrounded by four hundred and ninety-five acres of woods, vineyards and olive trees. The young owners—excellent riders themselves—with a passion for horses, offer a series of package rates ranging from a weekend to a week, including classes to improve riding skills for children and adults, courses on breaking in and training horses, and rides in the country. The house and its decor are rustic and the rooms are large and nicely arranged. The atmosphere is very warm, especially when guests gather together in the evening around the big table for a good meal, and a great chianti. This hotel is especially aimed at riders because you have to know and love horses to understand the philosophy of the Paretaio. But if you simply enjoy conviviality and the outdoors you will also like it here.

How to get there *(Map 14): 33 km south of Firenze via A1, Firenze-Certosa exit; towards SS Siena, Tavarnelle exit; road opposite restaurant "Passa Parola," towards S. Filippo.*

Villa Villoresi ★★★★

Via Ciampi, 2 – Colonnata
50019 Sesto Fiorentino (Firenze)
Tel. (055) 44 36 92 – Fax (055) 44 20 63
Sig.ra Villoresi de Loche

Rooms 28 with telephone, bath and WC (4 with TV). **Price** Single 150,000L, double 220-330,000L., suite 420,000L. **Meals** Breakfast 20,000L, served 7:00-10:30; half board 175-220,000 (per pers., 3 days min.). **Restaurant** Service 12:00-14:30, 20:00-22:00; closed Mon. (except for residents); menus 50-55,000L, also à la carte. Specialties: Penne al coccio, fagiano alla foglia di vite. **Credit cards** All major. **Pets** Dogs allowed. **Facilities** Swimming pool, parking. **Nearby** Sesto (Duomo and S. Maria dei Carceri), Castello dell'Imperatore in Prato, Firenze, dell'Ugolino golf course (18-hole) in Grassina. **Open** All year.

Eight kilometers from the center of Firenze, this villa used to be the property of noble Tuscan families. Today, the Villa Villoresi is a national monument and an amazing hotel. The present entrance to the villa is a one hundred and thirty-foot-long (40 meter) gallery, with renditions of Tuscan landscapes, painted in tempera by Alfredo Luzzi. The various salons, bars, reading rooms and music rooms are similar to the gallery. Some of the immense rooms have frescos and period furniture and open onto another loggia of pure Renaissance style, on the second floor. The other, less spectacular rooms, open onto the garden or the field. The only concession to modernity is the pool in the Italian-style garden, which you will really appreciate during the Florentine summer. Our only regret is the surroundings, which detract a bit from the charm of the place, but not at all from the beauty of the villa.

How to get there *(Map 14): 10 km northwest of Firenze, towards Prato-Calenzano.*

Villa Campestri ★★★

50039 Vicchio (Firenze)
Tel. (055) 84 90 107 – Fax (055) 84 90 108
Sig. Pasquali

Rooms 11 and 6 suites with telephone, bath or shower, WC, cable TV and minibar.
Price Single 130-160,000L, double 160-200,000L, suite 290-330,000L. **Meals**
Breakfast included, served 8:00-10:00; half board 120-140,000 (per pers., 5 days
min.). **Restaurant** Closed at noon (except Sun.) and Mon. Service 20:00-21:30;
menu 45,000L. Specialties: Tortelli del Mugello, vitella alla campaonola, coniglio
alle mele. **Credit cards** Amex, Visa, Eurocard and MasterCard. **Pets** Dogs allowed on
request. **Facilities** Swimming pool, parking. **Nearby** Firenze, Vespignano, Borgo S.
Lorenzo, S. Piero a Sieve, Scarperia, convent of Bosco ai Frati, Novoli, castello del
Trebbio, Pratolino, convent of Monte Senario in Bivigliano, Sesto Fiorentino and the
strada panoramica (panoramic road) dei Colli Alti (13 km to the N15 towards
Firenze). **Open** Apr. – Dec.

On the big road, we were taken aback by the urban growth
which, while not exactly uncontrolled, is still a little
depressing. But this disappears as you approach Mugello, where the
hills are gentler and greener than in Chianti, where the water
murmurs and flows in small brooks, streams and waterfalls, and
where wild boars and deer live in the valleys. In these surrowdings,
the hotel is like a precious stone in a case. Thanks to the
uncompromising care of its owners, it is in peak condition. The
interior and the cuisine, served in the restaurant, are both modern
and authenticelly Tuscan.

*How to get there (Map 14): 35 km northeast of Firenze. Via A1,
towards Bologna, Barberino exit di Mugello, towards Borgo San Lorenzo
and Vicchio. 3 km from Vicchio.*

Park Hotel ★★★★

Via di Marciano, 18
53100 Siena
Tel. (0577) 44 803 - Fax (0577) 490 20
Sig. Cadirni

Rooms 69 with air-conditioning, telephone, bath, WC, cable TV, safe and minibar. **Price** Single 242-330,000L, double 330-440,000L, suite 715-880,000L. **Meals** Breakfast 27,500-44,000, served 7:30-10:30. **Restaurant** Service 12:30-14:15, 19:30-22:30; à la carte 75,000L. Specialties: Seasonal Tuscan cuisine. **Credit cards** All major. **Pets** Dogs allowed. **Facilities** Swimming pool, tennis, parking. **Nearby** Siena (Piazza del Campo, Duomo, Piccolomini Library, the Baptistery, Pinacoteca),Sant'Antimo abbey, Monte Oliveto Maggiore abbey and the crestroad from Asciano to Siena, Convento dell'Osservanza, Torri abbey in Rosia, San Galgano abbey. **Open** Mar. – Dec. 1.

Built on a mountain pass, the old castle of Marciano has an exceptional view of Siena and the Tuscan countryside. This massive and imposing structure built by Peruzzi is now the Park Hotel. The salons, superbly furnished in Haute Epoque style, open onto a pretty inner courtyard, a replica of the famous Piazza del Campo. The restaurant is on the Italian-style garden, as are the loggia reserved for banquets. The rooms are comfortable—our favorites are on the *premier étage*. This hotel is very good, but its prices limit its guests to primarily businessmen and top level convention-goers.

How to get there *(Map 14): 68 km south of Firenze; take the Siena-North exit; then via Fiorentina to Perticcio and right, via di Marciano (5 km northwest of the center of the town).*

Hotel Certosa di Maggiano ★★★★

Strada di Certosa, 82
53100 Siena
Tel. (0577) 28 81 80 – Fax (0577) 28 81 89
Sig.ra Recordati

Rooms 6, and 12 suites with air-conditioning, telephone, bath, WC, TV and minibar. **Price** Single 400-500,000L, double 500-600,000L, suite 600-850,000L. **Meals** Breakfast 30,000L, served 7:15-11:00; half board +120,000L, full board +210,000L. **Restaurant** Service 13:00-14:30, 20:00-22:00; menus 80-140,000L, also à la carte. **Credit cards** All major. **Pets** Small dogs allowed (+50,000L) **Facilities** Heated swimming pool, tennis, parking. **Nearby** In Siena: Piazza del Campo (palio in July and Aug.), Duomo, Piccolomini Library, the Baptistery, Pinacoteca; Sant'Antimo abbey, Monte Oliveto Maggiore abbey and the crestroad from Asciano to Siena, Convento dell'Osservanza, Torri abbey in Rosia, San Galgano abbey. **Open** All Year.

Miraculously well preserved, the Maggiano monastery is the oldest monastery in Tuscany. Cardinal Petroni had this edifice for meditation built around 1300. Even today, it is very quiet. The cloister with its large arcades supported by stone columns, the silence of the surrounding countryside and the intimate and luxurious comfort all make this an enchanting place, so vast and initially so austere. The salons are furnished with soft, deep couches and carefully selected antiques. The library is full of old books. In the evening a profusion of candelabra illuminates the tables under the arcades. The rooms, few in number, open onto the still-unspoiled Tuscan countryside.

How to get there *(Map 14): 68 km south of Firenze, Siena-Sud exit, Porta Romana, on the right via Certosa.*

Grand Hotel Villa Patrizia ★★★★

Via Fiorentina, 58
53100 Siena
Tel. (0577) 50 431 – Fax (0577) 50 431
Sig. Brogi

Rooms 33 with telephone, bath, WC, TV and minibar. **Price** Single 260,000L,
double 360,000L. **Meals** Breakfast included, served 7:00-10:00, half board
40,000L, full board 50,000L. **Restaurant** Service 12:30-14:00, 19:30-21:30;
menus 50,000L, also à la carte. Specialties: Ribollita, pici alla senese.
Credit cards All major. **Pets** Dogs allowed. **Facilities** Swimming pool, tennis,
parking. **Nearby** Siena (Piazza del Campo, Duomo, Piccolomini Library, the
Baptistery, Pinacoteca), Sant'Antimo abbey, Monte Oliveto Maggiore abbey and
the crestroad from Asciano to Siena, Convento dell'Osservanza, Torri abbey in
Rosia, San Galgano abbey. **Open** All year.

In the 20s, the Patrizia was a minister's residence. This
beautiful patrician villa, retains its original charm. Enjoy the
tranquility of the grounds with its age-old trees and the rooms,
which look out onto the garden. The swimming pool allows
you to pleasantly escape the heat. The owner's mother, an
expert chef, will delight you with her culinary skills.

How to get there *(Map 14): 68 km south of Firenze, Siena-North exit;
then via Fiorentina to the intersection between viale Cavon and via Achille
Sclavo; 5 km northwest of the city center.*

Hotel Villa Scacciapensieri ★★★★

Via di Scacciapensieri, 10
53100 Siena
Tel. (0577) 41 441 – Fax (577) 27 08 54
Famiglia Nardi

Rooms 31 with air-conditioning, telephone, bath, WC, cable TV and minibar.
Price Single 160-210,000L, double 260-320,000L, suite 380-400,000L.
Meals Breakfast included, served 7:30-10:00; half board 220,000L, full board
370,000L. **Restaurant** Service 12:30-14:30, 19:30-21:00; closed Wed.; menus 50-
65,000L, also à la carte. Specialties: Tuscan cuisine, pici alla senese.
Credit cards All major. **Pets** Dogs allowed (40,000L). **Facilities** Swimming pool,
tennis, bus to Siena, parking. **Nearby** Siena (Piazza del Campo, Duomo,
Piccolomini Library, the Baptistery, Pinacoteca), Sant'Antimo abbey, Monte Oliveto
Maggiore abbey and the crestroad from Asciano to Siena, Convento
dell'Osservanza, Torri abbey in Rosia, San Galgano abbey. **Open** Mar. 15 – Jan. 6.

The Scacciapensieri, has an elegant, 18th–century facade, a
terrace at the edge of a beautiful flower garden, and a
marvelous view of Siena. The quiet, spacious rooms look out
onto the countryside. The tennis court and swimming pool are a
great place to unwind. The cuisine is simple and savory. The
two brothers who own the hotel make feel like home.

How to get there *(Map 14): 68 km south of Firenze, Siena-North exit;
stazione ferroviara (rail station) 3 km north of the city center.*

Hotel Antica Torre

53100 Siena
Via di Fiera Vecchia, 7
Tel. (0577) 22 22 55 – Fax (0577) 22 22 55
Sig.ra Landolfo

Rooms 8 with telephone, shower and WC (2 with TV). **Price** Single 90,000L, double 140,000L. **Meals** Breakfast 12,000L, served 8:00-10:30. **Restaurant** See p. 425-426. **Credit cards** All major. **Pets** Dogs not allowed. **Nearby** Siena, Abbey Sant'Antimo, Abbey Monte Oliveto Maggiore, Convento dell'Osservanza, Abbey Torri in Rosia, Abbey San Galgano. **Open** All year.

Just outside of Siena you will find one of the best hotels in Tuscany. This charming, affordable hotel in the center of town is so small and so discreet that we really had to dig it up. And what a find! It is a typical 16th century *casa torre*, on one of the quietest streets in Siena. A small central stairway (with beautiful 19th century portraits) leads to two rooms on every floor. They have travertine floors, wrought iron beds, antique furniture, engravings, and small, but well-equipped, bathrooms with showers. A former pottery store in the basement, serves as the breakfast room.

How to get there *(Map 14): SS Firneze-Siena, Siena-sud exit; then towards town center (Porta Romana).*

Hotel Santa Caterina ★★★

Via Enea Silvio Piccolomini, 7
53100 Siena
Tel. (0577) 22 11 05 – Fax (0577) 27 10 87
Sig.ra Minuti Stasi

Rooms 19 with air-conditioning, telephone, bath, WC, cable TV and minibar.
Price Single 110-150,000L, double 140-190,000L, triple 200-230,000L, for 4
pers. 220-260,000L. **Meals** Breakfast included, served 8:00-10:00. **Restaurant**
See p. 425-26. **Credit cards** All major. **Pets** Dogs allowed. **Facilities** Parking
(15,000L). **Nearby** Siena (Piazza del Campo, Duomo, Piccolomini Library, the
Baptistery, Pinacoteca), Sant'Antimo abbey, Monte Oliveto Maggiore abbey and
the crestroad from Asciano to Siena, Convento dell'Osservanza, Torri abbey in
Rosia, San Galgano abbey. **Open** Mar. 7 – Jan. 7.

The Hotel Santa Caterina is in a former private home in the
center of Siena, a few yards from the Porta Romana. The
facade is plain and the street corner location is not wonderful,
but the double pane windows make the rooms fairly
soundproof. All of the rooms are comfortably furnished and
have modern bathrooms. Ask for a room off the marvelous
flower garden, which overlooks the valley and the red rooftops
of Siena. This view is the most charming aspect of this hotel.

How to get there *(Map 14): 68 km south of Firenze, Siena-South exit;
then towards town center to Porta Romana via E.S. Piccolomini.*

Hotel Salivolpi ★★★

Via Fiorentina, 13
53011 Castellina in Chianti (Siena)
Tel. (0577) 74 04 84
Fax (0577) 74 09 98

Rooms 19 with telephone, bath or shower and WC. **Price** Double 125,000L.
Meals Breakfast included, served 8:00-10:00; half board 40,000L, full board
750,000L. **Restaurant** Service 12:30-14:00, 19:30-21:30; menus 50,000L, also à
la carte. Specialties: Ribollita, pici alla senese. **Credit card** Amex. **Pets** Dogs not
allowed. **Facilities** Swimming pool, parking. **Nearby** Firenze, Vineyards Chianti
Classico (S 222) from Impruneta to Siena, Castello di Meleto, Castello di Brolio
(Cappella S. Jacopo and Palazzo padronale), Siena. **Open** All year.

The Hotel Salivolpi consists of an old house and two modern
annexes, on the small road between Castellina and San
Donato. Nonethless, the hotel is very quiet. Once you are in the
garden or on the terrace you will be able to see the panoramic
view of the famous Gallo Nero vineyards. In the old house the
rooms have sloping walls and pretty, antique furniture. The
comfort, the friendly service, the swimming pool (a blessing on
hot summer days), and the very reasonable prices make the
Hotel Salivolpi a good place to stay if you want to explore
Chianti country.

*How to get there (Map 14): 21 km north of Siena via S222, exit
northwest of the town.*

Tenuta di Ricavo ★★★★

53011 Ricavo
Ricavo - Castellina in Chianti (Siena)
Tel. (0577) 74 02 21 - Fax (0577) 74 10 14
Sig. Lobrano

Rooms 23 with telephone, bath, WC, minibar and safe (15 with TV). **Price** Single 230,000L, double 280-360,000L, suite with balcony 420,000L. **Meals** Breakfast included, served 7:00-9:45. **Restaurant** «La Pecora Nera», by reservation. Service 19:30-21:45, closed Mon. and Tues., à la carte 40-60,000L, Specialties: Tuscan cuisine and very good Tuscan wines. **Credit cards** Visa, Eurocard and MasterCard. **Pets** Dogs not allowed. **Facilities** 2 swimming pools, parking (10,000L). **Nearby** Firenze, Vineyards Chianti Classico (S 222) from Impruneta to Siena, Castello di Meleto, Castello di Brolio (Cappella S. Jacopo and Palazzo padronale), Siena. **Open** Apr. – Oct.

The quiet and serenity of this hamlet, seems reserved for the privileged few. The splendid fragrant gardens, the swimming pools among the greenery, and the discreet service will ensure a dream vacation in this country residence. The regional cuisine and the wine cellar are good: meals are an important time of the day here (but smoking is not allowed in the dining room). Walks in the beautiful surrounding woods can be arranged.

How to get there *(Map 14): 25 km north of Siena, San Donato in Poggio exit, then towards Castellina in Chianti.*

Hotel Villa Casalecchi ★★★★

53011 Castellina in Chianti (Siena)
Tel. (0577) 74 02 40
Fax (0577) 74 11 11
Sig.ra Lecchini–Giovannoni

Rooms 19 with telephone, bath and WC. **Price** Double 265-340,000L.
Meals Breakfast included, served 8:00-10:30; half board 190-225,000L; full
board 220-225,000L (per pers.). **Restaurant** Service 12:30-14:30, 19:30-21:30;
menus 65-85,000L. Specialties: Tuscan cuisine. **Credit cards** All major.
Pets Dogs allowed. **Facilities** Swimming pool, tennis, parking. **Nearby** Firenze,
Vineyards Chianti Classico (S 222) from Impruneta to Siena, Castello di Meleto,
Castello di Brolio (Cappella S. Jacopo and Palazzo padronale), Siena. **Open** Apr. –
Oct.

Once the residence of a lord's family, this villa, on a wooded
hill, is very tranquil. Surrowded by trees, the tennis court
and the pretty swimming pool on the lawn, add to the peaceful
atmosphere. Rooms are pleasantly decorated with antique
Tuscan furniture. The regional cuisine and efficient service are
also very enjoyable. This hotel offers a restful stay to those who
want to visit the famous Chianti region.

How to get there (Map 14): 25 km north of Siena via S222, exit
northwest of the town.

Albergo Fattoria Casafrassi ★★★★

Casafrassi
53011 Castellina in Chianti (Siena)
Tel. (0577) 74 06 21 – Fax (0577) 74 10 47
Sig. Giunti

Rooms 22 with telephone, bath or shower and WC. **Price** Single 100-160,000L, double 150-250,000L. **Meals** Breakfast included, served 8:00-10:00; half board 45,000L (per pers., 3 days min.). **Restaurant** Service 13:00-14:30, 19:00-21:30; menu 45,000L, also à la carte. Specialties: Tuscan cuisine. **Credit cards** All major. **Pets** Dogs allowed (8,000L). **Facilities** Swimming pool, tennis, parking (10,000L). **Nearby** Firenze, Vineyards Chianti Classico (S222) from Impruneta to Siena, Castello di Meleto, Castello di Brolio (Cappella S. Jacopo and Palazzo padronale), Siena. **Open** Mar. 15 – Nov. 15.

Casafrassi is an 18th-century villa on a beautiful road which crosses the Chianti Classico vineyards called "The Chiantigiana." It has been carefully restored to the original spirit of the house. Almost all of the rooms are in the villa; they are comfortable, spacious, and filled with antique furniture. The restaurant serves fine regional specialties. At the edge of the grounds there is a swimming pool and a tennis court. This is a good place to come for a lengthly stay. The Albergo will be coming under new management, so we cannot say what changes this may incur.

How to get there *(Map 14): 10 km north of Siena via S222, exit northwest of the town. Casafrassi is south of Castellina.*

Hotel Belvedere di San Leonino ★★★

San Leonino
53011 Castellina in Chianti (Siena)
Tel. (0577) 74 08 87 – Fax (0577) 74 09 24
Sig.ra Orlandi

Rooms 28 with telephone, bath or shower and WC. **Price** Double 140,000L. **Meals** Breakfast included, served 8:00-10:00. **Restaurant** Service 19:30; menu 35,000L, also à la carte. Specialties: Bruschette toscane, gargallette confiori di zucca, lombo di miale al forno con fonduta di gorgonzola pecorino e funghi, semi treddo di ricotta e frutti di bosco. **Credit cards** Amex, Visa, Eurocard, MasterCard. **Pets** Dogs not allowed. **Facilities** Swimming pool, parking. **Nearby** Firenze, Vineyards Chianti Classico (S222) from Impruneta to Siena, Castello di Meleto, Castello di Brolio (Cappella S. Jacopo and Palazzo padronale), Siena. **Open** All year.

The Hotel San Leonino is surrowded by the beautiful countryside. The rooms are in several buildings; they are spacious, simply furnished and impeccably clean. The salon and the dining room on the ground floor have been modernized. The swimming pool at the end of the garden has a panoramic view of the valley. Staying here is a good way to get to know Tuscany, away from the hordes of tourists who periodically overrun Firenze and Siena.

How to get there (Map 14): 10 km north of Siena via S222, Badesse exit; 8 km south of Castellina, in Quercegrossa go left towards San Leonino.

Hotel Villa Belvedere ★★★

53034 Colle di Val d'Elsa (Siena)
Tel. (0577) 92 09 66
Fax (0577) 92 41 28
Sig. Conti

Rooms 15 with telephone, bath or shower and WC (13 with TV). **Price** Double 130-184,000L. **Meals** Breakfast 15,000L, served 8:00-10:00; half board 240-290,000L (per 2 pers.). **Restaurant** Service 12:30-14:00, 19:30-22:00; menu 38,000L, also à la carte. Specialties: Ravioloni tartufati, fFiletto Strozzi, fiorentina con fagioli al fiasco, rane fritte. **Credit cards** All major. **Pets** Dogs not allowed. **Facilities** Swimming pool, parking. **Nearby** Firenze, vineyards Chianti Classico (S222) from Impruneta to Siena, Castello di Meleto, Castello di Brolio (Cappella S. Jacopo and Palazzo padronale), Siena. **Open** All year.

This villa, visited of many kings in the past, has retained its noble and elegant style. Sunlight filters through the beautiful trees in the garden. On the ground floor, there is a pretty salon and an inviting dining room. The spacious and light rooms have simple, tasteful regional furniture. Avoid the rooms on the patio if you are not a morning person–breakfast is served there. Other excellent meals of regional specialties, notably risotto, are served on the terrace. You can fish for yourself in the nearby lake.

How to get there *(Map 14): 15 km northwest of Siena via highway; exit Colle di Val d'Elsa-South then S68; 2 km before the village.*

Castello di Spaltenna ★★★★

53013 Gaiole in Chianti (Siena)
Tel. (0577) 74 94 83
Fax (0577) 74 92 69
Sig. S. de Pentheny O' Kelly

Rooms 21 with air-conditiong, telephone, bath, WC, TV and minibar. **Price** Single 220,000L, double 260-320,000L, suite 385,000L. **Meals** Breakfast included **Restaurant** Service 12:30-14:30, 19:30-22:00, closed Mon. and Tues. lunch; menus 68-78,000L, also à la carte. Specialties: Porcellino di latte arrosto, tagliatelle fresche. **Credit cards** All major. **Pets** Dogs allowed (10,000L). **Facilities** Swimming pool, parking. **Nearby** Firenze, vineyards Chianti Classico (S222) from Impruneta to Siena, Castello di Meleto, Castello di Brolio (Cappella S. Jacopo and Palazzo padronale), Siena. **Open** Mar. 20 – Nov. 20.

This fabulous monastery, built between the 11th and the 13th centuries, has been bought by an Irishman. The very large rooms and look out onto the surrounding vineyards. The size, the height of the ceilings, and the large windows of the salons and the grand floor dining room are impressive. Seamus de Pentheny, the owner, is a great cook: he has studied with the greatest chefs in France other countries, which makes his savory cuisine as varied as it is refined.

How to get there *(Map 14): 28 km northeast of Siena via S408.*

Park Hotel Carvachione ★★★

53013 Gaiole in Chianti (Siena)
Tel. (0577) 74 95 50
Sig. Dabriel

Rooms 11 with, telephone, shower and WC. **Price** Double 185,000L.
Meals Breakfast included **Restaurant** See p. 427. **Credit cards** All major. **Pets**
Dogs allowed. **Facilities** Swimming pool. **Nearby** Firenze, vineyards Chianti
Classico (S222) from Impruneta to Siena, Castello di Meleto, Castello di Brolio
(Cappella S. Jacopo and Palazzo padronale), Siena. **Open** Mar. 15 – Oct.

The extremely confidential address of this hotel has, until
now, circulated almost exclusively by word of mouth. The
very small number of rooms and the particularly friendly
atmosphere here justifies the owner's reluctance to having too
much publicity. His guests are his friends and everything is done
to make each one feel at home. This old, fortified house
overlooking the valley and the castles of Chianti is on ten-acre
grounds. The rooms, although a little cramped, are cozy and
comfortable. The owners' enthusiasm for opera music can
disturb even good friends in the morning.

How to get there *(Map 14): 28 km northeast of Siena via S408.*

Castello di Uzzano

Via Uzzano, 5
50022 Greve in Chianti (Firenze)
Tel. (055) 85 40 32/33 - Fax (055) 85 43 75
Sig.ra De Jacobert

Rooms 6 apartments with kitchen, telephone, bath, WC, TV and minibar.
Price 1,500-2,500,000L per week. **Meals** Breakfast 18,000L, served 8:30-10:30.
Restaurant See p. 427. **Credit cards** All major. **Pets** Dogs and cats allowed.
Facilities Mountain biking, parking. **Nearby** Firenze, vineyards Chianti Classico
(S222) from Impruneta to Siena, Castello di Meleto, Castello di Brolio (Cappella S.
Jacopo and Palazzo padronale), Siena. **Open** All year (closed Sun.).

The Castello di Uzzano is on a 1,235-acre estate; 150 acres of
this is a vineyard. The castle was built around the year 1000
on an Etrusco-Roman site. It was redesigned by Orcagna and
enlarged during the Renaissance; between the 16th and 17th
centuries it was transformed into a villa. The present owners,
restored the Castle to full splendor. The comfortable, charming
apartments are on the courtyard. The furniture, paintings, old
engravings and fireplaces make atmosphere very warm. The
grounds and the maze in garden, in the 18th-century style, are
open to guests (except Sundays). For a souvenir, you can buy
items produced on the estate, such as wine, olive oil and brandy.
A visit to the castle with a wine tasting are a good idea even if
you don't stay here.

How to get there *(Map 14): 30 km south of Firenze via A1 Rome-Firenze,
Incisa-Valdarno exit; via A1 Milano-Bologna, Firenze-Certosa exit.*

Residence San Sano ★★★★

San Sano
(53010) Lecchi in Chianti (Siena)
Tel. (0577) 74 61 30 – Fax (0577) 74 61 56
Sig. and Sig.ra Matarazzo

Rooms 14 with telephone, shower, WC, TV and minibar. **Price** Double 170-190,000L. **Meals** Breakfast included, served 8:00-10:00. **Restaurant** Service 19:30; closed Sun.; menus 30,000L. Specialties: Tuscan cuisine. **Credit cards** All major. **Pets** Dogs allowed by request. **Facilities** Swimming pool, parking. **Nearby** Monteriggioni, Abbadia Isola, Colle di Val d'Elsa (colle Alta), Firenze, Siena, San Gimignano, Arezzo. **Open** Mar. 15 – Nov. 3.

Giancarlo and Heidi came all the way from Germany to restore this ancient fortress in the heart of Chianti country. They restored and decorated it perfectly. The polished furniture, the pink flagstone floors, the exposed beams and the stone arcades create a simple, authentic atmosphere. The rooms have modern, comfortable bathrooms and bear the name of the detail which makes them unique; the most charming and surprising is "the Nests Room" (which has been preserved intact but protected with a clever system of insulating glass). "The Room With A View" looks out on the small green valleys planted with grapevines. Fine regional cuisine is served only in the evening in the pleasant dining room, and delicious breakfasts await you on the terrace in summer.

How to get there *(Map 14): 20 km north of Siena via S408; then left towards Lecchi, then San Sano.*

Hotel Monteriggioni ★★★★

53035 Monteriggioni (Sienna)
Tel. (0577) 30 50 09 – Fax (0577) 30 50 11
Sig.ra Gozzi

Rooms 12 with air conditioning, telephone, bath, WC, TV and minibar. **Price** Single 200,000L, double 290,000L. **Meals** Breakfast included, served 9:00-10:00. **Credit cards** Amex, Visa, Eurocard and MasterCard. **Pets** Dogs allowed. **Nearby** Siena, Abbadia Isola, Colle Val d'Elsa, Basilica dell' Osservanza and chartreuse de Pontignano, San Gimignano; Volterra **Open** Feb. 16 – Jan. 14.

The towers of Monteriggioni rise like a mirage on the highway connecting Firenze and Siena. The beauty of the decapitated walls and towers, especially at sunset, will make you want get off the highway for a closer look. This small village is made up of what originally were old military buildings dating back to the time when Montérriggioni was still a Sienian garrison (the 8th century). The hotel, in the village, discreet is luxuly now. The rooms are all different and are very comfortable. We prefer the ones on the garden where breakfast is served in summer. Just across the street is one of the best restaurants in the region, Il Pozzo, which more than makes up for the lack of a restaurant in the hotel.

How to get there *(Map 14): 12 km north of Siena, on 4 Corsie, Colle di Val d'Elsa-Monteriggioni exit.*

La Chiusa

Via della Madonnina, 88
53040 Montefollonico (Siena)
Tel. (0577) 66 96 68 – Fax (0577) 66 95 93
Sig.ra Masotti and Sig. Lucherini

Rooms 6 and 6 apartments with telephone, bath, WC, TV and minibar.
Price Double 280,000L, suite 490-630,000L. **Meals** Breakfast included, served
8:30-10:30. **Restaurant** Service 12:30-15:00, 20:00-22:00; closed Tues.; menus
130,000L, also à la carte. Specialties: Collo d'oca ripieno, pappardelle Dania,
coniglio marinato al romarino, piccione al vinsanto. **Credit cards** All major.
Pets Dogs allowed. **Nearby** Montepulciano, Monticchiello, Montalcino, Terme in
Bagno Vignoli, Val d'Orcia villages (Castiglione d'Orcia, Rocca d'Orcia, Ripa
d'Orcia, Campiglia d'Orcia), Pienza, Collegiale San Quirico d'Orcia, Museo
Nazionale Etrusco in Siusi, Chianciano Terme, Siena. **Open** Mar. 20 – Nov. 10 and
Dec. 28 – Jan. 10.

La Chiusa is more than just a famous restaurant and inn—it's the
house of Dania, a gracious young woman whose charm plays
an important role in the reputation of this magical place. She
passionately loves her work and takes pleasure in receiving her
guests as if they were good friends. The delicious meals are
always prepared with fresh products from the farm. The rooms
and the apartments are very comfortable and very well kept. The
breakfasts, of homemade jellies and brioches and fresh fruit juices
are generous. When you watch the sun set over the Val di
Chiana and the Val d'Orcia, you will start planning your next
trip back.

How to get there *(Map 14): 60 km south of Siena via A1, Valdichiana
exit - Bettole, Torrita di Siena Montefollonico.*

La Saracina

Strada Statale, 146 (km 29,7)
53026 Pienza (Siena)
Tel. (0578) 74 80 22 – Fax (0578) 74 80 22
Sig. Don Mc Cobb

Rooms 5 and 1 apartment with telephone, bath, WC and TV. **Price** Double 230,000L, apartment 300,000L, suite 320,000L. **Meals** Breakfast included **Restaurant** See p.428. **Credit cards** All major. **Pets** Dogs not allowed. **Facilities** Swimming poll, tennis, parking. **Nearby** Pienza (Duomo, Palazzo Piccolomini), Montepulciano, Monticchiello, Montalcino, Terme in Bagno Vignoni, villages in Val d'Orcia (Collegiale San Quirico d'Orcia, Castiglione d'Orcia, Rocca d'Orcia, Ripa d'Orcia, Campiglia d'Orcia), Sant'Anna Camprena abbey (frescoes of Sodoma), Spedaletto, Chiusi, Cetona, Chianciano. **Open** All year.

The Saracina is in an old farmhouse on a small hill, which has a view of Pienza, Monticchiello and Montefollonico. The rooms are very beautiful; they are decorated with antique furniture and have large bathrooms and very comfortable salons. Everything has been done with exquisite taste. A savory breakfast is served in the shade of the pretty garden or on the terrace. Be sure to spend some time visiting the enchanting town of Pienza, which has remained intact since the Renaissance and is not a tourist trap. It was the work of Pope Pius II of Piccolomini, who wanted, with the help of architect B. Rossellino, to create the ideal town. Several palaces and the cathedral were built before the work was interrupted by the sudden death of the two sponsors. Fortunately, no one has disturbed the harmony of this small town which served as the set of Zefferelli's *Romeo and Juliet*.

How to get there *(Map 15): 52 km southeast of Siena via S2 to San Quirico then Pienza.*

Relais Il Chiostro di Pienza ★★★

Corso Rossellino, 26
53026 Pienza (Siena)
Tel. (0578) 74 84 00/42 – Fax (0578) 74 84 40
Sig.ra Bonifacci

Rooms 26 with telephone, bath or shower, WC, TV and minibar. **Price** Single 110,000L, double 170,000L, suite 220,000L. **Meals** Breakfast included **Restaurant** Service 13:00-14:30, 19:00-21:00, closed Mon.; menu, also à la carte. Specialties: regional cooking. **Credit cards** All major. **Pets** Dogs not allowed. **Facilities** Swimming pool, parking. **Nearby** Pienza (Duomo, Palazzo Piccolomini), Montepulciano, Monticchiello, Montalcino, Terme in Bagno Vignoni, villages in Val d'Orcia (Collegiale San Quirico d'Orcia, Castiglione d'Orcia, Rocca d'Orcia, Ripa d'Orcia, Campiglia d'Orcia), Sant'Anna Camprena abbey (frescoes of Sodoma), Spedaletto, Chiusi, Cetona, Chianciano. **Open** All year.

Pienza now has a long-awaited charming hotel, the Relais Il Chiostro di Pienza, in a 15th-century monastery in the heart of this historical town. The restoration is superb: You can see the arches, exposed beams, frescos, and of course, the cloister. The rooms are spacious and simply decorated. A deep quiet and serenity pervades the place. A restaurant will open in May 1996, but in the meantime you can have a very pleasant breakfast on the terrace. This place is ideal for exploring the magnificent small Renaissance town of Pienza, as well as the numerous Etrusco-Roman sites in the area.

How to get there *(Map 15): 52 km southeast of Siena via S2 to San Quirico then Pienza.*

Castello di Ripa d'Orcia ★★★

Ripa d'Orcia 53023 Castiglione d'Orcia (Siena)
Tel. (0577) 89 73 76 – Fax (0577) 89 80 38
Sig.ra Aluffi

Rooms 6 and 7 apartments with bath or shower and WC. **Price** Single 90,000L, double 95-135,000L, apart. 410-490,000L (2 pers., 3 nights), 620-730,000L (4 pers., 3 nights), 1,090-1,270,000L (4 pers., 7 nights). **Meals** Breakfast included **Restaurant** Service 19:30-22:00; closed Mon., also à la carte 35-45,000L. Specialties: Zuppa di pane, tortelloni al pecorino di Pienza, scottiglia di carni miste, trippa alla fiorentina, dessert della casa. **Credit cards** Not accepted. **Pets** Dogs not allowed. **Facilities** Parking. **Nearby** Val d'Orcia: Peinza, Montepulciano, Monticchiello, Montalcino and Sant' Antimo abbey, Terme de Bagno Vignoni, villages of the Val d'Orcia (Collegiale San Quirico d'Orcia, Castiglione d'Orcia, Rocca (d'Orcia, Ripa d'Orcia, Campiglia d'Orcia), Sant'Anna Camprena abbey, Spedaletto, Chiusi, Cetona, Chianciano. **Open** Mar. 2 – Jan. 7.

Ripa d'Orcia is one of those beautiful little hamlets, which has not changed since the Middle Ages. To get to the castle you must drive from San Quirico into the countryside for about 3 miles. Be patient, even if the road isn't in very good condition, its beautiful! In the heart of unspoiled surroundings, Ripa d'Orcia is worth a visit. You will quickly see a wall of cypress trees at the edge of the hamlet. Careful restoration has brought life back to some of the houses in the village, where you can now find rooms, apartments, a restaurant, and a superb meeting room. The level of comfort is, unfortunately, not as superb as the site. Although the apartments are equipped with all of the basics, we prefer the rooms, which are prettier and more comfortable.

How to get there *(Map 15): 45 km south of Siena (towards lago di Bolsena and Viterbo) via S2 to San Quirico and Ripa d'Orcia. A1, Val di Chiana or Chiusi-Chanciano exit and towards Pienza.*

Cantina Il Borgo

1996

Rocca d'Orcia 53023 Castiglione d'Orcia (Siena)
Tel. (0577) 88 72 80 – Fax (0577) 88 72 80 – Sig. Tanganelli

Rooms 3 with air conditioning, shower, WC and TV. **Price** 90-120,000L.
Meals Breakfast included, served 9:00-10:00. **Restaurant** Service 12:30-15:00,
19:30-21:30; closed Mon., à la carte 40,000L. **Credit cards** Amex, Visa, Eurocard,
MastercArd. **Pets** Dogs allowed. **Nearby** Val d'Orcia, Peinza, Montepulciano,
Monticchiello, Montalcino and Sant' Antimo abbey, Terme de Bagno Vignoni,
villages of the Val d'Orcia (Collegiale San Quirico d'Orcia, Castiglione d'Orcia,
Rocca (d'Orcia, Ripa d'Orcia, Campiglia d'Orcia), Sant'Anna Camprena abbey,
Spedaletto, Chuisi, Cetona, Chianciano. **Open** Feb. 16 – Jan. 14.

You can see the Rocca di Tentennano, the imposing military
fortress, towering above the Val d'Orcia from a distance. The
old Medieval town is discreetly set back, down below, as if to protect
itself from a few curious tourists. The village looks like it has been
asleep for centuries. The telephone booth (from which you can easily
call long distance) is the only reminder of the present. The restaurant,
the Cantina Il Borgo, is in one of the austere houses on the site—a
refurbished coach house—across from a superb octagonal, cited in texts
since the 12th century. The owner will welcome you simply, but
he's more than willing to share what he loves in this region with you:
its wine, cuisine, and the numerous trails which criss-cross the Val
d'Orcia. The three carefully prepared rooms have whitewashed walls,
wrought iron beds, antique furniture, and an array of fabrics
combining stripes and gingham, for a modern touch. The shower
rooms are comfortably equipped. This place is surprisingly nice.

*How to get there (Map 15): 50 km south of Siena (towards lago di
Bolsena and Viterbo) via S2, towards Castiglione d'Orcia and Rocca. A1,
Val di Chiana or Chiusi-Chanciano exit towards Pienza.*

Relais La Suvera ★★★★

La Suvera
53030 Pievescola di Casole d'Elsa (Siena)
Tel. (0577) 96 03 00/1/2/3 - Fax (0577) 96 02 20
Sig. Marioti

Rooms 20, and 12 suites, with telephone, bath, WC and cable TV. **Price** Single 280,000L, double 330,000L, suite 380-600,000L. **Meals** Breakfast included; half board +55,000L. **Restaurant** Service 20:00-23:00; also à la carte 70-80,000L. Specialties: Regional cuisine. **Credit cards** All major. **Pets** Dogs not allowed. **Facilities** Swimming pool, sauna, tennis, parking. **Nearby** Colle di Val d'Elsa, Abbadia Isola, Monteriggioni, Firenze, San Gimignano, Siena, dell'Ugolino golf course (18-hole) in Grassina. **Open** Apr. 1 – Oct.

There is no way to describe La Suvera without using superlatives. This papal villa, built in the 18th century, first belonged to an important Italian family, the Borgeses, then was bought several decades ago by Lucchinio Visconti, who passed it on to the Marquis de Ricci, the current owner. Today, La Suvera is both a luxury hotel and the sumptuous residence of a collector with a passion. The hotel consists of three buildings: The Oliviera and the Scederies have beautiful, very plush rooms, and the papal villa has suites, created by the marquis and his wife, which are perfect reconstitutions of a historical period or character; they are a collector's dream and a traveler's delight. The service at La Suvera is perfect, the cuisine excellent, and the gardens admirable.

How to get there *(Map 14): 61 km south of Firenze via SS Firenze-Siena, Colle di Val d'Elsa-sud exit, then via Grosseto; after 15 km, Pievescola.*

Hotel Villa San Lucchese ★★★★

50036 Poggibonsi (Siena)
Via S. Lucchese, 5
Tel. (0577) 93 42 31 – Fax (0577) 93 47 29
Sig. Ninci

Rooms 36 with air-conditioning, telephone, bath or shower, WC, TV, minibar and elevator. **Price** Single 100-180,000L, double 200-300,000L, suite 250-300,000L. **Meals** Breakfast included, served 7:30-10:00; half board 35,000L, full board 70,000L (per pers.). **Restaurant** Service 12:30-14:00, 19:30-22:00; closed Tues.; menu 50,000L, à la carte. Specialties: Tuscan cuisine. **Credit cards** All major. **Pets** Dogs not allowed. **Facilities** Swimming pool, tennis, parking. **Nearby** Firenze, Sienna, Colle Val d'Elsa, San Gimignano, Volterra, Monterrigioni Chianti Route. **Open** All year.

The hotel is ideally located in Poggibonsi, at the crossroads of the main cities of Tuscany, Florence and Siena. It is next to the San Lucchese monastery, overlooking the town and all of its commotion. This 15th century noble villa, has vast, light rooms and a pleasant classical decor. On the ground floor the restaurant opens onto a very large terrace, which looks out over the Val d'Elsa plain. In the garden, next to a grove of superb centenarian trees, there is a large pool. The hotel is well equipped for receptions.

How to get there *(Map 14): 19 km north of Siena. Superstrada «4 Corsie,» Poggibonsa exit. A1, Firenze Certosa exit.*

Albergo Borgo Pretale ★★★★

Borgo Pretale
53018 Sovicille (Siena)
Tel. (0577) 34 54 01 – Fax (0577) 34 56 25
Sig. Ricardini

Rooms 35 with telephone, bath, WC, TV and minibar. **Price** 160-175,000L (per pers.), suite 32,000L (per pers.). **Meals** Breakfast included, served 7:30-10:00; half board 60,000L (par pers., 3 days min.). **Restaurant** Service 20:00-21:30; menu: 60,000L, also à la carte. Specialties: Tuscan and Italian cuisine. **Credit cards** All major. **Pets** Dogs not allowed. **Facilities** Swimming pool, tennis, fitness center with sauna, mountain bikes, golf practice, parking. **Nearby** Villa Cetinale in Sovicille, Torri abbey in Rosia, San Galgano abbey, Siena. **Open** Mar. 16 – Nov. 14.

About eleven miles (18 km) from Siena, in a village which has retained its authenticity and its Tuscan colors, the Torre Borgo Pretale, has weathered nine centuries of history marvelously well. It is, in fact, in the heart of historic Tuscany. There are twenty-five wonderful rooms, a suite on the top floor of the tower and several apartments at garden level. The interior is comfortable and furnished with exquisite taste. The staff is very attentive. In summer, you can enjoy the club house, swimming pool, tennis court and other recreational facilities, even if you come for the Quattrocento pilgrimage.

How to get there *(Map 14): 18 km southeast of Siena via S73 towards Rosia.*

Relais Fattoria Vignale ★★★★

Via Pianigiani, 15
53017 Radda in Chianti (Siena)
Tel. (0577) 73 83 00 - Fax (0577) 73 85 92
Sig.ra Kummer

Rooms 30 with air-conditioning, telephone, bath, WC, TV and minibar.
Price Single 180-200,000L, double 270-330,000L. **Meals** Breakfast included
(buffet), served 7:30-10:30; half board 50,000L, full board 100,000L (per pers., 3
days min.). **Restaurant** Service 13:00-14:30, 19:30-21:00; closed Nov. 10 – Mar.
20; menus: 60-80,000L, also à la carte. Specialties: Seasonal and Tuscan cuisine.
Credit cards All major. **Pets** Dogs not allowed. **Facilities** Swimming pool, parking.
Nearby Siena, vineyard Chianti Classico (N 222), Impruneta, Firenze, dell'Ugolino
golf course (18-hole) in Grassina. **Open** Mar. 22 – Nov. 15.

This house, once owned by rich landowners, was entirely
renovated in 1983 by the present owners. You can feel the
meticulous fidelity to the past in the discreet decor, the vaulted
cellar, where can have breakfast, the immense fireplace in one of
the salons, the painted walls in the library, and the austerity of
the objects and furniture in the rooms. Connoisseurs should not
miss a chance to stop off at this beautiful hotel, which produces
excellent wine and has a special winelibrary available for
consultation by guests.

*How to get there (Map 14): 30 km north of Siena via S222 to Castellina
in Chianti, then S429.*

Podere Terreno

Volpaia - 53 017 Radda in Chianti (Siena)
Tel. (0577) 73 83 12 - Fax (0577) 73 83 12
Sig.ra Haniez

Rooms 7 with shower and WC. **Price** With half board 120,000L (per pers., 2 nights min. in high season). **Meals** Breakfast included, served 8:30-10:30. **Restaurant** Service 20:00; menu. Specialties: Tuscan and Mediterannean cuisine. **Credit cards** Amex, Visa, Eurocard, MasterCard. **Pets** Dogs allowed. **Facilities** Parking. **Nearby** Siena, Vineyard Chianti Classico (N 222), dell'Ugolino golf course (18-hole) in Grassina. **Open** All year.

This beautiful stone farmhouse is in the middle of a large estate of more than one hundred and twenty four acres with oak and chestnut trees, olive orchards and a vineyard, which produces quality wine and excellent olive oil. The old traditional Tuscan kitchen has been converted into a salon. The large couch in front of the fireplace, the rustic antique furniture and Marie-Sylvie's and Roberto's collections, all add to the decor. The very charming rooms are comfortable and decorated with taste and simplicity. Marie-Sylvie makes the jellies she serves for breakfast and Roberto supervises the kitchen. Meals are served around a large common table, accompanied by wine from the estate vineyards. The billiards room and library in the cellar are good places to spend a quiet moment alone, as is the arbor in the garden.

How to get there *(Map 14): 30 km north of Siena via S222 to Panzano in Chianti, towards Radda in Chianti. Before Radda, left towards Volpaia and Podere Terreno.*

Albergo Vescine

Vescine – 53017 Radda in Chianti (Siena)
Tel. (0577) 741 144 – Fax (0577) 740 263
Sig.ra Fleig

Rooms 25 with telephone, bath or shower, WC, TV, minibar. **Price** With half board 160,000L (per 1 pers.), 260-330,000L (per pers., double room or suite). **Meals** Breakfast included, served 7:30-10:00. **Credit cards** Amex, Visa, Eurocard, MasterCard. **Pets** Dogs allowed (10,000L). **Facilities** Parking. **Nearby** Siena, Vineyard Chianti Classico (N 222), San Gimignano, Firenze, dell'Ugolino golf course (18-hole) in Grassina. **Open** All year.

If you are looking for peace and quiet and are not afraid of solitude, Vescine is the place for you. This small hamlet in the heart of Chianti (on 185 acre grounds) has been transformed into a country inn; a unique setting for your visit to Tuscanny. Completely retsored and renovated, the buildings are connected by pretty little cobblestone paths abundantly lined with flowers. The young directrice has made this place a successful blend of Tuscan mildness and Germanic comfort. The rooms are simple and very functional. You can embellish your visit with many delights, from the swimming pool to the wine cellar with numerous vintage wines from the region.

How to get there *(Map 14): 30 km north of Siena via S222 to Panzano in Chianti, towards Radda in Chianti. Before Radda, left towards Volpaia.*

Hotel Relais Borgo San Felice ★★★★

San Felice
53019 Castelnuovo Berardenga (Siena)
Tel. (0577) 35 92 60 - Fax (0577) 35 90 89
Sig. Righi

Rooms 38 and 12 suites with telephone, bath, WC, TV and minibar. **Price** Single 277,000L, double 407,000L, suite 530,000L. **Meals** Breakfast included, served 7:30-10:30; half board 310-380,000L, full board 385-452,000L. **Restaurant** Service 12:30-14:00, 19:30-21:30; menus 75-100,000L. Specialties: Tuscan and Italian cuisine. **Credit cards** All major. **Pets** Dogs allowed. **Facilities** Swimming pool, tennis, parking. **Nearby** Castello delle quattro torri near by de Due Ponti, Castello di Brolio and Chianti vineyard via Meleto, Gaiole, Badia Coltibuono, Radda and Castellina in Chianti. **Open** Mar. – Oct.

A little square in front of a postcard chapel, small cobblestone streets lined with houses covered with flowers, cute gardens, stone stairways, beautiful Virginia creepercovered facades–you will find all this and more in Borgo San Felice, a Medieval Tuscan village. It feels like a village which has continued its agricultural activity of producing wine and olive oil. The houses are very tastefully decorated, with nice open spaces, shades of ochre and pretty furniture. A beautiful swimming pool, very professional service and an excellent restaurant make Borgo San Felice a hotel which we heartily recommend.

How to get there *(Map 14): 17 km east of Siena; in Siena, SS Siena-Perugia towards Arezzo, then 7 km to Montaperti.*

Hotel l'Antico Pozzo

Via San Matteo, 87
53037 San Gimignano (Siena)
Tel. (0577) 94 20 14 – Fax (0577) 94 21 17
Sig. Marro and Sig. Caponi

Rooms 18 with air-conditioning, telephone, bath, WC, cable TV, hairdryer, safe and minibar (whirl pool in suite). **Price** Single 130,000L, double 180,000L, suite 230,000L. **Meals** Breakfast included. **Restaurant** See p.428. **Credit cards** All major. **Pets** Dogs not allowed. **Nearby** San Gimignano (Church of sant'Agostino), piazza del Duomo, piazza della Cisterna, Palazzo del Popolo, Etruscan ancient city of Pieve di Cellole, Convent of S. Vivaldo, Certaldo, Pinacoteca and Visitation chapel (frescoes of Benozzo Gozzoli) in Castelfiorentino, Firenze, Siena, Volterra, Castelfalfi golf course (18-hole). **Open** All year.

Two talented young people with impeccable taste have restored this very beautiful 15th-century residence in the heart of San Gimignano. The house still has its original architecture and frescos. There is an old well inside the house, which is why the hotel has this name. Pretty, antique furniture and beautiful fabrics add to the atmosphere of elegance. If you ask for the fresco room, beware, it is unfortunately on the fire escape. The salon and breakfast room are very pleasant.

How to get there *(Map 14): 38 km northeast of Siena, in town center. Parking: Porta San Matteo (100 m).*

Hotel La Cisterna ★★★

Piazza della Cisterna, 24
53037 San Gimignano (Siena)
Tel. (0577) 94 03 28 – Fax (0577) 94 20 80
Sig. Salvestrini

Rooms 47 and 2 suites with telephone, bath or shower, WC, cable TV and safe.
Price Single 98,000L, double 131-166,000L, suite 196,000L. **Meals** Breakfast
included, served 7:30-10:00; half board 105,500-123,000L, full board 142,500-
1C0,000L (per pers.). **Restaurant** Service 12:30-14:30, 19:30-21:30; closed Tues.
and Wed. at noon; menus 50-70,000L. Specialties: Intercosta scaloppata al
chianti, specialita' ai funghi e ai tartufi. **Credit cards** All major. **Pets** Dogs not
allowed. **Nearby** San Gimignano (church of Sant'Agostino, piazza della Cisterna,
Palazzo del Popolo), Etruscan ancient city of Pieve di Cellole, Monastery of S.
Vivaldo, Certaldo, Pinacoteca and Visitation chapel (frescoes of Benozzo Gozzoli)
in Castelfiorentino, Firenze, Siena, Volterra, Castelfalfi golf course (18-hole).
Open All year (except Jan. 11 – Mar. 9).

This former convent, in the heart of the pretty town of San
Gimignano, was transformed into a hotel–restaurant at the
beginning of the century. It opens onto a square on one side,
and overlooks the Val d'Elsa and the sumptuous landscapes of
Tuscany on the other. The 18th–century Florentine furniture is
in perfect harmony with the architectural elegance of the place.
Le Terrazze, the restaurant, is famous for its fine regional cuisine
and wines, notably the Vernaccia di San Gimignano.

How to get there (Map 14): *38 km northeast of Siena, in town center.*
Parking: Porta San Matteo (200 meters).

Hotel Bel Soggiorno ★★★

Via San Giovanni, 91
53037 San Gimignano (Siena)
Tel. (0577) 94 03 75 - Fax (0577) 94 03 75
Sig. Gigli

Rooms 21 with air-conditioning, telephone, bath, WC, TV and 6 with minibar.
Price Double 120-135,000L, suite 160-180,000L. **Meals** Breakfast 10,000L,
served 8:00-10:00, half board about 110,000L, full board about 150,000L (per
pers.). **Restaurant** With air-conditioning. Service 12:15-14:30, 19:30-21:30;
closed Jan. 10 – Feb. 10; menu about 45,000L, à la carte. Specialties: Traditional
cuisine. **Credit cards** All major. **Pets** Dogs not allowed. **Facilities** Parking and
garage (15,000L). **Nearby** San Gimignano (church of Sant'agostino, piazza della
Cisterna, Palazzo del Popolo) Etruscan ancient city of Pieve di Cellole, Convent of
S. Vivaldo, Certaldo, Pinacoteca and Visitation chapel (frescoes of
Benozzo Gozzoli) in Castelfiorentino, Firenze, Siena, Volterra, Castelfalfi golf
course (18-hole). **Open** All year.

This very beautiful 13th-century house, in the center of San
Gimignano, has belonged to the family that also runs Le
Pescille, for five generations. A warm welcome awaits you here.
The rooms are unevenly charming: some are on the street and
others have a magnificent balcony overlooking the countryside
(Rooms 1, 2, and 6). The two suites (11 and 21) are the most
beautiful; they have small terraces overlooking the valley. The
restaurant also has an extraordinary view, and you can enjoy
excellent traditional cuisine, which has been the cause of Bel
Soggiorno's good reputation for several generations.

How to get there *(Map 14): 38 km northeast of Siena, in town center.*
Parking: Porta San Matteo (200 m).

276

Villa San Paolo ★★★★

53037 San Gimignano (Siena)
Tel. (0577) 95 51 00
Fax (0577) 95 51 13
Sig.ra Sabatini-Volpini and Sig. Squarcia

Rooms 18 with air-conditioning, telephone, bath, WC, cable TV and minibar.
Price Single 100-185,000L, double 140-265,000L. **Meals** Breakfast included,
served 7:30-10:30; half board 275-330,000L, full board 335-390,000L.
Restaurant "Leonetto" in Hotel Le Renaie (see p. 278). **Credit cards** All major.
Pets Dogs allowed. **Facilities** Swimming pool, tennis. **Nearby** San Gimignano
(Church of sant'Agostino), piazza del Duomo, piazza della Cisterna, Palazzo del
Popolo; etruscan ancient city of Pieve di Cellole, Monastery of S. Vivaldo, Certaldo,
Pinacoteca and Visitation chapel (frescoes of Benozzo Gozzoli) in Castelfiorentino,
Firenze, Siena, Volterra, Castelfalfi golf course (18-hole). **Open** All year (except
Jan. 10 – Feb. 10).

This small hotel in a beautiful villa is in the San Gimignano
countryside on large grounds full of pine and olive trees.
The owners also have a hotel next door, Le Renaie. There are
only a few rooms; all are air-conditioned and extremely
comfortable. The "winter-garden" decor is cheery and warm.
There is a superb pool with snack service and an unforgettable
view of the countryside around San Gimignano. There is no
restaurant, but you can always go the "Leonetto" next door. In
the local area, there are historical sites to visit and numerous trails
for hiking or horseback riding (there is a club a few miles away).

How to get there *(Map 14): 38 km northeast of Siena; 5 km north of San
Gimignano towards Certaldo.*

Hotel Le Renaie

53037 San Gimignano
Pancole (Siena)
Tel. (0577) 95 50 44 – Fax (0577) 95 51 26
Sig. Sabatini

Rooms 25 with telephone, bath, WC and TV. **Price** Single 90,000L, double 120-148,000L. **Meals** Breakfast 12,000L, served 8:00-10:00; half board 110-124,000L, full board 135,000L (per pers., 3 days min.). **Restaurant** Service 12:30-14:30, 19:30-22:00; closed Tues.; menus 30-60,000L, also à la carte. Specialties: Coniglio alla vernaccia, piatti al tartufi, piatti agli asparagi e ai funghi. **Credit cards** All major. **Pets** Dogs allowed. **Facilities** Swimming pool, tennis, parking. **Nearby** San Gimignano (church of Sant'agostino, piazza della Cisterna, Palazzo del Popolo), Etruscan ancient city of Pieve di Cellole, Convent of S. Vivaldo, Certaldo, Pinacoteca and Visitation chapel (frescoes of Benozzo Gozzoli) in Castelfiorentino, Firenze, Siena, Volterra, Castelfalfi golf course (18-hole). **Open** All year (except Nov. 5 – Dec. 5).

L e Renaie is in the countryside near San Gimignano. Recently constructed, it respects the traditional Tuscan materials and colors. Tiles, bricks, terra cotta and wood form a harmonious blend of textures and colors: pale pink and off-white colors predominate. The contemporary salon, with its large fireplace and a pretty little bar open onto a gallery surrounded by plants and flowers, particularly pleasant for having breakfast or a drink. The rooms are all comfortable and pleasant, but try to get the ones with a terrace overlooking the countryside.

How to get there *(Map 14): 38 km northeast of Siena; 6 km northwest of San Gimignano to Pieve di Cellole, then Pancole.*

Il Casolare di Libbiano

Libbiano
53037 San Gimignano (Siena)
Tel. (0577) 94 60 02 – Fax (0577) 94 60 02
Sig. Bucciarelli and Sig.ra Mateos

Rooms 5 with shower, WC and 1 suite with bath, WC. **Price** Double 210-230,000L, suite 260,000L. **Meals** Breakfast included, served 8:30-10:00; half board 250-300,000L. **Restaurant** Service 20:00. Specialties: Traditional Tuscan cuisine. **Credit cards** Not accepted. **Pets** Dogs allowed. **Facilities** Swimming pool, parking. **Nearby** San Gimignano (church of Sant'agostino, piazza della Cisterna, Palazzo del Popolo) Etruscan ancient city of Pieve di Cellole, Convent of S. Vivaldo, Certaldo, Pinacoteca and Visitation chapel (frescoes of Benozzo Gozzoli) in Castelfiorentino, Firenze, Siena, Volterra, Castelfalfi golf course (18-hole). **Open** Mar. – Oct.

In arid isolation at the end of a road lined with a few dust-coated bushes is the Libbiano, which has been renovated by the hand of a master. He used traditional materials—stone and terra cotta—in the salons and the rooms, which are neat and spacious and have old, comfortable furniture. There is a pool surrounded by olive and lemon trees and oleander bushes. The young man who runs the house is very kind and discreetly attentive. You will eat well here. Breakfasts are marvelously varied: fruit salads, ham and Tuscan bread served on a wood cutting board. In the common areas—the salon near the fireplace or on the terraces—there are many spots which lend themselves to reading, contemplation or simply *dolce far niente* (sweet idleness).

How to get there *(Map 14): 8 km from San Gimignano, towards Gambassi, left to Libbiano.*

Hotel Villa Arceno ★★★★

53010 San Gusmé – Castelnuovo Berardenga (Siena)
Tel. (0577) 35 92 92 – Fax (0577) 35 92 76
Sig. Mancini

Rooms 16 with telephone, bath, WC, TV and minibar. **Price** Single 250,000L,
double 400,000L, suite 508,000L. **Meals** Breakfast included, served 7:30-10:30;
half board 290-345L (per pers.). **Restaurant** Service 13:00-14:30, 20:00-22:00;
menus about 85,000L, also à la carte. Specialties: Italian and Tuscan cuisine.
Credit cards All major. **Pets** Dogs not allowed. **Facilities** Swimming pool, practice
golf course, tennis, parking. **Nearby** Siena, Arezzo, Monte San Savino, Monte
Oliveto abbey, crest road from Asciano to Siena. **Open** Mar. – Oct.

Getting to Castelnuovo Berardenga from Siena is no problem,
and along the way you will enjoy the marvelous landscape and
light that inspired Sienese painters. Finding the small hamlet of San
Gusmé, once outside of the village, is doable, but finding the Villa
Arceno is impossible without some help. When you are on the road,
look for a big arch with "Arceno" written on it. Drive through the
gate, follow the road through the woods, vineyards and olive trees,
and if, at this point, you haven't turned around and gone back
thinking you are lost, you will arrive at the villa. This beautiful 17th-
century country house is on a 24,700-acre estate; it is an old hunting
lodge which belonged to a rich Italian family until recently when it
was transformed into a very nice hotel. The 19 farms on the estate
were also carefully restored. The hotel is decorated with beautiful
fabrics. The rooms are spacious and comfortable, and the staff is very
welcoming.

How to get there *(Map 14): 25 km east of Siena via A1; Valdichiana or
Monte San Savino exit towards Monte San Savino, to Castelnuovo
Berardenga, San Gusmé.*

Locanda dell'Amorosa ★★★★

L'Amorosa
53048 Sinalunga (Siena)
Tel. (0577) 67 94 97 – Fax (0577) 67 82 16
Sig. Citterio

Rooms 11 and 4 suites with air-conditioning, telephone, bath, WC, TV and minibar. **Price** Standard 230,000L, superior 260,000L, luxury 480,000L, suite 530,000L. **Meals** Breakfast included, served 7:30-10:00. **Restaurant** Service 12:30-14:30, 20:00-21:15; closed Mon. and Tues. at noon; à la carte. Specialties: New regional cuisine, very good Italian wines. **Credit cards** All major. **Pets** Dogs allowed in room. **Facilities** Parking. **Nearby** Sinalunga (Collegiata di San Martino and church of S. Croce de Sinalunga), Museo Civico, Palazzo Comunale, Church Madonna delle Averce in Lucignano, Monte San Savino (loggia), Arezzo; Siena. **Open** All year (except Jan. 20 - Feb. 28).

After crossing the plain where Piero della Francesca was born, a long cypress-lined path will lead you to the entrance of the Locanda. Once you have gone through the vaulted archway, you will find enchanting old buildings built out of a mixture of stone, brick and the pink terra cotta of Siena. Quiet confort and good taste are the great luxuries of this inn, one of the most beautiful in Italy. The cuisine, made from numerous products from the farm, is excellent. The selection of wines from the region is also nice. Don't miss this place if you can afford it.

How to get there *(Map 15): 50 km southeast of Siena via S326; via A1, Val di Chiana exit; 2 km south of Sinalunga to L'Amorosa.*

La Frateria ★★★★

53040 Cetona (Siena)
Convento San Francesco
Tel. (0578) 23 80 15 – Fax (0578) 23 82 61

Rooms 7 with bath and WC. **Price** Single 220,000L, double 280,000L, suite 380-480,000L. **Meals** Breakfast included, served 7:30-10:00; half board 245-275,000L, full board 285-320,000L (per pers., 3 days min.). **Restaurant** Service 13:00, 20:00; closed Tues. except on request; menu: 100,000L. Specialties: New traditional cuisine. **Credit cards** Amex in the restaurant only. **Pets** Dogs not allowed. **Facilities** Parking. **Nearby** Montepulciano, Monticchiello, Montalcino, Terme de Bagno Vignoli, Val d'Orcia villages (Castiglione d'Orcia, Rocca d'Orcia, Ripa d'Orcia, Campiglia d'Orcia), Pienza, Collegiale San Quirico d'Orcia, Museo Nazionale Etrusco in Siusi, Chianciano Terme, Siena. **Open** All year (except Feb. by request).

A young Franciscan priest decided to restore an abandoned convent with the help of a community of troubled youth called "Mondo X." The result is nothing short of extraordinary. After a considerable amount of restoration, the convent once again has its chapels, cloisters with laurel flowers, meditation room, and very recently, dining hall. The garden is overloaded with clematis, camellias and azalies. In summer, the rose bushes and kiwi trees take over. The feeling here is harmony with nature. The cuisine in the restaurant consists of Tuscan specialties made exclusively with products from La Frateria's farm. The rooms are very nicely decorated and have a slightly monastic feel to them. If you didn't know that the founder of the order, Saint Francis of Assisi, had a taste for nice things, you might be surprised by so much elegance.

How to get there *(Map 15): 89 km of Siena, via A1, Chiusi exit; Chianciano Terme and S428 to Sarteano, towards Cetona.*

La Palazzina

Le Vigne 53040 Radicofani (Siena)
Tel. (0578) 55.771 – Fax (0578) 53.553
Sig. Innocenti

Rooms 10 with bath and WC. **Price** With half board 82-105,000L, full board 105-125,000L (per pers., 3 days min.). **Meals** Breakfast included, served 8:00-10:00. **Restaurant** Service 12:45-13:30, 20:00-20:30; menus: 35-45,000L. Specialties: Zuppe e vellutate di stagioni, pici, gnochetti agli aromi, tagliolini d'ortica arrosto alla cannella o alla mentta, mousse al limone, bianco mangiare alle mandorle. **Credit cards** All major. **Pets** Dogs allowed (15,000L). **Facilities** Swimming pool, parking. **Nearby** Montepulciano, Monticchiello, Montalcino, Terme de Bagno Vignoli, Val d'Orcia villages (Castiglione d'Orcia, Rocca d'Orcia, Ripa d'Orcia, Campiglia d'Orcia), Pienza, Collegiale San Quirico d'Orcia, Museo Nazionale Etrusco in Siusi, Chianciano Terme, Siena. **Open** All year (except 2nd week in Nov. and third week in Mar.).

The entrance to this Medician villa in Radicofini, faces a fountain whose water is said to give eternal youth. You will find this youth, or immortality of the spirit of Medicis, at La Palazzina; go out onto your balcony in the morning and experience it. The house has kept all of its grace and aristocratic simplicity. The fine cuisine is as organic (using products from the estate) as it is authentic (based on old Medician recipes). The environment, somewhat more austere than it is in nearby Firenze, provides an ideal setting for this residence with its beautiful, spacious, fragrant rooms.

How to get there *(Map 15): 80 km south of Siena by the via Cassia, to Radicofani. In Radicofani, towards Sarteano, then towards Celle sul Rigo (1.5 km).*

Hotel Villa San Michele ★★★★

Via della Chiesa, 462
San Michele in Escheto – Lucca
Tel. (0583) 37 02 76 – Fax (0583) 37 02 77
Sig. Signorelli

Rooms 22 with telephone, bath, WC, TV and minibar. **Price** Single 150-260,000L, double 240-340,000L, suite 380-410,000L. **Meals** Breakfast included (buffet), served 8:30-10:00. **Restaurant** See p. 429. **Credit cards** All major. **Pets** Dogs not allowed. **Facilities** Parking. **Nearby** Lucca (Duomo, S. Michele in Foro, S. Frediano, via Fillungo and via Guinigi, Villa Guinigi museum), Villa Mansi near Segromigno Monte, Villa Torrigiani near Camigliano, Villa Royale in Marlia, Pistoia, Pisa, Versiglialia golf course (18-hole). **Open** All year (except Jan. 1 – Feb. 10).

The Villa San Michele is about a mile outside of the city walls. It is an old 17th-century villa (restored in the 19th century), built on large grounds with green oak, cork-oak, olive trees and laurel bushes. The rooms are vast, have high arched ceilings and are appropriately decorated with 19th-century solid wood furniture. They are comfortable and decorated in a provincial motif. Above all, this hotel has atmosphere and is in a town worth seeing.

How to get there *(Map 14): Via A11 (towards Firenze); Lucca exit, then towards San Giuliano and Pisa; road for San Michele on the right.*

Villa La Principessa ★★★★

Via nuova per Pisa, 1616
Massa Pisana - 55050 Lucca
Tel. (0583) 37 00 37/38/39 - Fax (0583) 37 90 19
Sig. Mugnani

Rooms 44 with air-conditioning, telephone, bath, WC and TV, elevator, wheelchair access. **Price** Single 200-250,000L, double 290-330,000L, suite 320-360,000L. **Meals** Breakfast 22,000L, served 7:30-10:30. **Restaurant** Service 13:00-14:30, 20:00-22:00; closed Sun.; menus 45-65,000L, also à la carte. Specialties: Tortelli di radicchio, carpaccio di salmone, ravioli di mare. **Credit cards** All major. **Pets** Small dogs allowed in room. **Facilities** Swimming pool. **Nearby** Lucca (Duomo, S. Michele in Foro, S. Frediano, via Fillungo and via Guinigi, museum Villa Guinigi), Villa Mansi near Segromigno Monte, Villa Torrigiani near Camigliano, Villa Royale in Marlia, Pistoia, Pisa, Versiglialia golf course (18-hole). **Open** All year (except Jan. 7 – Feb. 9).

Through the years, this plant-covered villa in the middle of elegantly laid out grounds has maintained its importance. In 1805 Napolean gave the Duchy of Lucca to his sister, Elisa Baciocchi, who fostered an economic and cultural boom (she had the Piazza Napoleone designed). The duchy was then given to the Bourbon-Parme family in 1815; they transformed the Principessa into a prestigious address for illustrious guests. The rooms and salons are very comfortable, although the Baroque decor may not appeal to everyone's taste. Nonetheless, tine hotel is very luxurious.

How to get there *(Map 14): 3.5 km south of Lucca via SS12bis (towards Pisa); Massa Pisana exit.*

Villa La Principessa Elisa★★★★★

Via nuova per Pisa
Massa Pisana – 55050 Lucca
Tel. (0583) 37 97 37 – Fax (0583) 37 90 19
Sig. Mugnani

Rooms 2 and 8 suites with air-conditioning, telephone, bath, WC and TV.
Price Room for 1 pers. 220,000L, suite for 1 pers. 260-300,000L, suite for 2 pers.
350-360,000L. **Meals** Breakfast 22,000L, served 7:30-10:30. **Restaurant** Service
13:00-14:30, 20:00-22:00; closed Wed.; menus 45-65,000L, also à la carte.
Specialties: Tortelli di radicchio, carpaccio di salmone, ravioli di mare.
Credit cards All major. **Pets** Small dogs allowed in room. **Facilities** Swimming
pool, parking. **Nearby** Lucca (Duomo, S. Michele in Foro, S. Frediano, via Fillungo
and via Guinigi, museum Villa Guinigi), Villa Mansi near Segromigno Monte, Villa
Torrigiani near Camigliano, Villa Royale in Marlia, Pistoia, Pisa, Versiglialia golf
course (18-hole). **Open** All year.

The owners of the Principessa recently opened the Hotel
Principessa Elisa, less than 100 yards away. This old villa was
restored at the beginning of the 19th century by a Napoleanic
civil servant who followed the duchess Elisa Baciocchi to Lucca.
Using the 19th-century decor as a model, the suites and salons are
decorated with period fabrics, 19th-century mahogany furniture
and carpets based on illustrations and designs by P. Frey and
Braquenié. The woodwork was restored with pieces found in an
outbuilding in the garden. The dining room is in a Victorian-style
veranda on a lush garden, which has a variety of flowers, bushes
and aquatic plants growing near a creek. Refinement and comfort
pervade this very well-renovated house.

How to get there *(Map 14): 3.5 km south of Lucca via SS12bis (towards
Pisa); Massa Pisana exit.*

Hotel Tirreno ★★★

Viale Morin, 7
55042 Forte dei Marmi (Lucca)
Tel. (0584) 78 74 44 – Fax (0584) 787 137
Sig.ra Daddi Baralla

Rooms 59 with telephone, bath or shower and WC. **Price** Single 90,000L, double 150,000L. **Meals** Breakfast 16,000L, served 7:30-11:00; half board 135-145,000L, full board 165-195,000L. **Restaurant** Service 13:00-14:00, 20:00-21:00; menus 45-70,000L, also à la carte. Specialties Tuscan cuisine. **Credit cards** All major. **Pets** Dogs not allowed. **Nearby** Duomo de Carrara, Cave di marmo di Colonnata, cava dei Fantiscritti, Lucca, Pisa. **Open** Apr. – Sept.

The part of the hotel which is visible from the street is a little disconcerting–it is 70s' style–but there is a surprise deep in the garden: the outbuilding, an old 19th–century summer house. Don't plan to stay anywhere in Tirreno but here, in one of the rooms on the pretty garden (57, 58, and 60) or on the sea. The hotel is both centrally located in Tirreno and close to the beach. The service is meticulous and the Tuscan cuisine is great.

How to get there (Map 13): 35 km north of Pisa via A12 (Genova-Livorno); Versilia exit, Forte dei Marmi.

Azienda Costa d'Orsola

Orsola 54027 Pontremoli (Massa Carrara)
Tel. (0187) 83 33 32 – Fax (0187) 83 33 32

Rooms 14 with telephone and shower. **Price** Double 95-110,000L. **Meals** Breakfast included; half board 70-80,000L, full board 90-100,000L (per pers., 2 days min.). **Restaurant** Service 13:00-14:00, 20:00-21:00; closed Mon., menus 30-40,000L, à la carte. Specialties: Tuscan cuisine. **Credit cards** Diners, Visa, Eurocard and MasterCard. **Pets** Small dogs allowed. **Facilities** Swimming pool, tennis, parking. **Nearby** La Spezia, Cinqueterre, Val Lunigiana (Aula, Villafranca in Lunigiana), Appenin parmesan (Berceto, Cassio, Bardone, Fornovo di Taro Collechio, Parme). **Open** All year (except Jan.).

On the road from Tuscany to Liguria (from Parma to Spezia), don't hesitate to stop off and enjoy the hospitality of this little hamlet perched above Pontremoli. The Costa d'Orsola is a vast old farm recently transformed into an inn. The buildings are connected by a maze of stairways. The pleasant rooms, simply but prettily decorated, have a superb view of the Appenin Parmesan and the Val Lunigiana. The home-style cuisine is made from fresh ingredients from the farm and regional specialties such as "Testaroli," a delicious pasta dish. This is a great place for hikers and nature-lovers.

How to get there (Map 9): 35 km of La Spezia. Via A15 (La Spezial-Parma) Pontremoli exit; after the tollgate on the right and on left towards Costa d'Orsola.

Azienda Capobianco

Via Vecchia Pietrasantina, 11
55042 Albavola
Madonna dell'Acqua (Pisa)
Tel. (050) 89 06 71 - Fax (050) 89 06 71
Sig.ra Russo

Rooms 8 (4 with bath or shower). **Price** Single 30-35,000L (per pers.), double 60-70,000L. **Meals** Breakfast 8,000L, served about 8:30; half board 57-63,000L (per pers.). **Restaurant** Service about 20:00, menus 25-35,000L, also à la carte. Specialties: Tuscan cuisine. **Credit cards** Not accepted. **Pets** Dogs not allowed. **Nearby** Pisa, San Piero a Grado, Marina di Pisa, Calci and certosa di Pisa. **Open** All year.

The Azienda Capobianco is similar to the farm-inns in France that offer vacations in the country at unbeatable prices. It is in the countryside near Pisa, in the Miligrano and San Rossore Nature Reserve, on the banks of the Serchio. The rooms are comfortable, if a little bare; Only certain ones have bathrooms. A well-equipped equestrian center offers lessons and excursions on horseback to the nearby reserve. In the evening you can enjoy home-style regional cuisine. You won't feel too far from the charms of Tuscany because the sea, the countryside and historic towns are nearby.

How to get there (Map 14): 3 km northwest of Pisa, towards La Spezia.

Hotel Buriano ★★

Castello, 10
56040 Buriano - Montecatini Val di Cecina (Pisa)
Tel. (0588) 37 295 – Fax (0588) 37 295
Sig. Clamer

Rooms 13 (6 with bath or shower). **Price** Single 44,000L, double 63-88,000L.
Meals Breakfast 9,500L, served 8:00-10:00; half board 77-90,000L (per pers., 3
days min.). **Restaurant** Service 12:30, 19:30; menus 35-45,000L, also à la carte.
Specialties: Selvaggina, pasta, dolce e cucina casalinghe. **Credit cards** Not
accepted. **Pets** Dogs allowed. **Nearby** Volterra, San Gimignano, Siena, Lucca,
Marina di Cecina (beach), Pisa. **Open** Mar. – Sept.

In the very well preserved—and relatively tourist-
free—countryside you will find a more genuine Tuscany. This
solitary old farmhouse has been converted into a great inn. The
house is a lot less rustic than you might expect. The kitchen
extends into the large, pretty dining room, where there are
flowers on every table. The big plates of antipasti will give you a
taste of the savory cuisine to come. The rooms are all
impeccably well-kept, though not all of them have bathrooms.
Some have charming naive paintings on the walls. They all have
a nice view of the surrounding countryside and some look out
onto Volterra.

*How to get there (Map 14): 60 km northwest of Siena via SS (towards
Firenze); Colle di Val d'Elsa-South exit, towards Volterra to Saline di
Volterra. Buriano is 7 km away.*

Il Frassinello

56040 Montecatini Val di Cecina (Pisa)
Tel. (0588) 300 80
Fax (0588) 300 80
Sig.ra Sclubach Giudici

Rooms 4 and 1 apartment with shower. **Price** 90-120,000L (per 2 pers.).
Meals Breakfast 6,000L, served about 8:00-9:30. **Restaurant** In Hotel Buriano or
in Volterra (see p. 429). **Credit cards** Not accepted. **Pets** Dogs allowed.
Facilities Parking. **Nearby** Volterra, San Gimignano, Siena, Lucignano, Marina di
Cecina (beach), Pisa. **Open** Easter – late Sept.

An endlessly winding dusty path will bring you to this old
farmhouse whose charm is more comfortable than rustic. A
charming lady who withdrew from the world has created her own
little universe here. Little by little she surrounded herself with a decor
in her own image. There is a bronze angel over the kitchen door, an
incredible German chandelier over a wooden table, a terrace under a
wisteria for breakfast, a basin overflowing with water with the
fragrance of the mountains, and above all, an incredible deer farm,
equipped to receive guests. You can choose between comfortable
rooms with a shower room in the hallway, and a two room
apartment with a bathroom and kitchen, suitable for families.
Breakfast consisting of homemade bread and jelly and fresh eggs, is
served at a common table in the warm friendly kitchen. Located
several miles from Volterra, the Frassinello is not a place to stop off at,
but one where you will want to stay a while. You will no doubt, just
like us, feel sorry when you have to leave these deer families, who
will quietly watch you go without even moving an ear.

How to get there *(Map 14): 60 km northwest of Siena via SS (towards Firenze);*
Colle di Val d'Elsa-South exit, towards Volterra to Saline di Volterra.

Casetta delle Selve

56 010 Pugnano
San Giuliano Terme (Pisa)
Tel. (050) 85 03 59
Sig.ra Nicla Menchi

Rooms 6 with bath or shower and WC. **Price** Double 90,000L. **Meals** Breakfast 12,000L, served about 9:30. **Restaurant** See p. 429. **Credit cards** Not accepted. **Pets** Dogs allowed. **Facilities** Parking. **Nearby** Certosa di Calci, Pisa, Lucca. **Open** All year.

The Cassetta delle Selve may look modest, but you will absolutely love its breathtaking view and nice family atmosphere. With a shout of "Viva la Libertà", the very friendly Nicla will serve you breakfast on a marvelous terrace overlooking the sea and the rolling hills of Tuscany, Corsica and Gorgona in the distance. The rooms have been lovingly decorated. The owner, who runs a hotel by circumstance but is an artist at heart (her paintings are on the walls), has decorated the rooms herself, down to the smallest detail (from the rugs to the pillowcases). This is a good place to stay while visiting nearby Pisa and Lucca.

How to get there *(Map 14): 10 km south of Lucca, via A11 Lucca exit; then SS12 and SS12bis towards San Giuliano Terme; in Pugnano follow the small partly unpaved road.*

Hotel Villa di Corliano ★★★

Rigoli
Via Statale, 50
56010 San Giuliano Terme (Pisa)
Tel. (050) 81 81 93 – Fax (050) 81 83 41
Sig. Agostini della Seta

Rooms 18 with telephone (8 with bath, WC). **Price** Double 100-150,000L, suite for 4 pers. 250,000L. **Meals** Breakfast 18,000L, served 8:00-10:00. **Restaurant** On the property; menus, also à la carte. Specialties: Seafood. **Credit cards** Visa, Eurocard and MasterCard. **Pets** Dogs allowed. **Facilities** Parking. **Nearby** Santa Maria del Giudice, Pisa, Lucca. **Open** All year.

The Villa di Corliano is surrounded by vast grounds and has amazingly beautiful decor. The frescos, chandeliers, and uncommon furniture in the salons create a museum-like atmosphere that is extremely rare nowadays. The current owner has transformed the villa into a hotel to preserve it from the ravages of time and also to be able to continue living here himself. The rooms are large, comfortable and extremely quiet, though the bathrooms could be improved. There is a strange antiquated atmosphere, but the charm of the place and the owner's friendliness more than make up for this. The famous Pizan restaurant "Sergio" is now in an outbuilding of the castle; a special sampler dinner will allow you to try the best regional and house specialties, from the antipasti to the desserts. This address is unanimously appreciated by all who come here.

How to get there *(Map 14): 8 km north of Pisa via SS12bis to San Giuliano Terme, then northwest S12 towards Rigoli.*

Albergo Villa Nencini

Borgo San Stefano, 55
56048 Volterra (Pisa)
Tel. (0588) 86 386 – Fax (0588) 80 601
Sig. Nencini

Rooms 14 with telephone (11 with shower) and TV on request. **Price** Single 80,000L, double 105,000. **Meals** Breakfast 10,000L, served 7:00-11:00. **Restaurant** See p.430. **Credit cards** Visa, Eurocard, MasterCard. **Pets** Dogs allowed. **Facilities** Swimming pool. **Nearby** Volterra (Le Balze), San Gimignano, Lucignano, Siena. **Open** All year.

The Villa Nencini is just outside the walls of Volterra, an ancient Etruscan, Roman and medieval town, with "one of the most beautiful medieval squares in Italy," the Piazza dei Priori. On the edge of town, it has a great view of the valley. The house is very old; the interior is unpretentious and friendly. A wing has been added onto the house; the rooms there are more modern and more comfortable but the ones in the villa are more traditional and authentic. The very pretty garden and swimming pool overhanging the valley are good places to take in the marvelous panorama.

How to get there *(Map 14): 60 km northwest of Siena, via SS or A1; Colle di Val d'Elsa exit.*

Hotel Grotta Giusti ★★★★

Via Grotta Giusti, 17
51015 Monsummano Terme (Pistoia)
Tel. (0572) 51 165/6 – Fax (0572) 51 269
Sig. Mati

Rooms 70 with air-conditioning, telephone, bath, WC and TV. **Price** Single 120-140,000L, double 200-220,000L. **Meals** Breakfast included, served 7:30-10:00; half board 150-170,000L, full board 160-180,000L (per pers., 3 days min.). **Restaurant** Service 12:30-14:00, 19:30-21:00; menu 55,000L, also à la carte. Specialties: Tuscan and international cuisine. **Credit cards** All major. **Pets** Small dogs allowed. **Facilities** Swimming pool, tennis, health center (thermal swimming pool). **Nearby** Montecatini, Serra Pistoiese, Pistoia, Villa Mansi near Segromigno Monte, Lucca, golf course (18-hole) in Pievaccia and in Monsummano. **Open** Mar. – Nov.

This former residence of the rich poet Giusti is built around an amazing grotto with a stream of hot blue water. Giuseppe Verdi was often a guest at this house. You can still see some of the splendor of the original decor in the reception area. The rooms are functional, but the ones in the old building, which look out over the park, are by far the nicest. They all have hot running spring water, so ask for one with a bathtub. In addition, beautiful grounds with a spring water swimming pool, a tennis court and running trail make this hotel an ideal place for a relaxing stay.

How to get there *(Map 14): 37 km northwest of Firenze; 13 km west of Pistoia via A11, Montecatini exit; then S435 to Monsummano Terme.*

Grand Hotel e La Pace ★★★★★

Viale della Toretta, 1
51016 Montecatini Terme (Pistoia)
Tel. (0572) 758 01 – Fax (0572) 784 51
Sig. Tongiorgi

Rooms 136 and 14 apartments with telephone, bath, WC, TV and minibar.
Price Single 240-320,000L, double 380-490,000L. **Meals** Breakfast 30,000L,
served 7:30-10:30. **Restaurant** Service 12:30-14:00, 20:00-21:30, also à la carte.
Specialties: Tuscan cuisine. **Credit cards** All major. **Pets** Dogs allowed (fee).
Facilities Swimming pool, tennis, health center, parking. **Nearby** Pescia, church
in Castelvecchio, Collodi, Lucca, Pistoia, Firenze, Pisa, golf course (18-hole) in
Pievaccia and in Monsummano Terme. **Open** Apr. – Oct.

All of the traditional splendor of this 1870 palace is
completely intact. The hotel's sumptuous, thick carpeted
salons, first-class dining room with a baywindow and very
comfortable rooms, decorated in harmonious pastel colors, make
the atmosphere warm. On the superb five-acre grounds there is
a large heated swimming pool, a tennis court and a spa for
medically supervised mud baths, saunas, massages, ozone baths
and algae beauty treatments.

How to get there *(Map 14): 49 km northwest of Firenze; 15 km west
Pistoia via A11, Montecatini exit.*

Villa Lucia

Via dei Bronzoli, 144
51010 Montevettolini (Pistoia)
Tel. (0572) 62 8817 – Fax (0572) 62 8817
Sig.ra Vallera

Rooms 7 with bath or shower (6 with WC, 3 with TV). **Price** Single 130,000L, double 150,000L, suite 250,000L. **Meals** Breakfast included **Restaurant** For residents only, by reservation. Service 20:30; menu 30,000L. Specialties: Polenta, grilliata, risotto con verdure, pizze al forno. **Credit cards** Not accepted. **Pets** Dogs not allowed. **Nearby** Montecatini, Serra Pistoiese, Pistoia, Villa Mansi near Segromigno Monte, Lucca, golf course (18-hole) in Pievaccia and in Monsumanno. **Open** Nov. 15 – Apr. 15.

The Villa Lucia is part bed and breakfast and part Tuscan inn. Everything is pretty and authentically Tuscan, though there is a hint of California as well. This is no accident: it is run by a charming lady who caters to the many Americans who come here for the warm convivial atmosphere, the pretty copper beds, the regional furniture and a nice glass of *vinsanto* (fortified dessert wine) and *cantuccini* (almond biscuits). Her savory cuisine is based on house recipes. On summer evenings there are parties on the lawn. You may not make much progress with your Italian while you are here, but you are sure to have a great time.

How to get there *(Map 14): 40 km northwest of Firenze; 13 km west Pistoia via A11, Montecatini exit; then S435 to Monsummano Terme and little road for Montevettolini.*

Villa Vannini ★★★

Villa di Piteccio, 6
51030 Piteccio (Pistoia)
Tel. (0573) 42 031 – Fax (0573) 26 331
Sig.ra Vannini

Rooms 8 with bath or shower and WC. **Price** Double 120,000L. **Meals** Breakfast included, served 8:00-10:00; half board 180,000L (2 pers.). **Restaurant** Service 12:30-14:00, 20:00-22:30; menus 30-50,000L, also à la carte. Specialties: Tuscan cuisine. **Credit cards** Visa, Eurocard and MasterCard. **Pets** Dogs not allowed. **Nearby** Pistoia, Abetone, lake of Scaffaiolo, Corno alle Scale (1 945 m), Firenze, Lucca, golf course in Montecatini. **Open** All year.

On one of the hills of Pistoia, at an altitude of about a thousand feet (350 m), the Villa Vannini is a haven of peace. The linden tree-lined terrace overlooks the surrounding countryside. The rooms have flowers and the beds are perfumed. Enjoy the breakfasts of homemade jellies and the dinners, which are both simple and sumptuous. A warm welcome awaits you here in the heart of this relatively unexplored part of Tuscany.

How to get there *(Map 14): 6 km north of Pistoia via S66 to Ponte Calcaiola, then towards Piteccio; follow signposted road.*

Il Convento

Via San Quirico, 33
51030 Pontenuovo (Pistoia)
Tel. (0573) 45 26 51/2 – Fax (0573) 45 35 78
Sig. Petrini

Rooms 24 with telephone, bath, WC and TV. **Price** Single 95,000L, double 120,000L. **Meals** Breakfast 12,000L, served 7:30-9:30; half board 105,000L; full board 120,000L (per pers., 3 days min.). **Restaurant** Service 12:30-14:30, 19:30-22:00; closed Mon. and Jan. – Easter; menus 45-55,000L, also à la carte. Specialties: Tuscan cuisine **Credit cards** Visa, Eurocard and MasterCard. **Pets** Dogs not allowed. **Facilities** Swimming pool, parking. **Nearby** Pistoia, Lake of Scaffaiolo, Corno alle Scale (1 945 m), Firenze, Lucca, dell'Ugolino golf course (18-hole) in Grassina. **Open** All year.

This old Franciscan monastery, in keeping with its name, still has a small chapel and a tranquil atmosphere. Surrounded by a vast flower garden overlooking the plain, this charming hotel is a little old and could use some modernizing. But it is a pleasant place from which to visit Pistoia and the northern part of Tuscany. A pool above the garden is at your disposal. The restaurant serves very good, traditional Tuscan cuisine.

How to get there *(Map 14): 40 km northwest of Firenze; 5 km east of Pistoia to Pontenuovo.*

Hotel Villa Ombrosa ★★★

Via Massimo d'Azeglio, 18
San Marcello Pistoiese (Pistoia)
Tel. (0573) 63 01 56/63 23 57
Sig. Guerrini

Rooms 27 with bath and WC. **Price** Single: 40-60,000L, double 50-90,000L. **Meals** Breakfast 10,000L, served 8:00-10:00; half board 90,000L, full board 110,000L (per pers., 3 days min.). **Restaurant** Service 13:00, 20:00-21:00; menus 35-45,000L. Specialties: Tuscan cuisine. **Credit cards** All major. **Pets** Dogs allowed (fee). **Facilities** Parking (5,000L). **Nearby** Appennino Pistoiese: Cutigliano; Abetone, Pistoia. **Open** June 25 – Sept. 10.

La Villa Ombrosa is in San Marcello Pistoiese, a small vacation town in the Limestre Valley. It's altitude–over two thousand feet (600 m)–makes it the perfect place to escape from the summer heat of the cities. There are also some ski resorts in the Appenino Pistoiese. The historic center of Pistoia is worth visiting, especially the Duomo and the baptistry. The villa will remind you of an old family house: its old furniture smells of wax and the owner's paintings give the place a quaint nostalgic touch. You will find regional cuisine and a warm welcome here.

How to get there *(Map 14): 65 km northwest of Firenze; 30km northwest of Pistoia via S66 to San Marcello Pistoiese.*

Pardini's Hermitage Hotel ★★

Isola del Giglio
Cala degli Alberi
58013 Giglio Porto (Grosseto)
Tel. (0564) 80 90 34 – Fax (0564) 80 91 77
Sig. Pardini

Rooms 11 with air-conditioning, telephone, bath, WC and TV on request. **Price** with full board: 140-185,000L (per pers.). **Meals** Breakfast included, served about 8:00. **Restaurant** Service 13:30, 20:30. Specialties: cuisine with fresh products. **Credit cards** All major. **Pets** Dogs allowed. **Facilities** Sea-water swimming pool, health center, tennis, private beach, windsurfing, parking. **Nearby** Caldane beach, Cannelle beach, Giannutri island, scenic road though Giglio Porto, Giglio Castello and Campesse. **Open** Mar. – Sept.

This hotel, the most amazing on the island, is outside of the village (the hotel provides transportation to and from the port). The owner, who inherited this very pretty house from his father, is as welcoming as an old friend. The service is impeccable and the cuisine is excellent. There are several passageways to the sea through the rocks. There are also two or three sailing dinghies which will allow you to head offshore if you feel like being alone. The clientele is very mixed, but is composed mostly of regulars, which makes this a very convivial place.

How to get there *(Map 14): 53 km south of Grosseto; Ferry service from Porto San Stefano-Argentario (1hr.).*

Rifugio Prategiano ★★★

Via Prategiano, 45
58026 Montieri (Grosseto)
Tel. (0566) 99 77 03 – Fax (0566) 99 78 91
Sig. Paradisi

Rooms 24 with telephone, bath, WC and TV. **Price** Single 88-148,000L, double 61-103,000L. **Meals** Breakfast included; half board 83-129,000L (per pers.,3 days min.). **Restaurant** Service 13:00, 20:00; menus. Specialties: Tortelloni, cinghiale, acqua Cotta. **Credit cards** All major. **Pets** Dogs allowed. **Facilities** Swimming pool, riding, parking. **Nearby** Roman and Etruscan ruins of Roselle, Vetulonia, Montepescali, National Park of Maremma, Volterra. **Open** All year.

The Prategiano is on Montieri Hill, an old Medieval citadel deep in the High Maremma part of the little-known Métallifère Forest in Tuscany. The ambience is that of a mountain inn. The decor is very simple and rustic, as most of the hotel guests are horseback riders. There are riding lessons and daytime excursions for children and beginners, while more experienced riders can gallop through the Tuscan hills, crossing woods and forests to the deserted beaches of Punta Ala to get to Volterra. The setting is perfect and the owner is friendly and very careful about the security of his guests. This is the perfect address for those seeking a small adventure.

How to get there (Map 14): 50 km southwest of Siena via S73 to Bivio del Madonnino, then S441 (15km); on the right towards Montieri.

Hotel Il Pellicano ★★★★

58018 Porto Ercole (Grosseto)
Tel. (0564) 83 38 01
Fax (0564) 83 34 18
Sig. Fanciulli

Rooms 40 with telephone, bath, WC, TV and minibar. **Price** Double 284-830,000L,
suite 675-1,874,000L. **Meals** Breakfast included, served 7:30-10:30; half board
237-515,000L, full board 327-605,000L. **Restaurant** Service 13:00-14:30, 20:00-
22:00; menus 105-130,000L, also à la carte. Specialties: Risottino alle erbette,
fettuccine con scampi e zucchine, spaghetti al Pellicano. **Credit cards** All major.
Pets Dogs not allowed. **Facilities** Sea-water swimming pool, health center, tennis,
private beach, windsurfing, parking. **Nearby** Giannutri and Giglio islands,
Tombolo di Feniglia, Sovona, Sorano, Pitigliano. **Open** Mar. 29 – Nov. 2.

A small road in the mountains around Porto Ercole will lead
you to the Pellicano, a large red house surrounded by a
magnificent garden, which descends in a series of terraces to the
sea. There is a private beach on the rocks and a pleasant
swimming pool. Inside, the decor is elegant. Each of the rooms
has a small private terrace. An endless view of the sea on one
side and the unspoiled hills on the other make this luxury hotel
an oasis of tranquility. Prices vary according to the season.

How to get there *(Map 14): 55 km south of Grosseto via SS51, then
along the coast to Porto Ercole; then strada panoramica to Lo Sbarcatello.*

Hotel Cala del Porto ★★★★

Via del Porto
58040 Punta Ala (Grosseto)
Tel. (0564) 92 24 55 - Fax (0564) 92 07 16
Sig. Partigno

Rooms 36 and 5 apartments with telephone, bath, WC and minibar. **Price** Single 145-480,000L, double 280-740,000L, apartment 360-900,000L. **Meals** Breakfast 30,000L, served 7:30-10:30; half board 185-420,000L, 225-470,000L (per pers.,3 days min.). **Restaurant** Service 13:00-15:00, 19:30-21:30; menus 45-80,000L, also à la carte. Specialties: Mediterranean cuisine, seafood. **Credit cards** All major. **Pets** Dogs not allowed. **Facilities** Swimming pool, tennis (25,000L), parking. **Nearby** Tombolo, Massa Maritima, Volterra, National Park of Maremma, Punta Ala golf course (18-hole). **Open** May – Sept.

Punta Ala is the chic beach resort of Grossetto, which is at the tip of the Gulf of Follonica across from the Island of Elba. The Cala del Porto is a comfortable modern hotel with a beautiful flower garden. The rooms are elegantly furnished and have balconies with views of the historical island. Pleasant Tuscan-inspired cuisine is served on the beautiful terrace.

How to get there *(Map 14): 41 km west of Grosseto via S327, along the coast to Punta Ala.*

Piccolo Hotel Alleluja ★★★★

Via del Porto
58040 Punta Ala (Grosseto)
Tel. (0564) 92 20 50 - Fax (0564) 92 07 34
Sig. Partigno

Rooms 37 with air-conditioning and 5 apartments with telephone, bath, WC, safe and minibar. **Price** Single 250-530,000L, double 340-800,000L. **Meals** Breakfast 30,000L, served 7:30-10:30; half board 210-450,000L, 250-500,000L (per pers.,3 days min., oblig. in July – Aug.). **Restaurant** Service 13:00-14:30, 19:30-21:30; menus 75-85,000L, also à la carte. Specialties: Regional and international cuisine, seafood. **Credit cards** All major. **Pets** Dogs not allowed. **Facilities** Swimming pool, beach, tennis, parking. **Nearby** Tombolo, Massa Maritima, Volterra, National Park of Maremma, Punta Ala golf course (18-hole). **Open** All year.

The pink roughcast walls, tile roofs and exposed beams of this recently built hotel reflect the architect's respect for the region. An airy space opens onto the impeccably maintained lawns. The hotel is decorated with simple unpretentious furniture. The rooms open onto either an Italian–style terrace or a small garden on the lake. The numerous advantages of this hotel include a private beach, tennis courts and a nearby golf course.

How to get there *(Map 14): 41 km west of Grosseto via S327, along the coast to Punta Ala.*

Hotel Terme di Saturnia ★★★★

58050 Saturnia (Grosseto)
Provinciale della Follonata
Tel. (0564) 60 10 61 – Fax (0564) 60 12 66
Sig. Savelli

Rooms 92 with air-conditioning, telephone, bath or shower, WC, cable TV, safe, minibar and elevator. **Price** Single 230,000L, double 380,000L. **Meals** Breakfast 25,000L, served 7:30-10:00; half board 250-290,000L, 270-310,000L (per pers.,3 days min.). **Restaurant** Service 12:45-14:00, 20:00-21:15; closed Mon.; menus 70,000L, also à la carte. Specialties: Regional cuisine. **Credit cards** All major. **Pets** Dogs not allowed. **Facilities** Swimming pool, tennis, thermal baths, parking. **Nearby** Tombolo, Massa Maritima, Volterra, National Park of Maremma, Punta Ala golf course (18-hole). **Open** All year.

The Hotel Terme di Saturnia is located in the historical Saturnia woods, where legend has it that you can still hear the Etruscans, whose brilliant and mysterious civilization and language we know so little about. Tuscanny is named after the "Tusci", as the Etruscans were called, its first known inhabitants. Saturnia is also famous for its Renaissance heritage, and is surrounded by interesting vestiges such as Pitigliano, Sovana, and Sorano. The hotel is profoundly attached to this historical context, as well as the spring water which has flowed here from deep in the ground for thousands of years, beneficial for both body and mind. This is why the entire hotel is laid out around an immense pool, the centerpiece of a modern health and beauty complex. If you prefer, you can enjoy all of the comfort of the hotel, the garden, and the fine cuisine without doing a treatment. The staff, most of whom have worked there for more than 10 years, are very friendly and attentive.

How to get there *(Map 14): 57 km southeast of Grosseto via A1 (towards Roma) Manciano exit, then Montemerano, towards Saturnia.*

Albergo La Stellata

Pian del Bagno 58050 Saturnia (Grosseto)
Tel. (0564) 60 29 78 – Fax (0564) 60 29 34
Sig.ra Sciui

Rooms 13 (air-conditioning by request) with telephone, bath, WC, minibar. **Price** Single 110,000L, double 180,000L. **Meals** Breakfast 10,000L, served 8:00-10:00; half board 130-150,000L, full board 160-180,000L (per pers.). **Restaurant** Service 13:00-15:00, 20:00-23:00, menus 35,000L, à la carte. Specialties: Minestre, griglia, pesce, carni. **Credit cards** All major. **Pets** Small dogs allowed. **Facilities** Thermal baths of Saturnia, parking. **Nearby** Tombolo, Massa Maritima, Volterra, National Park of Maremma, Punta Ala golf course (18-hole). **Open** All year.

The thermal baths of ancient Saturnia date back to the Etruscan and Roman eras. Today, the Grand Hotel Terme di Saturnia offers a complete beauty and fitness program in a luxurious setting. The Albergo La Stellata is only five minutes away and is under the same management, so you can, enjoy the same services in a more casual environment. Isolated on one of the small hills of the Tuscan Maremma, this beautiful estate has elegant comfortable rooms. The staff is friendly and provides quality service. This is the ideal place for visiting Etruscan Tuscany.

How to get there *(Map 14): 45 km southeast of Grosseto via A1 (towards Roma) Manciano exit, Manciano, Montemerano, towards Saturnia.*

Azienda Saturnia Country Club

58050 Pomonte Scansano (Grosseto)
Tel. (0564) 59 91 88 – Fax (0564) 59 92 14
Sig. Frulloni

Rooms 20 with telephone, bath, WC, TV, minibar. **Price** Single 107,000L, double 174,000L. **Meals** Breakfast 14,000L, served 8:00-9:30. **Restaurant** Service 13:00-14:30, 20:00-21:30, menu 40,000L. Specialties: Regional cooking. **Credit cards** All major. **Pets** Dogs allowed (20,000L). **Facilities** Swimming pool, fishing, thermal baths, parking. **Nearby** Tombolo, Massa Maritima, Volterra, National Park of Maremma, Punta Ala golf course (18-hole). **Open** All year.

The Terme di Saturnia hotel group also has another place to stay: the *Azienda*, a beautiful working farm, several miles away. In addition to the usual accommodations, the Fattoria offers packages with daily excursions including horseback riding, hunting (wild boar, deer) and fishing (trout, eel and other fresh water fish), to help you get to know this ancient land. You can also go to the thermal baths. Whatever you choose, ask for the "Itinerari et Passagiate Ecologiche" brochure at the hotel, which lists a wealth of information on the artistic and ecological heritage of the region.

How to get there *(Map 14): 40 km southeast of Grosseto via A12 (towards Roma) Manciano exit, Manciano, Montemerano, towards Scansano.*

Grand Hotel Villa Parisi ★★★★

Via della Torre, 6 / via Ronolo Monti, 10
57012 Castiglioncello (Livorno)
Tel. (0586) 75 16 98 – Fax (0586) 75 11 67
Sig.ra Acerbi

Rooms 22 with air-conditioning, telephone, bath, WC and minibar. **Price** Single 110-250,000L, double 150-330,000L. **Meals** Breakfast included, served 8:00-10:00; half board 40,000L, 80,000L (per pers.). **Restaurant** Service 12:00-14:00, 20:00-22:00; menu 40,000L, also à la carte. Specialties: Italian and regional cuisine. **Credit cards** All major. **Pets** Small dogs allowed. **Facilities** Swimming pool, tennis, parking. **Nearby** Livorno (Monumento dei Quattri Mori, Via Grande), Santuario di Montenero. **Open** All year.

Villa Parisi is a turn–of–the–century villa has kept all of the flavor and color of the period. Set among pine trees on the sea, it is very quiet. The road ends abruptly on the rocks overhanging the sea and time seems to stop. The village seems to belong to children and proud adolescents who look at you as if you aren't supposed to be there. This is because they are spending the summer at their grandparents's villa and because they know how lucky they are to be in Castiglioncello. Villa Parisi is an oasis of bright, quiet, pastel rooms and Thonet armchairs facing the blue sea. Melancholy? It was just a cloud.

How to get there *(Map 14): 20 km south of Livorno, via A12; Rosignano Marittimo exit.*

Park Hotel Napoleone ★★★★

Isola d'Elba
57037 San Martino di Portoferraio (Livorno)
Tel. (0565) 91 85 02 – Fax (0565) 91 78 36
Sig. de Ferrari

Rooms 64 with air-conditioning, telephone, bath, WC, TV and minibar. **Price** Single 80-180,000L, double 160-360,000L. **Meals** Breakfast included, served 8:00-10:00; half board 90-225,000L, full board 125-265,000L (per pers., 3 days min.). **Restaurant** Open Apr. – Oct.; service 12:30-14:00, 20:00-21:30; menu 60,000L. Specialties: Italian and international cuisine. **Credit cards** All major. **Pets** Dogs not allowed. **Facilities** Swimming pool, private beach (30,000L), tennis, riding, parking. **Nearby** Portoferraio (Napoleon House), Villa Napoleone in San Martino, Madonna del Monte in Marciana, dell'Acquabona golf course (9-hole). **Open** Mar. 20 – Oct. 15.

The Park Hotel Napoleone is close to the Emperor's villa, which you can see from certain windows. The hotel itself has historical significance: it was built at the end of the last century by a famous aristocratic Roman family. It is surrounded by a lush garden dotted with white canvas chairs. The rooms are tastefully furnished. The hotel has a beautiful swimming pool, several horses and a private beach a few miles away. Being near the Imperial Villa has several drawbacks, however. The path is lined with small souvenir shops, but they disappear at nightfall.

How to get there *(Map 13): Ferry services from Livorno (2 hrs. 50 min.) or Piombino (1 hr.); the hotel is 6 km southwest of Portoferraio.*

Villa Ottone ★★★★

Isola d'Elba
Ottone – 57037 Portoferraio (Livorno)
Tel. (0565) 93 30 42 – Fax (0565) 93 32 57
Sig. Di Mario

Rooms 70 with air-conditioning, telephone, bath, WC, TV and minibar. **Price** Single 90-180,000L, double 180-350,000L. **Meals** Breakfast 20,000L, served 7:00-9:30; half board 105-230,000L, full board 125-250,000L (per pers., 3 days min.). **Restaurant** Service 12:45-13:45 (grill at the swimming pool 13:00-16:00), 19:30-21:00; menus 35-60,000L, also à la carte. Specialties: Italian and regional cuisine. **Credit cards** All major. **Pets** Dogs allowed (10,000L). **Facilities** Swimming pool, parking. **Nearby** Portoferraio (Napoleon House), Villa Napoleone in San Martino, Madonna del Monte in Marciana, dell'Acquabona golf course (9-hole). **Open** May 15 – Sept. 30.

This is the most charming beach hotel on the island of Elba. In the cool shade of the eucalyptus and laurel trees on the property, this 19th-century villa has something of the atmosphere of an old-fashioned colonial mansion in the South. In front of the hotel there is a terrace that leads to the hotel beach, the bay and the sea. One salon has emblazoned ceilings, the other is nice and large. The rooms in the main house look directly onto the sea. The ones in the newer part of the villa are very comfortably, furnished with beds and bamboo couches; all have small terraces looking onto the trees.

How to get there *(Map 13): Ferry service from Livorno (2 hrs. 50 min.) or Piombino (1 hr.); the hotel is at 11 km west of Portoferraio.*

Hotel Castel Freiberg ★★★★

Freiberg – Via Labers
39012 Merano (Bolzano)
Tel. (0473) 24 41 96 – Fax (0473) 24 44 88
Sig. Bortolotti

Rooms 35 with telephone, bath and WC (TV by request). **Price** Single 180-200,000L, double 290-340,000L. **Meals** Breakfast 20,000L, served 8:00-10:30. **Restaurant** Service 19:30-21:00; also à la carte. Specialties: Italian cuisine. **Credit cards** Amex, Visa, Eurocard, MasterCard. **Pets** Dogs not allowed. **Facilities** Indoor and outdoor swimming pool, tennis (15,000L), gymnasium, parking, garage. **Nearby** Castel Tirolo, Castel Scena, Castel Coira in Sluderno, Glorenza, Monte Maria abbey near Malles Venosta, Petersberg golf course in Karersee. **Open** Mid-Apr. – Oct.

This Medieval castle is at the top of a hill overlooking the valley of Merano. Palm trees and flowers fill the garden leading up to the entrance. Castel Freiberg has been restored with loving care by its owner and is now one of the best hotels in Italy. In the beautiful wood decorated dining room you can enjoy excellent cuisine before going into the salon with its painted vaulting and comfortable armchairs. You can admire the superb panorama of the Merano valley from the rooms, which are decorated with simple but elegant antique furniture. Castel Freiberg is an ideal place for those who love quiet, nature and the mountains.

How to get there *(Map 4): 28 km northwest of Bolzano via A22; exit Bolzano-South, then S38 to Merano. Sinigo, towards Scena, then via Labers (5km).*

Hotel Castel Labers ★★★

Via Labers, 25
39012 Merano (Bolzano)
Tel. (0473) 23 44 84 – Fax (0473) 234 146
Sig. G. Stapf-Neubert

Rooms 32 with telephone, bath or shower and WC (TV and minibar on request).
Price 90-135,000L (per pers.). **Meals** Breakfast included, served 7:30-10:00; half
board 110-165,000L (per pers., 3 days min.). **Restaurant** Service 12:00-14:00,
19:30-21:00; menus 35-70,000L, also à la carte. Specialties: Italian and Tyrolese
cuisine. **Credit cards** Amex, Visa, Eurocard, MasterCard. **Pets** Dogs allowed
(15,000L). **Facilities** Heated swimming pool, tennis (15,000L), gymnasium,
parking, garage. **Nearby** Castel Tirolo, Castel Scena, Castel Coira in Sluderno,
Glorenza, Monte Maria abbey near Malles Venosta, Petersberg golf course in
Karersee. **Open** Apr. 8 – Oct.

On a perfectly quiet site surrounded by vineyards, is Castel
Labers, a pretty Dolomite castle. An intimate atmosphere
and an unusually warm welcome await the traveler here.
Antique furniture and paintings decorate the salons and the
foyer. You can get to the rooms either by a charming stairway
or a pretty elevator. The rooms are comfortable and have old
fashioned charm—and they open onto dazzling panorama. The
service is attentive and efficient. The owners are true art and
music lovers and they sometimes organize concerts for hotel
guests.

How to get there *(Map 4): 28 km northwest of Bolzano via A22,
Bolzano-South exit; then S38 to Merano. Sinigo, towards Scena, then via
Labers (5 km).*

Hotel Pünthof ★★★

Steinachstrasse, 25
39022 Merano – Lagundo (Bolzano)
Tel. (0473) 44 85 53 – Fax (0473) 44 99 19
Sig.ra Wolf

Rooms 15 with telephone, bath or shower, WC, TV and minibar. **Price** With half board 120-140,000L (in double per pers.). **Meals** Breakfast 25,000L, served 7:30-11:00. **Restaurant** Service 19:00-24:00; menu 35,000L, also à la carte. Specialties: Tyrolese and Italian cuisine. **Credit card** Diners. **Pets** Dogs not allowed. **Facilities** Swimming pool, sauna (30,000L), tennis (9-16,000L), parking. **Nearby** Castel Tirolo, Castel Scena, Castel Coira in Sluderno, Glorenza, Monte Maria abbey near Malles Venosta, Petersberg golf course in Karersee. **Open** Mar. 15 – Nov. 15.

The Hotel Pünthof is on the famous Roman road, Caludia Augusta, only a few miles from the Merano health spa. This old country house (which has belonged to the same family since the 17th century) is surrowded by vineyards and fruit trees. It is a wonder of good taste, tradition and comfort. The rooms are spacious and have old–fashioned decor, waxed wood floors and antique regional furniture. In a small town, which is a part of Merano, this charming hotel is the ideal place for a *villegiatura* vacation in southern Tyrol.

How to get there (Map 4): 28 km northwest of Bolzano via A22, Bolzano-South exit; then S38 to Merano. Lagundo is 2 km west of Merano.

Hotel Castel Rundegg ★★★★

39012 Merano–Maia alta (Bolzano)
Tel. (0473) 23 41 00 – Fax (0473) 23 72 00
Sig. Sinn

Rooms 30 with telephone, bath, WC, TV and minibar. **Price** Double 135-258,000L (per pers.), suite 151-258,000L (per pers.). **Meals** Breakfast included, served 7:30-10:00; half board 200-313,000L (per pers., 3 days min.). **Restaurant** Service 12:00-13:00, 19:00-20:00; menus 70-120,000L, also à la carte. Specialties: Tyrolese cuisine. **Credit cards** All major. **Pets** Dogs allowed. **Facilities** Swimming pool, sauna (20,000L), health center, fitness, parking. **Nearby** Castel Tirolo, Castel Scena, Castel Coira in Sluderno, Glorenza, Monte Maria abbey near Malles Venosta, Petersberg golf course in Karersée. **Open** All year (except Jan. 9 – 31).

Castel Rundegg, with its robust body and pointed roofs, is typical of Trentino. It has been transformed into a "beauty farm" and hotel. Two musician angels will greet you at the front desk. The prettiest rooms are in the castle itself; they open onto the splendid landscape of Merano. The others are in the outbuildings and are just as comfortable; they have terraces and direct access to the swimming pool and sauna via luxurious red velvet hallways. The lounge chairs set up in the garden and the health Spa make this the perfect place to unwind. Prices are somewhat high, which is why there are many older people among the clientele. Come here to let yourself be pampered for a day or two, even if you are not yet ready for retirement.

How to get there *(Map 4): 28 km northwest of Bolzano via A22, Bolzano-South exit, then S38 to Merano.*

Hotel Oberwirt ★★★★

Casa di Salute Raphael
39020 Merano – Marling (Bolzano)
Tel. (0473) 47 111 – Fax (0473) 47 130
Sig. Joseph Waldner

Rooms 40 with telephone, bath or shower, WC, TV and minibar. **Price** With half board 110-150,000L (in single), 110-145,000L (in double), 155-185,000L (in suite, per pers., 3 days min.). **Meals** Breakfast 20,000L, served 7:30-11:00. **Restaurant** Menus 42-62,000L, also à la carte. **Credit cards** All major. **Pets** Dogs allowed (13,000L). **Facilities** Indoor and outdoour swimming pool, sauna, tennis, riding, golf course (9-hole), parking. **Nearby** Castel Tirolo, Castel Scena, Castel Coira in Sluderno, Glorenza, Monte Maria abbey near Malles Venosta, Petersberg golf course in Karersee. **Open** Mar. 15 – Nov. 11.

The Hotel Oberwirt is in Marling, a village on the outskirts of Merano, near the racetrack in the hills of the town. It has been run by the same family for two centuries, so there is no lack of professionalism. The hotel only has about forty rooms, all comfortably furnished in traditional and more modern styles. Our favorite is the one in the tower. The traditional *Stube* and the salons have the warmth of Tyrolean style. The Franz Liszt salon was the workplace of the famous musician during the summer of 1874. The hotel has two covered, heated swimming pools and a farm where you can go horseback riding; you can also do a week-long tennis clinics on the grounds (around $675 for half board per person per week). The region offers wonderful possibilities for hikes in the woods.

How to get there *(Map 4): 28 km northwest of Bolzano via A22, Bolzano-South exit; then S38 to Merano. Marlengo is 4 km south of Merano, next to the hippodrome.*

Hotel Schloss Korb ★★★★

Missiano
39050 San Paolo Appiano (Bolzano)
Tel. (0471) 63 60 00 – Fax (0471) 63 60 33
Famiglia Dellago

Rooms 56 with telephone, bath, WC and TV. **Price** Double 220-280,000L.
Meals Breakfast included, served 7:30-10:00; half board 140-220,000L, full
board 170-250,000L (per pers.). **Restaurant** Service 12:00-14:00, 19:00-21:00;
menu 60,000L, also à la carte. Specialties: Regional and Italian cuisine.
Credit cards Not accepted. **Pets** Dogs not allowed. **Facilities** Parking and garage
(15,000L). **Nearby** Wine road (N 42) from Appiano to the Caldaro Lake, Bolzano.
Open Apr. – Nov. 5.

On top of a hill, the Schloss Korb is an old castle which has a
superb view and is surrounded by vineyards, which make
it absolutely quiet. It is decorated in a Baroque style reminiscent
of the Tyrol. Colors, hand crafted objects, a profusion of gilded
wood and bouquets of flowers give the place a look of
comfortable luxury. You can go for a pleasant walk to the ruins
of a neighboring castle where a picnic is served with wine from
the property, in a small shelter set up for hotel guests.

How to get there *(Map 4): 13 km west via S42 to San Paolo, then
towards Missiano.*

Schloss Freudenstein

Via Masaccio, 6
39057 Appiano (Bolzano)
Tel. (0471) 66 06 38 - Fax (0471) 66 01 22

Rooms 15 with telephone, bath and WC. **Price** With half board 135-160,000L (per pers.). **Meals** Breakfast included. **Restaurant** For residents only. Service 12:30-13:00, 19:30-20:00; menus. Specialties: Regional cuisine. **Credit cards** Not accepted. **Pets** Dogs not allowed. **Facilities** Swimming pool, parking. **Nearby** Wine road (N 42) from Appiano to the Caldaro Lake, Bolzano, Santa Giustina Lake, Santuario de San Romedio and lake of Tavon. **Open** Apr. 1 – Nov. 10.

The back country of Bolzano is a very beautiful region of vineyard-covered hills along Caldaro Lake. The castle overlooks this beautiful southern Tyrolean landscape. The arches, columns and loggias of the castle create elegant spaces around the small cobblestone courtyard. Inside, the simplicity of the decor preserves the original spirit of the castle. The rooms and bathrooms are very comfortable. There is a swimming pool in the garden. You will find traditional breakfasts, dinners and regional wines at incomparable prices here.

How to get there (Map 4): 10 km southwest of Bolzano.

Pensione Leuchtenburg ★★

Klughammer, 100
39052 Caldaro sulla Strada del Vino (Bolzano)
Tel. (0471) 96 00 93 – Fax (0471) 96 00 93
Sig. Sparer

Rooms 17 and 1 suite with shower and WC. **Price** Double 110,000L, suite 220,000L. **Meals** Breakfast included; half board 18,000L (per pers.). **Restaurant** For residents. **Credit cards** Not accepted. **Pets** Dogs allowed. **Facilities** Private beach, windsurfing, gymnasium, mountain biking, parking. **Nearby** Wine road (N 42) from Appiano to the Caldaro Lake, Appiano, Merano, Petersberg golf course. **Open** Mar. – Nov. (closed Wed.).

The *pensione* is in the outbuildings of the Leuchtenberg castle. It is a very pleasant house with pretty arbor-covered courtyards and a large terrace, filled with flowers, on the lake. The interior, is simple decor, but charming. The tavern is typical of the region and the rooms are decorated with pretty painted wood furniture. A private beach, sailboards and mountain bikes are at the disposal of hotel guests at no charge. This is a good place for a nice vacation at a low price.

How to get there: *(Map 4) 25 km south of Merano, via A22, Ora-Lago Caldaro exit (Kaltern); on the left bank of the lake.*

Berghotel Zum Zirmerhof

39040 Redagno (Bolzano)
Oberradein, 59
Tel. (0471) 88 72 15 - Fax (0471) 88 72 25
Sig. Perwanger

Rooms 32 with bath or shower and WC. **Price** With half board 101-145,000L, 140-180,000L (suite), full board 20,000L (per pers., 3 days min.). **Meals** Breakfast 17,000L, served 8:00-10:00. **Restaurant** For residents only. Service 12:00, 19:30; closed Mon., menus 40-60,000L. **Credit cards** Not accepted. **Pets** Dogs allowed. **Facilities** Parking. **Nearby** Wine road (N 42) from Appiano to the Caldaro Lake, Appiano, Merano, Petersberg golf course. **Open** Dec 26 – Mar. 29 and Mai 21 – Nov. 4.

Away from the hordes of tourists, the Redagno region and the Monte Corno Reserve have not lost any of their traditional, natural beauty. This inn, which opened in 1890, was a popular vacation spot for the aristocracy and upper classes of Vienna and Berlin and a place where intellectuals came for inspiration. The rooms are cosy and comfortable, the *stube* and the family library still have that "Magic Mountain" atmosphere, and the great "Sala Grimm" the work of Ignaz Sthol, has kept its beautiful frescos. The fine cuisine of the house restaurant is still influenced by the recipes of the *nonna* Hanna Perwanger, of German origin, who loved the Upper Adige very much. Friendly service is a priority here, as is the happiness of the guests.

How to get there *(Map 4): 40 km south of Bolzano via A22, Egna Ora exit towards Cavalese to Kaltenbruno; after on your left towerds Redagno.*

Hotel Monte San Vigilio

Pawigl 37
San Vigilio 39011 Lana (Bolzano)
Tel. (0473) 51 236 – Fax (0473) 51 410
Sig. Gapp

Rooms 40 with telephone, bath or shower and WC. **Price** With half board 65-93,000, full board 75-98,000L. **Meals** Breakfast included, served 8:00-10:00. **Restaurant** Service 12:00-14:00, 19:00-20:30; menus. 27-38,000L, also à la carte. Specialties: Filetto al funghi, trute. **Credit cards** Not accepted. **Pets** Dogs not allowed. **Facilities** Heated swimming pool, riding, parking. **Nearby** Skiing, Castel Tirolo, Castel Scena, Castel Coira in Sluderno, Glorenza, Abbey of Monte Maria near Malles Venosta, Petersberg golf course in Karersee. **Open** All year (except Nov. 7 – Dec. 19).

This chalet is the perfect place for mountain lovers. The obligatory access by cable car will satisfy even the most demanding apecionados of rest and fresh air. Decorated with naive paintings, this chalet is undoubtedly one of the most charming places in this guide. There is a nice family atmosphere, warmly fostered by the manager, who willingly acts as a guide for guests who want to explore one of the many hiking trails in the area. The lifts work during the summer too, so you can get to beautiful natural sites and shelters where it is pleasant to stop and rest for awhile. The rooms all have a superb panoramic view. The cuisine is simple and good. This place is ideal for a family vacation.

How to get there *(Map 4): 30 km northwest of Bolzano via S38 towards Merano to Postal, then Lana; in Lana take the cable car (in summer 8:00-19:00, in winter 8:00-18:00).*

Park Hotel Laurin ★★★★

Via Laurin, 4
39100 Bolzano
Tel. (0471) 31 10 00 – Fax (0471) 31 11 48
Sig. Havlik

Rooms 96 with air-conditioning, telephone, bath or shower, WC, cable TV, minibar, fax and PC outlets. **Price** Single 175-250,000L, double 255-375,000L. **Meals** Breakfast included, served 7:30-10:30. **Restaurant** Service 12:00-14:00, 19:00-22:00; menus 38-56,000L, also à la carte. Specialties: Regional and Italian cuisine. **Credit cards** Amex, Visa, Eurocard, MasterCard. **Pets** Dogs allowed (20,000L). **Facilities** Heated swimming pool, parking. **Nearby** Wine road (N 42) from Appiano to Caldaro Lake, Bolzano, Castel Roncolo and Sarentina valley to Vitipeno. **Open** All year.

This old palace in the center of Bolzano, six hundred and fifty feet (200 meters) from the train station, remains an important address for a clientele of businessmen and upper-class families. The dining room, salons and guest rooms are large and "international palace" style. The hotel has every modern convenience and a very attentive personnel. *La Belle Epoque* is one of the best known restaurants in the region. The rooms look out onto the grounds and are all decorated with contemporary paintings from the hotel's own collection. The swimming pool, hidden in a box of greenery and coolness, is very pleasant. This establishment confirms the advantages of tradition.

How to get there *(Map 4): 140 km north of Verona via A22, Bolzano-South or North exit toward the stazione (railway station).*

Hotel Castel Guncina

39100 Bolzano
Tel. (0471) 28 57 42
Fax (0471) 463 45
Sig. Lanthaler

Rooms 18 with telephone, shower and WC. **Price** Double 77-176,000L. **Meals** Breakfast included, served 7:00-10:00. **Restaurant** Service 11:00-13:00, 19:00-21:00; closed Tues.; menus, also à la carte. **Credit cards** Not accepted. **Pets** Dogs not allowed. **Facilities** Swimming pool, tennis (15,000L), parking. **Nearby** Wine road (N 42) from Appiano to the Caldaro Lake, Bolzano, Castel Roncolo and Sarentina valley to Vitipeno. **Open** All year (except Jan.).

The Castel Guncina overlooks Bolzano and the valley and is just as romantic as can be. Surrounded by vineyards, so typical of the region, this curious edifice, with its lordly manor appearance, houses an opulent, comfortable hotel with slightly over elaborate decor. The restaurant is frequented by a clientele of regulars who also come here to swim and play tennis. The rooms all have the same decor, but are more or less spacious according to where they are located. Ask for the ones on the top floor looking out over the valley. It is hard to imagine that Bolzano, which seems so far, is only a mile and a half away.

How to get there *(Map 4): 154 km north of Verona via A22, Bolzano-South exit; 2 km west of town center via Cardone.*

Hotel Turm ★★★★

39050 Fié Allo Sciliar (Bolzano)
Tel. (0471) 72 50 14 – Fax (0471) 72 54 74
Sig. Pramstrahler

Rooms 23 with telephone, bath, WC and TV. **Price** Single 90-134,000L, double 170-278,000L. **Meals** Breakfast included, served 8:00-10:00; half board 107-161,000L, full board 130-187,000L (per pers.). **Restaurant** Service 12:00-14:00, 19:00-22:00; closed Sun. evening; menus 38-60,000L, also à la carte. Specialties: Regional cuisine. **Credit cards** Amex, Visa, Eurocard and MasterCard. **Pets** Dogs allowed (17,000L). **Facilities** Heated swimming pool, garage (7,000L). **Nearby** Alpe di Siusi (1996 m) and Seceda (2500 m) by cable car, Castelrotto, Val Gardena, Bolzano. **Open** Dec. 20 – Nov. 15.

This hotel is in Fié, a small village in Val Gardena, a superb region just below the spectacular and impressive Mount Sciliar. It is in the old town hall, right in the middle of Fié and has been run by the same family for three generations. Very comfortable and nicely decorated interior, it has antique furniture and a large collection of paintings. Most of the rooms are cozy and tastefully furnished and have a superb view of the mountains. Stefano, the owner's son and manager of the restaurant, is also an excellent cook: his fine inventive cuisine skillfully blends the particularities of regional cuisine with the sophistication of recipes of the great French chefs. In the summer, this is a marvelous place for hiking around the lake and in the winter, you can go cross–country skiing, skating and downhill skiing at Alpe di Suisi, only twenty minutes away.

How to get there *(Map 5): 16 km east of Bolzano (via A22 Bolzano-North exit) via S49 to Prato all'Isarco, then Fié.*

Hotel Cavallino d'Oro ★★★★

Piazza Kraus
39040 Castelrotto (Bolzano)
Tel. (0471) 706 337 – Fax (0471) 707 172
Sig. and Sig.ra Urthaler

Rooms 20 with telephone, bath, WC, TV and safe. **Price** Single 55-80,000L, double 80-120,000L. **Meals** Breakfast included, served 7:30-11:00; half board 65-95,000L, full board 95-130,000L. **Restaurant** Service 11:30-14:00, 18:00-21:00; closed Sun. dinner; menus 20-50,000L, also à la carte. Specialties: Italian and regional cuisine. **Credit cards** All major **Pets** Dogs allowed (fee). **Facilities** Heated swimming pool, parking. **Nearby** Skiing, Alpe de Siusi, Val Gardena, Ortisei. **Open** All year (closed Tues.).

The Cavallino d'Oro is a traditional inn typical of Southern Tyrol. It is in Castelrotto, a village in the Val Gardena where Ladin is still spoken and where the inhabitants still dress in traditional costume and live in houses with painted facades. The *stube* (locale) is friendly and the restaurant features local specialties. The rooms are very well kept. In the summer, a small terrace is set up on the square, the prettiest spot in the village. This still relatively unvisited region is worth exploring, especially at these prices.

How to get there *(Map 5): 26 km northeast of Bolzano via S12 to Ponte Gardena, then towards Castelrotto.*

Hotel Adler ★★★★

Via Rezia, 7
39046 Ortisei (Bolzano)
Tel. (0471) 79 62 03 – Fax (0471) 79 62 10
Famiglia Sanoner

Rooms 100 with telephone, bath, WC, TV and minibar. **Price** Single 200-218,000L, double 203-400,000L. **Meals** Breakfast included, served 7:00-10:00; half board 21,000L, full board 42,000L (per pers.). **Restaurant** Service 12:00-14:00, 19:00-21:30; menus 25-35,000L, also à la carte. Specialties: Tyrolese cuisine. **Credit cards** Amex, Visa, Eurocard, MasterCard **Pets** Dogs allowed. **Facilities** Heated indoor swimming pool, tennis (16,000L), sauna, health center, garage, parking. **Nearby** Alpe di Siusi (1996 m) and Seceda (2500 m) by cabble car, Castelrotto, Val Gardena, Bolzano. **Open** May 15 – Oct. 20, Dec. 15 – Apr. 15.

In the center of Ortisei, this hotel, born from the fusion of two buildings with very different architectural styles, is an island of greenery and quiet. It is also the meeting place for German tourists staying in the region. In summer and winter it is frequented by a clientele of regulars for whom solitude and proximity to the slopes are not priorities; they enjoy the animated ambience of the little village of Ortisei. All of the rooms have been redone.

How to get there *(Map 5): 35 km east of Bolzano via A22; Chiusa exit (or S12 to Ponte Gardena), then S242 to Ortisei.*

Uhrerhof Deur ★★★

Bulla 39046 Ortisei (Bolzano)
Tel (0471) 79 73 35 – Fax (0471) 79 74 57
Famiglia Zemmer

Rooms 7 and 3 apartments with telephone, bath or shower, WC and TV.
Price Single 100-140,000L, apartment 50-60,000L (per pers.). **Meals** Breakfast
included, served 7:00-10:00; half board 110-140,000L (per pers., 3 days min.).
Restaurant By request, service 19:00; menus 30-50,000L. **Credit cards** Visa,
Eurocard, MasterCard **Pets** Dogs not allowed. **Facilities** Sauna, hammam,
solarium (15,000L), parking. **Nearby** Alpe di Siusi (1,996 m) and Seceda (2,500
m) by cable car, Castelrotto, Val Gardena, Bolzano. **Open** All year.

R ewarding is when the discovery of a place like this by
accident. You start thinking that you are all alone in the
world, then a little civilization appears, and the hope is that in
the two wooden houses above a valley on a road which ends in
a waterfall, there will be enough modern conveniences...There
are more than enough at Uhrerhof Deur. Not only do the
rooms have a superb view, but there is also a sauna, a steam
bath, an old *stube* (locale), linen tablecloths and very good
cuisine. The attention you get here will make you feel like a
king. But there is one condition: smokers stay away!

How to get there *(Map 5): 35 km east of Bolzano via A22; Chiusa or
Bolzano-North exit (or S12 to Ponte Gardena), then S242 to Ortisei.
Bulla is 5 km of Ortisei.*

Hotel Elephant ★★★★

39042 Bressanone (Bolzano)
Via Rio Bianco, 4
Tel. (0472) 83 2750 – Fax (0472) 83 65 79
Sig. Falk

Rooms 44 with telephone, bath, WC and TV. **Price** Single 100-115,000L, double 200-230,000L. **Meals** Breakfast 22,000L; half board 194,000L, full board 230,000L (per pers., 3 days min.). **Restaurant** Service 12:00-14:15, 19:00-21:15; closed Mon.; menus 65,000L. Specialty: Piatto Elephante **Credit cards** All major. **Pets** Dogs allowed in room (11,000L). **Facilities** Heated swimming pool, parking (11-15,000L). **Nearby** Plose (2504 m), Convent of Novacella, Val Gardena (castle of Velturno, Chiusa, Ortisei). **Open** Mar. – Nov. 10, Dec. 25 – Jan. 7.

The many Episcopal monasteries and castles around Bressanone testify to the artistic, cultural and spiritual influence this town had on the region during the 18th–century. The Hotel Elephant is the ideal base for exploring the area. The paneled reception rooms are decorated with antique furniture, tapestries and rugs. The rooms are all very comfortable and most of them look out onto the swimming pool or the mountains (only certain rooms face north). The cuisine is remarkable and the personnel is excellent. The hotel has consistently lived up to its reputation since 1550 when a convoy with an elephant, given to the Emperor Ferdinand of Habsbourgby the King of Portugal, stayed here.

How to get there *(Map 5): 40 km northeast of Bolzano via A22; Bressanone exit. The hotel is northwest of town center: from via Roma, via Fichini, then via Rio Bianco.*

Hotel La Perla ★★★★

Via Centro, 44
39033 Corvara in Badia (Bolzano)
Tel. (0471) 83 61 33 - Fax (0471) 83 65 68
Famiglia Costa

Rooms 52 with telephone, bath, WC and TV. **Prices** Single 130-280,000L, double 220-520,000L, suite 280-620,000L. **Meals** Breakfast included, served 7:30-12:00; half board 128-278,000L (per pers., 3 days min.). **Restaurant** "La Stua de Micheli" Service 12:00-14:00, 19:00-22:00; menus 48-68,000L. Specialties: Rotolo di salmone e rombo con salsetta al limone, mezzelune di crauti e speck con burro dorato, sella di capriolo in salsa di maggiorana, terrina di ricotta con frutti freschi. **Credit cards** Amex, Visa, Eurocard and MasterCard **Pets** Small dogs allowed. **Facilities** Heated swimming pool, tennis (12-28,000L), sauna, fitness, garage, parking. **Nearby** Skiing, Val Badia, great road of Dolomites (N 48), Ortisei. **Open** Dec. 3 – Apr. 17, July – Sept.

The Hotel La Perla is a real gem. A beautiful chalet in a quiet part of the center of Corvara, it is perfect in every way. It is more elegant than rustic, and it manages to maintain a certain intimacy despite the numerous services worthy of a grand hotel (sauna, hairdresser, wine cellar, heated pool). Just twenty seven miles (45 km) from Cortina d'Ampezzo, this place is great all year round.

How to get there *(Map 5): 65 km east of Bolzano via A22; Chiusa exit (or S12 to Ponte Gardena), then S242 to Corvara via Ortisei.*

Hotel Armentarola ★★★

Via Prè de Vi, 78
39030 San Cassiano (Bolzano)
Tel. (0471) 84 95 22 – Fax (0471) 84 93 89
Famiglia Wieser

Rooms 50 with telephone, bath or shower, WC, safe and TV. **Price** With half board single 160-200,000L, double 280-400,000L, suite 320-440,000L, with full board 110-160,000L (per pers.). **Meals** Breakfast included, served 7:30-11:00; half board 125-258,000L (per pers., 3 days min.). **Restaurant** Service 11:00-13:30, 19:00-21:00; menus 35-60,000L. Specialty: Regional cuisine. **Credit cards** Not accepted **Pets** Dogs allowed (20,000L). **Facilities** Indoor swimming pool, tennis, riding, sauna, solarium, garage (10,000L). **Nearby** Skiing, Cortina d'Ampezzo, great road of Dolomites (N 48), Ortisei. **Open** Dec. 8 – Apr. 14, July 14 – Oct. 8.

The story of the Armentarola began with the Wieser family in 1938, when Paolo and Emma transformed the family chalet into an inn. It is isolated at an altitude of 5,200 feet (1,600 meters), in an enchanting landscape of pastures and woods with the Dolomites in the background, but the Armentarola has continually adapted to the changing standards of modern comfort, while keeping all of its original charm intact. There are plenty of well-organized leisure activites here all year round. In summer, you can play tennis and go horseback riding, and in winter, you can swim in the covered swimming pool or take the ski lift from the hotel, which is linked to the large ski *caroussel* of the upper Badia Valley. Enjoy the grandeur of nature at this hotel, only a few kilometers from Cortina d'Ampezzo.

How to get there *(Map 5): 75 km east of Bolzano via S12, S242d and S242 towards Selva di Valgardena; then S243 to Corvara and S244.*

Ansitz Heufler Hotel ★★★

39030 Rasun di Sopra (Bolzano)
Tel. (0474) 49 62 88
Fax (0474) 49 81 99
Sig. Pallhuber

Rooms 8 with telephone, bath or shower and WC. **Price** Double 160-230,000L, suite +30,000L. **Meals** Breakfast included, served 8:00-11:00; half board 90-108,000L, full board 32,000L (per pers., 3 days min.). **Restaurant** Service 12:00-14:00, 18:00-21:30; closed Wed.; menus 40-50,000L. Specialties: Regional cuisine. **Credit cards** All major. **Pets** Dogs allowed (8,000L). **Facilities** Parking. **Nearby** Anterselva Lake, Monguelfo, Braeies Lake, Cortina d'Ampezzo via Carbonin (N51), skiing in Plan de Corones (private bus from the hotel). **Open** All year except Mai 11 – 31 and Nov.5 – Dec. 3.

This small 14th-century castle is one of the nicest hotels in this guide. It is not unusual to see similar places by the side of the road when traveling in this region, but it is quite surprising to find one with an interior that has been so well preserved through the centuries. Even more surprising is the warm friendly atmosphere in the kind of place where grandiosity so often interferes with comfort. The guest rooms are cozy and have nice antique furniture. The blond wood-paneled salon is particularly convivial: it has a large couch and ceramic stove. This is a nice place for skiing at plan de Corones (free skibus service), with special rates for «white week» («settimane bianhe»).

How to get there *(Map 5): 87 km northeast of Bolzano via A22, Bressanone exit; then S49 to Brunico; then road towards valley of Anterselva.*

Parkhotel Sole Paradiso ★★★★

Via Sesto, 13
39038 San Candido - Innichen (Bolzano)
Tel. (0474) 913 120 - Fax (0474) 913 193
Famiglia Ortner

Rooms 41 with telephone, bath or shower, WC and TV. **Price** Single 75-160,000L, double 150-320,000L. **Meals** Breakfast included (buffet), served 8:00-10:30; half board 105-185,000L, full board 135-220,000L (per pers., 3 days min.). **Restaurant** Service 12:30-13:30, 19:00-20:30; menus 40-50,000L. Specialtie: Schlutzkrapfen, maccheroni alla boscaiola, trota del vivaio Kaiserschmarrn. **Credit cards** Visa, Eurocard and MasterCard. **Pets** Small dogs allowed. **Facilities** Indoor swimming pool, tennis (15,000L), sauna, garage (15,000L). **Nearby** Lago di Braeies, lago di Misurina, Croda Rossa, Tre cime di Lavaredo, Cortina d'Ampezzo. **Open** Dec. 22 – Apr. 10, June 14 – Oct. 6.

The architecture and the red and yellow colors of this large chalet will remind you, if you need to be reminded, that you are only a few miles from the Austrian border. The warm cozy atmosphere of a mountain home pervades the hotel. The walls are covered with blond wood and the ceiling and table lamps are made of very beautiful sculpted wood. The rooms have large canopy beds, heavy drapes and pretty flower-covered balconies with nice views of the Val Pusteria. The hotel is very wellequipped for leisure activities: There is a tennis court, a heated swimming pool open year round, cross-country ski trails and a ski shuttle bus which stops just in front of the hotel.

How to get there *(Map 5): 110 km northeast of Bolzano via A22, Bressanone exit; then S49 to San Candido.*

Ansitz Zum Steinbock

38, San Stefano
39040 Villandro (Bolzano)
Tel. (0472) 84 31 11 – Fax (0472) 84 31 11
Sig. and Sig.ra Kirchbaumer

Rooms 17 with telephone, bath or shower and WC (3 with TV). **Price** Single 65,000L, double 110,000L. **Meals** Breakfast included, served 8:00-10:00; half board 65,000L (per pers., 3 days min.). **Restaurant** Service 12:00-14:00; closed Mon.; menus, also à la carte. Specialties: Regional cuisine. **Credit cards** All major. **Pets** Dogs allowed. **Facilities** Parking. **Nearby** Bressanone, Plose (2504 m), convent of Novacella, Val Gardena: castle of Velturno, Chiusa, Castelrotto, Ortisei. **Open** Mar. 10 – Jan. 12 and Mon..

From the highway to Brenner you can see small villages with castles in the mountains. If the urge to see them is strong, get off at Chiusa, where a narrow road will quickly lead you up. Villandro is one of these pretty and unpretentious, little resort towns, with a castle that welcomes both the traveler passing through and the family on vacation. The decor is traditional, and the rooms are comfortable. The hotel is simple but adorable, authentic and well kept by young professionals. It is a nice place to stop off at for a breath of pine scented fresh air along your way.

How to get there *(Map 5): 27 km northeast of Bolzano via A22, Chiusa exit.*

Albergo Accademia ★★★★

Vicolo Colico, 4-6
38100 Trento
Tel. (0461) 23 36 00 – Fax (0461) 23 01 74
Sig.ra Fambri

Rooms 43 with air-conditioning, telephone, bath or shower, WC, cable TV and minibar. **Price** Single 170,000L, double 240,000L. **Meals** Breakfast included, served 7:30-10:30; half board 18,000L, full board 32,000L (per pers., 3 days min.). **Restaurant** Service 12:30-14:30, 19:30-22:30; closed Sun.; menus 45-55,000L, also à la carte. Specialties: Storione affumicato con finferli crudi, ravioli fatti in casa, carrello dei bolliti, panna cotta al caffè. **Credit cards** All major. **Pets** Dogs allowed. **Facilities** Parking. **Nearby** Trento (Piazza del Duomo and cathedral, Museo Risorgimento), Lake Garda, Brenta Dolomites, Lake Toblino, La Paganella (summit reached by cable car, 7,000L), the "Ormeri" di Segonzaro. **Open** All year.

The Albergo Accademia is in an old house from the Middle Ages on a small square in this pretty neighborhood of this medieval town. The decor is resolutely modern, but highlights what remains of the original architecture and a few antique pieces. The rooms are large, light, quiet and very comfortable. The hotel restaurant is renowned for its innovative cuisine, including local specialties. The old inner courtyard is now a garden where breakfast is served and the terrace is a nice place from which to enjoy the view of the rooftops, the towers and the bell-towers of Trento. This is a charming address in a town that is really worth the trip.

How to get there *(Map 4): 101 km north of Verona via A22, Trento exit; the hotel is located in the town center.*

Lido Palace Hotel ★★★★

Lago di Garda
Viale Carducci, 10
Riva del Garda (Trento)
Tel. (0464) 55 26 64 - Fax (0464) 55 19 57
Sig. Genetin

Rooms 62 with telephone, bath or shower, WC and TV. **Price** Double 180-240,000L. **Meals** Breakfast included, served 7:30-10:00; half board 110-140,000L, full board 130-160,500L (per pers., 3 days min.). **Restaurant** Service 12:30-14:00, 19:30-21:00; menu 38,500L. Specialties: International and Italian cuisine. **Credit cards** All major. **Pets** Small dogs allowed (9,000L). **Facilities** Swimming pool, tennis, parking. **Nearby** Lake Garda, Monte Bastione (1502 m) by cable car, Cascade of Varone, Lake of Tenno, Trento. **Open** Apr. – Oct.

The main attraction of the Lido is its proximity to the small port of Riva del Garda. The grounds are next to the public garden and the lakeside docks where you will find a quaint 19th-century spa atmosphere. The building is from the same period and has been very tastefully renovated. The rooms are bright and simple; from them you can see the lake through the foliage of cedar trees. A family atmosphere pervades the hotel despite its conventional, classic appearance.

How to get there *(Map 4): 50 km southwest of Trento; 87 km north of Verona via A22; Marco exit, then S240.*

Albergo Castel Pergine ★

38057 Pergine Valsugana (Trento)
Tel. (0461) 53 11 58 – Fax (0461) 53 11 58
Sig. and Sig.ra Schneider-Neff

Rooms 21 with telephone (12 with shower and WC). **Price** Single 70,000L, double 140,000L. **Meals** Breakfast 10,000L, served 8:00-9:30; half board 70-95,000L, (per pers., 2 days min.). **Restaurant** Service 12:00-14:30, 19:00-22:00; closed Mon. lunch; menus 35-55,000L. Specialties: Regional cooking. **Credit cards** Not accepted. **Pets** Dogs allowed. **Facilities** Parking. **Nearby** Caldonazzo Lake (San Cristoforo al Lago), Canal of the Brentaby (N47) after Primolano, Trento. **Open** May 15 – Oct. 31.

This former residence of the Bishops of Trento, built in the 8th century, is perfect for a quiet restful vacation. It is at the top of a wooded hill overlooking the valley, surrounded by the Dolomites and Lake Caldonazzo. The grounds, hidden behind high walls, are a nice place for reading. The rooms are decorated with period furniture. The lake's proximity is convenient for water sports. The Castello also has a good restaurant that has helped make it famous.

How to get there (Map 4): 11 km east of Trento via S47. The hotel is 2 km from the center of town.

Palace Hotel ★★★★

Casa di Salute Raphael
38050 Roncegno (Trento)
Tel. (0461) 76 40 12 – Fax (0461) 76 45 00
Sig. Quaiatto

Rooms 85 with telephone, bath or shower, WC and TV. **Price** Single 130,000L, double 190,000L. **Meals** Breakfast included, served 7:30-10:00; half board 145,000L, full board 160,000L (per pers., 3 days min.). **Restaurant** Service 12:30-14:00, 19:30-21:30; menus 35-45,000L, also à la carte. Specialties: Tronco de pontesel, cumel alla paesana. **Credit cards** Amex, Visa, Eurocard, MasterCard. **Pets** Dogs not allowed. **Facilities** Indoor swimming pool, tennis, squash, gymnasium, parking. **Nearby** Ruins of the castles of Borgo Valsugana, Canal of the Brenta (N47) after Primolano, Trento. **Open** Apr. – Oct.

Built at the beginning of the century on twelve and a half acres, the Palace Hotel still has all of the elegance and the picturesque quality of that time. It has long been the summer meeting place for the Italian aristocracy. The salons and the dining room testify to its past. It has been completely renovated and has all the requisite amenities of a four-star hotel, including a squash court, a health center with an indoor pool and a sauna. This blend of old-fashioned elegance and modern efficiency is the main appeal of this hotel.

How to get there *(Map 5): 33 km east of Trento via S47.*

Hotel Cipriani – Palazzo Vendramin ★★★★

Isola della Giudecca, 10
30133 Venezia
Tel. (041) 520 77 44 – Fax (041) 520 39 30 – Sig. Rusconi

Rooms 104 with air-conditioning, telephone, bath, WC, safe, cable TV and minibar.
Price Single 650-850,000L, double 850-1,200,000L. **Meals** Breakfast included, served
7:00-10:30. **Restaurant** Service 12:30-15:00, 19:30-22:30; à la carte. Specialties:
Vitello Cipriani, scampi "Carlina." **Credit cards** All major. **Pets** Small dogs allowed.
Facilities Swimming pool, tennis (25,000L), sauna (22,000L), turkish bath, private
port, parking. **Nearby** Piazza San Marco, Grand Canal, Gallery of the Academy, Ca'
d'Oro, Guggenheim collection, scuola di San Rocco, scuola di San Giorgio degli
schiavoni, the Ghetto, the Lido and lagoon, Murano (venetian glass), Burano (center of
lacemaking), Torcello (S. M. Assunta, S. Fosca), Venetian villas (cruise along the
Brenta Canal with the boat "Il Burchiello" or by rented car: Amex), traditions (Carnival
of Venice, the Regata Storica (Sept.), the Mostra of Venice (Aug.-Sept.), Biennale of
Venice), al Lido Alberoni golf course (18-hole). **Open** All year.

The Cipriani is an incredibly luxurious hotel on the island of
Giudecca, facing Venice and the lagoon. The salons are
sumptuous. The terrace-bars look out on marvelously well-kept
gardens. The rooms, with their pink marble bathrooms are
extremely comfortable. We hesitate between the ones with a
view of the island of San Giorgio and the ones with small patios
in the back of the garden. We should also mention the
impeccable service and the friendly personnel the famous fine
cuisine served by candlelight on the terraces by the water facing
the lagoon and the spectacular sea-water swimming pool.
Adjoining the hotel, the Palazzo Vendramin offers luxury suites
with a view of San Marco or the gardens of Cassanova.

How to get there *(Map 5): On Isola della Giudecca.*

Bauer Grünwald – Grand Hotel ★★★★★

Campo San Moise, 1459
30124 Venezia
Tel. (041) 520 70 22 – Fax (041) 520 75 57
Sig. Puppo

Rooms 215 with air-conditioning, telephone, bath, WC, safe, cable TV and minibar. **Price** Single 200-350,000L, double 300-620,000L. **Meals** Breakfast included, served 7:00-10:30. **Restaurant** Service 12:30-14:30, 19:00-22:30; menu: 80,000L, also à la carte. Specialties: Risotto alla torcellana, fegato alla veneziana. **Credit cards** All major. **Pets** Dogs allowed (50,000L). **Nearby** Piazza San Marco, Grand Canal, Gallery of the Academy, Ca' d'Oro, Guggenheim collection, scuola di San Rocco, scuola di San Giorgio degli schiavoni, the Ghetto, the Lido and lagoon, Murano (venetian glass), Burano (center of lacemaking), Torcello (S. M. Assunta, S. Fosca), Venetian villas (cruise along the Brenta Canal with the boat "Il Burchiello" or by rented car: Amex), traditions (Carnival of Venice, the Regata Storica (Sept.), the Mostra of Venice (Aug.-Sept.), Biennale of Venice), al Lido Alberoni golf course (18-hole). **Open** All year.

The Bauer Grünwald was born out of Italian unity: a young Venetian man, Jules Grünwald, married Miss Bauer. First they opened a tavern, which was a great success, and then they built the Grand Hotel. The difference between the Bauer and other palaces in Venice is its "class": An atmosphere of quiet luxury reigns here. Only a few steps from Piazza San Marco, it also has the advantage of having a terrace on the Grand Canal, where you can dine by candlelight facing the Salute and the island of San Giorgio.

How to get there *(Map 5): Near Piazza San Marco, along the Grand Canal.*

Gritti Palace Hotel ★★★★★

30124 Venezia
Campo Santa Maria del Giglio, 2467
Tel. (041) 79 46 11 – Fax (041) 520 09 42
Sig. Balaudo

Rooms 85 and 11 suites with air-conditioning, telephone, bath, WC, safe, cable TV and minibar. **Price** Single 481-553,000L, double 732,600-897,600L, suite 1,821,600-2,701,600L. **Meals** Breakfast included, served 7:00-10:30. **Restaurant** Service 12:30-15:00, 19:30-22:30; menu: 100-140,000L, also à la carte. Specialties: Bresaola Gritti Palace, i risotti del Gritti, scampi fritti in erbaria. **Credit cards** All major. **Pets** Small dogs allowed in room. **Nearby** Piazza San Marco, Grand Canal, Gallery of the Academy, Ca' d'Oro, Guggenheim collection, scuola di San Rocco, scuola di San Giorgio degli schiavoni, the Ghetto, the Lido and lagoon, Murano (venetian glass), Burano (center of lacemaking), Torcello (S. M. Assunta, S. Fosca), Venetian villas (cruise along the Brenta Canal with the boat "Il Burchiello" or by rented car: Amex), traditions (Carnival of Venice, the Regata Storica (Sept.), the Mostra of Venice (Aug.-Sept.), Biennale of Venice), al Lido Alberoni golf course (18-hole). **Open** All year.

E rnest Hemingway wrote of this 15th–century palace built by Andrea Gritti, "The best hotel in Venice, which is a town made of grand hotels." Its splendid and famous terrace on the Grand Canal is a magic place. Everything here, from the rooms and suites to the salons and dining rooms, emanates luxury and refinement. The restaurant is also one of the best in Venice. If you are planning to stay at the Gritti, try to get a room on the Grand Canal so you can enjoy the show for longer.

How to get there *(Map 5): Near San Marco, on the Grand Canal.*

Hotel Monaco e Grand Canal ★★★★

San Marco – Calle Vallaresso, 1325
30124 Venezia
Tel. (041) 520 02 11 – Fax (041) 520 05 01
Sig. Zambon

Rooms 72 with air-conditioning, telephone, bath, WC, safe, cable TV and minibar.
Price Single 330-350,000L, double 470-520,000L, on the canal 550,000L, suite
700-900,000L. **Meals** Breakfast included, served 7:00-10:30. **Restaurant** Service
12:30-15:00, 19:30-22:00; à la carte. Specialties: "Cape sante" gratinate, ravioli
di magro al burro e salvia, scampi Ca' d'Oro e riso pilaf, fegato alla veneziana con
polenta, zabaglione con amaretti. **Credit cards** All major. **Pets** Small dogs allowed.
Nearby Piazza San Marco, Grand Canal, Gallery of the Academy, Ca' d'Oro,
Guggenheim collection, scuola di San Rocco, scuola di San Giorgio degli schiavoni, the
Ghetto, the Lido and lagoon, Murano (venetian glass), Burano (center of lacemaking),
Torcello (S. M. Assunta, S. Fosca), Venetian villas (cruise along the Brenta Canal with
the boat "Il Burchiello" or by rented car: Amex), traditions (Carnival of Venice, the
Regata Storica (Sept.), the Mostra of Venice (Aug.-Sept.), Biennale of Venice), al Lido
Alberoni golf course (18-hole). **Open** All year.

The elegant atmosphere, plush salons, flowering patio and
small but very well decorated rooms make this one of the
great hotels of Venice. It also has a superb terrace on the Grand
Canal, where you can have lunch and dinner. The restaurant is
excellent, but very expensive. In the summer, it is nicer to have
a room on the interior patio. If you really want to have a view
of the Grand Canal, try to get room farthest from the *vaporetto*
station at the foot of the hotel. Our favorite is Room 308. Prices
are reasonable, especially off-season.

How to get there (Map 5): Near Piazza San Marco.

Londra Palace ★★★★

San Marco – Riva degli Schiavoni, 4171
30124 Venezia
Tel. (041) 520 05 33 – Fax (041) 522 50 32
Sig. Samueli

Rooms 57 with air-conditioning, telephone, bath, WC, safe, cable TV, whirl pool and minibar. **Price** Double 300-500,000L, suite 400-600,000L. **Meals** Breakfast included, served 7:00-11:00. **Restaurant** Service 11:30-16:00, 19:00-24:00; menus: 70-93,000L, also à la carte. Specialties: Italian and Venitian cuisine. **Credit cards** All major. **Pets** Dogs not allowed. **Nearby** Piazza San Marco, Grand Canal, Gallery of the Academy, Ca' d'Oro, Guggenheim collection, scuola di San Rocco, scuola di San Giorgio degli schiavoni, the Ghetto, the Lido and lagoon, Murano (venetian glass), Burano (center of lacemaking), Torcello (S. M. Assunta, S. Fosca), Venetian villas (cruise along the Brenta Canal with the boat "Il Burchiello" or by rented car: Amex), traditions (Carnival of Venice, the Regata Storica (Sept.), the Mostra of Venice (Aug.-Sept.), Biennale of Venice), al Lido Alberoni golf course (18-hole). **Open** All year.

On the edge of the San Marco basin close to several large palaces, the recently renovated Londra Palace has again found its place among the grand hotels of Venice. This neo-Gothic palace built in the second half of the 19th century once hosted d'Annunzio and Tchaikovsky. The rooms are decorated with antique furniture and beautiful objects. We strongly encourage you to ask for the rooms on the lagoon, facing the island of San Giorgio Maggiore. The hotel also has a fine restaurant, *Do Leoni*. You will find that all of this luxury comes at a reasonable price.

How to get there *(Map 5): Near Piazza San Marco.*

Hotel Gabrielli Sandwirth ★★★★

San Marco - Riva degli Schiavoni, 4110
30122 Venezia
Tel. (041) 523 15 80 - Fax (041) 520 94 55 - Sig. Perkhofer

Rooms 110 with telephone, bath, WC, safe and TV. **Price** Single 295,000L, double 520,000L. **Meals** Breakfast included, served 7:00-12:00; half board 620,000L, full board 680,000L. **Restaurant** "Trattoria al Buffet" Service 12:00-14:30, 19:00-21:30. Specialties: Buffet of Italian and Venetian cuisine. **Credit cards** All major. **Pets** Dogs allowed. **Nearby** Piazza San Marco, Grand Canal, Gallery of the Academy, Ca' d'Oro, Guggenheim collection, scuola di San Rocco, scuola di San Giorgio degli schiavoni, the Ghetto, the Lido and lagoon, Murano (venetian glass), Burano (center of lacemaking), Torcello (S. M. Assunta, S. Fosca), Venetian villas (cruise along the Brenta Canal with the boat "Il Burchiello" or by rented car: Amex), traditions (Carnival of Venice, the Regata Storica (Sept.), the Mostra of Venice (Aug.-Sept.), Biennale of Venice), al Lido Alberoni golf course (18 holc). **Open** Feb.   Nov.

This old 13th-century Veneto-Gothic palace is on the Riva degli Schiavoni, among some of the most luxurious hotels in Venice. It has been expanded to incorporate two other medieval houses and the interior is now a real maze. The rooms are decorated in a classical style and are very comfortable. The ideal is to get one with a loggia on the San Marco Basin, facing the San Giorgio Church. There is no trace of the old palace left in the modern decor of the bar, but this hotel is the only one on the Riva degli Schiavoni with an inner courtyard and a palm tree-shaded rose garden where you can dine by candlelight and Venetian lanterns. There is also a terrace on the roof with a view of the Grand Canal and the lagoon.

How to get there *(Map 5): Near Piazza San Marco.*

Hotel Metropole ★★★★

San Marco – Riva degli Schiavoni, 4149
30122 Venezia
Tel. (041) 520 50 44 – Fax (041) 522 36 79
Sig. Beggiato

Rooms 73 with air-conditioning, telephone, bath, WC, safe, TV and minibar. **Price** Single 190-380,000L, double 290-530,000L, suite 380-560,000L. **Meals** Breakfast included, served 7:00-10:30; half board 51,000L, full board 102,000L. **Restaurant** Service 12:30-15:00, 19:00-22:00; buffet: 51,000L. Specialties: Italian and Venetian cuisine. **Credit cards** All major. **Pets** Small dogs allowed. **Nearby** Piazza San Marco, Grand Canal, Gallery of the Academy, Ca' d'Oro, Guggenheim collection, scuola di San Rocco, scuola di San Giorgio degli schiavoni, the Ghetto, the Lido and lagoon, Murano (venetian glass), Burano (center of lacemaking), Torcello (S. M. Assunta, S. Fosca), Venetian villas (cruise along the Brenta Canal with the boat "Il Burchiello" or by rented car: Amex), traditions (Carnival of Venice, the Regata Storica (Sept.), the Mostra of Venice (Aug.-Sept.), Biennale of Venice), al Lido Alberoni golf course (18-hole). **Open** Feb. – Nov.

We will say this up front: this hotel, in one of the most busy parts of Venice, is more pleasant off-season. Behind its slightly banal facade you will find it deliciously quaint. The salon is vast and pleasant and the breakfast room on the canal is exquisite. In the hallways you will find pretty collections of objects, mirrors and Venetian paintings. The rooms are fairly spacious and look like the rest of the hotel. The ones on the top floor have small terraces with a phenomenal view of the rooftops of Venice.

How to get there *(Map 5): Near Piazza San Marco.*

Pensione Accademia – Villa Maravegie

Dorsoduro, 1058
30123 Venezia
Tel. (041) 521 01 88 – 523 78 46 – Fax (041) 523 91 52
Sig. Dinato

Rooms 27 with telephone, bath or shower and TV. **Price** Single 110-145,000L, double 165-225,000L. **Meals** Breakfast included, served 7:15-10:30. **Restaurant** See p.433-437. **Credit cards** All major. **Pets** Dogs not allowed. **Nearby** Piazza San Marco, Grand Canal, Gallery of the Academy, Ca' d'Oro, Guggenheim collection, scuola di San Rocco, scuola di San Giorgio degli schiavoni, the Ghetto, the Lido and lagoon, Murano (venetian glass), Burano (center of lacemaking), Torcello (S. M. Assunta, S. Fosca), Venetian villas (cruise along the Brenta Canal with the boat "Il Burchiello" or by rented car: Amex), traditions (Carnival of Venice, the Regata Storica (Sept.), the Mostra of Venice (Aug.-Sept.), Biennale of Venice), al Lido Alberoni golf course (18-hole). **Open** All year.

This "villa of wonders" is one of the landmarks of Venice. It was the Russian consulate until 1930 and it has kept all the richness of its historic past. Its 17th–century facade, period furniture and wisteria-covered terrace give it a charming atmosphere. The quietest rooms are the ones on the garden where breakfast is served. The service is impeccable. One minor problem is that you must reserve a long time in advance, as the hotel is very much in demand by its international clientele.

How to get there *(Map 5): Vaporetto No.1 to Accademia stop, No.2 to Zattere stop.*

Hotel Bel Sito & Berlino ★★★

San Marco – Campo Santa Maria del Giglio, 2517
30124 Venezia
Tel. (041) 522 33 65 – Fax (041) 520 40 83
Sig. Serafini

Rooms 38 with air-conditioning, telephone, bath or shower and WC (30 with minibar). **Price** Single 158,000L, double 242,000L, triple 3110,000L. **Meals** Breakfast included, served 8:00-10:00. **Restaurant** See p. 433-437. **Credit cards** Amex, Visa, Eurocard, MasterCard. **Pets** Dogs allowed. **Nearby** Piazza San Marco, Grand Canal, Gallery of the Academy, Ca' d'Oro, Guggenheim collection, scuola di San Rocco, scuola di San Giorgio degli schiavoni, the Ghetto, the Lido and lagoon, Murano (venetian glass), Burano (center of lacemaking), Torcello (S. M. Assunta, S. Fosca), Venetian villas (cruise along the Brenta Canal the "Il Burchiello" or by rented car: Amex), traditions: Carnival of Venice, the Regata Storica (Sept.), the Mostra of Venice (Aug.-Sept.), Biennale of Venice; al Lido Alberoni golf course (18-hole). **Open** All year.

The Hotel Bel Sito is in San Marco near Gritti. The rooms are furnished in Venetian style and are comfortable, air-conditioned and quiet, especially the ones on the canal. Our favorite ones are in the front, however: notably, Rooms 30 and 40, which are sunny and have flowering balconies and a view of the Baroque sculptures of the church of Santa Maria del Giglio. Breakfast and bar service on the terrace will allow you to enjoy the magic atmosphere unique to Venice. The hotel has an extra room used only when the hotel is fully booked, so if you agree to take it you should know that you will be charged the regular price.

How to get there *(Map 5): Vaporetto No. 1, Santa Maria del Giglio stop.*

346

Hotel Do Pozzi ★★★

Via XXII Marzo, 2373 – Calle do Pozzi
30124 Venezia
Tel. (041) 520 78 55 – Fax. (041) 522 94 13
Sig.ra Salmaso

Rooms 35 with telephone, bath or shower, TV and minibar. **Price** Single 115-160,000L, double 160-240,000L. **Meals** Breakfast included, served 7:00-10:30; half board 35,000L, full board 70,000L (per pers.). **Restaurant** Service 12:00-15:00, 18:45-22:30; closed Fri., Dec., Jan.; menu: 35,000L, also à la carte. Specialties: Venetian and Italian cuisine. **Credit cards** All major. **Pets** Dogs allowed. **Nearby** Piazza San Marco, Grand Canal, Gallery of the Academy, Ca' d'Oro, Guggenheim collection, scuola di San Rocco, scuola di San Giorgio degli schiavoni, the Ghetto, the Lido and lagoon, Murano (venetian glass), Burano (center of lacemaking), Torcello (S. M. Assunta, S. Fosca), Venetian villas (cruise along the Brenta Canal the "Il Burchiello" or by rented car: Amex), traditions: Carnival of Venice, the Regata Storica (Sept.), the Mostra of Venice (Aug.-Sept.), Biennale of Venice, al Lido Alberoni golf course (18-hole). **Open** All year (except Jan.).

After ploughing your way through the crowds on the small commercial streets of the San Marco quarter, it is easy to miss the little cul de sac which leads to the Hotel Do Pozzi. Hidden in one of those tiny squares so typical of Venice, the hotel is sheltered from the crowds. The rooms and bathrooms are small, modern and well equipped. The *campullo* full of flowers makes the hotel feel like an inn, there is also a restaurant, *Da Raffaele*. In summer, you can dine next to the canal and in winter, in a large picturesque room with a fireplace, decorated with old weapons and copper.

How to get there *(Map 5): Vaporetto, San Marco stop. In the via XXII* Marzo, *behind the Museo Correr, on a very small street.*

Hotel Flora ★★★

Via XXII Marzo, 2283 a
30124 Venezia
Tel. (041) 520 58 44 - Fax (041) 522 82 17 - Sig. Romanelli

Rooms 44 with air-conditioning, telephone, bath or shower and WC. **Price** Single 205,000L, double 280,000L. **Meals** Breakfast included, served 7:30-10:00. **Restaurant** See p. 433-437. **Credit cards** All major. **Pets** Dogs allowed. **Nearby** Piazza San Marco, Grand Canal, Gallery of the Academy, Ca' d'Oro, Guggenheim collection, scuola di San Rocco, scuola di San Giorgio degli schiavoni, the Ghetto, the Lido and lagoon, Murano (venetian glass), Burano (center of lacemaking), Torcello (S. M. Assunta, S. Fosca), Venetian villas (cruise along the Brenta Canal the "Il Burchiello" or by rented car: Amex), traditions: Carnival of Venice, the Regata Storica (Sept.), the Mostra of Venice (Aug.-Sept.), Biennale of Venice, al Lido Alberoni golf course (18-hole). **Open** All year.

At the end of a small hidden street not far from the Piazza San Marco you will find the Hotel Flora, a true oasis of cool, quiet greenery. The decor is of mostly English inspiration, a vestige of the time when the clientele was primarily British. If you make your reservation early enough, you might be able to have a room on the garden. All the bathrooms are tiny. The salon and the dining room are delightful but there is nothing like breakfast in the verdant garden around the fountain. The Saint Moses Church near the hotel has many 17th and 18th-century paintings, including a Tintoretto and a "Cène" by Palma le Jeune.

How to get there (Map 5): *Vaporetto, San Marco stop. In the via XXII* Marzo, *behind the Museo Correr, on a very small street.*

Hotel La Fenice et des Artistes ★★★

Campielo de la Fenice, 1936
30124 Venezia
Tel. (041) 523 23 33 – Fax (041) 520 37 21
Sig. Appollonio

Rooms 68 with air-conditioning, telephone, bath or shower, WC and TV. **Price** Single 190,000L, double 295,000L, suite 320-400,000L. **Meals** Breakfast included, served 7:30-10:30. **Restaurant** "Taverna La Fenice", see p.433-437. **Credit cards** All major. **Pets** Dogs allowed. **Nearby** Piazza San Marco, Grand Canal, Gallery of the Academy, Ca' d'Oro, Guggenheim collection, scuola di San Rocco, scuola di San Giorgio degli schiavoni, the Ghetto, the Lido and lagoon, Murano (venetian glass), Burano (center of lacemaking), Torcello (S. M. Assunta, S. Fosca), Venetian villas (cruise along the Brenta Canal the "Il Burchiello" or by rented car: Amex), traditions: Carnival of Venice, the Regata Storica (Sept.), the Mostra of Venice (Aug.-Sept.), Biennale of Venice, al Lido Alberoni golf course (18-hole). **Open** All year.

The hotel is on a quiet little square, behind the Fenice Theatre. It consists of two pretty houses connected by a patio where you can have a nice breakfast or unwind after hours of running around Venice. The rooms are all comfortable, but ask for one of the three rooms with terraces, which are also the most pleasant ones: Rooms 354, 355, and 406. The hotel has no restaurant, but it is next door to the famous *Taverna La Fenice*, a Venice classic.

How to get there *(Map 5): Near La Fenice.*

Hotel Panada ★★★

30124 Venezia
Calle dei Specchieri, 646
Tel. (041) 520 90 88 - Fax (041) 520 96 19

Rooms 48 with air-conditioning, telephone, bath or shower, WC and TV. **Price** Single 160-220,000L, double 200-320,000L, triple 250-390,000L, 300-460,00L (4 pers.). **Meals** Breakfast included, served 7:00-11:00. **Restaurant** See p.433-437. **Credit cards** All major. **Pets** Dogs allowed. **Nearby** Piazza San Marco, Grand Canal, Gallery of the Academy, Ca' d'Oro, Guggenheim collection, scuola di San Rocco, scuola di San Giorgio degli schiavoni, the Ghetto, the Lido and lagoon, Murano (venetian glass), Burano (center of lacemaking), Torcello (S. M. Assunta, S. Fosca), Venetian villas (cruise along the Brenta Canal the "Il Burchiello" or by rented car: Amex), traditions: Carnival of Venice, the Regata Storica (Sept.), the Mostra of Venice (Aug.-Sept.), Biennale of Venice, al Lido Alberoni golf course (18-hole). **Open** All year.

The hotel is on the hard to find calle dei Specchieri, just a few yards from the Basilica of San Marco (northeast of the Torre dell'Orologio). It is worth the effort, though because it would be hard to find anything better (at this price) right in the heart of Venice. As soon as you walk in, the noise and the crowds fade in the distance. The hotel is quiet and comfortable. The rooms are cozy and have Venetian-style furniture in different pastel shades. All have comfortable bathrooms. There is no restaurant, but there is a bar, "Ai Speci," which is very popular with locals. This is a good place to relax, to meet friends for a drink or to have a light meal.

How to get there *(Map 5): Vaporetto No. 1 and 82, 52, San Marco stop. Behind Basilica of San Marco.*

Hotel Ai due Fanali ★★★

30120 Venezia
S. Croce, 946
Tel. (041) 71 84 90 – Fax (041) 78 83 44
Sig.ra Ferron

Rooms 16 with telephone, bath or shower, WC, TV and minibar. **Price** Single 100-220,000L, double 150-280,000L. **Meals** Breakfast included, served 8:00-10:30. **Restaurant** See p.433-437. **Credit cards** Amex, Visa, Eurocard and MasterCard. **Pets** Dogs not allowed. **Nearby** Piazza San Marco, Grand Canal, Gallery of the Academy, Ca' d'Oro, Guggenheim collection, scuola di San Rocco, scuola di San Giorgio degli schiavoni, the Ghetto, the Lido and lagoon, Murano (venetian glass), Burano (center of lacemaking), Torcello (S. M. Assunta, S. Fosca), Venetian villas (cruise along the Brenta Canal the "Il Burchiello" or by rented car: Amex), traditions: Carnival of Venice, the Regata Storica (Sept.), the Mostra of Venice (Aug.-Sept.), Biennale of Venice, al Lido Alberoni golf course (18-hole). **Open** All year.

A pretty hotel has just opened in the old church school of San Simeon Grando, conveniently located in the Santa Croce sestiere? Very close to Santa Lucia station and the Piazzale Roma parking lot. The vast interior spaces of the building have allowed for the creation of an ample reception area decorated with period furniture. Breakfast is served in the adjoining the breakfast room, or on the third floor terrace when the weather gets warm. The somewhat smaller but very comfortable rooms are decorated in simple Venetian-style elegance. Some have a nice view of the Grand Canal.

How to get there *(Map 5): Vaporetto No. 1 Riva di Biario stop.*

Hotel Pausania ★★★

Dorsoduro, 2824
30123 Venezia
Tel. (041) 522 20 83 – Fax (041) 52 22 989
Sig. Gatto

Rooms 26 with air conditioning, telephone, bath or shower, WC, TV and minibar. **Price** Single 90-200,000L, double 150-295,000L. **Meals** Breakfast included, served 7:30-10:30. **Restaurant** See p.433-437. **Credit cards** Amex, Visa, Eurocard and MasterCard. **Pets** Small dogs allowed. **Nearby** Piazza San Marco, Grand Canal, Gallery of the Academy, Ca' d'Oro, Guggenheim collection, scuola di San Rocco, scuola di San Giorgio degli schiavoni, the Ghetto, the Lido and lagoon, Murano (venetian glass), Burano (center of lacemaking), Torcello (S. M. Assunta, S. Fosca), Venetian villas (cruise along the Brenta Canal the "Il Burchiello" or by rented car: Amex), traditions: Carnival of Venice, the Regata Storica (Sept.), the Mostra of Venice (Aug.-Sept.), Biennale of Venice, al Lido Alberoni golf course (18-hole). **Open** All year.

Away from the hustle and bustle of the Venetian streets especially in the summer when the town is overrun with tourists, the Hotel Pausania is a haven of peace, despite its proximity to the Ca' Rezzonico, near the *vaporetto*. Most of the rooms are on an enclosed garden surrounded by the neighboring palaces. Breakfast is served in a veranda on the garden. You will be welcomed warmly here.

How to get there *(Map 5): Vaporetto No. 1, Ca' Rezzonico stop.*

Hotel San Cassiano Ca' Favretto ★★★

S. Croce, 2232
30133 Venezia
Tel. (041) 524 17 68 – Fax (041) 72 10 33 – Sig. Maschietto

Rooms 36 with air-conditioning, telephone, bath or shower, WC and TV. **Price** Single 150-218,000L, double 250-311,000L, triple 320-402,000L. **Meals** Breakfast included, served 7:30-10:30. **Restaurant** See p.433-437. **Credit cards** All major. **Pets** Dogs allowed. **Nearby** Piazza San Marco, Grand Canal, Gallery of the Academy, Ca' d'Oro, Guggenheim collection, scuola di San Rocco, scuola di San Giorgio degli schiavoni, the Ghetto, the Lido and lagoon, Murano (venetian glass), Burano (center of lacemaking), Torcello (S. M. Assunta, S. Fosca), Venetian villas (cruise along the Brenta Canal the "Il Burchiello" or by rented car cf Amex). **Open** All year (except May).

On the *vaporetto* from the station to Rialto, the excited shouts of the tourists on board is overwhelming. You will not find this surprising as you yourself will want have a hundred houses, live on a hundred terraces and lean out of a hundred windows. The Hotel San Cassiano just across from the Ca' d'Oro, is breathtaking. This red palace, flaunting itself by the side of the canal, will enchant you. Prominent Venetian families, the Corners and the Bragadins, lived here before the famous 19th-century painter Giacomo Favretto took it over. What remains of this romantic period is the small private pontoon, the terrace on the Grand Canal and several pretty rooms (be sure to get one on the canal). But you will also find a certain decadence here and some rooms are a little dusty. This hotel will suit those who don't mind some laxity, which is, nonetheless, more than made up for by the charm of the place.

How to get there *(Map 5): Vaporetto No. 1, St. Stae stop.*

Hotel Marconi ★★★

S. Polo, 729
30125 Venezia
Tel. (041) 522 20 68 – Fax (041) 522 97 00
Sig. Maschietto

Rooms 28 with air-conditioning, telephone, bath or shower, WC, TV and minibar. **Price** Single 150-218,000L, double 250-311,000L, triple 320-402,000L. **Meals** Breakfast included, served 7:30-10:00. **Restaurant** See p.433-437. **Credit cards** All major. **Pets** Dogs allowed. **Nearby** Piazza San Marco, Grand Canal, Gallery of the Academy, Ca' d'Oro, Guggenheim collection, scuola di San Rocco, scuola di San Giorgio degli schiavoni, the Ghetto, the Lido and lagoon, Murano (venetian glass), Burano (center of lacemaking), Torcello (S. M. Assunta, S. Fosca), Venetian villas (cruise along the Brenta Canal the "Il Burchiello" or by rented car: Amex), traditions: Carnival of Venice, the Regata Storica (Sept.), the Mostra of Venice (Aug.-Sept.), Biennale of Venice, al Lido Alberoni golf course (18-hole). **Open** All year.

The Hotel Marconi is just a few yards from the Rialto on this "Riva del Vin," where you can find nice *osterias* and authentic *bacari* (wine bars). One of the best bargains in town, it has been meticulously decorated in Venetian style without being overdone. There is gilded wood, tassels and crimson cushions. The hotel blends the charm of tradition with modern comfort (the air conditioning is especially welcome because of the noise and the heat). Its proximity to the Rialto and the fish market make this area very noisy and crowded, not only with tourists, but with Venetians doing their shopping. In any case, don't miss this typically Venetian promenade, which this hotel will allow you to enjoy to the fullest.

How to get there *(Map 5): Vaporetto No. 1, Rialto stop.*

Hotel Agli Alboretti ★★

Dorsoduro - Rio Terrà Foscatini, 884
30123 Venezia
Tel. (041) 523 00 58 - Fax (041) 521 01 58 - Sig.ra Linguerri

Rooms 20 with air-conditioning, telephone, bath or shower, WC and TV.
Price Single 130,000L, double 200,000L. **Meals** Breakfast included, served 7:30-
9:30; half board 150-180,000L (per pers.). **Restaurant** 17:00-23:00; closed Wed.,
3 weeks between July and Aug., Jan., Apr. 15 – Oct. 15 the restaurant is open
12:30-14:00; menus: 45-65,000L, also à la carte. Specialties: Venetian cuisine,
very good Italian wines. **Credit cards** Amex, Visa, Eurocard, MasterCard. **Pets**
Dogs allowed. **Nearby** Piazza San Marco, Grand Canal, Gallery of the Academy, Ca'
d'Oro, Guggenheim collection, scuola di San Rocco, scuola di San Giorgio degli
schiavoni, the Ghetto, the Lido and lagoon, Murano (venetian glass), Burano
(center of lacemaking), Torcello (S. M. Assunta, S. Fosca), Venetian villas (cruise
along the Brenta Canal the "Il Burchiello" or by rented car: Amex). **Open** All year.

The entrance to the Hotel Agli Alboretti has a blond wood
parquet floor and an atmosphere, which is as warm as the
welcome Isabella and Federica Linguerri will give you. The
rooms are all pleasant, though some are larger than others. The
most charming ones are on the interior gardens, such as Room
18, and especially Room 15, which has a balcony big enough to
have breakfast on. The daughter owner's, Anna, is a certified
wine-waitress and runs the restaurant with a talented chef. She
will help you select the right wine, which you can order by the
glass, to accompany dishes. The dining room is pleasant, but the
interior terraces and the *pergola* are really charming. This hotel is
the best value in Venice.

How to get there *(Map 5): Vaporetto No. 1 and 82, Accademia stop.*

Hotel Santo Stefano ★★

San Marco – Campo San Stefano, 2957
30124 Venezia
Tel. (041) 520 01 66 – Fax (041) 522 44 60
Sig. Gazzola

Rooms 11 with telephone, bath, WC, TV, safe and minibar (air-conditioning on request). **Price** Single 120-150,000L, double 160-250,000L, suite 200-300,000L. **Meals** Breakfast included, served 8:30-10:00. **Restaurant** See p.433-437. **Credit cards** Visa, Eurocard, MasterCard. **Pets** Dogs not allowed. **Nearby** Piazza San Marco, Grand Canal, Gallery of the Academy, Ca' d'Oro, Guggenheim collection, scuola di San Rocco, scuola di San Giorgio degli schiavoni, the Ghetto, the Lido and lagoon, Murano (venetian glass), Burano (center of lacemaking), Torcello (S. M. Assunta, S. Fosca), Venetian villas (cruise along the Brenta Canal the "Il Burchiello" or by rented car cf Amex), traditions: Carnaval of Venice, the Regata Storica (Sept.), the Mostra of Venice (Aug.-Sept.), Biennale of Venice, al Lido Alberoni golf course (18-hole). **Open** All year .

The prices at the Hotel Santo Stefano make it a particularly interesting address. It is in a 15th-century Gothic-style house nicely on the charming Campo San Stefano. The rooms are pleasant. Certain ones are on the Campo San Stefano, which is certainly one of the liveliest places in town. On the ground floor is the lobby, an adorable breakfast room and a flowering patio.

How to get there (Map 5): Vaporetto No. 82 San Samuele stop - No. 1, Accademia stop.

Pensione Seguso ★★

Zattere, 779
30123 Venezia
Tel. (041) 522 23 40 – Fax. (041) 522 23 40
Sig. Seguso

Rooms 36 with telephone (16 with bath or shower, 10 with WC), elevator, wheelchair access. **Price** With half board 260-290,000L. **Meals** Breakfast included, served 8:00-10:00. **Restaurant** Service 13:00-14:00, 19:30-20:30; closed Wed.; menu: 40,000L. Specialties: Home Venetian cooking. **Credit cards** All major. **Pets** Dogs allowed. **Nearby** Piazza San Marco, Grand Canal, Gallery of the Academy, Ca' d'Oro, Guggenheim collection, scuola di San Rocco, scuola di San Giorgio degli schiavoni, the Ghetto, the Lido and lagoon, Murano (venetian glass), Burano (center of lacemaking), Torcello (S. M. Assunta, S. Fosca), Venetian villas (cruise along the Brenta Canal the "Il Burchiello" or by rented car: Amex). **Open** Mar. – Nov.

In the Dorsoduro quarter, slightly back from the streets crowded with tourists, you will find the last real pensione in Venice. We hope it will stay that way, at least as long as the Segusos are still there. It is not luxurious, but there is a lot of atmosphere. The rooms still have their original turn-of-the-century furniture and the bathrooms are old fashioned, but the house is friendly and warm. A true pensione means obligatory half-board with dinner served at a fixed time without a choice about what is served. But far from being a constraint, this is just one more charming thing about the place. Simple, family-style cuisine is served in two very quaint rooms by staff wearing black uniforms and white aprons. The Pensione Seguso is one of the few remaining institutions of Venice of old.

How to get there *(Map 5): Vaporetto No. 1 and 82, Accademia stop - No. 52 and 82, Zattere Gesuati stop.*

La Residenza ★★

Campo Bandiera e Moro, 3608
30122 Venezia
Tel. (041) 528 53 15 – Fax (041) 523 88 59
Sig. Tagliapietra

Rooms 15 with shower, WC, TV and minibar. **Price** Single 145,000L, double 200,000L. **Meals** Breakfast included, served 7:30-9:30. **Restaurant** See p. 433-437. **Credit cards** All major. **Pets** Dogs not allowed. **Nearby** Piazza San Marco, Grand Canal, Gallery of the Academy, Ca' d'Oro, Guggenheim collection, scuola di San Rocco, scuola di San Giorgio degli schiavoni, the Ghetto, the Lido and lagoon, Murano (venetian glass), Burano (center of lacemaking), Torcello (S. M. Assunta, S. Fosca), Venetian villas (cruise along the Brenta Canal the "Il Burchiello" or by rented car: Amex), traditions: Carnival of Venice, the Regata Storica (Sept.), the Mostra of Venice (Aug.-Sept.), Biennale of Venice, al Lido Alberoni golf course (18-hole). **Open** Jan. 6 – Nov. 5.

The Residenza is a 15th-century palace located between the Piazza San Marco and the old Arsenal, away from the tourist circuit. Its marvelous facade is embellished by a central balcony with five windows opening onto a beautiful square. The imposing salon has a grand piano and beautiful antique furniture and is the main attraction of the hotel. The rooms are more simply decorated but are nonetheless pleasant and comfortable. It is very close to the *Corte Sconta*, one of the best restaurants in Venice.

How to get there *(Map 5): Riva degli Schiavoni, Vaporetto No. 1, Arsenale stop.*

Locanda Fiorita ★

30124 Venezia
San Marco - Campiello Nova (S. Stefano), 3457
Tel. (041) 523 47 54 - Fax (041) 522 80 43
Sig Gasparini-Nironi

Rooms 10 with telephone, 8 with shower and WC. **Price** Single 60-90,000L, double 90-120,000L. **Meals** Breakfast included, served 8:30-10:00. **Restaurant** See p. 433-437. **Credit cards** Amex, Visa, Eurocard, MasterCard. **Pets** Dogs not allowed. **Nearby** Piazza San Marco, Grand Canal, Gallery of the Academy, Ca' d'Oro, Guggenheim collection, scuola di San Rocco, scuola di San Giorgio degli schiavoni, the Ghetto, the Lido and lagoon, Murano (venetian glass), Burano (center of lacemaking), Torcello (S. M. Assunta, S. Fosca), Venetian villas (cruise along the Brenta Canal the "Il Burchiello" or by rented car: Amex), traditions: Carnival of Venice, the Regata Storica (Sept.), the Mostra of Venice (Aug.-Sept.), Biennale of Venice, al Lido Alberoni golf course (18-hole). **Open** All year.

Between the Academy bridge and San Marco, sheltered from the hordes of tourists following this route and entrenched in a quiet little campo, the "Flowering" Locanda is the ideal point of departure for all of your excursions. The rooms are simply decorated–standard but functional. The location, the price and the quiet make it one of the more soughtafter places in the city of the Doges, so you must not only reserve long in advance, you must also have your reservation confirmed. The service is what you might expect from a hotel which is always completely full.

How to get there *(Map 5): Vaporetto No. 82, San Samuele stop - No. 1 Accademia stop, towards Piazza S. Stefano.*

Pensione Alla Salute Da Cici

Fondamenta Cà Balla, 222
30123 Venezia
Tel. (041) 523 54 04 – Fax. (041) 522 22 71
Sig. Cici

Rooms 38 with telephone, shower and WC. **Price** Single 100,000L, double 170,000L. **Meals** Breakfast included, served 7:30-10:00. **Restaurant** See p.433-437. **Credit cards** Not accepted. **Pets** Dogs not allowed. **Nearby** Piazza San Marco, Grand Canal, Gallery of the Academy, Ca' d'Oro, Guggenheim collection, scuola di San Rocco, scuola di San Giorgio degli schiavoni, the Ghetto, the Lido and lagoon, Murano (venetian glass), Burano (center of lacemaking), Torcello (S. M. Assunta, S. Fosca), Venetian villas (cruise along the Brenta Canal the "Il Burchiello" or by rented car: Amex), traditions: Carnival of Venice, the Regata Storica (Sept.), the Mostra of Venice (Aug.-Sept.), Biennale of Venice, al Lido Alberoni golf course (18-hole). **Open** Carnival – Nov. 7, 2 weeks at Christmas.

Alla Salute "da Cici" is one of the old *pensiones* of Venice, in one of the most poetic places in the town–on a canal behind the Salute. Though the house has lost some of its traditional appearance, the old family furniture is still in the large rooms. The rooms don't all have bathrooms, but they are impeccably well kept. Ask for the ones on the canal; the neighborhood is very quiet. Despite a kitchen just waiting to be used and an inner courtyard, the restaurant remains closed. But the bar service in the small adjoining garden is great.

How to get there (Map 5): Vaporetto No. 1, La Salute stop. Take No. 52, Zattere stop. Take No., 82 Accademia stop.

Palazetto da Schio

30123 Venezia
Dorsoduro 316/B – Fondamenta Soranzo
Tel. (041) 523 79 37 – Fax (041) 523 79 37
Contesse da Schio

Rooms 2 apartments with 2 rooms, air-conditioning, lounge, kitchen, bath, telephone and TV. **Price** 900,000L (1 week). **Meals** Breakfast included, served 8:00-10:00. **Restaurant** See p. 433-437. **Credit cards** Amex, Visa, Eurocard, MasterCard. **Pets** Dogs not allowed. **Facilities** Swimming pool, tennis, parking. **Nearby** Piazza San Marco, Grand Canal, Gallery of the Academy, Ca' d'Oro, Guggenheim collection, scuola di San Rocco, scuola di San Giorgio degli schiavoni, the Ghetto, the Lido and lagoon, Murano (venetian glass), Burano (center of lacemaking), Torcello (S. M. Assunta, S. Fosca), Venetian villas (cruise along the Brenta Canal the "Il Burchiello" or by rented car: Amex), traditions: Carnival of Venice, the Regata Storica (Sept.), the Mostra of Venice (Aug.-Sept.), Biennale of Venice, al Lido Alberoni golf course (18-hole). **Open** All year.

If you are traveling with your family and plan to spend more than two nights in Venice, a pleasant apartment in the center of town is undoubtedly the most economical option. The small but charming Palazetto da Schio is in a palace, close to the Academy. It is a good place to relax after a day of sightseeing. There are two light, spacious apartments. The antique family furniture creates an atmosphere which is both Romanesque and intimate. The owners are very nice and live downstairs on the "noble floor" of the house. Staying here will allow you to live like a Venetian for a while (without having to go to the Rialto market as a tourist). You will also enjoy both the intimacy of a home and the comfort of a hotel (maid service is available for all of your household needs). A deposit and references are required.

How to get there *(Map 5): Vaporetto No. 1 and 82, La Salute stop.*

Albergo Quattro Fontane ★★★★

Lido - Via delle Quattro Fontane, 16
30126 Venezia
Tel. (041) 526 02 27 - Fax (041) 526 07 26
Famiglia Friborg-Bevilacqua

Rooms 61 with air-conditioning, telephone, bath, WC and TV. **Price** Single 240-290,000L, double 330-400,000L. **Meals** Breakfast included, served 7:00-10:30; half board 205-270,000L, full board 250-310,000L. **Restaurant** Service 13:00-14:30, 19:45-22:30; menus: 60-80,000L, also à la carte. Specialties: Seafood. **Credit cards** All major. **Pets** Dogs allowed. **Nearby** Piazza San Marco, Grand Canal, Gallery of the Academy, Ca' d'Oro, Guggenheim collection, scuola di San Rocco, scuola di San Giorgio degli schiavoni, the Ghetto, the Lido and lagoon, Murano (venetian glass), Burano (center of lacemaking), Torcello (S. M. Assunta, S. Fosca), Venetian villas (cruise along the Brenta Canal the "Il Burchiello" or by rented car: Amex). **Open** Apr. 20 – Oct. 20.

For those who would like to see a different Venice, the Albergo Quattro Fontane is a fabulous villa in the Lido run by two very friendly sisters, heiresses of great Venetian voyagers, one with a passion for Africa and the other for South America. A fabulous collection of memorabilia from their travels decorates the salons of the villa. Everything is perfectly elegant and comfortable here: the well-kept gardens, the shaded flagstone terraces with wicker furniture, the personalized rooms on the garden and the impeccably served Venetian cuisine. The annex built in the style typical of the islands of the lagoon, has newer and even more comfortable rooms.

How to get there *(Map 5): Vaporetto via the Lido from Piazza San Marco.*

Hotel Villa Mabapa ★★★★

Lido – Riviera San Nicolo, 16
30126 Venezia
Tel. (041) 526 05 90 – Fax (041) 526 94 41
Sig. Vianello

Rooms 62 with air-conditioning, telephone, bath, WC and TV. **Price** Single 110-260,000L, double 180-380,000L. **Meals** Breakfast included (buffet), served 7:30-10:00; half board 40,000L, full board 75,000L (per pers., 3 days min.). **Restaurant** Service 12:30-14:00, 19:30-21:30; menu: 40,000L, also à la carte. Specialties: Venetian cuisine, seafood. **Credit cards** All major. **Pets** Small dogs allowed in room. **Facilities** Parking. **Nearby** Piazza San Marco, Grand Canal, Gallery of the Academy, Ca' d'Oro, Guggenheim collection, scuola di San Rocco, scuola di San Giorgio degli schiavoni, the Ghetto, the Lido and lagoon, Murano (venetian glass), Burano (center of lacemaking), Torcello (S. M. Assunta, S. Fosca), Venetian villas (cruise along the Brenta Canal the "Il Burchiello" or by rented car: Amex). **Open** All year.

It is possible to find a bit of quiet country in Venice, even in the middle of August. These are the two major attractions of this property, built in the Lido in 1930 and subsequently transformed into a hotel. It is still run by the same family; the name Mabapa comes from the first syllables of "mama, bambini, papa." The interior of the villa still looks like a private house. The most charming rooms are the ones on the second floor of the main house. In the summer you can have your meals in the garden on the lagoon. A bit far from the center of town, but close to the Lido beach and convenient *vaporetto* (ferry) service, the Mabapa is a nice refuge for those who fear the tourist frenzy of Venice in the summer.

How to get there *(Map 5): Vaporetto via the Lido from Piazza San Marco.*

Locanda Cipriani ★★★

Isola Torcello – Piazza Santa Fosca, 29
30012 Venezia
Tel. (041) 730 150 – Fax (041) 735 433 – Sig. Brass

Rooms 6 with air-conditioning, telephone, bath, WC and TV. **Price** With half board 260,000L, full board 350,000L (per pers.). **Meals** Breakfast included, served 7:00-12:00. **Restaurant** Service 12:00-15:00, 19:00-22:00; menus: 60-80,000L, also à la carte. Specialties: Risotto alla torcellana, zuppa di pesce. **Credit cards** Amex, Visa, Eurocard, MasterCard. **Pets** Dogs not allowed. **Nearby** Piazza San Marco, Grand Canal, Gallery of the Academy, Ca' d'Oro, Guggenheim collection, scuola di San Rocco, scuola di San Giorgio degli schiavoni, the Ghetto, the Lido and lagoon, Murano (venetian glass), Burano (center of lacemaking), Torcello (S. M. Assunta, S. Fosca), Venetian villas (cruise along the Brenta Canal the "Il Burchiello" or by rented car: Amex), traditions: Carnival of Venice, the Regata Storica (Sept.), the Mostra of Venice (Aug.-Sept.), Biennale of Venice, al Lido Alberoni golf course (18-hole). **Open** Mar. 19 – Nov. 4 and Christmast, New Year and Carnival (closed Tues.).

Giuseppe Cipriani discovered this old inn on the island of Torcello while driving a visiting couple around the lagoon. It was love at first sight and he ended up buying it. The Locanda has four rooms and is known for its fine cuisine, notably the fish specialties. The exterior has kept its rustic flavor, but the salons and rooms are elegantly decorated. Meals are served in the garden or in the gallery with arcades. It is hard to stay very long in Torcello, where there's only the Santa Fosca Church and the superb Veneto–Byzantine Santa Maria Assunta Cathedral, but this old inn's isolation and charm make it well worth spending at least one evening here. Reservations are a must.

How to get there (Map 5): From San Marco, boat via Torcello (30-45min.).

Villa Ducale ★★★

30031 Dolo (Venezia)
Tel. (041) 42 00 94 – Fax (041) 42 00 94

Rooms 11 with air-conditioning, telephone, bath or shower, WC, cable TV, safe and minibar. **Price** Single 120-160,000L, double 160-220,000L. **Meals** Breakfast included (buffet), served 7:00-11:00; half board 60,000L, full board 120,000L (per pers., 3 days min.). **Restaurant** Service 12:00-14:30, 19:00-22:00; closed Wed.; menu: 40,000L, also à la carte. Specialties: Seafood. **Credit cards** Amex, Visa, Eurocard, MasterCard. **Pets** Dogs allowed. **Facilities** Parking. **Nearby** Riviera del Brenta and Palladian Villas (S11) between Padua and Venice (Villas Ferretti-Angeli in Dolo), Villa Venier-Contarini-Zen in Mira Vecchia, Palais Foscarini in Mira, Villa Widmann, Ca' della Nave golf course (18-hole) in Martellago. **Open** All year.

The Villa Ducale is, alas, next to a rather noisy road. But the building is magestic. The lobby has marvelous decorated ceilings and is very elegant. The rooms have beautiful period furnitureare very comfortable and they are air-conditioned and soundproofed, so traffic noise from the road is not a problem. The hotel provides quality round-the-clock service and has a fine restaurant. In this sublime setting you will feel like you are in a waking dream, especially if you are lucky and have a room with a terrace facing the grounds.

How to get there *(Map 5): 22 km west of Venezia via A4, Dolo-Mirano exit; 2 km east of town center via S11, towards Venezia.*

Hotel Villa Margherita ★★★★

Via Nazionale, 416/417
30030 Mira Porte (Venezia)
Tel. (041) 426 58 00 – Fax (041) 426 58 38
Famiglia Dal Corso

Rooms 19 with air-conditioning, telephone, bath or shower, WC, cable TV, safe
and minibar. **Price** Single 140-160,000L, double 190-275,000L. **Meals** Breakfast
included, served 7:30-10:30; half board 175,000L, full board 220,000L (per pers.)
Restaurant Service 12:00-14:30, 19:00-22:00; closed Tues. dinner, Wed.; à la
carte. Specialties: Seafood, Venetian cuisine. **Credit cards** All major. **Pets** Small
dogs allowed. **Facilities** Parking. **Nearby** Riviera del Brenta and Palladian Villas
(S11) between Padua and Venice (Villas Ferretti-Angeli in Dolo), Villa Venier-
Contarini-Zen in Mira Vecchia, Palais Foscarini in Mira, Villa Widmann, Ca' della
Nave golf course (18-hole) in Martellago. **Open** All year.

This old 17th-century patrician villa is ideally on the tourist
circuit of villas which rich Venetians built on the banks of
the Brenta. It is luxuriously decorated; and particular attention
has been paid to architectural details such as the quality of
materials used, the studied mixture of antique and contemporary
furniture, the richness of the decor with frescos, the *trompe l'œil,*
the drapes and the fabrics. The surrounding fields and the small
number of rooms, make this hotel a very quiet place. The
personnel is charming and discreet and the price is justified.

How to get there *(Map 5): 15 km west of Venezia via A4, Dolo-Mirano
exit; then S11 towards Mira Porte.*

Hotel Bellevue ★★★★

Corso Italia, 197
32043 Cortina d'Ampezzo (Belluno)
Tel. (0436) 88 34 00 – Fax (0436) 86 75 510
Famiglia Melon

Rooms and apartments 20 with telephone, bath, WC, cable TV, safe, minibar and elevator. **Price** Double 290-480,000L. **Meals** Breakfast included, served 7:00-11:00; half board 185-300,000L (per pers.). **Restaurant** "Il Meloncino al Bellevue," via del Castello, closed May – Nov.; Service 12:30-14:00, 19:30-21:00; menus: 30-70,000L, also à la carte. Specialties: Italian cuisine. **Credit cards** All major. **Pets** Dogs not allowed. **Facilities** Garage. **Nearby** Skiing, excursions by cable car to the Tofana (10,543 feet) and to the Cristallo, Ghedina lake, Misurina lake, Tiziano's house in Pieve di Cadore. **Open** All year (except May).

The historical Hotel Bellevue has been one of the most popular inns in Cortina with celebrities since the beginning of the century. It is the jewel of this famous resort. Wood—used as the main decorative element in the hotel—is paneled, painted, parqueted and sculpted, and the result is magnificent. Most of the work has been done by hand using traditional techniques, which gives the entire hotel an atmosphere of elegant warmth. Beautiful fabrics by Pierre Frey and Rubelli complement the regional antique furniture. You will find the same atmosphere in the restaurant, which as excellent cuisine. This hotel is a model of simplicity and good taste—the essential ingredients of what we call "class."

How to get there *(Map 5): 168 km north of Venezia via A27 to Alemagna, then S51 to Cortina d'Ampezzo.*

Hotel Pensione Menardi ★★★

Via Majon, 110
32043 Cortina d'Ampezzo (Belluno)
Tel. (0436) 24 00 – Fax (0436) 86 21 83
Famiglia Menardi

Rooms 51 with telephone, bath or shower, WC and cable TV. **Price** Single 70-
150,000L, double 120-280,000L. **Meals** Breakfast 10,000L, served 7:30-10:00;
half board 90-180,000L, full board 100-200,000L (per pers.). **Restaurant** Service
12:30-14:00, 19:30-21:00, menu: 35,000L. Specialties: Italian cuisine.
Credit cards Visa, Eurocard, MasterCard. **Pets** Dogs not allowed.
Facilities Garage. **Nearby** Skiing, excursions by the cable car to the Tofana
(10,543 feet) and to the Cristallo, Ghedina lake, Misurina lake, Tiziano's house in
Pieve di Cadore. **Open** Dec. 22 – Apr., June 17 – Sept. 18.

The Hotel Menardi is an old postal inn. It is charming: as
soon as you enter the village you can't help noticing this
pretty building with light green wood balconies covered with
flowers in the summer. You will find the same charm and
warmth inside the house is wood with regional decor. Don't get
the wrong idea from its location next to the road; the hotel has
large grounds in the back. The quietest rooms are on the garden
and have a nice view of the Dolomites. The kindness of the
Menardi family and their dedication to running their hotel well
has earned them a clientele of regulars. The prices are also
particularly good, considering the quality of the service.

How to get there *(Map 5): 168 km north of Venezia via A27 to*
Alemagna, then S51 to Cortina d'Ampezzo.

Franceschi Park Hotel ★★★

Via Battisti, 86
32043 Cortina d'Ampezzo (Belluno)
Tel. (0436) 86 70 41 - Fax (0436) 2909
Famiglia Franceschi

Rooms 49 with telephone, bath or shower, WC and TV. **Price** Double 200-380,000L, apartment 264-760,000L. **Meals** Breakfast included, served to 10:00; half board 80-275,000L (per pers.). **Restaurant** (non smoking) service 12:30-13:45, 19:30-20:45; menus: 42-70,000L. Specialties: Italian cuisine. **Credit cards** All major. **Pets** Dogs not allowed. **Facilities** Tennis, sauna, turkish bath, beauty, parking. **Nearby** Skiing, excursions by the cable car to the Tofana (10,543 feet) and to the Cristallo, Ghedina lake, Misurina lake, Tiziano's house in Pieve di Cadore. **Open** Dec. 20 – Easter, June 21 – Sept. 22.

This pretty turn-of-the-century building has housed the Franceschi family hotel for three generations. It is on large grounds with a pretty garden, near the center of town. The hotel has kept its old-time flavor. Woodwork, parquet floors and blond wood exposed beams make the atmosphere very warm, as does the furniture and the large Austrian stove. The cozy, comfortable rooms have the same decor. This hotel is ideal for a family vacation.

How to get there *(Map 5): 168 km north of Venezia via A27 to Alemagna, then S51 to Cortina d'Ampezzo.*

Villa Marinotti

Via Manzago, 21
32040 Tai di Cadore (Belluno)
Tel. (0435) 322 31 – Fax (0435) 333 35
Sig. and Sig.ra Giacobbi de Martin

Suites 5 and 2 bungalows, with telephone, bath and WC. **Price** Suite 110-130,000L (per 1 pers.), 150-180,000L (per 2 pers.), bungalow 250-795,000L. **Meals** Breakfast included, served until 10:00. **Restaurant** Open in summer only. Service 19:30-21:00; menu. Specialties: Home cooking. **Credit card** Amex. **Pets** Small dogs allowed. **Facilities** Tennis (10,000L), sauna (20,000L), parking. **Nearby** Skiing in Pieve di Cadore (2 km) and in Cortina d'Ampezzo (25 km), Tiziano's house in Pieve di Cadore, the Great Dolomite Road. **Open** July – Sept.

The owners of this house had the fortunate idea of transforming the family chalet into a small hotel, which is still a precious secret. The house has only five rooms, or rather five suites, as each one has a small, private salon. Simplicity and good taste pervade the decor (the "Rosa" suite is the nicest one). The house is surrounded by large grounds, which have a tennis court and a sauna. Breakfasts are excellent. You can now have dinner at the restaurant at the chalet. You can expect a warm welcome here.

How to get there *(Map 5): 34 km north of Belluno via S51.*

Golf Hotel ★★★★

Via Oslavia, 2
34070 San Floriano del Collio (Gorizia)
Tel. (0481) 88 40 51 – Fax (0481) 88 40 52
Comtesse Formentini

Rooms 14 and 1 apartment (3 pers.) with telephone, bath or shower, WC and TV.
Price Single 150-190,000L, double 270,000L, apart. 390,000L. **Meals** Breakfast
included **Restaurant** Service 12:00-14:00, 20:00-21:30; closed Mon. and Tues.
lunch; menus 70-80,000L, also à la carte. Specialties: Regional cuisine. **Credit
cards** All major. **Pets** Dogs allowed. **Facilities** Swimming pool, tennis, golf (9
holes), parking. **Nearby** Fortress of Gradisca d'Isonzo, Gorizia castle, Trieste,
Cividale (medieval city), Duomo of Grado and of Aquileja. **Open** Mar. – Dec.

Two houses of the San Floriano castle make up this hotel.
Each of the rooms bears the name of one of the famous of
regional wines. They are all furnished in a blend of styles, from
17th-century to Biedermeier, like in old family houses where
each generation has left its mark. The hotel has a nine-hole golf
course with a practice and putting green. The restaurant Castello
Formentini is next to the castle and is one of the region's finest.

How to get there *(Map 6): 47 km northwest of Trieste via A4, Villesse-
Gorizia and San Floriano exit.*

Haus Michaela ★★★

32047 Sappada (Belluno)
Borgata Fonta, 40
Tel. (0435) 46 93 77 – Fax (0435) 46 93 77
Sig. Piller Roner

Rooms 20 with telephone, shower, WC, cable TV. **Price** Single 60-90,000L, double 120-140,000L, suite 140-180,000L. **Meals** Breakfast included, served 8:00-10:00; half board 70-115,000L, full board 80-130,000L (per pers. 3 days min.). **Restaurant** Service 12:30-13:30, 19:30-20:30; menus 35,000L. Specialties: regional cooking. **Credit cards** Visa, Eurocard, MasterCard. **Pets** Dogs not allowed. **Facilities** Swimming pool, sauna, parking. **Nearby** Skiing, Cortina d'Ampezzo, Titien house in Pieve di Cadore. **Open** All year except late May – June 16 and late Oct. – Dec. 12.

Haus Michaela is located in Sappada, a beautiful town on the outskirts of Venetia, where you can already feel the charms of Austria (just 5 km away). It extends down to the floor of a valley dominated by the majestic furrowed summits and sharp peaks of the Dolomites. You can enjoy the mountains to the fullest here year round: it is a fine ski resort in the winter and a marvelous vacation spot in summer. Among the many hiking trails don't miss the one going up to the sources of the Piave, the legendary river which is the main supplier of the lagoon of Venice and flows through all of Venetia. The hotel offers simply decorated but highly comfortable rooms, and three large studios ideal for family vacations. Hotel facilities include a heated pool, a complete health care complex with Turkish baths, and a restaurant featuring local and Tyrolian specialties, notably a wide variety of deer dishes.

How to get there *(Map 12): 169 km north of Venezia. A27, Vittorio Veneto exit, then towards Cortina, then towards Sappada.*

Albergo Leon Bianco ★★★

Piazzetta Pedrocchi, 12
35122 Padova
Tel. (049) 65 72 25 – Fax (049) 875 61 84
Sig. Morosi

Rooms 22 with air-conditioning, telephone, bath or shower, WC, TV and minibar. **Price** Single 98-119,000L, double 142-155,000L. **Meals** Breakfast 15,000L, served 7:30-10:30. **Restaurant** See p. 439. **Credit cards** All major. **Pets** Dogs allowed (12,000L). **Facilities** Parking (25,000L). **Nearby** Padua: Piazza delle Erbe and Palazzo della Ragione, Basilica di San Antonio, Chiesa degli Eremitani, Cappella degli Scrovegni (frescoes of Giotto); Pallandian villas: tour in car from Padua to Venice via the Brenta Riviera-N 11 (Villa Pisani, Villa "La Barbariga," villa Foscari) by boat *Il Burchiello*; Villa Simes in Piazzola sul Brenta; Villa Barbarigo in Valsanzibio; Praglia abbey; Pétrarque's house in Arqua Petrarca; Valsanzibio and Frassanelle golf course (18-hole). **Open** All year.

You will find the post-modern facade of this hotel—one of the oldest in Padua—behind the famous Café Pedrocchi. Breakfast is served on a terrace overlooking the town. The rooms, in pastel shades, blend antique and modern furniture and contemporary engravings. The clientele dines at the Michelangelo, a nearby restaurant belonging to the same family. The service there is perfect, too.

How to get there *(Map 5): 37 km east of Venezia via A4, Padova-East exit; then towards town center, Palazzo della Ragione.*

Hotel Regina Margherita ★★★★

Viale Regina Margherita, 6
45100 Rovigo
Tel. (0425) 36 15 40 – Fax (0425) 313 01
Sig. Albertin

Rooms 22 with telephone, bath or shower, WC, TV and minibar. **Price** Single 80-100,000L, double 100-140,000L, suite 200,000L. **Meals** Breakfast 10,000L (buffet), served 7:00-10:00. **Restaurant** Service 12:00-15:00, 19:30-23:00, closed Aug. 4 – 21; menus 35-50,000L, also à la carte. Specialties: Seafood, zuppa di vongole, filetto di branzino con scampi ed olive. **Credit cards** All major. **Pets** Dogs allowed (12,000L). **Facilities** Piano-bar, parking. **Nearby** Villa Badoer (Palladio), Villa Bragadin, Villa Molin in Fratta Polesine, Abbey of the Vangadizza in Badia Polesino, Padua, Ferrara. **Open** All year.

This charming hotel and its excellent restaurant are in a very pretty Art Deco villa. In the center of the little town of Rovigo, on a beautiful and slightly old-fashioned residential avenue, the Hotel Regina Margherita has recently been tastefully renovated. The stained glass, in vogue in the 1930s, has been preserved, along with some beautiful pieces of furniture which, combined with pretty, warm colors, make the salons and the lobby particular charming. The rooms, some of which are on the garden, are pleasant, comfortable and particularly well kept. The hotel restaurant deserves special mention for its remarkable setting, service and cuisine.

How to get there *(Map 11): 45 km south of Padova via A13, Boara exit.*

Hotel Villa Cipriani ★★★★

Via Canova, 298
31011 Asolo (Treviso)
Tel. (0423) 95 21 66 - Fax (0423) 95 20 95
Sig. Kamenar

Rooms 31 with air-conditioning, telephone, bath or shower, WC, TV and minibar.
Price Single 250-280,000L, double 320-370,000L, 50,000L with view, 70,000L
with balcony. **Meals** Breakfast 22-38,000L, served 7:00-10:30; half board
110,000L (per pers.). **Restaurant** Service 12:30-14:30, 20:00-22:00, also à la
carte. Specialties: Risotto Asolo, pasta, seafood. **Credit cards** All major.
Pets Dogs allowed (12,000L). **Facilities** Parking. **Nearby** Possagno (casa and
tempio del Canova d'Antonio Canova), Villa Barbaro in Maser, Villa Rinaldi-
Barbini, Villa Emo in Panzolo. **Open** All year.

The Villa Cipriani is in one of the prettiest villages in
Venetia, Asolo where the Italian actress Eleonora Duse
lived and died. Its ochre facade with semi-circular openings
overlooks a marvelous garden where a lovely lawn and flowers
surround a Virginia creeper covered well. The comfortable
rooms have large beds, flowered tapestries and very beautiful
views of the surrounding countryside. Avoid the ones on the
street side and ask for Rooms 101 and 102, which have terraces.
Breakfast is delicious, especially the croissants baked by a master
baker. You can enjoy lunch or dinner by candlelight at tables
under a striped tent. This place seems too good to be true.

How to get there *(Map 5): 65 km northwest of Venezia; 35 km
northwest of Treviso via S348 to Montebelluna, then S248 to Asolo;
towards Bassano, D/Grappa.*

Hotel Abbazia ★★★

Via Martiri della Libertà
31051 Follina (Treviso)
Tel. (0438) 97 12 77 - Fax (0438) 97 00 01
Sig.ra de Marchi Zanon

Rooms 17 and 7 suites with air-conditioning, telephone, bath, WC, cable TV and minibar. **Price** Single 130,000L, double 200-220,000L, suite 140,000L (per pers.). **Meals** Breakfast included, served 8:00-12:00. **Restaurant** In Miane see p. 440 or Lino in Solighetto see p. 381. **Credit cards** All major. **Pets** Dogs not allowed. **Facilities** Swimming pool, tennis, sauna, parking. **Nearby** Abbey of Follina, from Conegliano (white wine road to Valdobbiadene (Spumante), red wine road to Roncade), Palladian villas tour, Treviso, Venice, Asolo, Pian del Cansiglio golf course (9-hole) in Vittorio Veneto. **Open** All year.

The Hotel Abbazia is a pretty, 17th-century house in the soft green Venetian Pre-Alps, facing a splendid Cistercien abbey. It is a small, luxurious hotel that offers everything you can imagine in terms of comfort, service and elegance. The rooms, some of which have pretty flower-filled terraces, are vast and each one is differently with antique furniture, pretty engravings decorated and soft, quiet colors. This dream house does not have a garden, but Follina is in the heart of the marvelous province of Trévise, which is filled with often undiscovered villas and Paladian farms. If you stay four nights in July and August you'll get one night free.

How to get there *(Map 5): 40 km north of Treviso. Via A4, A27 Vittorio Veneto exit towards Lago Revine; Follina is located at 15 km.*

Villa Conestabile ★★★

Via Roma, 1
30037 Scorzé (Venezia)
Tel. (041) 44 50 27 – Fax (041) 584 00 88
Sig.ra Martinelli

Rooms 19 with telephone, bath or shower, WC, TV and minibar. **Price** Single 100,000L, double 150,000L. **Meals** Breakfast included, served 7:00-10:00, half board 110-130,000L (per pers.). **Restaurant** Service 12:30-14:00, 19:30-22:00; closed Sun.; menu: 38,000L, also à la carte. Specialties: Venetian cuisine. **Credit cards** Amex, Visa, Eurocard, MasterCard. **Pets** Dogs allowed. **Facilities** Parking. **Nearby** Riviera del Brenta and Palladian Villas (S11) between Padua and Venice (Villas Ferretti-Angeli in Dolo, Villa Venier-Contarini-Zen in Mira Vecchia, Palais Foscarini in Mira, Villa Widmann), Ca' della Nave golf course (18-hole) in Martellago. **Open** All year.

This villa, a vacation house for a noble Venetian family since the 15th century, was badly damaged during WWII. In 1960 it was restored into a hotel. The rooms are furnished in a slightly provincial way, but they are large and quiet. Here you will find all of the charm of a country hotel, only 12 miles (20km) from Venice and 18 miles (30km) from Padua.

How to get there *(Map 5): 28 km northeast of Padova by A4, Padova-East exit towards Treviso.*

Villa Stucky ★★★★

Via Don Bosco, 47
31021 Mogliano Veneto (Treviso)
Tel. (041) 590 4 5 28 – Fax (041) 590 45 66
Sig. Pianura

Rooms 20 with air-conditioning, telephone, bath (7 with whirlpool), WC, cable TV, video, safe and minibar. **Price** Single 170,000L, double 270,000L, suite 330-370,000L. **Meals** Breakfast 15,000L, served 7:00-10:30. **Restaurant** Service 12:30-14:30, 19:30-22:30, à la carte. **Credit cards** All major. **Pets** Dog not allowed. **Facilities** Parking. **Nearby** Venice, Treviso and Palladian villas, Villa Condulmer golf course (18-hole). **Open** All year.

Villa Stucky is an 18th-century Venetian villa built by the Countess Seymour. It had become pretty run down until major renovations were undertaken to transform it into the luxury hotel it is today. It has twenty rooms, which all took out onto the grounds, but are all different. Each one has decor that corresponds to the name it bears. "Princess Sissi" is precious with pastel colors; others are simpler and more elegant. In the ones on the top floor you can sleep in the moonlight, thanks to a skylight which you can open.

How to get there (Map 5): 12 km south of Treviso via S13.

Relais El Toula ★★★★★

Paderno di Ponzano – Via Postumia, 63
31050 Ponzano Veneto (Treviso)
Tel. (0422) 440 751 – Fax. (0422) 440 754
Sig. Zamuner

Rooms 10 with telephone, bath, WC, cable TV and minibar. **Price** Single 220-250,000L, double 320-360,000L, suite 400,000L. **Meals** Breakfast 25,000L, served 7:00-11:30; half board 272,000L, full board 347,000L (per pers., 3 days min.). **Restaurant** Service 12:00-14:30, 20:00-22:00; menus: 80-100,000L, also à la carte. Specialties: Italian cuisine. **Credit cards** All major. **Pets** Dogs allowed. **Facilities** Swimming pool, parking. **Nearby** Villa Lattes in Istrana, Villa Barbaro Maser, Villa Emo Fanzolo di Vedelago, from Conegliano, white wine road to Valdobbiadene (Spumante), red wine road to Roncade, Treviso; Villa Condulmer golf course (18-hole). **Open** All year.

This residence was conceived in the dreams of Count Giorgio, its former owner, who entertained artists and socialites here. The hospitality of the great Venetian villas is represented by the Relais El Toula, which has a discreet and extremely courteous staff. The grounds, the swimming pool, the room decor and the restaurant all add to the charm of the place. The restaurant features regional specialties and the wine cellar is exceptional.

How to get there *(Map 5): 37 km north of Venezia. 7 km north of Treviso via S13 to Ponzano Veneto, then towards Paderno (2 km).*

Villa Giustinian ★★★★

Via Giustiniani, 11
31019 Portobuffolé (Treviso)
Tel. (0422) 85 02 44 – Fax (0422) 85 02 60

Rooms 40 and 8 suites with air-conditioning, telephone, bath, WC, TV and minibar. **Price** Single 120,000L, double 200-220,000L, suite 350-450,000L. **Meals** Breakfast 14,000L, served 7:30-10:30. **Restaurant** Service 12:30-14:30, 19:30-22:30, à la carte. **Credit cards** All major. **Pets** Dogs not allowed. **Facilities** Parking. **Nearby** Venice, from Conegliano (White Wine Road to Valdobbiadene (Spumante), Red Wine Road to Roncade), Treviso. **Open** All year.

The Villa Giustinian is in Portobuffolé, a beautiful Medieval village on the border between Venetia and Frioul. Around 1700, a noble Venetian family built this magnificent villa in a classical architectural style on a large piece of land. The interior is sumptuously Baroque, with stucco, frescos of the Veronese school and trompe l'œil. In this grandiose decor you will nonetheless find an intimate atmosphere. A superb stairway leads up to the comfortable rooms of different sizes; they are tastefully decorated. The suites are as big as ballrooms and have Venetian furniture. The presidential suite, which has a bed in a sculpted alcove, is amazing. You will really like the restaurant and its excellent wine list.

How to get there *(Map 5): 40 km northeast of Treviso, towards Oderzo, Mansué and Portobuffolé.*

Locanda Da Lino ★★★

31050 Solighetto (Treviso)
Tel. (0438)84 23 77 - Fax. (0438) 98 05 77
Sig. Lino Toffolin

Rooms 17 with telephone, bath, WC, TV and minibar. **Price** Single 90,000L, double 110,000L, suite 130,000L. **Meals** Breakfast 15,000L, served 8:00-11:00; half board 140,000L, full board 170,000L (per pers., 3 days min.). **Restaurant** Service 12:00-15:00, 19:00-22:00; closed Mon. and Christmas; menus: 50-60,000L, also à la carte. Specialties: Tagliolini alla Lino, spiedo, faraona con salsa peverada, dolci della casa. **Credit cards** All major. **Pets** Dogs allowed. **Facilities** Parking. **Nearby** Venice, Villa Lattes in Istrana, Villa Barbaro Maser, Villa Emo Fanzolo di Vedelago, Treviso, Villa Condulmer golf course (18-hole). **Open** All year (except July).

Da Lino is, a character who regularly makes news in his village of Solighetto. He started by opening a restaurant, which quickly put the town, in the beautiful countryside of Montello and at the foothills of the Pre-Alps, between Venice and Cortina, famous for its Prosecco and its Marzemino sung by Don Juan, on the map. His painter, novelist and poet friends, among whom Zanzotto is the most faithful, have an open table and it is here that the great singer Toti del Monte came to spend her last days. In her memory, Lino has created the *Premio Simpatia*, a cultural event. Marcello Mastroainni, on the back cover of the book «Que Bonta» dedicated to Lino, boasts the atmosphere of well being of the house. The rooms bear the names of regulars and friends: "Marcello" (Mastroainni) and "Marta Marzotto" are comfortable and decorated with originality. In the restaurant, there are two rooms frequented by regulars; one is bigger and more touristy.

How to get there (Map 5): 33 km northwest of Treviso.

Hotel Villa Condulmer ★★★★★

Via Zermanese
31020 Zerman Mogliano Veneto (Treviso)
Tel. (041) 45 71 00 – Fax (041) 45 71 34
Sig. Zuindavide

Rooms 45 with air-conditioning, telephone, bath, WC, TV and minibar.
Price Single 150,000L, double 220,000L, suite 350,000L. **Meals** Breakfast
included, served 7:30-10:30. **Restaurant** Service 12:00-13:30, 19:30-21:30;
menus: 70-80,000L, also à la carte. Specialties: Regional cuisine. **Credit cards**
All major. **Pets** Dogs not allowed. **Facilities** Swimming pool, tennis, golf (27
holes), riding, parking. **Nearby** Venice, Treviso, Venetian and Palladian Villas.
Open All year.

This beautiful 18th-century house, built on the ruins of an
old monastery, offers a dream vacation. The salons with
period frescos and furniture, the Italian-style garden and the
beauty of the grounds contribute to its elegance. The cuisine
changes each season with different chefs. The sports facilities are
exceptional: tennis, golf and horseback riding adding to the
pleasant and comfortable environment here.

How to get there *(Map 5): 18 km north of Venezia via A4, Mogliano
Veneto exit; then towards Zerman.*

Locanda al Castello ★★★

Via del Castello, 20
33043 Cividale del Friuli (Udine)
Tel. (0432) 73 32 42/73 40 15 – Fax (0432) 70 09 01
Sig. Balloch

Rooms 10 with telephone, bath or shower, WC and TV. **Price** Single 85,000L, double 110,000L. **Meals** Breakfast 10,000L; half board 85,000L, full board 110,000L (per pers, 3 days min.) **Restaurant** Service 12:00-14:30, 19:00-22:00; closed Wed.; menu: 40,000L, also à la carte. Specialties: Antipasti misti di pesce e di selvagigina, pesce e carne ai ferri. **Credit cards** All major. **Pets** Dogs allowed. **Facilities** Parking. **Nearby** Cividale (Tempietto, Duomo and Archeological Museum), Udine, Villa Manin in Passariano, golf course (9-hole) in Lignano, golf course (9-hole) in Tarvisio. **Open** All year (except 1st 2 weeks in Nov.).

In this part of Frioul there's a limited choice of nice places to stay: this is why the Locanda del Castello is appealing. It has several cozy, old-fashioned, slightly provincial rooms and a friendly family atmosphere. Go to the restaurant during the week because on Sunday, apart from a few merry Austrians, the room fills up with locals who come here with their families for Sunday lunch. Take advantage of your time here to go visit nearby Cividale–it's well worth the detour.

How to get there *(Map 6): 17 km east of Udine via A23, Udine exit; then towards Cividale (1.5 km from Cividale).*

Hotel Gabbia d'Oro ★★★★★

Corso Porta Borsari, 4a
37121 Verona
Tel. (045) 800 30 60 – Fax (045) 59 02 93
Sig.ra Balzarro

Rooms 27 and suites with air-conditioning, telephone, bath, WC, TV and minibar.
Price Single 350-400,000L, double 380-400,000L, suite 450-980,000L.
Meals Breakfast 40,000L, served 7:30-11:00. **Restaurant** See pp. 438-439.
Credit cards All major. **Pets** Small dogs allowed. **Nearby** Verona (Piazza delle Erbe,
Piazza dei Signori, the Arena, Juliet's House, Arche Scaligere, Church of San Zeno,
Castelvecchio), Opera Festival of Verona in the Arena mi-July–mi-Aug., Lago di
Garda, Villa Boccoli-Serego in Pedemonte, Villa della Torre in Fumane, Soave, Castle
Villafranca di Verona; golf course (18-hole) in Sommacampagna. **Open** All year.

The luxurious Hotel Gabbia d'Oro is a discreet 14th–century
palace. At first glance it seems like a secret place. The
entrance is barely distinguishable from the street. There are two
small salons with superb exposed beams, very beautiful period
furniture and nice armchairs around an old fireplace. The
courtyard, with pretty flowers, is surrounded by rooms which are
not very large, but are very luxurious. On the top floor there is a
peaceful terrace from which you can see the rooftops of the old
town. The service is as nice as the setting. Alas, nothing is
perfect–the prices are high, but justifiably so. The hotel is in a
historical pedestrian area. If you come by car, a taxi (at the hotel's
expense) will accompany you to the nearest garage–one less thing
to worry about.

How to get there *(Map 4): Via A4, Verona-South exit. Via A22,
Verona-West exit. The hotel is in front of Piazza delle Erbe.*

Hotel Aurora

37121 Verona
Piazza Erbe, 4a
Tel. (045) 59 47 17 – Fax (045) 801 08 60
Sig.ra Rossi

Rooms 19 with air-conditioning, telephone, bath or shower, WC, 5 with TV and elevator. **Price** Single 100-130,000L, double 120-150,000L, suite 200-280,000L. **Meals** Breakfast included, served 7:30-10:00. **Restaurant** See pp. 438-439. **Credit cards** All major. **Pets** Dogs allowed. **Nearby** Verona (Piazza delle Erbe, Piazza dei Signori, the Arena, Juliet's House, Arche Scaligere, Church of San Zeno, Castelvecchio), Opera Festival of Verona in the Arena mi-July–mi-Aug., Lago di Garda, Villa Boccoli-Serego in Pedemonte, Villa della Torre in Fumane, Soave, Castle Villafranca di Verona, golf course (18-hole) in Sommacampagna. **Open** All year except in May.

The Albergo Aurora is on the Piazza dell'Erbe in the heart of the town (a pedestrian area). It is very well kept and very comfortable (air-conditioning and well-equipped shower room). The service is discreet and charming and the prices are very competitive. There is one sour note, however, the decor and the lighting are reminiscent of a train station. So, should you decide to come here, choose the front rooms with a view of the piazza (they are the smallest but there are plans to enlarge them). The terrace, which looks out on those famous sun umbrellas, is a wonderful place to sit back and relax.

How to get there *(Map 4): A4, Verona-sud exit; A22, Verona-ouest exit.*

Hotel Villa del Quar ★★★★

Via Quar, 12
37020 Pedemonte – Verona (Verona)
Tel. (045) 680 06 81 – Fax (045) 680 06 04
Sig.ra Acampora Montresor

Rooms 22 with telephone, bath, WC, TV and minibar. **Price** Single 150-195,000L, double 2250-350,000L, suite 350-510,000L. **Meals** Breakfast included, served 7:30-10:00. **Restaurant** Service 12:30-14:00, 19:30-22:00; menus: 120,000L. Specialties: Zuppa di funghi con scampi, frittura del mare e dell'orto, coulins di fichi in salsa di amarone. **Credit cards** All major. **Pets** Dogs allowed. **Facilities** Swimming pool, parking **Nearby** Verona (Piazza delle Erbe, Piazza dei Signori, the Arena, Juliet's House, Arche Scaligere, Church of San Zeno, Castelvecchio), Opera Festival of Verona in the Arena mi-July–mi-Aug., Lago di Garda, Villa Boccoli-Serego in Pedemonte, Villa della Torre in Fumane, Soave, Castle Villafranca di Verona, golf course (18-hole) in Sommacampagna. **Open** All year.

The Hotel Villa del Quar is on the rich plain of the famous Valpolicella vineyards, less than 12 miles (20 km) from Verona. It has been lovingly restored by its owners. The simplicity of the decor highlights the antique furniture and the objects so carefully selected by the owners. The plush, elegant rooms are also perfect in their simplicity. You will find this same subtle sensitivity in the cuisine. The staff is exceptional and the service excellent.

How to get there *(Map 4): 5 km northeast of Verona, via Trento; before Parona take the Valpolicella road towards Pedemonte. Via A4, Verona-North exit, highway towards S. Pietro in Cariano, right (towards Verona) to Pedemonte.*

Foresteria Serègo Alghieri

37020 Gargagnano di Valpolicella (Verona)
Tel. (045) 770 36 22 – Fax (045) 770 35 23
Sig. Piero Alvise Serègo Alighieri

Apartments 8 with air-conditioning, telephone, bath, 7 with WC, TV and minibar. **Price** 2 pers. 250,000L (1 night), 170,000L (1 night during 1 week); 3 pers. 360,000L (1 night), 250,000L (1 night during 1 week); 4 pers. 460,000L (1 night), 320,000L (1 night during 1 week). **Meals** Breakfast 10,000L, served 8:00-10:00. **Restaurant** See p. 438-439. **Credit cards** All major. **Pets** Dogs allowed. **Facilities** Parking. **Nearby** Verona (Piazza delle Erbe, Piazza dei Signori, the Arena, Juliet's House, Arche Scaligere, Church of San Zeno, Castelvecchio), Opera Festival of Verona in the Arena mi-July–mi-Aug., Lago di Garda, Villa Boccoli-Serego in Pedemonte, Villa della Torre in Fumane, Soave, Castle Villafranca di Verona, golf course (18-hole) in Sommacampagna. **Open** All year (except Jan.).

Go up the long path lined with majestic cypress trees and you will soon see a massive residence with a large enclosed courtyard of flagstones in the middle of the Valplolicella vineyards. Dante used to come here on vacation when he lived in Verona. The Casal dei Ronchi was bought in 1353 by his eldest son, Pietro, and has been the home of the poet's descendants ever since. Today it is a prosperous estate with a working farm with wine and oil you can taste during your stay here. Eight elegantly decorated apartments are available (for 2 to 4 people). Between Lake Garda and Verona, and Venice less than 60 miles away, this villa is a magical, rare delight.

How to get there *(Map 4): 20 km of Verona via A4, Verona-north exit; then towards S. Ambrogio di Valpolicella.*

Relais Villabella ★★★

Villabella 37047 San Bonifacio (Verona)
Tel. (045) 61 01 777 – Fax (045) 61 01 799
Sig. Cherubin and Sig. Arabbi

Rooms 10 with telephone, bath, WC, TV and minibar. **Price** Single 160,000L, double 245,000L, suite 285,000L. **Meals** Breakfast included; half board and full board 190-225,000L (per pers., 3 days min.). **Restaurant** Service 12:00-14:00, 19:30-22:00; menus:50-80,000L. **Credit cards** All major. **Pets** Dogs not allowed. **Facilities** Parking. **Nearby** Verona (Piazza delle Erbe, Piazza dei Signori, the Arena, Juliet's House, Arche Scaligere, Church of San Zeno, Castelvecchio), Opera Festival of Verona in the Arena mid-July–mid-Aug., Lago di Garda, Villa Boccoli-Serego in Pedemonte, Villa della Torre in Fumane, Soave, Castle Villafranca di Verona, golf course (18-hole) in Sommacampagna. **Open** All year (except Aug. 1 – 20).

The Relais Villabella is a low structure with lateral wings called *barchesse*. It is a beautiful red color and it is elegant and perfectly integrated into the country setting. In this pleasant and somewhat rustic countryside you will be pleasantly surprised by so much refinement and harmony. The rooms have been carefully decorated: You will find the same hues of green, faded pink and turquoise in the silk curtains, bedspreads, door trimmings and armchair hems. The charming dining room opens onto the fragrant outdoors. You can finish up the evening at the piano-bar, listening to pretty music in a beautiful room, open to the night.

How to get there *(Map 4): 20 km west of Vierona, via A4, Soave exit; Villabella is located near the highway.*

Hotel Gardesana ★★★

Lago di Garda
Piazza Calderini, 20
37010 Torri del Benaco (Verona)
Tel. (045) 722 54 11 - Fax (045) 722 57 71
Sig. Lorenzini

Rooms 34 with air-conditioning (in July and Aug.), telephone, bath or shower, WC and TV; elevator. **Price** Single 50-80,000L, double 70-140,000L. **Meals** Breakfast 20,000L, served 7:00-11:00. **Restaurant** Service 19:00-23:00; menus: 45-85,000L, also à la carte. Specialties: Seafood. **Credit cards** All major. **Pets** Dogs not allowed. **Facilities** Parking. **Nearby** Cap San Vigilio (Villa Guarienti), Verona, degli Ulivi golf course (18-hole) in Marciaga. **Open** Mar. – Oct. 25, Dec. 26 – Jan. 15.

This 15th-century harbormaster's office faces the ruins of the Scalinger castle built on the other side of the port. From the terrace, where breakfast and dinner are served, you can look down onto the small port on Garde Lake. The rooms all have identical decor; ask for one on the third floor overlooking the lake—it is quieter. The famous restaurant attracts clientele from outside of the hotel and on certain evenings it celebrities from the world of art, literature, show business and sports host the dinner. Torri del Benaco is one of the most charming places on the lake. André Gide enjoyed his stay here and Room 23 bears his name. The owner and his family will make you feel at home too.

How to get there *(Map 4): 39 km northwest of Verona via A4, Peschiera exit; Via A22, Affi-Lago di Garda exit.*

Villa Michelangelo ★★★★

Via Sacco, 19
36057 Arcugnano (Vicenza)
Tel. (0444) 55 03 00 – Fax (0444) 55 04 90
Sig. Leder

Rooms 34 and 2 suites with air-conditioning telephone, bath or shower, WC, TV and minibar. **Price** Single 180-200,000L, double 260-285,000L, suite 380-395,000L. **Meals** Breakfast included, served 7:00-10:30. **Restaurant** Service 13:00-14:30, 20:00-22:00, closed Sun.; à la carte. **Credit cards** All major. **Pets** Small dogs allowed (30,000L). **Facilities** Swimming pool, parking. **Nearby** Palladian and Venetian Villas (Villa Valmarana, La Rotonda), Vicenza, Colli Berici golf course (18-hole) in Brendola free. **Open** All year.

The Villa Michelangelo was built on an incontestably beautiful site. The spacious and very comfortable rooms have been furnished and decorated with almost maniacal care, especially the two suites. Off to the side and down below the hotel, there is a pool with a superb view of the vineyards. The Villa Michelangelo has the advantage of being in the heart of Venetia, equidistant from Venice, Padua and Verona. It is also a very practical place to stay while you visit the famous villas built by Palladio.

How to get there *(Map 5): 30 km northwest of Padova via A4, Vicenza-West exit; then south towards Arcugnano via the Donsale dei Berici.*

Relais Ca' Masieri ★★★★

Via Massieri, 16
36070 Trissino (Vicenza)
Tel. (0445) 49 01 22 – Fax (0445) 45 04 55
Sig. Vassena

Rooms 51 (5 with air-conditioning) with telephone, bath or shower, WC, TV and minibar. **Price** Single 100,000L, double 140,000L, suite 180,000L. **Meals** Breakfast 14,000L, served 7:30-11:00. **Restaurant** Service 12:30-14:00, 19:30-22:00; closed Sun. and Mon. noon; menus: 70-90,000L, also à la carte. Specialties: Insalata di capesante, bigoli al torchio, filetto bollito. **Credit cards** Amex, Visa, Eurocard and MasterCard. **Pets** Dogs allowed. **Facilities** Swimming pool, parking. **Nearby** Villa Marzotto in Trissino, Montecchio Maggiore (view of the castello di Bellaguardia and castello della Villa called castles of Romeo and Juliet), Villa Cordellina-Lombardi, Vicenza. **Open** All year (except 3 weeks from early Jan. – mid-Feb.).

This house, which still functions as a farm, is ideally on the circuit of Palladian villas. Truly beautiful, it seems perfect, down to the last detail. Eight very modern and extremely comfortable rooms (excellent bedding, beautiful bathrooms, very well designed lighting) are in the outbuildings, where you can sleep as long as you like in the deep silence there. In the evening, the simple, delicious cuisine will keep you at the hotel. After dinner, you can enjoy a glass of *Torcolato* and listen to the crickets sing. In the morning, breakfast is served on the terrace where you can view the hills, valleys and two castles, one of which the poet L. da Porta attributed to Romeo, the other to Juliette.

How to get there *(Map 4): 20 km northwest of Vicenza via A4, Montecchio Maggiore exit; then 15 km towards Valdagno.*

Hotel Duchi d'Aosta ★★★★

Piazza Unità d'Italia, 2
34121 Trieste
Tel. (040) 76 000 11 - Fax (040) 36 60 92
Sig. Fort

Rooms 48 with air-conditioning, telephone, bath or shower, WC, TV and minibar.
Price Single 248-260,000L, double 330,000L, suite 525-548,000L.
Meals Breakfast included, served 7:00-10:30. **Restaurant** Service 12:30-14:30,
19:30-22:30; menus: 50-70,000L, also à la carte. Specialties: Seafood. **Credit
cards** All major. **Pets** Dogs allowed. **Facilities** Garage (37,000L). **Nearby** Trieste
(Piazza dell'Unita, Roman theater, Cathedral of S. Giusto, the port), Castello di
Miramare, Grotta Gigante, Church of Monrupino. **Open** All year.

Like the rest of the town of Trieste, the Hotel Duchi d'Aosta
has the nostalgic charm of one of those places with a
fabulous history, which is now overlooked. It is a palace from
another century, where you might expect to see some rich
Austro-Hungarian family with its entourage, stopping off for an
evening on the way to Venice, enter one of the plush salons. It
is an excellent hotel with vast, pleasant rooms, equipped with
every modern convenience. The service is in the fine and all too
rare tradition of the international hotels of yesteryear. The
trilingual personnel is omnipresent, attentive, friendly, discreet
and efficient. The restaurant is also excellent. The hotel is right
in the center of the old part of Trieste, only a few minutes away
from the fort.

How to get there *(Map 6): Via A4, Trieste-Costieza exit.*

RESTAURANTS

R E S T A U R A N T S

BASILICATA
CALABRIA

Maratea

Taverna Rovita, via Rovita 13, tel. (0973) 876 588 – Closed November-March 15 – 35-50,000L. A pretty restaurant on a narrow street in the

historical center of Maratea. It serves regional cuisine, has a good wine cellar – **Za' Mariuccia**, on the port, tel (0973) 876 163 – Closed Thursday except in the summer and from December to February – 50-80,000L. Wide variety of fish specialties.

Fiumicello

5km from Maratea
La Quercia, tel. (0973) 876 907 – Closed October-Easter – 30-40,000L. It Serves seafood and traditional regional Italian cuisine in a romantic atmosphere. Meals are served in a rustic but elegant dining

room, or in the garden in the shade of the big oak tree.

Matera

Il Terrazzino, Bocconcino II, vico San Giuseppe 7, tel. (0835) 332 503 – Closed Tuesday – 40,000L. The town's amazing vestiges of the Troglodyte period are worth seeing. Terrazzino is a great place to stop in for a family meal. Matera has some of the best bread in Italy.

LOCAL SPECIALTIES

Il Buongustaio, piazza Vittorio Veneto 1 – It features smoked ham from Lauria, Picerno, and Palazzo San Gervasio, and the *Aglianico* wine.

Potenza

Taverna Oraziana, via Orazio Flacco 2, tel. (0971) 21 851 – Closed Sunday, August – 40-50,000L. This classic restaurant has long been the haunt of town notables who come for rich hearty regional cuisine. *Aglianico dei Vulture* is a good local wine.

Altomonte

Barbieri, via San Nicolas 32, tel. (0981) 948 072 – A famous restaurant, regional cooking.

Bottega di Casa Barbieri, has a very good selection of regional

products such as the *Ciro classico*, one of the best wines of Calabria.

Cosenza

Da Giocondo, via Piave 53, tel. (0984) 29 810 – Closed Sunday, August – 30,000 L. It is very small, so reservations are a must.

Castrovillari

La Locanda di Alia, via Jetticelle 69, tel. (0981) 46 370 – Closed Sunday – 50-70,000L. It is located a few miles from the ancient Greek town of Sibari, and serves traditional Calabrian cuisine in a very lovely decor.

Reggio di Calabria

Bonaccorso, via Nino Bixio 5, tel. (0965) 896 048 – Closed Monday, August 45-50,000L. Italian and French cuisine with some Calabrian specialties, *fettucine, cinzia, semifreddi* – **Conti**, via Giulia 2, tel (0965) 29 043 - Closed Monday - 45-60,000L. It has 2 rooms, one is elegant, the other more casual with a piano bar.

Gallina

2km from Reggio di Calabria
La Collina dello Scoiattolo, via Provinciale 34, tel. (0965) 682 255 – Closed Wednesday, November - 40,000L. There is an avalanche of *antipasti,penne all'imbriacata* and very good desserts, in pleasant surroundings, but it is always overcrowded.

Soverato

Il Palazzo, Corso Umberto I 40, tel. (0967) 25 336 – Closed Monday, November – 40,000L. Old very well restored and tastefully decorated palace and features regional cuisine. In the summer, meals are served in the garden.

Catanzaro Lido

La Brace, 102 via Melito di Porto Salvo, tel. (0961) 31 340 – Closed Monday, July – 40-60,000L. A pretty restaurant with a panoramic view on the Gulf of Squillace, fine cuisine (spaghetti with zucchini flowers, octopus ravioli, homemade pie) and a good selection of Calabrian wine.

C A M P A N I A

Napoli / Naples

La Cantinella, via Cuma 42, tel. (081) 764 86 84 – Closed Monday, August – 70-120,000L. It has a nice view on Vesuvius and serves elegant cuisine in the great Neopolitan tradition – **La Sacrestia**, via Orazio 116, tel. (081) 7611051 – Closed Monday, August – 70-100 000L. People come here religiously for its elegant simplicity, very good cuisine, and great Campanian wines – **Amici Miei**, via Monte di Dio 78, tel. (081) 764 6063 Closed Monday, August – 40,000L. Has good traditional family-style cuisine and a friendly atmos-

phere – **Ciro a Santa Brigida**, via Santa Brigida 71, tel. (081) 5524 072 – Closed Sunday, Christmas, August – 60,000L. People come here to enjoy simple authentic Neopolitan cuisine – **Ciro a Mergellina**, via Mergellina, 21, Find the pushcart vender wandering on the boardwalk, and try his *Ostrecaro Ficico* and other seafood specialties – **Bellini**, via Santa Maria di Costantinopoli 80, tel. (081) 459 774 – Closed Wednesday, August – 45,000L. Has good pizza and other Neopolitan specialties – **Giuseppone a Mare**, via F. Russo 13, tel. (081) 575 60 02. Typically Neopolitan restaurant in an inlet in Posilippe which serves seafood specialties – **Dante et Beatrice**, piazza Dante 44, tel. (081) 549 94 38. Typical Neopolitan trattoria – **Bersagliera**, Borgo Marino, tel. (081) 764 60 16, faces the Castel dell'Ovo, on the small port of Santa Lucia. It is is famous, so you must

reserve – **Al Poeta**, piazza Giacomo, 134, is the in restaurant for young Neopolitans.

CAFFE' – BARS

Scaturchio, piazza San Domenico Maggiore – Closed Thursday. The best place to try real traditional rum cake and *brevettata* (chocolate cake) **Bar Marino**, via dei Mille, 57 – **Caffe' Latino**, Gradini di Chiesa, 57, the best *espresso* – **Bilancione**, via Posillipo, 238, Closed Wednesday, the best ice creams in Naples –

Gambrinus, via Chiaia 1, is an old Neopolitan cafe, once closed down by the fascist regime and transformed into a bank, now restored in the finest tradition.

LOCAL SPECIALTIES, CRAFTS

Pintauro, via S. M. di Constantinopoli and vico d'Affuto, has made *sfogliatelle,* a specialty of the house since 1848 – **Light**, via Chiaia, 275, is a coral boutique – **Marinella**, via Chiaia, 287 is where you can find the same silk ties as Don Corleone!

Pompeii

Il Principe, piazza B. Longo 8, tel. (081) 850 55 66 – Closed Monday, August 1–15 – 60,000L. You will find only the best, the most elegant, and the most expensive here - **Zi Caterina**, via Roma – Closed Tuesday, June 28-July, more traditional and less expensive.

Caserta

Antica Locanda-Massa 1848, via Mazzini, 55, tel. (0823) 321 268 – serves regional specialties, with service in the garden in the summer. It is only about thirty kilometers from Naples. Don't miss the Palazzo Reale and the Parco-Giardino in Caserta.

CASERTA VECCHIA (10 km away) **La Castellana**, Closed Thursday - 20-50,000L – It is rustic, regional, and has a cool terrace in the summer.

Capri

CAPRI:

La Capannina, via Le Botteghe 12 b, tel. (081) 8370 732 – Closed Wednesday, November 7-March 15 – 50-75,000L. It is elegant and serves very good fish from Capri – **La Pigna**, via Roma 30, tel. (081) 837 0280 – Closed Tuesday October 15-Easter – 50-60,000L. It has been a wine bar since 1876, and is today one of the most popular restaurants on the island. It has an elegant room, a beautiful garden with lemon trees, and a view on the Bay of Naples – **Luigi**, ai Faraglioni, tel. (081) 837 0591 – Closed October-Easter – 60-80,000L. It has good cuisine, a flower-covered terrace, and a great view. Take a walk to the Faraglioni, the famous rocks across from Capri, a half an hour away on foot, or go there by boat from Marina Piccola **Pizzeria Aurora**, via

Fuorlovado 18, tel. (081) 837 0181 – Closed Tuesday, December 10-March 10 – 40-50,000L. Excellent cuisine by Peppino.

ANACAPRI

Da Gelsomina, à Migliara 72, tel. (081) 837 14 99 Closed Tuesday, February 1-15. You can see the sea and the gulf from the terrace through the vineyards and the olive trees.

CRAFTS

Capri Flor, via Tragara, is a nursery. Capri will make you start dreaming about gardens, and Carthusia **Carthusia**, via Matteotti 2, will about perfumes – **Massimo Godericci** offers a large selection of pottery and fine Italian china.

Ischia

ISCHIA PONTE

Giardini Eden, via Nuova Portaromana, tel. (081) 993 9091 Closed the evening, October-April – 40-50,000L. Away from the hordes of tourists, come have a quiet lunch and enjoy good southern Italian cuisine in this garden full of exotic flowers – **Gennaro**, via Porto, tel (081) 992 917, has a lively, convivial, typical regional atmosphere.

ISCHIA-FORIO

La Romantica, via Marina 46, tel. (081) 997 345 Closed Wednesday, January – 30-60,000L. It serves seafood cuisine in an elegant classical setting.

BAGNO-LIDO PORTO-D'ISCHIA, **Alberto** tel. (081) 981 259 – Closed Monday evening, November–March 40, 000L. This friendly trattoria has a veranda on the beach, regional cuisine, and good house wine by the pitcher.

Ravello

Garden, via Boccaccio 4, tel. (089) 857 226 – Closed Tuesday in the winter – 30-45,000L. In the summer, you can dine on the picturesque terrace with a view on the gulf.

Sorrento

O Parrucchiano Corso Italia 71, tel. (081) 878 13 21, Closed Wednesday in the winter - 35-50,000L. It has been the "must-see" of Sorrento for more than a century now. Be sure to end your meal with a *limoncello*, the liquor of the house – **Il Glicine**, via Sant'Antonio 2, tel. (081) 877 2519 – Closed Wednesday off season, January 15 - March 1– 30-50,000L. Elegant, friendly, reservations necessary – **La Pentolaccia**, via Fuorimura 25, tel. (081) 878 5077 Closed Thursday – 35,000L. A classic restaurant in the heart of town serving traditional cuisine.

CRAFTS

Handkerchiefs, via Luigi di Maio 28 sells beautiful handkerchiefs, one of the specialties of Sorrento, monogrammed to your specifications.

Sant'Agata Sui Due Golfi

9 km from Sorrento **Don Alfonso 1890**, piazza Sant'Agata, tel. (081) 878 0026 – Closed Monday off season., Tuesday, January 10–February 25 – 70-95,000L. It is the best restaurant in Campania, and in Italy, superbly located on a little hill between Sorrento and Amalfi, featuring traditional cuisine made with produce fresh from the market.

Vico Equense

Pizza A Metro Da Gigino, via Nicotera 10, tel. (081) 879 8426 – 35,000L, has a wide selection of delicious pizzas and local specialties – **San Vicenzo** in Montechiaro (3km), tel 802 8001 – Closed Wednesday in the winter.

Salerno

Vicolo della Neve, Vicolo della Neve 24, tel. (089) 225 705 – Closed Wednesday, Christmas – 30,000 L. Despite its name, it is not a pizzaria, and serves fine local traditional cuisine made with fresh produce from the grounds – **Al Fusto d'Oro**, via Fieravecchia 29, unpretentious pizzeria and seafood dishes – **La Brace**, lungomare Trieste 11, tel. 225 159 - Closed Wednesday and from 20. to 31 December.

Paestum

Nettuno, closed in the evening, Monday except July, August, Christmas – 30-50,000L. It is on the archaeological site and has a lovely dining room and terrace with a view on the temples. It is closed Mondays and Christmas.

Palinoro

Da Carmelo, in Iscia, tel. (0974) 931 138 – Closed Monday off season, October, November – 30-35,000L. It has a rustic dining room, a pretty verdant garden, and traditional cuisine with seafood specialties.

Positano

San Pietro, via Laurito 2, 2km from

Positano, tel. (089) 875 455 – Dinner on the terrace perched on a rocky crag is magic. The view is sublime and the cuisine delicious – **Chez Black**, via Brigantino 19, tel. (089) 875 036 – Closed November-January – 30-45,000L is a charming place near the beach, serving pizzas, grilled fish, and spaghetti – **Da Constantino**, via Corvo 95, tel. (089) 875 738 – Closed November- December – 20,000L is 5 km from Positano, and has a marvelous view on the sea. A minibus will take you to the restaurant. Reservations are a must in the summer.

Praiano
9km from Positano
La Brace, via G. Capriglione, tel.

(089) 874226 – Closed October 15- March 15, Wednesday off season. You can enjoy a superb view of Posiatno and the *faraglioni* of Capri from the terrace.

Amalfi

Da Gemma, via Cavalieri di Malta, tel. (089) 871 345 – Closed Tuesday, Jan. 15–Feb. 15 – 35-45,000L. An old restaurant where you can have delicious Neopolitan specialties such as *genovese*, along with good regional wines – **Il Tari'**, via Capuano, tel. (089) 871 832 – Closed Tuesday, Nov. – 20,000L. Good seafood specialties – **La Caravella**, via M. Camera, tel/. (089) 871 029, Closed Tuesday and Nov.. Here is another classic Amalfi address. Reservations are required.

EMILIA ROMAGNA

Bologna

I Carracci, via Manzoni 2, tel. (051) 270 815 – Closed Sunday, August – 60-80,000L. It features fine cuisine for elegant suppers – **Il Battibecco**, via Battibecco 4, tel. (051) 223 298 – Closed Sunday between Christmas and New Year's Day, August 10-20 – 60-90,000L. It has delicious risottos, spaghetti with clams, and roast beef pie – **Il Bitone**, via Emilia Levante 111, tel. (051) 546 110 – Closed Monday, Tuesday, August – 55,000L. The favorite restaurant of the Bolognese. There is a large garden where you can have tea in the summer – **Diana**, via Indipendenza 24, tel. (051) 231 302 – Closed Monday, August – 50,000 L. A traditional restaurant with classic cuisine – **Rodrigo**, via della Zecca 2-h tel 22 04 45 – Closed Sunday, August 4–24. Excelent – **Rosteria Da Luciano**, via Nazario Sauro 19, tel. (051) 231 249. Closed Tuesday evening, Wednesday, August, Christmas and New Year – 35-80,000 L. One of the best restaurants in Bologna, reservation – **Torre de' Galluzzi'**, corte de'

Galluzzi 5-A, tel. (051) 267 638. Located inside the old tower, fine meat and fish dishes – **Rostaria Antico Brunetti**, via Caduti di Cefalonia 5, tel. (051) 234 441 – 40,000L. A very old restaurant with delicious pasta, and good *lambrusco* – **Antica Trattoria del Cacciatore**, Casteldebole, tel. (051) 564 203 Closed Monday, August, January – 50,000 L. Located 7km west of Bologna, it is a rustic but very chic trattoria, with fine cuisine.

LOCAL SPECIALTIES

Bottega del vino Olindo Faccioli, large selection of wines. Among Emilian wines, try the young and bubbly *Lambrusco,* and the *Sangiovese* – **Brini**, via Ugo Bassi, 19-C, is great for its wide selection of cheeses, and of course the famous *parmigano regiano* - **Salsamenteria**

Tamburini, via Caprarie 1, features ham from Parma, *mortadelle* and *culatello*, reputed to be the best Italian salami – **Casa della Sfoglia**, via Rialto 4. Here they make traditional Bolognese pasta and tagliatelles, invented, legend has it, for the wedding of Lucrecia Borgia and the Duke of Ferrara in 1487.

Imola

30km from Bologna
San Domenico, via Sacchi 1, tel. (0542) 29 000 – Closed Monday, January 1-13, July, August 1–22 – 90-130,000L. Gourmets from all over the world come here for the San Domenico pilgrimage as well as for this restaurant's ingenious interpretation of regional Italian cuisine.

Brisighella

La Grotta, via Metelli 1, tel. (0546) 81 829 – Closed Tuesday, January, June 1–15 – 30-55,000L. La Grotta shares the gastrionomic honors of this very pretty little town with **Gigiolé**, piazza Carducci 5, tel. (0546) 81 209, Closed February, July 1–15. Several gest rooms.

Ferrara

Grotta Azzurra, piazza Sacrati 43, tel. (0532) 209 152 – Closed Wednesday, Sunday evenings, January

2-10, August 1-15 – 40,000L. The decor is Mediterranean, but the cuisine is traditional northern Italian, with some Emilian specialties – **Vecchia Chitarra**, via Ravenna 13, tel. (0532) 62 204 – Closed Tuesday, August 1–15 – 30,000L. Regional specialties and home made pasta – **La Provvidenza**, corso Ercole I d'Este 92, tel. (0532) 205 187 – Closed Monday, August – 40-60,000L. The interior resembles a farmhouse with a little garden full of regular customers. You will need a reservation **Enoteca Al Brindisi**, via degli Adelardi II. The Guinness Book of World Records says this is the oldest tavern in the world. Benvenuto Cellini, the Titien was said to have frequented this "Hostaria del Chinchiolino". There are wine tastings and wine is also sold here.

Argenta

34km from Ferrara

Il Trigabolo, piazza Garibaldi 4, tel. (0532) 804 121 – Closed Sunday evening, Monday – 100-130,000L. A good place to enjoy fine cuisine in Emilia-Romagna.

Modena

Bianca, via Spaccini 24, tel.(059) 311 524 – Closed Saturday at noon, Sunday, August, Christmas holidays – 45-65,000L. You will like this trattoria and the authentic cuisine served here – **Fini**, rua Frati Minori 54, tel. (059) 223 314 – Closed Monday, Tuesday, August, Christmas – 60-75,000L. Fini's *tortellini* and *zamponi* are almost as famous as the Ferraris of Modena.

Ravenna

Tre Spade, via Faentina 136, tel. (0544) 500 5222 – Closed Sunday nights, Monday – 55,000L. It features Italian cuisine from different provinces in a pretty decor – **La Gardèla**, via Ponte Marino 3, tel. (0544) 217 147 – Closed Thursday, August 10-25. It serves savory cuisine **Al Gallo**, via Maggiore 87 tel 213 775 - Closed Monday nights, Tuesday, Christmas, Easter. Reservation – **Enoteca Ca' de Ven**, via Ricci 24 – Closed Monday. This wine bar in an old palace offers wine tasting and sales, and light meals.

Parma

La Greppia, via Garibaldi 39, tel. (0521) 233 686 – Closed Monday,

Tuesday, July – 50-70,000 L. Near the Opera, and has very good Italian cuisine and a cheery decor. Reservations are recommended – **L'Angiol d'Or**, vicolo Scutellari 1, tel. (0521) 282 632 – Closed Sunday, Christmas, August 14-15, January 10–20. At the corner of the piazza del Duomo – You can enjoy savory cuisine and the illuminated baptistry at night in this elegant restaurant – 65,000L – **Croce di Malta**, Borgo Palmia, tel. 235 643. A small restaurant with innovative cuisine

and a terrace in the summer – **La Filoma**, via XX Marzo 15, tel. (0521) 234 269 – Closed Sunday, August – 40-50,000L. One of our favorites with an intimate atmosphere and personalized regional cuisine **Il Cortile**, borgo Paglia 3, tel. 285 779. Closed Sunday, Monday noon, August 1–22 – 30-40,000L. Reservations are recommended – Gallo d'Oro, Borgo della Salina 3, tel. (0521) 20 80 46 A tavern. Try their famous *culatello de Parme, maltaglioti,* and *tortellini.* **Vecchio Molinetto,** viale Milazzo 39, tel 526 72. Traditional trattoria .

AROUND PARMA

Sacca di Colorno, 15km from Parma **Le Stendhal**, tel. (0521) 815 493 - Closed Tuesday, January 1-15, July 20-August 10. If you are following the footsteps of Fabrice del Dongo, try the Stendhal.

Noceto, 14km from Parma : **Aquila Romana**, via Gramsci 6, tel. (0521) 62 398, Closed Monday, Tuesday, 15 July 15-August 15, 30-50,000L. An old postal inn, famous for its regional specialties inspired by old recipes.

Busseto, 35km from Parma, **Ugo** via Mozart 3. Country atmosphere.

Polesine Parmense, Santa Franca 6km from Busseto: **Da Colombo**, tel. (0524) 98 114 – Closed Monday evening, Tuesday, January, July 20–August 10 - 40,000 L. It is famous, so you'd better reserve.

Zibello, 10km from Busseto: **Trattoria La Buca**, tel. (0524) 99 214, Closed Monday evening, Tuesday, July 1-15 45,000 L. It is very popular, so you will need a reservation.

Berceto, 50km from Parma **Da Rino**, piazza Micheli 11 tel. (525) 64 306 – Closed Monday, December 20-February 15 – 30-60,000L. The masters of the mushroom in season, and of ravioli of all sorts year round.

Reggio nell'Emilia

5 Pini-da-Pelati, viale Martiri di Cervarolo 46, tel. (0522) 5536 63 – Closed Tuesday evening, Wednesday, August 1-20 – 45-70,000L – **La Zucca**, piazza Fontanesi 1/L, tel. 437 222 – Closed Sunday, January 5-12, August – **Enoteca Il Pozzo**, viale Allegri 6/A. It has wine tasting and sales, and a restaurant with garden.

Sant'Arcangelo di Romagna, **Zaghini**, piazza Gramsci – Closed Monday, 30,000L.

LATIUM ABRUZZI

Roma / Rome

Il Caminetto, viale Parioli 89, tel. (06) 808 3946 – Closed Thursday, August – 50,000L. Success has not spoiled the quality of this restauran – **La Campana**, vicolo della Campana 18, tel. (06) 686 7820 – Closed Monday, August – 35-45,000 L. One of the oldest, if not the oldest trattoria of the capital, with good Roman cuisine and good house wine – **Il Bacaro**, via degli Spagnoli 27. Près du Panthéon, tel. (06) 686 4110 – Closed Sunday – 60,000L. near the Pantheon and has an elegant bistro decor – **L'Eau Vive**, via Monterone 85, tel. (06) 654 1095 Closed Sunday, August 10-20 – 20-70,000L. Missionary sisters serve their specialties every day (near the Pantheon) – **Nino**, via Borgognona 11, tel. (06) 679 5676 – Closed Sunday – 50,000L. Near the stairs of the Piazza di Spagna, it is frequented by local artists and writers who come here for Tuscan specialties and the "Mont Blanc", a house dessert. – **Osteria Margutta**, via Margutta 82, tel. (06) 679 8190 – Closed Sunday – 40,000L. Friendly trattoria with a nice atmosphere, very close to the Piazza di Spagnanice, closed Sundays. There are many galleries and antique shops on this street where Fellini used to live – **Otello alla**

Concordia, via della Croce, tel. (06) 679 1178 – Closed Sunday. Is a charming house with an arbor in the summer, decent cuisine, and a trendy atmosphere – **Pino e Dino**, piazza di Montevecchio 22, tel. (06) 686 1319 Closed Monday, August – 70,000L. Is an intimate place near the Piazza Navona, hidden behind heavy curtains on this Renaissance square so dear to Raphael and Bramante, where Lucrecia Borgia formented numerous intrigues. Reservations are necessary – **Quirino**, via delle Muratte 84, tel. (06) 679 4108 – Closed Sunday and 10 days in August – 40,000L – **Majella**, 45 piazza Sant'Appolinare 45, tel. (06) 65 64 174, Closed Sunday. The restaurant is in a beautiful old house, and features – **Tre Scalini**, Close to the Piazza Navona and facing the Bernin fountain, it is a great place for breakfast, with delicious *tartuffo,* a typically Italian atmosphere and family-style cuisine – **La Rosetta**, via della Rosetta 9, tel. (06) 686 1002 – Closed Saturday noon, Sunday, August – 80-100,000L (near the Pantheon) is well known for its fish specialties – **Checchino dal 1887,**

Via Monte Testaccio 30, tel. (06) 574 63 18 – Closed Sunday evening, Monday, August, Christmas – 60-80,000L. You will dine on typically Roman cuisine under an old vaulted ceiling. The specialty is *coda alla vaccinara* and the wine cellar is very good – **Papa' Giovanni**, via dei Sediari 4, tel. (06) 686 1002 – Sunday, August – 80,000L. Between Palazzo Madama and the Pantheon, serves Roman-style "nouvelle cuisine" – **Antica Pesa**, 18, via Garibaldi, tel. (06) 58 09 236, Closed Sunday – You can dine in a room with frescos painted by customer-artists or on the patio. The house specialty is *trittico di pastaciutta* – **Il Giardino**, 29 via Zucchelli, Closed Monday. near the Piazza Barberini is one of the best trattorias in town, with low prices – **La Carbonara**, piazza Campo dei Fiori, tel. (06) 68 64 783, Closed Tuesday. One of the most beautiful market places in Rome, featuring fish specialties – **Abruzzi**, via del vaccaro 1 tel.(06) 679 38 97 – Closed Saturday. A marvelous classic restaurant – **El Tartufo**, vicolo Sciarra, tel. (06) 678 02 26 – Closed Sunday. An authentic place. The *Navone* meal is a true delight.

DINNERS IN THE TRASTEVERE

Romolo, via di Porta Settimania, tel. (06) 581 8284 – Closed Monday, August. Dine by candlelight in the garden Raphael used to visit. The interior is also has charm and atmosphere – **Sabatini I**, piazza Santa Maria in Trastevere 10, tel. (06) 582 026 – Closed Wednesday and two-weeks in August – 60,000L. It is the most famous and popular restaurant in the Trastevere. If it is full, you can always try the **Sabatini II**, vicolo di Santa Maria in Trastevere 18, tel. (06) 5818307 – **Checco er Carettiere**, via Benedetta 10, tel. (06) 574 6318 – Closed Sunday evening, Monday, August, Christmas – 50-75,000 L – An osteria typical of the Trastevere with a decor reminiscent of the time when the *carettieri* came here, and very good Roman cuisine with old recipes – **La Tana de Noiantri**, via della Paglia 13, Closed Tuesday. friendly and inexpensive, with simple cuisine and tables on the sidewalk in the summer – **Alberto Ciarla**, piazza San Cosimato – Closed Sunday, August, January – 50-95,000L.

PIZZERIAS

Pizzeria Berninetta, via Pietro Cavallini 14, tel. (06) 360 3895 – Closed Monday, August, open only in the evening – 25,000L is also very popular, a good place for pizza, *crostini,* and pasta – **Pizzeria Da Fieramosca ar Fosso**, piazza de Mercanti 3, tel. (06) 589 0289 – Closed Sunday – open only in the evening – 20-30,000L. The best pizzeria in the Trastevere – **Pizzeria San Marco**, via Taano 29, tel. (06) 687 8494 – Closed Wednesday, August – 20,000L. It has fine, crisp Roman pizza and a clientele of Roman yuppies who won't think twice about having champagne with their pizza. There is a good selection of wines too – **Ivo a Trastevere**, via di San

Francesco a Ripa 150. Delicious pizzas in a tiny room.

CAFFE' – BARS

near the piazza Navona : **Antico Caffè della Pace**, via della Pace 6, has turn of the century artistic atmosphere, and is frequented in the evening by a hip intellectual crowd – **Tre Scalini**, piazza Navona, is across

from the Bernin fountain, and has the best *granita di caffe* and *tartufo*.
Enoteca Navona, piazza Navona offers wine tasting and *crostini*.

near the via Veneto : **Gran Caffè' Doney**, via Veneto 39, was born in Florence in 1822, moved to Rome in 1884 and to the Via Veneto in 1946. Coctails, salads, and pastries are served here – **Harry's Bar**, via Veneto 148. Like its brothers, it is chic and elegant.

near the piazza del Popolo : **Casina Valadier**, Pincio, Villa Borghese. The chic terrace restaurant is a great place to enjoy a superb view at sunset, good cocktails and fine ice cream when the weather gets warm – **Caffè' Rosati**, piazza del Popolo, serves sandwiches and pastries. The large terrace has been completely overrun.

near the piazza di Spagna : **Caffè' Greco**, via Conditi 86. Casanova

mentioned this place in his memoirs, and Stendhal, Goethe, and D'Annunzio have all been here. You can have small sandwhiches in a nice Napolean III-style decor. Try the *paradiso,* a house specialty – **Babington**, on the Piazza di Spagna, this is a something of a local institution for having English tea.

Le Cornacchie, piazza Rondanini. This place has style, an upbeat friendly atmosphere, and family-style cuisine.

THE BEST CAPPUCCINO: **Caffe' San Eustachio**, piazza San Eustachio **La Tazza d'Oro**, via degli Orfani, near the piazza del Pantheon.

THE BEST GELATI: **Giolitti**, Offici del Vicario 40.

THE OLDEST BAKERY IN ROME: **Valzani**, via del Moro 37.

SHOPPING

Gamarelli, via Santa Chiara 34 - Closed Saturday, sells religious accessories. Lay people come here to buy their famous socks, violet for bishops, and red for cardinals – **La Stelletta**, via delle Stelletta 4, is great for costme jewelry – **Aldo Fefe**, via delle Stelleta 20b. Closed Saturday, sells beautiful cardboard boxes – **Papirus**, via Capo le case, has a large selection of elegant stationery – **Libreria antiquaria Cascianelli**, largo Febo 14, is specialized in old and modern works on Rome, across from the Hotel Raphaël **Limentani**, via Portico d'Ottavia 25 is in the old ghetto, in a basement, and offers a wide selection of household linens.– **Ai Monasteri**, corso Rinascimento 72, sells liquors, elixirs, and other products produced by monastic orders, in a beautiful Neo-Gothic decor – **Trimani Wine Bar,** via Cernaia 37-B is a good place for tasting and buying fine Italian food products.

Antique Shops via del Babbuino, via dei Coronari, in the Corso Emanuele distric.

Tivoli

Le Cinque Statue, via Quintilio Varo 1, tel. (0774) 20 366 – Stop in while visiting the Villa d'Este gardens in Tivoli – **Sibella**, via della Sibella 50, tel. (0774) 20281 – 45,000L. has the same beautiful interior and garden which Chateaubriand admired in 1803.

Villa Adriana

Albergo Ristorante Adriano, , tel. (0774) 529 174 – Closed Sunday evening –has terra cotta walls, Corinthian columns decorating the interior, and a beautiful shady garden in the summer, a nice place to relax after visiting Hadrian's villa.

Frascati, 22km from Roma

Cacciani, via Armando Diaz 13, tel. (06) 9420 378 – Closed Monday, January 7-17, August 17-27– 50,000L. Thirty years of great Roman cooking, delicious house wine and a beautiful terrace in the summer make this place well worth the trip – **Cantina Comandini**, via E. Filiberto – Closed Sunday. A good place to buy wine and has a nice wine bar – **Pasticceria Renato Purificato**, piazza del Mercato or **Bar degli Specchi** , via Battisti 3,

Try the lady-shaped *biscottini*.
Villa Simone, via Toricella 2 at Monteporzio Catone. You will find the best *Frascati* of the region and very good olive oil here.

Castel Gandolfo, 22km from Roma

Sor Campana, corso della Repubblica – Closed Monday, is one of the oldest restaurants of the region

Anagni

Del Gallo, Via V. Emanuele 164, tel. (0775) 727 309, has a long family tradition of fine regional cuisine.

Alatri

La Rosetta, via Duomo, 35, tel. (0775) 43 45 68 – Closed Tuesday, November 5-30.

L'Aquila

Tre Marie, via Tre Marie, tel. (0862) 413 191 – Closed Sunday evening, Monday. This historical monument has a superb decor, very good cuisine, and a delicious dessert "Tre Marie". Ernesto, (Ai benefattori del Grillo), piazza palazzo 22, tel. (0862) 2 10 94, closed Sunday and Monday, August; After having *Sagnarelle alla pastora, pastasciutta,* or *bigolo al torchio,* be sure to visit the two "botti a camera", superb rooms where wine is stored.

Isola di Ponza

Da Mimi, Terrazza Mari, via dietro la chiesa, tel. (0771) 80 338 – 50,000L, is one of the best restaurants on the island – **Eéa**, via Umberto 1 and **La Kambusa**, via Banchina Nuova 15, serve regional cuisine.

Viterbo

Il Grottino, via della Cava 7, tel. (0761) 308 188 – Closed Tuesday, June 20-July 10 – 50,000L.– **Aquilanti**, La Quercia, 3km, tel. (0761) 341 701 - Closed Sunday evening, Tuesday, August 1-20 – 50,000L. You will need a reservation for this classic regional restaurant with a beautiful "Etruscan room" among the other more modern ones.

L I G U R I A

Genova / Genoa

Gran Gotto, via Fiume 11r, tel. (010) 564 344 – Closed Saturday noon, Sunday, August – 60-80,000L. This is the chic restaurant of the town with an elegant decor and very good classic Ligurian cuisine – **Giacomo**, Corso Italia, tel. (010) 369 67 – Closed Sunday, August – 65-80,000L. It is an elegant place with a beautiful view on the sea – **Il Cucciolo**, viale Sauli 33, tel. (010) 546 470 – Closed Monday, August – 40-50,000L, has great Tuscan cuisine. If you don't know your way around town, you'd better come by taxi – **La Buca (di San Matteo)**, via Davide Chiossone 5 r., tel. (010) 29 48 10 – Specialties: *pasta e fagioli, pappardelle al sugo, trippe, fiorentine alla brace* – **Ferrando** in San Cipriano on the hill tel. (010) 75 19 25 – Closed Sunday, Monday and Wednesday evening. Specialties: mushroom dishes.

CAFFE' IN GENOVA

Caffe' Mangina, via Roma 91, Closed Monday. You can admire the equestrian statue of Victor Emmanuel II on Corvetto Square from this elegant cafe – **Caffe' Klainguti**, piazza Soziglia 98. This is one of Italy's historical cafés.

San Remo

Da Giannino, lungomare Trento e Trieste 23, tel. (0184) 504 014 – Closed Sunday evening, Monday, May 15-31 – 80-90,000L. This is the chic gourmet restaurant of the town – **Pesce d'oro**, corso Cavalotti 300, tel. (0184) 576 332 – Closed February 15 March 15, Monday 65,000L. It has some of the best food on the Italian Riviera – **Osteria del Marinaio da Carluccio**, via Gaudio 28, tel. (0184) 501 919 – Closed Monday, October, December – 70-90,000L. This very small osteria serves excellent seafood cuisine to a distinguished clientele. Reservations are a must.

Cervo

35km from San Remo
San Giorgio, via Volta 19, tel. (0183) 400 175 – Closed Tuesday, Christmas vacation – 50-60,000L. This adorable little restaurant serves seafood *antipasti* , excellent cuts of meat, and *zabaione.*

Finale Ligure

Osteria della Briga, altipiano delle Marie, tel. (019) 698 579 – Closed Tuesday, Wednesday – 20-25,000L. It has a rustic family atmosphere, and memorable *lasagne alle ortiche* and *grappe "al latte" .*

Rapallo

Da Monique, lungomare Vittorio Veneto 6, tel. (0185) 50 541 – Closed Tuesday, February – 45-50,000L. It is the most famous seafood restaurant of the port – **U Giancu**, in San Massimo 3km, tel. (0185) 260 505 – Closed Wednesday, Thursday noon, October 4-13, November 13-December 6 – 30,000L. Nice country atmosphere, and service on the terrace in the summer.

Santa Margherita Ligure

Trattoria Cesarina, via Mameli 2, tel. (0185) 286 059 – Closed Wednesday, December – 85,000L, is one of the better restaurants on the Ligurian coast, with excellent service – **Trattoria l'Ancora**, via Maragliano 7, tel. (0185) 280 559 – Closed Monday, January, February. serves a mostly local clientele. Marinated spaghetti is a house specialty.

Portofino

Il Pistoforo, Molo Umberto 1, tel. (0185) 269 020 – Closed Tuesday, Wednesday noon, January, February – 70-100,000L. It serves fish soup, fish stew, and grilled fish in the shade of the centuries-old *pistoforum.* - **Puny**, piazza M. Olivetta 7, tel. (0185) 269 037 – Closed Thursday – 45-70,000L. It is a classic Portofino restaurant, with a nautical decor and a beautiful view of the port **Delfino**, piazza M. dell' Olivetta 40, tel. (0185) 269 081 – Closed Thursday, November, December 75 000L. One of the most stylish restaurants of this port town - **Da Ü Batt**i, vico Nuovo 17, tel. (0185) 269 379, is a small fish trattoria. Reservations are a must. **Splendido Restaurant,** tel. (0185) 269 551 closed from November to April. Fine Italian cuisine on an enchanting site with a superb view.

C A F F E ' — B A R S
Bar Sole, piazza Olivetta. People come here for sandwiches, cocktails, to see and be seen – **Caffe' Excelsior**, piazza M. Olivetta. A good place to drink expresso and read the morning paper.

Ameglia

18km from La Spezia

Paracucchi, at 4,5km, via Sarzana-Marinella, viale XXV Aprile 60, tel. (0187) 64 391 - 80,000L - Closed Monday, January. This is a good place to stop off for a meal on the way to Firenze or Milano.

Sestri Levante

Fiammenghilla Fieschi, at Erigox, Riva Trigoso 2 km via Pestella 6, tel. (0185) 481 041 – Closed Monday at noon off season – 50-85,000L. It has very good traditional cuisine and a pretty garden – **Portobello**, via Portobello 16, tel. (0185) 415 66 – Closed Wednesday.

Portovenere

La Taverna del Corsaro, lungomare Doria 102, tel. (0187) 900 622 – Closed Tuesday, November, June 1-22 – 60,000L. There is a very nice view of the island of Palmaria from the dining room. The cusisne is based on fish fresh and produce from the market as well as local specialties.

L O M B A R D Y

Milano / Milan

Giannino, via Amatore Sciesa 8, tel. (02) 551 955 82 – Closed Sunday, August – 60-100,000L. You will enjoy some of the finest gourmet cuisine in Lombardy here in this classic chic Milanese restaurant – **Peck**, via Victor Hugo 4, tel. (02) 876 774 Closed Sunday, January 1-10, July 1-

10- 60,000L .It features traditional and creative cuisine, with a snack bar at street level, and the restaurant in

the basement – **Trattoria Milanese**, via Santa Marta 11 tel. (02) 864 519 91 – Closed Tuesday, it is true to tradition – **Trattoria Bagutta**, via Bagutta 14, tel. (02) 7600 27 67 – Closed Sunday, August, Christmas holidays 60-100,000L. The sequential rooms are decorated with characatures. This is undoubtedly the most famous trattoria in town (a litterary award is given here every year). Although the cuisine is nothing to write home about, the decor is nonetheless attractive.– **Osteria del Binari**, via Tortona 1, tel. (02) 8940 9428 – Closed at noon, Sunday, August 10-20 – 50 000L. This is an atmosphere restaurant, with a very convivial dining room, a very shady garden, and somewhat traditional cuisine – **Pizzeria il Mozzo**, via

Marghera (angle via Ravizza), tel. (02) 498 4746 – Closed Wednesday, August. Open until 2 am. It has a rustic decor, good home-style cuisine, and an elegant clientele – **Peppermoon**, via Bagutta 1, near by Via Spiga et Montenapoleone. Pizzas, risotto – **Masuelli San Marco,** viale Umbria, tel. 551841 38, Closed Sunday, Monday noon, Christmas holidays, August 15-September 15 – 50 000 L, **Alfredo Gran San Bernardo** via Borghese 14 tel. (02) 3319000, closed Christmas, August, Sunday,

Saturday in June and July - 65-99,000L, **Trattoria della Pesa**, via Pasubio, tel. (02) 65 55 74. Closed Sunday, August, 70;000L. The four G. Armani's best adresses to taste the *risotto all'osso buco* – **Rigolo**, largo Treves angle via Solferino, tel. (02) 8646 3220 – Closed Monday, August 30-50,000L. It is in the Brera quarter, and is frequented by

a stylish crowd of regulars. Another plus, it is open Sundays – **Don Lisander,** via Manzoni 12, tel. (02) 7602 0130 – 68-105 000L – Closed Saturday evening and Sunday. The restaurant is especially nice in the summer, as it serves fine cuisine to its upscale clientele on a very pleasant canvas-covered terrace with an Italian-style decor and flowering plants. You will need a reservation – **Franco il Contadino**, via Fiori Chiari 20, tel. (02) 8646 3446 – Closed Tuesday, Wednesday at noon, July – 45-60,000L. It has a nice atmosphere and is frequented by artists. It is open Sundays – **Torre di Pisa**, via Fiori Chiari 21, tel. (02) 874 877 – Closed Sunday – 40-50,000L. It is a Tuscan restaurant frequented by designers and people from the fashion industry – **Boeucc**, piazza Belgioioso 2, tel. (02) 760 20224, Closed Saturday, Sunday at noon, Christmas holidays, August. 60-80,000L. Reservations are necessary for this chic restaurant, where you can dine on the terrace as soon as the weather permits.

D O P O   S C A L A

Le Santa Lucia, via San Pietro all'orto 3, tel. (02) 760 23155. - **Biffi**

Scala, piazza della Scala, tel. (02) 86 66 51, closed Sunday and Chrismas, 10.-20 August. - **Don Carlos,** Don

Carlos is the restaurant at the superb Grand Hotel (de Milan?) where Verdi spent his last days. The atmosphere is appropriately theatrical.

C A F F E ' - B A R S

Cova, via Montenapoleone 8, is the most elegant café in Milan, and serves teas, coffee, pastries, champagne, and cocktails – **Pozzi**, piazza Cantore 4, glacier. features a wide assortment of ice cream and sherbert – **Pasticceria Marchesi**, via santa Maria alla Porta, 1. This is a good place for a coffee and an Italian croissant with jelly. They have made the best holiday pastries, (Panattone at Chrismas and Colombe at Easter) since 1824.- **Bar del Comparlno**, the original Frescos and Liberty-style mosaics have recently been restored in this historical landmark, the former haunt of Toscanini, Verdi, and Carrà – **Caffè Milano**, via San Fermo, 1 in the Brera quarter, very pleasant for the lunch. Menu: 25 000L.

T E A   R O O M S

Sant Ambrœus, corso Matteoti 7, spécialité l'Ambrogitto, is the most elegant tearoom in Milan, but there is also **Biffi**, corso Magenta 87, **Taveggia**, via Visconti di Modrone 2, **Galli**, corso di Porta Romana 2 which has delicious candied chestnuts.

S H O P P I N G

Casa del formaggio, via Speronari 3, has a wide asssortment of cheeses from all over Italy – **Peck**, via Spadari 9, is still the finest gourmet food store in Milano – **La Fungheria di Bernardi**, viale Abruzzi 93, has a wonderful variety of fresh and canned mushrooms – **Enoteca Cotti**, via Solferino 32 – **Memphis Design** for Ettore Sottsass' creations – **De Padova** corso Venezia 14, modern furniture by Vico Magistretti and Gae Aulenti – **High Tech**, piazza 25 Aprile 14 - **Pratesi**, via Montenapoleone 27, supplies the finest house linen – **Libreria Rizzoli,** galleria Vittorio Emanuele 79, has rare French publications and art books - **Libreria Hoepli**, via Hoepli 5, has modern works, manuscripts, and authentic signatured drawings.

Bergamo

Lio Pellegrini, via San Tomaso 47, tel. (035) 247813 – Closed Monday, Tuesday at noon, January 4-11, August 2-24 – 50-90,000L. Resevation advised – **Taverna del Colleoni**, piazza Vecchia 7, tel. (035) 232 596 – Closed Monday, August – 50-70,000L. It serves regional cuisine in a Renaissance decor. The *tagliatelle* and the *filetto alla Colleoni* are house specialties. There is also **Il**

Gourmet, via San Vigilio, 1 tel. (035) 25 61 10 - Closed Tuesday, January 1-6 – 40-60,000L.- **La Marianna**, largo Colle Aperto 2/4, tel. (035) 23 70 27 - closed Monday, from January 1 to 14. You can dine on a beautiful flower-covered terrace when the weather is nice.

Brescia

La Sosta, via San Martino della Battaglia 20, tel. (030) 295 603 – Closed Monday, August – 50-80,000L. The handsome 17th century building and fine cuisine make it worth stopping off here for a meal.

Cremona

Ceresole, via Ceresole 4, tel. (0372) 23 322 – Closed Sunday evening, Monday, January, August – 60-80,000L. It is considered to be something of an institution in this town famous for its violins. If you are interested, you can visit the Antonio Strativari Museum – **Antica Trattoria del Cigno**, via del Cigno 7, tel. (0372) 21 361 – Closed Sunday, January, July 20- October 4 30,000L. In the shadow of the Torrazzo, this old trattoria is the favorite of the inhabitants of Cremona .

Mantova / Mantua

San Gervasio, via San Gervasio 13, tel. (0376) 35 05 04 - Closed Wednesday, August 12-31 – 40-70,000L - **L'Aquila Nigra**, vicolo Bonacolsi 4, tel. (0376) 350 651. Closed Sunday, Monday, Christmas, August, 45,000L. It is famous for its

cuisine, which you will enjoy in a beautiful decor of frescos in a former monastery - **Cento Rampini**, p.delle Erbe, tel. 366 349. It is nicely located under the portico of the Palazzo Comunale, and has service on the terrace.

Pavia

Antica Trattoria Ferrari da Tino, via del Mille 111, tel. (0382) 31033 – Closed Sunday evening, Monday, August – 35-70,000L. This traditional country trattoria serves savory cuisine.

Certosa di Pavia

Vecchio Mulino, via al Monumento 5, tel. (0382) 925 894 - Closed Sunday evening, Monday, January 1-10, August 1-20 – 60-80,000L. This is a good place to dine when visiting the famous monastery. Be sure to make a reservation- **Chalet della Certosa**, opposite the Certosa - Closed Monday, January.11-24

M A R C H E

Ancona

Passetto, piazza IV Novembre, tel. (071) 33 214 – Closed Wednesday, August 45-75,000 L. There is a nice view of the Adriatic from the terrace which is open in the summer.

Pesaro

Da Teresa, viale Treste 180, tel. (0721) 30 096 – Closed Monday, November – 60,000L. The restaurant serves fine cuisine in an elegant setting with a view of the sea.

Urbino

Il nuovo Coppiere, via Porta Maja 20, tel. (0722) 320 092 – Closed Wednesday, February – 30,000 L. regional specialties – **Self-Service Franco**, via de Possio – Closed Sunday – 15,000 L. Located near the museum, it has reasonable prices **Vecchia Urbino**, via dei Vasari 3, tel. (0722) 4447, Closed Tuesday off season – 40-60,000 L. It serves regional cuisine, (the *formaggio di fossa* is remarkable) in a pleasant room in the Viviani Palace.

Ascoli Piceno

Gallo d'Oro Corso V. Emanuele 13, 3 salles modernes - Closed Sunday evening, Monday, August. Regional dishes are served in three modern rooms near the Duomo – **Tornassaco**, piazza del Popolo 36, Closed Wednesday, July. – **Caffe' Meleni**, piazza del Popolo. Local pastries. Sartre and Hemingway used to come here.

Perugia

Osteria del Bartolo, via Bartolo 30, tel. (075) 5731 561 – Closed Sunday, January 7-15, July 25-August 7 – 60,000L. Very good home-style cuisine and old Umbrian dishes – **La Taverna**, via delle Streghe 8, tel. (075) 5724 128 – Closed Monday – 40,000L. Country cuisine in a large room with a vaulted ceiling – **Del Sole**, via delle Rupe 1, tel. (075) 65 031 – Closed Monday, December 23-January 10– 35,000L. A beautiful old room with a vaulted ceiling and service on the panoramic terrace in the summer.

C A F F E ' — B A R S

Caffe' del Cambio, corso Vannucci 29. It can get pretty crowded in this student cafe. **Pasticceria Sandri**, corso Vannucci 32, for pastry buffs.

Assisi

Buca di San Francesco, via Brizi 1, tel. (075) 812 204 – Closed Monday, February, July – 30,000L. It serves traditional Umbrian cuisine in a Medieval palace with a pretty garden in the summer – **Medio Evo**, via Arco del Priori 4, tel. (075) 81 3068 Closed Wednesday, January, July – 45,000L. It has beautiful architecture and meticulously fine cuisine – **La Fortezza**, Vic. Fortezza 2-B, tel. (075) 812 418 – Closed Thursday – 30,000L. Some vestiges of the ruins of the typical Roman house it was built on remain. The cuisine is Umbrian-style.

LOCAL SPECIALTIES

Bottega del Buongustaio, via S. Gabriele 17. A small, well-stocked grocery store where you can find the famous black Norcian truffles.

Gubbio

Taverna del Lupo, via G. Ansidei 21, tel. (075) 927 43 68 – Closed Monday off season, January. It serves delicious local specialties in a beautiful Medieval tavern decor – **Alle Fornace di Mastro Giogio,** via Mastro Giogio 3, tel 927 55740 – Closed Sunday evening, Monday, February, 60,000L.

Spello

Il Cacciatore, via Giulia 42 – Closed Monday, July 6-20, 35,000L. Pleasant trattoria with a beautiful terrace – **Il Molino**, piazza Matteotti – Closed Tuesday.

Spoleto

Il Tartufo, piazza Garibaldi 24, tel. (0743) 40 236 – Closed Wednesday, August 15-10 – 35-70,000L. This is

an excellent tavern serving regional cuisine. The house specialty is *fettucine al tartufo* – **Tric Trac da Giustino**, piazza del Duomo, tel. (0743) 44 592 – 20-50 000L. very busy during the "Two World Festival". IN CAMPELLO SUL CLITUNNO, 9km from Spoleto – **Casaline**, tel. (0743) 62 213 Closed Monday – 45,000L. After your visite of Tempietto sul Clitunno. Have lunch in this country inn after visiting the Tempietto sul Clitunno. The cuisine is made with local products, and the *crostini* with truffles are marvelous.

Orvieto

Giglio d'Oro, piazza Duomo 8, tel. (0763) 41 903 – Closed Wednesday – 40-70,000L – **Grotte del Funaro**, v. Ripa Serancia 41, a regional restaurant **Dell'Ancora**, via di Piazza del Popolo 7, tel. (0763) 42 766 – Closed Thursday, January – 35 000L. Local home-style cuisine.

LOCAL SPECIALTIES

Dai Fratelli, via del Duomo 11, it has all kinds of cheese and the famous Umbrian sausages and ham.

P I E D M O N T VALLE D'AOSTA

Torino / Turin

Vecchia Lanterna, corso Re Umberto 21, tel. (011) 537 047 – Closed Saturday noon, Sunday, August 10-20 – 80-97,000L. This is one of the best restaurants in Italy. The owner, Armando

Zanetti, is constantly experimenting with new flavors, but also does an admirable job with traditional recipes. The wine cellar is superbly well stocked with Italian wines – **Del Cambio**, piazza Carignano, tel. (011) 546 690 - closed Sunday and August-85/110000L- located in the historical center of Turin, birthplace of the unification of Italy, this restaurant has kept all of the luster of the old days when Cavour came to eat here every day. The atmosphere, cuisine, and service are straight out of the 19th century.- **Mina**, via Ellero 36, tel. (011) 696 3608 – Closed Sunday evening, Monday, July – 50,000L. It serves genuine Piemontian home-style cuisine (*antipasti, sformati, finanzeria*) – **Trattoria della Posta**, strada Mongreno 16, tel. (011) 8980 193 – Closed Sunday evening, Monday, July 10-August 20. It is famous for its cheeses and its excel-

lent wine cellar – **Al Gatto Nero**, corso Turati 14, tel. (011) 590 414 - closed Sunday and August - 700000L. Specialties: *assassini*. - **Tre Galline,** via Bellezia 37, tel. (011) 436 65 53 - Closed Sunday, Monday noon - 50,000L. Typical Piemontian cuisine – **Salsamentario**, via Santorre di Santarosa 7-B – tel. (011) 819 50 75 – Closed Sunday evening, Monday,

August 15-22. There is a large buffet for 35,000 L, just next door to a caterer– **Il Ciacalon** viale 25 Aprile, tel. (011) 661 09 11 – Closed Sunday, August 11-24, located near the fairgrounds, beautiful restaurant with a simple friendly atmosphere – **Ostu Bacu**, corso Vercelli 226, tel. (011) 265 79 Closed Sunday. Typical Piemontian cuisine served in a rustic family atmosphere.

C A F F E ' — B A R S

In the land of Vermouth, Martini and Cinzano, the before-dinner coctail in Turin is something of a ritual.
Caffe' Baratti e Milano, piazza Castello 29. This chic Art Nouveau cafe has been open since 1875 – **Caffe' Mulassano**, piazza Castello 15. his large cafe has a lot of atmosphere, and delicious *tramezzini*

(small sandwhiches) – **Caffe' San Carlo**, piazza San Carlo 156. opened in 1822, and used to be the meeting point of the European intellegensia – **Caffe' Torino**, piazza S. Carlo, still has its quiet salons frequented by Cesare Pavese, James Stewart, and many other celebrities – **Caffe' al Bicerin**, piazza della Consolata 5. has had famous customers such as Alexander Dumas who perhaps came to try the famous *bicerin*, a house specialty made from chocolate, coffee, milk, and sugar cane syrup. **Caffe Il Florio**, via Po, called "caffe dei condini" because it used to be a meeting place for the most conservative people of the time. Try the *Sabaione, gelato al gianduia.*

LOCAL SPECIALTIES

Stratta, piazza San Carlo 191 specialties: *caramelle alla gioca di gelatinases*, "marrons glacés", *amaretti, meringhe con panna montata* - **Peyrano**, corso Moncalieri 47, is a laboratory for the famous Turinese chocolates, *givu, diablottini*, and the most famous *giandujotti*, also sold at the pastry shop Peyrano-Pfatisch, corso V. Emanuele II, 76 – **Cantine Marchesi di Barolo**, via Maria Vittoria sells Piedmont wines *Barolo Barbera, Barbaresco, Gattinara, l'Asti Spumante* of course, and the *grappe*.

Carmagnola

29 km from Turin
La Carmagnole, via Sottotenente Chiffi 31, tel. (011) 971 26 73 - Dine in an old palace, reservations a must.

Lozanzé

46 km from Turin
Panoramica, Lungo Tanaro, 4 tel. (0125) 66 99 66 - closed Saturday noon, Sunday evening, Christmas. This is still one of the best restaurants in Piedmont.

Asti

Gener Neuv, Lungo Tanaro 4, tel. (0141) 557 270 – Closed Sunday evening, Monday, August, Christmas 85,000L. This is one of the best places for traditional Piedmont cuisine – **L'Angolo del Beato**, via Guttuari 12, tel (0141) 531 668, Closed Wednesday, August – 50,000L. A beautiful old house, reservation advised – **Il Cenacolo**, viale al Pilone 59, tel. (0141) 511 00 – Closed Monday et Tuesday at noon, January 10-20 and August 5–20 – 40,000L. Savory regional cuisine is served in this intimate reasturant. Reservations required.

IN CASTIGLIOLE D'ASTI, 15km from Asti, **Guido**, Piazza Umberto I 27, tel. (0141) 966 012 – Closed at noon, Sunday, August 1-24, December 22-January 10 – 100,000L. Elegantly reinvented specialties of Langhe are served here. By reservation only.

Canelli

29 km from Asti
San Marco, via Alba 136, tel. (0141) 82 35 44 - closed Tuesday evening, Wednesday, from July 20 to august 13. A la carte:.... Great cuisine, you will need a reservation.

Cannobio

Del Lago, in Carmine Inferiore 3 km away, tel. (0166) 948 775 – Closed November, February - 60-100 000L réservation. This restaurant on a lake offers very good classical cuisine.

Aosta

Le Petit Restaurant, Hotel du Cheval Blanc, via Clavalité, 20, tel. (0165) 262 214 – Closed Wednesday, November 20-December 20 – 80,000L. One of the best restaurants in the valley – **Le Foyer** Corso Ivrea 146, tel. (0165) 32136 - Closed Monday evening, Tuesday, July 5-20, January 15-31 – 50,000L. Local specialties are served in this friendly comfortable restaurant. IN SAINT CHRISTOPHE, **"Casale"**, 12 km from Aosta, regione Candemine, tel. (0165)

541 203, closed Monday, holidays, January - 75000L. The house specialties and wine cellar are worth the trip.

Breuil-Cervinia

Les Neiges d'Antan, 4 km away, tel. (0166) 948 775 – Closed Monday, July, October, November – 35-90,000L. This is the best restaurant with the best wine cellar in Cervinia. The charming hotel is also mentioned in this guide – **Cime Bianche**, tel. (0166) 949 046 – 30-50,000L, is on the ski slopes in the win-

ter, and serves regional cuisine in a pretty mountain decor, with a superb view on the Matterhorn – **Le Mattherhorn**, tel. (0166) 948 518. is in the center of town, and serves pizzas, steaks, and fish – **Hostellerie des guides**, is open from 7 am to midnight, and is famous for its Irish coffee.

Courmayeur

Le Vieux Pommier, piazzale Monte Bianco 25, tel. (0155) 842 281, Closed Monday, October. Regional cuisine in a warm friendly setting – **Pierre Alexis 1877**, via Marconi 54, tel (0155) 84 35 17 – Closed October, November, Monday (except August), Tuesday at noon from December to March – **Al Camin**, via dei Bagni, tel (0155) 841 497 - Closed Tuesday off season, November, Mountain atmosphere and home-style cuisine – **Caffe' Della Posta**, via Roma 41. It is a hundred-year-old bar where you can drink traditional Alpine alcohols and cocktails, comfortably installed in plush sofas. (*Grappas*, *Genepi*).

Entrèves

4km from Courmayeur
La Maison de Filippo, tel. (0165) 89 668 – Closed Tuesday, June 1-July 15, Nov., 50,000L. You must make a

reservation for this famous tavern.

Planpincieux Val Ferret
7km from Courmayeur

La Clotze, tel. (0165) 89 928 –
Closed Wednesday, June, November
45,000L. Good regional cuisine.

La Palud Val Ferret
5km from Courmayeur

La Palud-da-Pasquale, tel. (0165)
89 169 – Closed Wednesday,
November – 30-40,000L. Regional
and mountain specialties.

Plan–de–Lognan Val Veny
12km from Courmayeur

Le Chalet del Miage, Closed July,
September. Mountain-style cuisine.

Cogne

Lou Ressignon, rue des Mines 22,
tel. (0165) 74 034. It has excellent
cuts of meat, *fonduta, carbonara*
(meat cooked in beer) and also delicious cheeses and desserts.

Verres

Chez Pierre, via Martorey 43, tel.
(0125) 929 376 – Closed Monday
and Tuesday except August - 50-
80,000L. This adorable litttle restaurant, 22 miles (37km) from Aoste,
has a friendly atmosphere and regional cuisine.

PUGLIA / APULIA

Alberobello

Trullo d'Oro, via Cavallotti 31, tel.
(080) 721 820 – Closed Monday,
January 7- February 8 – 25-60,000L.

It is picturesque, with a country-style
decor and regional cuisine.– **Il Poeta
Contadino**, via Indipendenza 21, tel.
(080) 721 917 – Closed Sunday eve-

ning, Monday, January, June – 50-
80,000L. Excellent cuisine

Bari

Nuova Vecchia Bari, via Dante
Alighieri 47, tel. (080) 521 64 96 –
Closed Friday, Sunday evening –
50,000L. Pugilian cuisine is served in
this rustic former oil press house –
La Pignata, corso Vittorio Emanuele
173, tel. 523 24 81 – **Deco'**, largo
Adua 10, tel. 524 60 70. Elegant.

Lecce

Gino e Gianni, via Adriatica à 2
km, tel. (0832) 45 888 – Closed
Wednesday – 45,000L. Traditional
cuisine in this theatrical-looking
town **Il Satirello**, tel (0832) 376
121 - Closed Tuesday. It is in an old
farmhouse with a beautiful garden
when the weather is warm, 9km from
the road to Torre Chianca.

Martina Franca

Da Antonietta, via Virgilio 30, tel. (080) 706 511 – Closed Wednesday off season – 25,000L. Flavorful cuisine **Rosticceria Ricci**, via Cavour 19. Excellent cuts of meat – **Trattoria delle Ruote**, via Ceglie 4,5km, tel. (080) 883 74 73 – Closed Monday – 30-45,000L. A nice place with limited seating so be sure to make a reservation – **Caffe' Tripoli**, piazza Garibaldi, is a wonderful old cafe serving pastries and almond paste – **Bar Derna**, piazza Settembre 4. Delicious pastries.

Polignano al Mare

Grotta Polazzese, via Narcisso 59, tel. (080) 740 0677 – 65-90,000L. It serves lobster and fish dishes inside a natural grotto in the summer.

S A R D I N I A

Alghero

Le Lepanto, via Carlo Alberto 135, tel. (079) 979 116 – Closed Monday off season 50,000L. After your visit to the Grottos of Neptune, you will undoubtedly be delighted to have a lobster Lepanto or to try other regional specialties here – **Al Tuguri**, via Majorca 113 or **Dieci Metri**, vicolo Adami 37.

Santa Teresa Gallura

Canne al Vento, via nazionale 23, tel. (0789) 754 219 – Closed October, November, Saturday off season *Zuppa galurese, antipasti del mare*, seafood delicacies cooked

with love.

Nuoro

Canne al Vento, viale Repubblica 66, tel. (0784) 201 762. It has a nice selection of meat and fish.

Monte Ortobene

7 km from Nuoro
Dai Fratelli Sacchi, tel. (0784) 31200. The Sacchi brothers warmly welcome their guests with savory cuisine.

Dorgali

Il Colibri, via Gramsci 44, tel. (0784) 960 54, Closed December-February, Sunday from October to May – 20-30,000L. This is a good place to stop off for a Sardinian meal on your way to visit the Dolmen Mottore and the Grottos di Ispinigoli.

Olbia

Ristorante dell' hotel Gallura, corso Umberto 145, tel. (0789) 246 48. It has served fish and seafood dishes cooked with delicious simplicity for more than fifty years – **Leone et Anna**, via Barcelona 90, tel. (0789) 263 33 – Closed January, Wednesday off season Sardinian cuisine, fish, and some Venetian specialties.

Cagliari

Dal Corsaro, viale Regina Margherita 28, tel. (070) 664 318 – Closed Sunday, August – 60,000L. If you spend a night in Cagliari before moving on down the coast, you can come here for high quality authentic Sardinian cuisine – **Antica Hostaria**, via Cavour 60, tel. (070) 665 870 – Closed Sunday, August. It is one of the nicest restaurants in Cagliari. Antonello Floris has skillfully adapted traditional recipes, and his wife Lilly makes great desserts.

Isola San Pietro–Carloforte

Al Tonno di Cosa, via Marconi 47, tel. (0781) 855 106. It serves delicious local cuisine (*tonno alla carlofortina*, "casca" regional couscous) on a terrace overlooking the sea – **Miramare**, piazza Carlo Emanuele 12, tel. (0781) 85 653, Carlofortan, Sardinian, and Arab specialties.

Porto Cervo

Il Pescatore, sul molo Vecchio, tel. (0789) 92 296 – Closed October-May, open in the evening only – 65,000L. You can have dinner by candlelight on a flower-covered terrace – **Bar degli archi**, piazzetta degli Archi. People come here for breakfast, a sandwhich at noon, and a drink in the evening – **Pevero Golf Club**, Pevero, tel. (0789) 96 210 – Closed November-April – 80,000L. This is one of the nicest golf courses. The cuisine served in the clubhouse restaurant is elegant and light, just like the clientele.

Isola la Maddalena

La Grotta, via Principe di Napoli 3, tel. (0789) 737 228 - Closed November 30-50,000L. Seafood – **Mangana**, via Mazzini, tel (0789) 738 477 – Closed Wednesday, December 20-January 20 – 45-60,000L. There are all-fish meals here, too.

Oristano

Il Faro, via Bellini 25, tel. (0783) 700 02 – Closed Sunday, July 11-25; 60,000L. Inventive cuisine based on regional recipes.

Palermo

Renato l'Approdo, via Messina Marina 28, tel. (091) 630 2881 – Closed Wednesday, August 10-25 – 50-70,000L. One of the best restaurants on the island, featuring dishes made from old Silicioan recipes. – **La Scuderia**, viale del Fante 9, tel. (091) 520 323 – Closed Sunday evening – 55,000L. It has one of the prettiest terraces in town. Dinners here are exquisite – **Charleston,** Piazza Ungheria 30, tel (091) 321 366 – Closed Sunday, June

–September - 80,000L. Very good cuisine in a beautiful Liberty-style decor – **Al Ficondindia**, via Emerico Amari 64, tel. (091) 324 214 – Closed Thursday 25,000L. A country tavern serving local regional cuisine - **Gourmand's**, via Libertà 37-E, tel (091) 323 431, elegant, and fine cuisine. Smoked fish is a house specialty. – IN MONREALE, 8km from Palermo, **La Botte**, contrada Lenzitti 416, tel. (091) 414 051 – Closed Monday, July, August – 45,000L. Delicious cuisine. Don't miss the superb cathedral – IN MONDELLO, 11 km of Palerme, **Charleston le Terrazze**, viale Regina Elena, tel. (091) 450 171, opened from June to September. On the most elegant beach of Palermo. It is the summer quarters of the *Charleston* of Palermo, with an superbly elegant terrace on the sea – **Gambero Rosso**, via Piano Gallo 30, tel. (091) 454 685 Closed Monday, November – 45,000L. This trattoria serves good seafood dishes.

CAFFE' – BARS
Caffe' Mazzara, via Generale Magliocco 15. Tomaso di Lampedusa wrote many chapters of "the Cheetah" here - **Bar du Grand**

Hotel des Palmes. – **Bar du Grand Hotel des Palmes** The hotel has been dropped from our selection because the rooms are overpriced, but the superb salons are still worth a visit.

Cefalù
La Brace, via XXV Novembre 10, tel. (921) 23 570 – Closed Monday, December 15-January 15. This small restaurant offers traditional Italian cuisine.

Messina
Alberto, via Ghibellina 95, tel (090) 710 711. Alberto Sardella has served marvelous cuisine here since his return from the U.S. 30 years ago. One of his specialties is *spiedini di pesce spada* – **Pippo Nunnari**, via Ugo bassi 157 - Closed Monday, June – 50,000L.

Taormina
La Griglia, corso Umberto 54, tel.(0942) 239 80 – Closed Tuesday, November 20-December 20 – 40,000L , serves carefully prepared country-style regional cuisine – **Rosticepi**, via S. Pancrazio, 10 – tel (0942) 24149, is the trattoria of Toarmina – **Giova Rosy Senior**, corso Umberto 38, tel. (0942) 24 411 – Closed Thursday, January. There is a large cart of antipasti and fish on a lovely jasmin-covered terrace – **Ciclope**, corso Umberto, tel. (0942) 232 63 – Closed Wednesday. 25-35,000L. One of the best Sicilian-style trattorias.

Catania

La Siciliana, via Marco Polo 52-A, tel.(095) 376 400, Closed Monday, August 15–31 - 70,000L. One of their specialties, the *Rippiddu nivicatu*, is a miniature Etna **Costa Azzura**, via de Cristofaro à Ognina à 4 km, tel. 494 920 - Closed Monday. A beautiful terrace for the summer; seafood - ACIREALE 16km, **Panoramico**, Sta Maria Ammalati. Closed Monday. View of Etna and wonderful *pastaciutta al raguttiino di mare*, the "castellane di Leonardo"

Siracusa

Darsena, riva Garibaldi 6, tel. (0931)66 104 – Closed Wednesday – 25-50,000L. Seafood – **Archimede**, via Gemellaro 8, tel. (0931) 69 701 – 40-60,000L. Trattoria – **Don Camillo**, via Maestranza 92-100, tel (0931) 66 104 – Closed Sunday - 50,000L - **Amnesye**, a good new restaurant in Siracusa.

Agrigente

Le Caprice, strada panoramica dei Tempi 51 – Closed Friday, July 1-15, It overlooks the Valley of the Temples – **Taverna Mosé**, contrada San Biagio 6, has a terrace with a view on the Junon temple. They serve spaghetti that Pirandello is said to have liked! – **Trattoria del Vigneto**, via Cavalieri Magazzeni 11, tel. (0922) 414 319 – Closed Tuesday, November – 25-30,000L. The best place to dine after visiting the Valley of the Temples.

Eolie-Lipari

Filippino, piazza Municipo, tel. (090) 981 1002 – Closed Monday except in summer, November 15-December 15 – 45,000L. Traditional cuisine, and the best fish on the island – **E Pulera**, via Stradale Diana 51, tel. (090) 981 1158 – Closed November-May – 35-65,000 L. You can dine under a charming pergola. Reservations are a must.

Eolie-Vulcano

Lanterna Bleu, Porto Ponente, via Lentia, tel. (090) 985 2287 – 40,000L. The best one on this small untamed island, good fish

T U S C A N Y

Firenze / Florence

Enoteca Pinchiorri, via Ghibellina 87, tel. (055) 242 777 – Closed Sunday, Monday at noon, August, February, Christmas and New Year's 125-150,000L. This upscale expensive restaurant is beautifully decorated, has a lovely flower-covered patio, one of the best wine cellars and some of the finest cuisine and in Italy – **Trattoria Coco Lezzone**, via del

Parioncino 26r, tel. (055) 287 178 – Closed Sunday, Tuesday evening, August, Christmas – 45-80,000L. You will find simple perfection here is a row of small rooms where regulars and locals rub elbows with international celebrities. The manager announces the delicious specialties of the day one after another as they are prepared. You don't have to try them all, but you will be tempted to.

– Da Gannino, piazza del Cimatori, tel. (055) 214 125 – Closed Sunday, August. This typical little osteria near the Signoria has service on the small square in the summer – **l Latini**, via Palchetti, tel. (055) 210 616, Closed Sunday, August – 30,000L. Hidden on a back street, people stand on line a glass of wine in hand while waiting to be seated in this noisy convivial restaurant. There is a common table, *prosciutto* and *vitello arosto*, a house specialty. – **Il Cibreo**, via dei Macci 118r, tel. (055) 234 1100 – Closed Sunday, Monday, August, Christmas 60,000L. It serves Italian-style nouvelle cuisine in a trendy atmosphere, not far from Santa Croce – **Trattoria Cammillo**, borgo San Iacopo 57, tel. (055) 212 427 – Closed Wednesday, Thursday, August 1-7, Christmas. This is one of most popular trattorias in town, serving traditional Florentine-style cuisine with a few innovations, such as the curried *tortellini* – **Mamma Gina**, borgo S. Iacopo 37, tel. (055) 296 009 – Closed Sunday, August – 30-40,000L. Traditional cuisine – **Cantinone del Gallo Nero**, via San Spirito 6, tel. (055) 218 898 – 25,000L. It has great *Crostini*, *Chianti*, and *Tiramisu*. It is in a cellar a few yards away from and opposite Cammillo, and the entrance can be a little hard to find – **Sostanza**, via della Porcellàna, tel. (055) 212 691 – Closed Saturday, Sunday, August – 40,000L. Tiny restaurant-grocery sto-

re with good local specialties – **13 Gobbi,** Via del Porcellana 9 r, tel. (055) 2398 769. Enjoy local cuisine around tables with benches in this softly lit restaurant – **Sabatini**, via de Panzani 9-a, tel. (055) 282 802 – Closed Monday 70,000L. The house antipasti will give you a taste of good classic Tuscan cuisine – **Da Noi**, via Fiesolana, 46 r, tel. (055) 242 917 – Closed Sunday, Monday, August, Christmas – 50,000L. This small elegant restaurant serves creative cuisine and seafood – **Dino**, via Ghibellina 51 r, tel. (055) 241 452 – Closed Sunday evening, Monday, August – 35-50,000L. One of the oldest restaurants in Florence, where each day Tuscan tradition is renewed with products fresh from the market – **Cantinetta Antinori**, piazza Antinori 3, tel. (055) 292 234. Hidden in the courtyard of the Antinori palace near the town hall. People come here for simple meals and good Tuscan wine – **Buca Lipi**, via del Trebbio 1 r, tel. (055) 213 768 Closed Wednesday, August – 30-50,000L. This picturesque cellar serves local cuisine – **Buca Mario**, piazza Ottaviani, 16 l, tel. (055) 214 179 – Closed Wednesday et August – 30-50,000L. Typical regional cuisine and wine – **Le Fonticine**, via Nazionale 79 r, tel (055) 282 106. is a large country-style restaurant with walls covered with paintings, Tuscan cuisine, and a few Emilian delicacies. The only drawback is that the tables are a little too close – **Campannina di Sante**, piazza Ravenne, tel (055) 68 8343. It has a nice view of the Ponte Vecchio and the Signoria tower. It serves only fish dishes. There is a very pretty walk you can take in the evening along the Arno to the da Verrazzano bridge – **Antico Fattore**, via Lambertesca 1, tel. (055) 238 12 15 – Closed Sunday, Monday, August – 35,000L. Family trattoria near the Uffizi Museum serving traditional Tuscan specialties – **Fagioli**, Corso Tintori 47 r, tel. (55) 244 285 – Closed Saturday, Sunday, August, Christmas – 30-40,000L. Typical regional specialties prepared by a real Tuscan – **Giubbe Rosse**, piazza della Repubblica, 13 – A very nice gallery-restaurant.

CAFFE' – BARS

Rivoire, piazza della Signoria. It has a large terrace on the most beautiful square in the world, a nice place to have sandwhiches and pastries and relax after visiting the Offices. It is famous for its *gianduiotti* and the *Cantucci di Prato* which is great with a glass of *Vino Santo* – **Giacosa**, via Tornabuoni 83. ice place to have cappuccino and pastries. It is always crowded – **Vivoli**, via Isola delle Strinche – Closed Monday. Very good ice cream and pastries. **Dolce Vita**, piazza del Carmine. The meeting place for hip young Florentines – **Gilli,** piazza della Repubblica. It has a Belle Epoch interior, and a large terrace on the busiest square in Florence, sheltered by palm trees. **Paszkowski**, piazza della Repubblica 6, concert cafe and restaurant.

Pineider, piazza della Signoria 13r, used to supply Napolean and Verdi with paper, and has continued to make stationery and desk sets for the rich and famous, and esthetes who come here to buy ink or to have their stationery monogrammed – **Taddei**, via Sta Margherita 11, pretty hand-crafted leather goods store – **Boutique de la Leather**

School, also sells items made in the neighboring schools – **Bottega Orafa di Cassigoli e Costanza**, via degli Ramaglienti 12 and **Gusceli Brandi-marte**, via Bartolini 18, personalized handcrafted jewelry – **Officina Profumo Farmaceutica di Santa Maria Novella**, is in a 14th century chapel, and sells perfumes, cologne, elixirs, and soap. You can visit the superb back rooms

by appointment – **Bizzarri**, via Condotta 32r, sells hardware and herb. The Via de' Tornabuoni is where you can find boutiques. For silk and traditional Florentine Renaissance brocade, try, **Antico Sattificio Fiorentini**, via Bartolini. For embroidered handkerchiefs, or house linens, go to **Loretta Caponi**, borgo Ognissanti 10-12r - **Procacci**, via de' Tornabuoni, sells quality groceries, **Gastronomia Palmieri**, via Manni 48 r and **Gastrononomia Vera**, piazza Frescobaldi 3r, has sausages and ham, wine, cheeses and other Tuscan products.

Prato

Il Piraña, via Valentini 110, tel. (0574) 25746 – Closed Saturday noon, Sunday et August – 70-80,000L. Fine cuisine in a modern elegant decor – **Trattoria Lapo**, piazza Mercatale. Simple and inexpensive – **Tonio**, piazza Mercatale 161, tel. (0574) 21 266, Closed Sunday, Monday, August.

Siena

Cane e Gatto - Osteria Castel Vecchio, via Pagliaresi: two good trattorias on a small street across from the art museum – **Guido,** Vic. Pettinaio, 7 tel. (0577) 28 00 42 – Closed Wednesday, January 10-25, July 15-30 - The most genuine cuisine – **Al Mangia**, or **Il Campo** piazza del Campo 43 – 45-50,000L. Its location on the famous Place del

Campo makes it worth the visit, but it is not a tourist trap – **Nello La Taverna**, via del Porrione 28, tel. (0577) 289 003 – Closed Monday,

February – 25- 50,000L. Taverne frequented by Siene families, with fine cuisine and a selection of Tuscan wine. – **Osteria Le Logge**, via del Porrione 33, tel. (0577) 480 13 – Closed Sunday – 40-50,000L. Excellent cuisine – **Grotta Santa Caterina da Bogoga,** via della Galluzza 26, tel. (0577) 282 208 – Closed Sunday evening, Monday, July – 30,000L. Country-style cuisine and atmosphere – **Antica Trattoria Botteganova**, strada Chiantigiana, tel. (0577) 284 230 – Closed Sunday, Monday at noon, 20 days between July and August – 40,000L. This very pleasant restaurant is worth the trip: the cuisine and service are meticulously well done.

CHIANTI COUNTRY

Fiesole
5km from Firenze

Trattoria Cave di Maiano, in Maiano 3 km away, via delle cave 16, tel. (055) 591 33 – Closed Thursday, Sunday evening, August – 35,000L. In the summer you can dine on large wooden tables on a shady terrace, and in the winter, in a picturesque tavern setting.

Bagno a Ripoli
9km from Firenze

Cent'Anni, via Centanni 7, tel. (055) 630 122 – Closed Saturday noon, Sunday, August – 50,000L. This pretty restaurant has a lovely garden. The traditional Tuscan dishes served here are a family affair. Mamma Luciani does the cooking, her son Luciano makes the pastries, and Silvano takes care of the wine.

Settignano
7km from Firenze

Caffe' Desiderio is an old cafe dating from the end of the 19th century, where you can have coffee, chocolate, pastries, and cocktails while enjoying a superb view of the Fiesole hills.

Serpiolle
8km from Firenze

Lo Strettoio , via di Serpiolle 7, tel (055) 4250 044 – Closed at noon and Sunday, Monday, August. is in a beautiful room in an old villa which still has an olive oil press (which is why it has this name). The atmosphere is elegant, and the seasonal cuisine is served by *cameriere* dressed in black with white collars.

Carmignano
22km from Firenze

Da Delfina, Artimino 6km, via della Chiesa, tel. (055) 871 8175 – Closed

Monday evening, Tuesday, August, January 1-15. Mamma Delfina oversees the entire operation, and everything comes from the family estate (vegetables, eggs, and poultry) and is homemade, notably the unforgettable *pappardelle*.

San Casciano in Val di Pesa
18km from Firenze

La Biscondola, in Mercatale tel. (055) 821 381 – Closed Monday, Tuesday at noon, November – 40-50,000L - **La Tenda Rossa**, in Cerbaia, 6 km, tel. (055) 826 132 – Closed Wednesday, Thursday at noon, August 5-28 – 75,000 L. This small family-run restaurant serves savory cuisine prepared with the freshest ingredients.

Monterriggioni
15km from Siena

Il Pozzo, piazza Roma 2, tel. (0577) 304 127 – Closed Sunday evening, Monday, January, July 30-August 15;

40-50,000L. This excellent restaurant has a wide selection of wines and regional gourmet cuisine.

San Piero a Sieve
21km of Siena

Villa Ebe, borgo San Lorenzo, tel. (0551) 845 7507 – Closed Monday –

40,000L. The village and the countryside alone are worth the trip, but it's Signora Ebe's fresh pasta that makes this place truly irrestable.

Castellina in Chianti
26km from Siena

Antica Trattoria La Torre, tel. (0577) 740 236 – Closed Friday, September 1-15 – 30-45,000L. The longstanding family tradition of serving fine cuisine made with local products is contiuned here

Gaiole in Chianti
28km from Siena

Badia, in Coltibuono,5km, tel. (0577) 749 424 – Closed Monday, November-December 15 – 45,000L. The Benedictine tradition of humanism and fine gourmet cuisine continues here in this very pleasant place.

Colle Val d'Elsa
25km from Siena

Arnolfo, piazza Santa Caterina 2, tel. (0577) 920 549 – Closed Tuesday, August 1-10, January 10–February 10 – 60-85,000L. On the trail of San Gimignano and Volterra, Arnofolo is a good place to stop off for a meal. The young chef in charge of the kitchen serves traditional and innovative cuisine.

Monteoliveto Abbey Asciano
37km from Siena

La Torre, is a tavern in the Abbey gardens, a very pleasant place to wait for the Abbey to reopen after lunch. Tables are set up under the trellis as soon as the weather permits., sandwiches and meals are served. Menus: 25-50,000L - Closed Tuesday – **Osteria della Pievina**, stratale 438, Lauretana, Asciano. This is an atmosphere restaurant with fine cuisine and a good wine cellar, a nice place to stop off at during your indispensable drive on the spectacular ridge road from Asciano to Siena.

Montefollonico

60km from Siena
La Chiusa, via Madonnina, tel. (0577) 669 668 – Closed Tuesday, except from August to September, 5 January 5-March 19, November 5-December 5 – 80-120,000L. Here you will enjoy delicious cuisine prepared by a pretty woman, and a good wine cellar, in a charming setting.

Montepulciano

66km from Siena
Ristorante rustico Pulcino, strada per Chianciano, tel. (0578) 716 905. Dishes with fresh ingredients accompanied by the best wines.

Pienza

52km from Siena
La Buca delle Fate, corso il Rossellino 38a, tel. (0578) 74 84 48 - closed Monday, from January 10 to 20, July 15 to 31. Authentic Tuscan cuisine copiously served in a rustic setting. – **Dal Falco**, piazza Dante Alighieri 7, tel. (0465) 74 85 51 – Closed Friday, July 12-20 and November 10-30 – 25-35,000L. It serves house delicacies in a family atmosphere – **Il Prato**, piazza Dante Alighieri 25, tel. (0465) 74 86 01 – Closed Wednesday, July 1-20. Friendly atmosphere and regional cuisine.

San Gimignano

38km from Siena
Le Terrazze, piazza della Cisterna, tel. (0577) 575 152 – Closed Tuesday, Wednesday noon –

40,000L. Tuscan specialties and a nice view of the Elsa Valley - **Dorando'**, vicolo dell' oro, 2 – Closed Monday. Elegant atmosphere and very good cuisine, right near the Duomo – 50,000L – **La Griglia**, tel. 940005 – Closed Thursday. A nice view on the valley

Arezzo

Buca di San Francesco, via San Francesco, tel. (0575) 23 271 – Closed Monday evening, Tuesday, July – 55,000L. Delicious cuisine in a Renaissance decor thick with atmosphere– **Al Principe**, 7 km from Giovi, tel. 362 046 – Closed Monday, July 20-August 20 – 50,000L. An old trattoria in the tradition.

Cortona
28km from Arezzo

La Loggetta, piazza Pescheria 3 – Closed Monday, January – 35,000 L **Il Falconiere**, in S. M. a Bolena 3 km away. Closed Wednesday - 60,000L.

Lucignano
27km from Arezzo

Osteria da Toto, piazza Tribunale 6, tel. (0575) 836 988 – Closed Tuesday, November, February. This is a nice place in a beautiful village.

Lucca

Buca di Sant' Antonio, via della Cervia 1, tel. (0583) 55 881 – Closed Sunday evening, Monday, July – 50,000L. One of the best restaurants in the region, with a warm intimate decor
Antico Caffe' delle Mura, piazzale Vittorio Emanuele 2, tel. (0583) 47

962 – Closed Tuesday, 20 days in January, 10 days in August – 40,000L. This old cafe serves hearty regional cuisine - **Da Giulio in Pelleria**, via delle Conce 45, tel. (0583) 55 948 – Closed Sunday, Monday, August 1-15, Christmas – 25,000L. Flavorful genuine local family-style cuisine – **Solferino**, San Macario in Piano, 6km, tel. (0583) 59 118 – Closed Wednesday, Tuesday evening, two weeks in August, Christmas – **Vipore**, in Pieve Santo Stefano 9 km away, tel. (0583) 39 4107 – 60,000L. Closed Monday, Tuesday evening. This 18th century farmhouse has been transformed into an adorable restaurant with a nice view of the Lucca plain.

Pugnano San Giulano Terme

Le Arcate, tel. (050) 850 105 – Closed Monday, August - Tuscan cuisine in a pretty rustic decor with an lovely pergola – **Sergio** the famous Pisan restaurant, has opened up at the Villa di Corliano, in Rigoli San Guiliano Terme.

Pisa

Al Ristoro dei Vecchi Macelli, via Volturno 49, tel. (050) 20 424 – Closed Wednesday, Sunday at noon, August 10-20 – 60,000L - Personalized cuisine – **Sergio**, lungarno Pacinotti 1, tel. (050) 58 0580 – Closed Sunday, Monday noon, January – 70-95,000 L. The best place in Pisa, with market-fresh inventive cuisine and delicious desserts – **Emilio**, via Roma 26, tel. (050) 562 131 – Closed Friday – 25-45,000L. Between the Arno and the Tower, this is a nice place to have lunch, with a large buffet of *antipasti* – **Da Bruno**, via Bianchi 12, tel. (050) 560 818 – Closed Monday evening, Tuesday, August 5-18. 25-60,000L. It serves traditional cuisine in a friendly setting - **Lo Schiaccianoci**, via Vespucci 104, tel 21024 – Personalized local cuisine.

Volterra

60km from Pisa

Da Beppino, via delle Prigioni 15, tel. (0588) 86 051 – Closed Wednesday, January 10-20. Traditional trattoria in a historical center – 30,000L. **Etruria**, piazza dei Priori 8, tel. (0588) 86 064 – Closed Thursday, November, 45,000L. The restaurant is located in an old palace.

Livorno

La Barcarola, viale Carducci 63, tel. (0586) 402 367 – Closed Sunday, August – 40-60,000L. The best Livornan specialties: caciucco, fish soup, and *loup a la livournaise* in a 1900 palace – **Gennarrino**, via Santa Fortunata 11, tel (0586) 888 093 – Closed Wednesday, February - 45,000L. This is a good classic restaurant – **Il Fanale**, Scali Novi Lena 15, tel. (0586) 881 346 – Closed Tuesday – 50,000L. Reservation advised.

Isola d' Elba

Publius, Poggio (Marciana), tel. (0565) 99 208, Closed October 15-Easter – 35-70,000L. Reputed to be the best restaurant on the island, with a beautiful view of the sea – **Rendez-vous da Marcello**, in Marciana Marina, piazza della Vittoria 1, tel. (0565) 95251 – 45,000L - Closed Wednesday - January 10–February 10.

DOLOMITES

Trento

Chiesa, via Marchetti 9, tel. (0461) 238 766 – Closed Wednesday evening, Sunday, August 10-25 – 60-80,000L. The specialties vary according to the seasons. During the apple season, all the dishes are made with them. In the spring, there are many early vegetables, and in the summer, fine fresh water fish from the lake – **Orso Grigio**, via degli Orti 19, tel. (0461) 984 400 – Closed Sunday January 1-15. Fine French-style cuisine, with a beautiful garden in the summer – **Hostaria del Buonconsiglio**, via

Suffragio 23, tel. (0461) 986 619 – Open in the evening only except on Sunday – 30,000L. Rustic and friendly – **Birreria Forst**, via Oss Mazzurana 38, tel. (0461) 235 590 – Closed Monday – 30,000L. Good place for lunch, either at the bar, or in the back room – **Le Bollicine**, via dei Ventuno 1, tel. (0461) 983 161 – Closed Sunday, August – 35,000L. Restaurant and tavern on the road to Buon Consiglio Castle - IN CIVEZZANO, 6 km from Trento, **Maso Cantanghel**, via Madonnina 33, tel. (0461) 858 714 – Closed Sunday, Easter, August 35,000L. This beautiful old farmhouse located just outside of town, has been nicely restored, and offers carefully prepared cuisine and attentive service.

C A F F E ' – B A R S

Caffe' Campregher, via Mazzini. Delicious cocktails made with *Spumante,* a sparkling regional wine.

Calavino
19km from Trento
Castel Toblino, tel. (0461) 44 036. Located in a marvelous landscape of mountains and lakes, this beautiful castle on Lake Garde now has a res-

taurant in one of its most charming rooms.

Riva del Garda
28km from Trento
Vecchia Riva, via Bastione 3, tel. (0464) 555 061 – Closed Tuesday off season – 50,000L. Elegant, with meticulous service and cuisine – **Bastione** via Bastione 19-A, tel (0464) 552 652 - Closed Wednesday, November 4-December 11 – 30,000L. Typically Trentinan cuisine in a warm friendly atmosphere. You will need a reservation.

Madonna di Campiglio
Prima o Poi, Pozze 8, tel. (0465) 57 175 – Closed Wednesday, June. In a small wooden house a few miles from the center of town, the Recagni family awaits you with hearty mountain cuisine – **Rifugio Malghette,** Pradalago, tel. (0465) 41 144 – Closed September 20-Christmas, May-June 10 – 30,000L. This warm friendly castle is located in the Andamello-Brenta Reserve. The best time of year to visit the forest is at the beginning of July when the rhododendrons are in bloom. The mushroom and blueberry risotto and homemade pasta are always a delight.

Bolzano
Da Abramo, piazza Gries 16, tel. (0471) 280 141 – Closed Sunday and August – 45-65,000L. elegant Restaurant – **Chez Frederic**, via

Armando Diaz 12, tel. (0471) 271 011 – 35,000L. It serves French-inspired cuisine. Dining in the shaded courtyard in the summer is especially pleasant. – **Castel Mareccio**, via Claudia de' Medici 12, tel. (0471) 979 439. An elegantly rustic castle surrounded by vineyards.

LOCAL SPECIALTIES

Antica Salumeria Salsamenteria Guiliano Masé, via Goethe 15 has homemade *spek tirolese, salami di selvagina*, and other delicacies

Bressanone

Fink, Portici Minoni 4, tel. (0472) 83 48 83 – Closed Wednesday, July 1-15. Typical mountain cuisine in an old palace located under the Medieval arcades of the center of Bressanone – **Oste Scuro**, vicolo

Duomo 3, tel. (0472) 353 43 – Closed Sunday evening, Monday, January 10-February 5 – 40,000L. Tyrolean cuisine in a Baroque dining room, and on a beautiful terrace in the summer.

Fie allo Scilliar

Tschafon, Fié di Sopra 57, tel. (0471) 72 5024 – open in the evening only, Closed Monday, January 9-22,

November 1-14. If you are a fan of French cuisine, you can expect a warm welcome from Therese Bidart. If you come on a Wednesday between October and April, try her extraordinary fish buffet.

Merano

Andrea, via Galilei 44, tel. (0473) 237 400 – Closed Monday, February 4-25 – 45-85,000L. Its reputation has crossed the Dolomites. Reservations are a must for this elegant restaurant **Flora**, via Portici 75, tel. (0473) 231 484 – Closed Sunday, Monday at noon, January 15-February 28 – 55-85,000L. Sophisticated Tyrolean and Italian cuisine – **Villa Mozart**, via San Marco 26, tel. (0473) 30 630 – 115-130,000L – Closed January, February, open in the evening only on request. Modern Tyrolean cuisine is served in a this very beautiful house with Hoffmann furniture –

Terlaner Weinstube, via Portici 231, tel. (0473) 235 571 – Closed Wednesday. Typical restaurant serving regional cuisine.

LOCAL SPECIALTIES

Casa del Miele Schenk, via casa di Risparmio 25. Honey, royal jelly, and an assortment of hand-crafted candles.

Santa Gertrude - Val D'ultimo
28 km from Merano

Genziana, via Fontana Bianca 116, tel. (0473) 79 133 – Closed Wednesday, November-December 26 – 50,000L. One of the best, and certainly one of the highest (2000 meters) restaurants in Italy.

Villabassa

Friedlerhof, via Dante 40, tel. (0474) 75 003 – Closed Tuesday, June – 40,000L. 23km from Brunico, Lovely restaurant with Tyrolean meals and decor, 23 km from Brunico.

Ortisei

Ramoser, via Purger 8, tel. (0471) 796 460 – Closed Thursday – 40,000L. This warm friendly restaurant, one of the best in Val Gardena, serves authentic regional cuisine – **Janon**, via Rezia 6, tel. (0471) 796 412 – Closed Tuesday, November – 30,000L. Typically Tyrolean cuisine and good desserts.

Venezia / Venice
near San Marco

RESTAURANTS:

Harry's Bar, calle Vallaresco 1323, tel. (041) 528 577 – Closed Monday, January 4-February 15 – 110,000L. The *Bellini, carpaccio,* and *risotto*

are house specialties famous all over the world. The best table is the one near the bar. Reservations are a must.

Trattoria alla Colomba, Piscina-Frezzeria 1665, San Marco, tel (041) 522 11 75 – 70,000L. One of the most popular trattorias in Venice. It has excellent cuisine and works by contemporary artisits on the walls – **Antico Martini**, across from the opera, tel. (041) 522 41 21 – Closed Tuesday, Wednesday noon – 75,000L, delicious – **Taverna La Fenice**, campiello della Fenice 1936, tel. (041) 522 38 56 – Closed Sunday, January. It has all the refinement you could hope for, the perfect place to dine after a show at the Fenice – **Al Teatro,** Campo San Fantin 1917, tel. (041) 523 72 14 – Closed Monday – 40,000L. The walls of this pizzeria-tobacco shop are covered with dedications from actors and performers who come after their shows – **La Caravella**, via XXII Marzo, tel (041) 520 71 31 – Closed Wednesday in winter - 75,000L **Vini da Arturo**, calle degli Assassini 3656, tel. (041) 528 69 74. Only seven tables which you must reserve if you want to stand a chance of having the excellent meat served here – **Da Raffaele**, San Marco 2347, tel. (041) 523 23 17. You can dine near a large fireplace in the winter. In the summer the tables are set up along a picturesque little canal on a gondola route. – **Do Forni**, calle

dei Specchieri 457, tel. 523 77 29 - closed Thursday in winter and end of November-beginning of December.- 60-90000L.

CAFFE' ET BACARI

Florian, piazza San Marco 56 – Closed Wednesday. Travelers and Venetians have appreciated its sumptuous interior and large terrace on the shady side of Saint Mark Square since 1720. Specialties: cocktails, the *Bellini* in summer, the *Tintoretto* in winter – **Quadri,** piazza San Marco. is across the square on the sunny side, and is also very elegant – **Caffe' Lavena**, piazza San Marco 134. Despite the fact that it is 200 years old, the Lavena holds its own with its two illustrious neighbors – **Caffe' Paolin**, campo San Stefano, 2692 San Marco. has a large sunny terrace on the campo where you can enjoy the best ice cream in town or a *spritz* (*Prosecco* and *bitter*) - **Vino Vino**, Ponte delle Veste 2007A, is a small bar popular with gondoliers who come here to take a break, just a few steps away from the Fenice Theatre. There is a good selection of Italian wine, which you can enjoy along with a dish of *pasta e fagioli* – **Enoteco Volto,** calle Cavalli, 4081 San Marco 4081 – tel. (041) 522 89 45. is the ideal place for lunch. You can have delicious little sandwiches on rye bread along with an *ombre* (white venetian wine), or other equally good wines such as *Brunello, Barello,* or *Barbaresco*. There is also a wide assortment of beers – **Al Bacareto**, San Samuele 3447, crowed.

near Rialto, Cannaregio, San Polo

RESTAURANTS

Trattoria Madonna, calle de la Madonna 594, tel. (041) 522 38 24 – 40,000L. One of the most typically Venetian trattorias, but it can be difficult to find a table here – **Al Graspo de Ua**, calle de Bombaseri 5094, tel. (041) 522 36 47 – Closed Monday, Tuesday, July 25-August 10 – 70,000L. It has a picturesque decor and lives up to its reputation as the best seafood restaurant in town. - **Vini da Gigio**, near Ca' d'Oro, tel. (041) 528 51 40 - Closed Monday - 45,000L – **Ai Mercanti,** Pescheria Rialto, tél (041) 324 02 82, Closed Sunday - 60,000L – **Alla Madonna**, Rialto, tel. (041) 522 38 24 – Closed Wednesday - 50,000L – **Osteria da Fiore**, calle

del Scaleter, tel. (041) 72 13 08, Closed Sunday, Monday, Christmas, August – Seafood - Reservation advised – **Da Ignazio**, calle del Saoneri tel. (041) 523 48 52 Closed Saturday - 60,000L – **Caffè Orientale,** Rio Marin, calle del Caffettier, tel. (041)

71 98 04 – Closed Sunday evening, Monday – 60,000L.

BACARI

Do Mori, calle dei Do Mori, near the Rialto brige. The one place you must not miss in this quarter. Careful, it closes at 13:00 for lunch. – **Do Spad**e, calle Le do Spade, an extension of des do Mori street. Counter service – **Osteria Al Million** S. Giovanni Crisostomo, 5841 – Closed le Wednesday. One of the oldest bacari in Venise. Try *Soave* or *Prosecco* if you like while wine, or *Valpolicella* or *Bardolino* if you prefer red, to go with you *molecche* (soft crab) or *cichetti* – **Ca d'Oro** or alla Vedova, calle del Pistor, a classic bar behind Ca d'Oro.

near Dorsoduro Accademia

RESTAURANTS

Locanda Montin, fondamenta di Borgo 1147, tel. (041) 522 71 51 – Closed Tuesday evening, Wednesday – 30,000L. It is located very close to the Guggenheim Foundation, and serves traditional cuisine. In the summer, the tables are set up under an arbor in the large courtyard – **Ai Gondolieri,** Dorsoduro 366 – San Vio, tel. (041) 528 63 96 – Closed Tuesday – 50,000L – **Agli Alboretti,** Dorsoduro, Accademia, tel. (041) 523 00 58 – Open in the evenig only, closed Wednesday – 60,000L.– **Le Riviera**, di G. Canton, Dorsoduro

1473, tel. (041) 522 762 - across from Stucky Mills, is run by a former Maitre d' from Harry's. The clientele of regulars, politicians and show business initiates reserve their tables on the platform to enjoy the house seafood delicacies.- 50-60000L.

CAFFE' ET BACARI

Cucciolo, Zattere 782, a large sunny terrace and very good coffee – **Linea d'ombra**, Zattere 19, near La Salute, piano-bar in the evening – **Il Caffé**, campo S. Margherita 2963, a very small bar, with a 1900 decor and per-colator – **De Maravegie**, calle de la Toletta 1185, near the Accademia museum, good breakfasts with fresh squeezed fruit, vices.

between riva degli Schiavonni and giardini

RESTAURANTS

Corte Sconta, calle del Pestrin 3886, tel. (041) 522 70 24 – Closed Sunday, Monday – 60,000L. This subtly ele-gant restaurant serves truly excellent cuisine. It is the best place in Venice, frequented by a clientele of intellec-tuals and artists, who have had no trouble keeping it relatively secret, as it is not very easy to find – **Al Cavo**, campiello della Pescaria 3968, tel. (041) 522 38 12 – Closed Wednesday, Thursday, January, August – 50,000L. Another good restaurant – **Hostaria da Franz**, fondamenta San Isepo 754, tel. (041) 522 0861 – Closed Tuesday off season, January 50-60,000L. Seafood. In the summer the tables are set up along the canal.

la Giudecca

RESTAURANTS

Harry's Dolci, fondamenta San Biagio, tel. (041) 522 48 44 – Closed Monday, November 10- March 10 – 70,000L. This is the summer head-quarters of ultra-chic Venetians –

L'Altanella. As you walk along the canal on the Giudecca, you will notice the small Virginia creeper-covered terrace of the Altanella, where you can have Venetian family-style cuisine.

SHOPPING

Stefano Zanin has sculpted gold-leaf picture frames – **Renato Andreatta** has frames for mirrors or pictures, and masks – **Mondonovo**, ponte dei Pugni, 3063 - Dorsoduro. Giano Lavato makes superb masks, and also does work for the theater.

At the **Legatoria Piazzesi** S. Maria del Giglio 2511 you will find marbled and traditional "carta varese" hand printed stationery, and other Venitian handicrafts, old-fashioned book bindings, and beautiful collectors' items.

Antichita` V. Troïs, Campo S. Maurizio Superb Fortuny fabrics – **Rubelli,** palais Cornerspinelli, Campo S. Gallo. Superb damask, silks, and brocades – **Delphos, et Venetia Studium**, campo S. Fantin, 1997, have dresses, handbags, and Fortuny scarves in a wide assortment of colors, as well as lamps created by Fortuny – Chez **Mazzaron,** sells handmade lace including the famous "Venitian stitch" – **Jesurum,** Ponte della Canonica S. Marco, offers house linens and old lace in an old 12th century church – La **Pantofola** calle della Mandola - S. Marco 3718 sells the velvet shoes which gondoliers used to wear.

Pauly, piazza S. Marco, beautiful glass art objects – **L'Isola**, campo S.-Moise, glass art objects of Carlo Moretti – **Rigattieri,** calle de la Mandola, glass art objects of Seguso, Barovier and Toso, Venini... **Archimede Seguso**, piazza San Marco – **Industie Veneziane** and **Battiston**, calle Vallaresco 1320 have the famous "Harry's Bar" pitchers here.

Codognato, calle del Ascension, sells antique Art-Deco, Cartier, Fabergé, and Tiffany jewelry - **Nardi**, piazza S. Marco, is one of the best jewelers and has a superb series of Othellos, each one of a kind – **M. Antiquités,** sells jewels by Monica Zecchi, silk velvet dresses and capes by Mirella Spinella.

Enoteca Al Volto, calle Cavalli 4081, has good selection of Veneto wines – **Pasticceria Dal Col**, San Marco 1035 has all kinds of traditional Venitian candies.

Murano

Ai Frati, tel (041) 736 694 – Closed Thursday, February. This is the

oldest osteria in Murano serving typically Venetian meals.The terrace on the grand canal is particularly pleasant in the summer.

Torcello

Locanda Cipriani, tel (041) 735433 Closed Tuesday, du 10 au 20 March –

70,000L. It has the simplicity and high elegance of the Cipriani tradition **Ponte del Diavolo**, tel. (041) 730 401 Closed Thursday, March-November 15 – 40-60,000L. A pleasant inn serving seafood specialties. In the summer you can dine in a pretty garden.

Burano

Osteria ai Pescatori, tel. (041) 730 650 – Closed Monday, January – 50,000L. Boasts two centuries of activity and fidelity to authentic *buranella* cuisine, a pretty dining room, and a small garden for warm sunny days – **Al Gato Nero-da Ruggero**, tel. (041) 730 120 – Closed Monday, January 8-

30, October 20-November 20 – 50,000L. Regional cuisine atmosphere.

Verona

Arche, via delle Arche Scaligere 6, tel. (045) 800 7415 – Closed Sunday, Monday noon, January – 80,000L. Across from the famous Della Scala mausoleum this old tavern is also a marvelous elegant restaurant – **Il Desco**, via Dietro San Sebastiano 7, tel. (045) 595 358 – Closed Sunday, Christmas, Eastern, June – 70,000L. In the historical center of Verona, you can enjoy Italain-style nouvelle cuisine and a very nice wine cellar – **12 Apostoli**, vicolo Corticella San Marco 3, tel. (049) 596 999 – Closed

Sunday evening, Monday, January 2-8, June 20–30 – 85,000L. This is the "must-see" of Verona – **Nuovo Marconi**, via Fogge 4, tel.(045) 591 910 – Closed Sunday, July - 70,000L. an elegant restaurant with fine Italian cuisine and friendly service.- **Re Teodorico**, piazzale Castel San Pietro, tel. (045) 49 990 – 55,000L. It has a nice view of Verona and the Adige – **Torcoloti**, via Zambelli 24 , tel. (045) 800 6777 - Closed Sunday, Monday evening 50,000L. Elegant atmosphere – **Quo Vadis**, via Leoni 13 - 25,000L, is an old garage transformed into a pizzeria, off of the Via Cappello (where Juliette's house is located).– **Bottega del Vino**, via scudo di Francia 3, tel. (045) 80 04 535, is a pleasant wine bar with classic cuisine in a cheery informal atmosphere. – **Osteria dal Duca**, via Arche Scaligere 2, tel. (045) 59 44 74. The clientele is made up of regulars who come for the *pastisada de caval* (horse stew), the specialty of Verona.

cuisine made from fresh products from the market. In the summer you can dine by candlelight in the garden **El Toula'**, via Belle Parti 11,tel. (049) 8751822 – Closed Sunday, Monday evening, August – 65-80,000L. People always love the elegant but conventional Toula' – **Il Michelangelo**, corso Milano 22, tel. (049) 65 60 88 – Closed Saturday noon, Monday, August 10-20 – 45,000L. Reservation advised.

C A F F E ' — B A R S

C A F F E ' — B A R S

Caffe' Dante, piazza dei Signori. has a warm friendly atmosphere and opens onto the superb square surrounded by palaces and the Loggia del Consiglio. – **Campidoglio**, piazzetta Tirabosco 4. A yuppie bar in a former convent with its original frescos. – **Enotheque Dal Zovo**, Vicolo San Marco in Foro, 7 - has a large selection of wines to taste, *amarone* and *reciota*.

Caffe' Pedrocchi, piazzetta Pedrocchi. opened in 1831 by Antionio Pedrocchi and was once the most elegant cafe in Europe. Its salons are green, white, and red, like the Italian flag. Don't miss this place.

Padova / Padua

Antico Brolo, Vicolo Cigolo 14, tel. (049) 664 555 – Closed Sunday, August 1-20 – 70-100,000L. It serves

Dolo

19km from Padoue

Locanda alla Posta, tel. (041) 410 740 – Closed Monday – 55,000L. Seafood restaurant.

Vicenza

Scudo di Francia, Contrà Piancoli 4, tel. (0444) 323322 – Closed Sunday evening, Monday, August – 40,000L. Enjoy Venetian delicacies in a Venetian-style palace, near the piazza Signori in Vicenza – **Cinzia e Valerio**, piazzetta Porto Padova 65, tel. (0444) 505 213 – Closed Monday, January et August – 70,000L. Seafood restaurant – **Gran Caffe' Garibaldi**, piazza dei Signori 5, tel. (0444) 544 147 – Closed Tuesday evening, Wednesday, November – 35,000L. You can either have a drink and a small sandwich on one of the marble tables in a beautiful spacious room on the ground floor, or enjoy classic Italian cuisine in the restaurant upstairs. – **Osteria Cursore**, stradella Cursore 10, tel. (0444) 32 35 04. Friendly and popular.

Treviso

Le Beccherie, piazza Ancillotto 10, tel. (0422) 56 601 – Closed Thursday evening, Friday noon, July 20-30. One of the oldest and most prestigious restaurants in town, and is doing its part to revive the great culinary tradition of the region – **Al Bersagliere**, via Barberia 21, tel. (0422) 541 988 – Closed Sunday, Saturday noon, January, January 1-10, August 1-10. good Trevisan cuisine. The menu changes from day to day – **El Toula' da Alfredo**, via Collalto 26, tel. (0422) 540 275 – Closed Sunday evening, Monday, August. This is where the famous chain of Toula' restaurants began.

Miane

Da Gigetto, via A. de Gasperi 4, tel. (0438) 960020 – 20,000L. An excellent restaurant in a luxurious country-style setting, serving fine innovative Italian cuisine inspired by nouvelle cusisne, but without the drawbacks of its French counterpart. The wine cellar is excellent, as is the service.

Belluno

Al Borgo, via Anconetta 8, tel. (0437) 926 755 – Closed Monday evening, Tuesday, June – 35,000L. It combines fine cuisine and culture in a beautiful Venetian villa on the border between Veneto and Alto Adigea. *Mel, 14km from Belluno*
Antica Locanda al Cappello, piazza Papa Luciani, tel. (0437) 753 651 – Closed Tuesday evening, Wednesday, 2 weeks in July – 30,000L. The old sign still outside this17th century palace testifies to its past as a postal inn. Cuisine based on old recipes is served here.

Cortina d' Ampezzo

Bellavista-Meloncino, in Gillardon, tel. (0436) 861 043 – Closed Tuesday, June, November – 50,000L. A small restaurant, very popular among the regulars at the resort. From the center of Cortina, follow the signs to Falzarego – **El Toulà**, Ronco 123, tel. (0435) 3339 – Closed Monday, December 20-

April 12, July 20-August 31 – 90,000L. The elegant restaurant of Cortina – **Baita Fraina**, Fraina, tel. (0436) 3634 – Closed Monday, October, November, May, June – 40,000L. This chalet deep in the mountains has a warm convivial atmosphere and family-style cuisine **Da Beppe Sello,** via Ronco 67 – tel. (0436) 3236 - 40-50,000L. We like the hearty cuisine served in this small three star chalet-hotel, in the pretty Tyrolean-style dining room or on a terrace in the summer – **Da Leone e Anna**, via Alverà 112, tel. (0436) 2768 – 50-60,000L. Sardinian delicacies – **Il Meloncino al Lago**, lago Ghedina, tel. (0436)

860 376, Closed Tuesday, July, November. It serves good authentic cuisine in a rustic but elegant chalet in a very beautiful natural setting.

C A F F E ' – B A R S

Bar del Posta, Hotel de la Poste, piazza Roma. Quiet atmosphere and a small bar which Hemingway loved. The *Dolomite* is the house cocktail.

Udine

Alla Vedova, via Tavagnacco 8, tel. (0432) 470 291 – Closed Sunday eve-

ning, Monday, August – 45,000L. Savory cuisine in a friendly atmosphere.

Trieste

Harry's Grill, Hotel Duchi d'Aosta, piazza dell' Unita d'Italia, tel. (040) 62 081 – 90,000L. The hotel bar is the meeting point for the town businessmen, and the restaurant is also very popular for its seafood specialties – **Ai Fiori**, piazza Hortis 7, tel. (040) 300 633 – Closed Sunday, Monday, June 15-July 15 – 40,000L. Elegant seafood restaurant – **Suban**, via Comici 2, tel. (040) 54 368 – Closed Monday, Tuesday, 20 days in August – 60,000L. When it opened in 1865, it was a country inn. The town has now surrounded it, but the interior remains unchanged. Try the delicious herb risotto. In the summer, meals are served under a lovely pergola – **Elefante Bianco**, riva Tre Novembre 3, tel. (040) 365 784 Closed Saturday noon, Sunday – 35-75,000L. You must reserve if you want to stand a chance of getting a table – **Al Granzo**, piazza Venezia 7, tel. (040) 306 788 – Closed Wednesday – 50,000L. Try to get a table facing the very picturesque fish market – **Al Bragozzo**, riva Nazario Sauro 22, tel. (040) 303 001 – Closed Sunday, Monday, June 25-July 10. One of the most popular restaurants of the port.

C A F F E ' – B A R S

Caffe' degli Specchi, piazza dell'Unita de' Italia, is on the largest square in Trieste, a good starting point for your visit to the town. Have a drink in the evening and watch the sun go down over the sea – **Caffe' San Marco** opened in 1904 under the

Austro-Hungarian Empire. It has been recently restored to recreate the atmosphere of days gone by when it was a literary cafe where Umberto Saba, Italo Svevo, and more recently contemporary writers such as Claudio Magris and Giorgio Voghera would gather. To celebrate this reopening, the San Marco has teamed up with the Hungaria in Budapest and the Florian in Venice, two other cafes which have played an important role in the cultural life of the center of Europe – **Para Uno**, via Cesare Battisti 13, has marvelous cappuccino.

INDEX

A

E

F

G

Z